D0432532

ADVANCES IN FOOD RESEARCH

VOLUME 32

ADVANCES IN FOOD RESEARCH

VOLUME 32

Edited by

C. O. CHICHESTER
University of Rhode Island
Kingston, Rhode Island

B. S. SCHWEIGERT
University of California
Davis, California

Editorial Board

ACADEMIC PRESS, INC.
Harcourt Brace Jovanovich, Publishers
San Diego   New York   Berkeley   Boston
London   Sydney   Tokyo   Toronto

ACADEMIC PRESS, INC.
1250 Sixth Avenue
San Diego, California 92101

United Kingdom Edition published by
ACADEMIC PRESS INC. (LONDON) LTD.
24-28 Oval Road, London NW1 7DX

LIBRARY OF CONGRESS CATALOG CARD NUMBER: 48-7808

ISBN   0-12-016432-9   (alk. paper)

PRINTED IN THE UNITED STATES OF AMERICA
88 89 90 91   9 8 7 6 5 4 3 2 1

CONTENTS

A Review of Aseptic Processing

E. L. Mitchell

Convective Heat Transfer to Fluid Foods in Cans

M. A. Rao and R. C. Anantheswaran

Selenium in Foods

Gerald F. Combs, Jr.

Chemistry of Maillard Reactions: Recent Studies on the Browning Reaction Mechanism and the Development of Antioxidants and Mutagens

Mitsuo Namiki

Food versus Biomass Fuel: Socioeconomic and Environmental Impacts in the United States, Brazil, India, and Kenya

David Pimentel, Alan F. Warneke, Wayne S. Teel, Kimberly A. Schwab, Nancy J. Simcox, Dan M. Ebert, Kim D. Baenisch, and Marni R. Aaron

Factors Influencing Food Selection in the American Diet

Carol I. Waslien

ADVANCES IN FOOD RESEARCH, VOL. 32

A REVIEW OF ASEPTIC PROCESSING

E. L. MITCHELL

Scholle Corporation
Irvine, California 92715

I. INTRODUCTION

In the last decade, there has been phenomenal growth in the production of aseptic products in the United States. This growth involves the use of flexible packaging for both consumer-size and institutional-size (bag-in-box) containers. The principal products for consumer-size containers have been juice drinks and juices, but there are numerous other aseptic products available in consumer-sized containers such as soups, sauces, milk, milk products, puddings, tomato paste, tomato sauce, yogurt-type products, apple sauce, gravies, juice concentrates, baby foods, and more recent introductions of nutritional supplements and tofu. The principal products for institutional use are tomato paste and tomato catsup; however, numerous other products are available, such as tropical fruit purees (guava, papaya, mango, passion fruit), pineapple juice concentrate, deciduous fruit puree concentrates (apricot, pear, peach), apple juice, pizza sauce, fruit particulates (peach, apple, strawberry, apricot), and citrus concentrate. Over 1 billion aseptic food containers were produced in 1984 in the United States, and it is estimated that by 1990, production will be 10 billion containers, a sizeable increase if attained. Aseptic processing or packaging is an outstanding technical achievement in the food industry. The following will trace the events leading up to where we are in 1987.

WHAT IS ASEPTIC PROCESSING OR ASEPTIC PACKAGING?

Aseptic processing is the ability, hour after hour, to bring sterile products together with sterile packages for filling and closing or sealing in a sterile environment (Scheme 1).

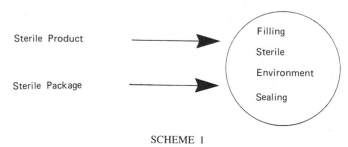

SCHEME 1

Successful aseptic systems require the following conditions:

1. Equipment or a system which will sterilize the product and keep it sterile throughout the process.
2. Equipment which can be sterilized and kept sterile throughout the packing period.
3. Constant availability of sterile packages.

In the following pages, different aseptic systems will be discussed. Each one will involve the steps as shown in Scheme 1, but may vary considerably in how they achieve these conditions. [Author's Note: In searching the literature for the materials for this review, I have found that most of the material available is in narrative form. I have made an effort to include the quantitative information that is available. In addition, my own comments are narrative in nature. As a result, this contribution is more narrative than those normally found in this series.]

II. EARLY ERA: 1927–1961

A. C. OLIN BALL: THE HCF PROCESS

In 1927, the state of the art for processing low-acid products in can or glass containers was the use of a retort in which the product was processed at 240–250°F. The container was in a stationary position in the retort. As a result, products in the outside areas of the can received much more heat treatment than products in the central areas of the container. The finished, processed foods had significant color and flavor changes from this process. These changes were particularly noticeable in milk products. It was also known that increasing the processing temperature naturally decreased the time necessary for sterilization. A typical process for a low-acid food was and is as follows:

> 600.0 seconds at 250°F
> 170.0 seconds at 260°F
> 52.0 seconds at 270°F
> 13.0 seconds at 280°F
> 3.6 seconds at 290°F

The use of lower processing times and higher temperatures would produce better products, but, unfortunately, neither the technology nor the equipment necessary to make use of these high processing temperatures was available. For example, 280°F requires steam pressure in excess of 35 psig, and 290°F requires steam pressure in excess of 40 psig. It was impractical to design retorts and containers which would stand up to these high pressures. Also, for most products, there was the serious problem of overcooking the outside portions of the product before the center portions were sterilized.

However, the American Can Company Research Department in Maywood, Illinois, felt there must be a way to capture this high lethality of high-temperature sterlization. Under the direction of C. Olin Ball, work was initiated in 1927 which led to the development of the HCF process. The process was named from the initial letters of the words *heat, cool,* and *fill*. These words describe the exact procedure used in the process.

According to Ball and Olson (1957a) the process "provides for the operations of sterilizing empty containers, sterilizing and cooling covers for the containers, sterilizing a food material in bulk, putting the sterilized food into the sterilized containers and applying the sterilized covers to seal the containers. All operations in handling the sterilized objects until after the containers are sealed are performed under aseptic conditions which are maintained in closed chambers by the presence of steam and a pressure greater than that of the outside atmosphere."

It was necessary for the product to be liquid or semiliquid because heating and cooling were accomplished by pumping the food through heat exchangers utilizing steam for heating and water for cooling in a continuous operation. Containers and covers were sterilized with saturated steam and then introduced into the sterile chamber by means of rotary pocket valves whose surfaces were kept continuously sterile by protecting them from contact with the outside atmosphere. The filling–closing machine was sterilized prior to use with saturated steam at 20 psig or more. The pressure required for sterilization of the filler–sealer made it necessary to provide heavy construction of these units.

Numerous pilot tests were run on many different products, and at times, the HCF pilot plant unit was shipped to customer premises for further testing. Finally, in 1938, two HCF units were installed for commercial production of chocolate-flavored milk beverage. According to Ball and Olson (1957b) "the product was heated to 300°F in less than 15 seconds and was cooled immediately [and] the product quality was most desirable as compared to unacceptable product quality when the chocolate beverage was processed in a retort." The two canning lines had a capacity of 300 8-oz cans per min. Ball (1936) was granted U.S. Patent 2,029,303 for the process, and the process is described therein.

The HCF process did not expand beyond these two commercial lines for chocolate milk, and these lines are no longer in operation. A number of reasons were given for the lack of expansion (Ball and Olson, 1957a):

1. high cost of the equipment;
2. inflexibility with respect to can size;
3. to clear jams in the can-closing machine required 1½ hr and, unfortunately, jams did occur more often than desired.

While the HCF machine was not a commercial success, it was a great success in that it was the initiator of all that has followed, and we must look to C. Olin Ball as the pioneer of aseptic processing.

B.   THE AVOSET PROCESS

The Avoset process (Ball and Olson, 1957b) was developed by George Grindrod at the Avoset plant located in the San Joaquin Valley of California that produced a cream product which was introduced in 1942 under the Avoset label.

The process was unique in that it utilized a filling and closing area around which the air had been treated to remove bacteria and was further protected by ultraviolet (UV) lamps. The area was enclosed by a wall with only one opening for the conveyor to carry the finished containers out of the room. There was a slight positive pressure in the enclosed area to provide for only outward flow of air from the opening for the conveyor. Sterilization was accomplished by heating the product with direct steam injection to a temperature of 260–280°F. Product was cooled in a heat exchanger type cooler.

Containers were sterilized in retorts using saturated steam. The retorts extended through the wall of the filling and closing room, and a retort door was installed on each end of the retort. Unsterilized cans were loaded into the retort from the door on the outside the room with the inside door closed. After sterilization with steam, containers were removed from the retort by opening the inside door and keeping the outside door closed. Closures for the containers were sterilized in a similar manner. The retort method of sterilization was eventually discarded and replaced by a continuous hot-air system in which the conveyor went through the wall and the sterilized containers were discharged into the sterile filler area. The speed of the operation was 75–100 containers per min, and an excellent cream product was produced.

Unfortunately, like the HCF process, the Avoset process is no longer in operation, but it served as the second stepping stone in the evolution of aseptic processing.

C.   WILLIAM MCKINLEY MARTIN: THE DOLE ASEPTIC PROCESS

The Dole aseptic process involved four separate operations (Martin, 1948):

1. sterilization of the product by flash heating and cooling in a tubular heat-exchange system;
2. sterilization of the containers and covers with superheated steam;
3. aseptic filling of the cold, sterile product into the sterile containers; and
4. application of sterile product to the filled containers and sealing the same in an atmosphere of either saturated or superheated steam.

Before the start of operations, the heat-exchange equipment, pipelines, pumps, and other handling equipment were sterilized utilizing hot water at 260–325°F. The filling area and can-closing machine were sterilized by superheated steam at 400–600°F. During operation, sterility was continuously maintained in these areas by the superheated steam.

Product sterilization and cooling were accomplished by pumping through a heat-exchange system utilizing principles of short, high-temperature sterilization processes (Martin, 1951). The empty containers entered the system on a cable conveyor and were sterilized by superheated steam at 400–450°F for sufficient time to obtain sterilization of the can. Time was regulated by the speed of the conveyor. Covers were sterilized in a special apparatus built into the cover feed of the closing machine.

The filler was directly above the cable carrying the empty cans and was located between the sterilizing area and the closing machine in the same enclosure. The filler was a slit-type filling nozzle, and as the cans moved continuously below the nozzle, the product was delivered into the cans. With the cans moving lip to lip under the filler nozzle, there was very little waste. Problems arose when there was a jam in the closing machine, which did happen infrequently. When it did happen, product would overflow the stationary cans onto the floor, and it was necessary to shift from product to acidified water and overflow the acidified water until the jam had been cleared.

The use of superheated steam in the system produced an outward flow of steam through entrance and exit ports as well as through other openings in the system which effectively prevented airborne bacteria from entering the system. This principle also made it unnecessary to use mechanical valves for passing empty containers and covers into the system and the sealed containers out of the system. The use of superheated steam eliminated the need for equipment designed to withstand pressures of 20 psig or greater.

Sterilization tests with inoculated cans were carried out under widely differing conditions over a period of nearly 2 years. The National Canners Association, San Francisco, California (relocated to Berkeley, California and now in Dublin, California as the National Food Processors Association), particularly C. T. Townsend, cooperated in many of these tests. Cans and covers were inoculated with spores of heat-resistant bacteria, allowed to dry for 24 hr, and then passed through the aseptic canning machine at various speeds so as to control the sterilization times. The cans thus sterilized were packed with nutrient broths, which were prepared in accordance with formulas in general use for the specific organisms, and the sterilization treatment given the broths in the canning process was sufficient for complete sterilization. The canned samples were incubated and the spoilage determined in accordance with standard practice. Most of the tests included 48 samples. Some pertinent data collected is in Tables I–IV.

Tables I and II show that with superheated steam, the critical sterilization time was 40–60 sec for cans inoculated with spores as shown. Table III shows that seaming-head sterilization was completed in 30 min under the conditions shown. Further work on the resistance of bacterial spores to superheated steam was performed by (Collier and Townsend, 1956). The resistance characteristics of three bacterial spores to superheated steam was determined and is shown in Table IV.

Martin attempted to and did overcome many of the obstacles which prevented the success of the HCF unit. The use of superheated steam at atmospheric pressure eliminated the need for the equipment with rotary valves for passing empty cans into the system and finished cans out the system. The use of atmo-

TABLE I

STERILIZATION OF CANS AND COVERS INOCULATED WITH ORGANISM NCA 3679 (30,000 SPORES PER CAN)[a]

| Code[b] | Sterilization | | | | Days of sample incubation at 87°F (percent swells) | | | | |
| | Cans | | Covers | | | | | | |
	Time (sec)	Temperature (°F)	Time (sec)	Temperature[c] (°F)	15	32	65	152	292
6	120	457	10	385	0	0	0	0	0
7A	120	457	10	386	0	0	0	0	0
8A	60	432	10	389	0	0	0	0	0
9A	30	300	10	388	5	12.5	15.0	17.5	17.5
10B	120	455	15	386	0	0	0	0	0
11B	120	452	30	369	0	0	0	0	0
12B	120	451	45	359	0	0	0	0	0
13B	—	—	10	358	9.5	100	—	—	—

[a] After Martin (1948).

[b] A, Cans inoculated; B, covers inoculated.

[c] Average values for temperatures recorded by three thermocouples mounted between superheated steam jets and covers.

TABLE II

STERILIZATION OF CANS INOCULATED WITH ORGANISM NCA 3679
(10,000 SPORES PER CAN)[a,b]

| | Sterilization | | | | |
| | Cans | | Covers | | Incubation of |
Code[c]	Time (sec)	Temperature (°F)	Time (sec)	Temperature (°F)	samples at 87°F (percent swells)
60A	20	280	60	360	100.0
60AH	20	340	60	360	100.0
62A	40	380	60	360	14.6
63AH	40	390	60	360	2.1
64A	60	430	84	375	0.0
65AH	60	435	84	375	0.0
66A	80	440	111	380	0.0
67AH	80	440	111	380	0.0
68B	40	390	60	360	8.3

[a] After Martin (1948).

[b] Cans inadvertently cross-inoculated with organisms, NC1518, through action of ants attracted by sugar added to the inoculum as an adhesive to assist in making the inoculum stick to the can.

[c] Codes: A, cans inoculated; B, covers inoculated; H, cans preheated.

TABLE III

SEAMING HEAD INOCULATED WITH ORGANISM NCA 3679 AND STERILIZED WITH
SUPERHEATED STEAM (340 MILLION SPORES)[a,b]

| | Sterilization of seaming head | | Days of sample incubation at 87°F (percent swells) | | | | | |
Code	Time (min)	Temperature (°F)	7	14	21	40	68	119
107	—	—	30.0	100.0	—	—	—	—
108	0	198	0	14.6	18.7	35.4	39.6	39.6
109	15	257	0	2.1	2.1	4.2	6.3	6.3
110	30	260	0	0	0	0	0	0
111	45	258	0	0	0	0	0	0
112	60	271	0	0	0	0	0	0
113	75	282	0	0	0	0	0	0

[a] After Martin (1948).

[b] Spore suspension containing 5% cane sugar as adhesive sprayed into seaming head and allowed to dry 24 hr (three spray applications).

TABLE IV

RESISTANCE OF THREE BACTERIAL SPORES TO SUPERHEATED STEAM[a]

| | | Resistance | |
| | | | F^c 350 |
Organism	Type	Z^b	(min)
B. *stearothermophilus* FS 1518	Thermophilic flat sour	26	0.708
B. *polymyza* PSO	Mesophilic gas-producing facultative anaerobe	28	0.667
PA 3679	Putrefactive anaerobe	60	0.625

[a] After Collier and Townsend (1956).
[b] Change in degrees Fahrenheit for a 10-fold change in death rate.
[c] Lethal time in minutes at reference temperatures.

spheric pressure negated the need for high-pressure construction. Closing machine jams were removed in much less time, and it was possible to run different sizes of containers within limits. The equipment was simpler and investment cost was much less for the Dole system as compared to the HCF unit.

In the early 1950s the first commercial line was installed for soups (primarily split pea soup); soon after, a second installation was utilized for specialty sauces (white, cheese, and Hollandaise). Both of these installations were made in California, but soon after, numerous other Dole units were in operation worldwide, and the list of aseptically packed products soon included milk, evaporated milk, chocolate drink, banana puree, sour cream, puddings, fruit puree concentrates, various sauces, eggnog, ice cream mixes, and others.

Havighorst (1951) reported as follows on the use of the Dole system with split-pea soup. The soup was heated to 285–295°F in approximately 3.53 sec and then held for 8.8 sec, after which the soup was cooled to 90°F in 14.0–17.0 sec. The Dole unit uses a valveless filler for straight-line filling. The process compares to 40–70 min at 240–250°F for similar products normally processed.

Product quality is the same for large and small containers. This is especially important in products which are difficult to process because of heat sensitivity or poor heat-transfer properties.

Products were available in both consumer- and institutional-sized (#10) packages. The products were of excellent quality, but for some reason the consumer was not enamored with many of the aseptically processed products and many were discontinued.

So as we came into the 1960s, we found a rather slow aseptic industry. Certain products, particularly specialty products, had found small niches and were surviving.

D. BULK PACKS: 55-GALLON DRUMS

In the late 1940s and early 1950s there was increasing use of tomato-paste and fruit-puree concentrates for remanufacturing purposes. These remanufactured products included tomato catsup, barbecue sauce, fruit nectars, fruit drinks, and others. The biggest volume involved products from tomato paste. The product used in remanufacture was packed in #10 cans (approximately 7 pounds of product per can) and #12 cans (approximately 9 pounds of product per can). The process for these nonaseptically processed products was long and inefficient. Initially, by means of heat exchangers, the product was heated to 190–205°F and filled into the can at that temperature. The can was then closed (the lid was put on the can) and the container was held for 2–10 min to effect sterilization of product and container. After sterilization the container was water cooled, usually in a continuous rotary cooler. Cooling of these products was (and is) very slow and required 60–90 min in the cooler. The slow cooling rate is due to the following factors:

1. The product is very thick and there is no agitation of product during cooling to assist in heat transfer.
2. Heat transfer is by conductance only.
3. The slow rate of heat transfer by conductance is further decreased by the large amount of insoluble solids present.

Upon discharge from the cooler, the outer portions of product had cooled to 80–100°F while the interior portions of the container still had a temperature of 150–180°F, with average can temperatures of 90–115°F. After discharge from the cooler, an additional 3–6 hr were required for the can contents to equilibrate to the average temperature (90–115°F). Thus, the cooling of these products in the normal process used was very inefficient and, on occasion, could reduce the quality of the product.

Customers using large numbers of #10 and #12 containers were showing an increasing interest in a larger container. In 1955, Rheem Manufacturing Company (a manufacturer of metal bodies including metal drums), Thermovac Company (a manufacturer of food-processing equipment), and Thornton Canning Company (a processor of tomato paste) joined together with a common desire to process tomato paste satisfactorily in 55-gallon drums. William Martin, the same William Martin who developed the Dole aseptic process, was hired as a consultant. By late 1956, a pilot plant aseptic drum filler was in place at the Thornton Canning Company. A few drums were packed from the pilot plant unit in 1957, and a commercial aseptic drum filler was installed for the 1958 season.

Spoilage problems required a design change in the drum, and shipping problems required a second design change in the drum. Finally, the package, the aseptic process, and the aseptic filler all came together to make a successful unit known as the Thermovac Sterilpac Drum Filling System. Early installations were used almost exclusively for tomato paste. Tomato paste, which had been heated to 190–205°F in a heat exchanger, was pumped to the hot holding tank of the system. Before the paste reached the hot holding tank, there was a steam injection heater in the line to guarantee that the paste was up to proper temperature— an additional precaution to guarantee sterility of the product. From the hot holding tank, the product was pumped to the vacuum flash separator where, by means of a 26- to 28-in. vacuum in the separator, the tomato paste was instantly cooled to 90–100°F. Prior to the start of operation, the "cold side" was sterilized using saturated steam at 250°C. The cold side consisted of the flash separator, aseptic pump, and piping (including the piping to each of four filling nozzles).

The empty drums were loaded into a retort, and the unit was set up to run 4 drums in the retort on each cycle. The empty drums were sterilized in the retort as follows: 45 sec vent plus 1 min, 45 sec at 35 pounds steam pressure. After the sterilization was completed, the retort was put under a 20 to 25-in. vacuum, at which point cool sterile tomato paste was pumped into the drums. Filling was by means of retractable nozzles which retracted into position immediately above the 4.5-in. opening in the top for filling; when the fill was completed, the nozzles retracted out of position, sealing heads with magnetically held closures were lowered onto the 4.5-in. opening, and the drum was sealed by a swadging operation. Each drum had a filling nozzle and sealing head; thus, there were four fill nozzles and four sealing heads. At the completion of the sealing operation, the front and back doors of the retort automatically opened, and the filled drums were automatically discharged. Empty drums (4) were put in place manually, the retort doors again automatically closed, and the cycle was repeated: 5 to 6 cycles were possible per hour, or 20 to 24 drums per hour. Figure 1 will assist in understanding the equipment and process.

Steam seals were installed on the cold side of the process to protect any area where air leakage might take place, including aseptic pumps, divert valves, sanitary fittings, sight glasses, instrument probes, rotating shafts, and scraped-surface heat exchangers.

This was the first instance of vacuum flash cooling in an aseptic processing system. Pumping tomato paste through heat exchangers for cooling developed very high back pressures in the system. It was much simpler to utilize vacuum flash cooling and escape this high back pressure. Today, both heat exchangers and flash coolers are used for these aseptic drum systems, but the greatest volume utilizes flash coolers. Concern has been expressed that there is greater chance of contamination from airborne microorganisms with vacuum flash cooling systems, but actual commercial operation of the two systems has not shown any difference in the two methods.

There was a steady increase in use and production of aseptically packed

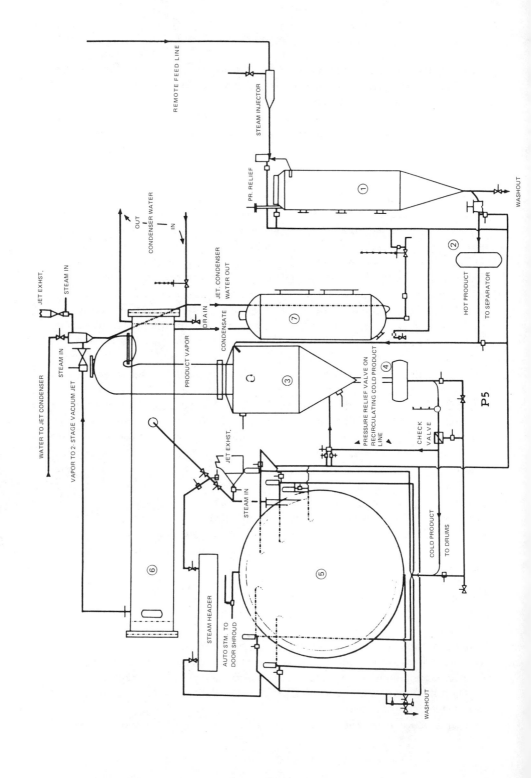

tomato paste and other products. The Sterilpac unit was eventually replaced by the FranRica Drum Filler. Sterilization and filling of the drums was accomplished by means of a "bell-jar" arrangement which fitted onto and sealed the top of each drum. Steam was added to the drum by means of the bell-jar arrangement. Sterilizing time was 1¾ min vent plus 45 sec at 15–18 psig steam pressure. At the completion of the sterilization cycle, steam pressure was reduced to where only a slight positive pressure remained. A retractable fill tube was then inserted almost to the bottom of the drum. As the drum was filled with paste, the fill tube automatically rose in the drum. When the fill was completed, the fill tube retracted and the drum was sealed utilizing a swadging tool similar to units used in the Thermovac equipment. The capacity of the unit was 15–17 drums per hr. Product-sterilizing procedures were identical for either the Thermovac or FranRica system.

Because of the high consistency of tomato paste, the FranRica filling system was superior to the Thermovac systems for obtaining uniform fills in the drum. Many systems have been installed worldwide, and production of well over 1 million drums per year was achieved.

E. BULK TANKS

A patent was granted to Dixon *et al.* (1963), wherein they state

Our patent is for a process in which tomato juice, for example, or concentrate or pulp may be charged into vessels which may be permanent storage vessels or transportation vessels such as trucks or tank cars, and withdrawn when required for use. Essentially it is a bulk method of handling, transporting and storing such products as distinguished from canning. . . . According to our invention, storage tanks of suitable size, often of many thousand gallons capacity . . . are filled with a fluid to displace oxygen, water generally being used. Then as the water or other fluid is drained out, it is replaced with nitrogen or other inert gas which need not be sterile. It is then sterilized with a nontoxic sterilizing medium which is recirculated through the system and then withdrawn, leaving the tank filled with nitrogen or inert gas above atmospheric pressure at all times. When the oxygen has thus been replaced with inert gas, the liquid or semi-liquid vegetable product or concentrate which has been sterilized, is pumped into the tank displacing the inert gas. Thus the product is kept from contact with air or organisms which might cause spoilage. If steam is used as a sterilizing fluid, low pressure steam is then preferably used for such period of time as may be required to assure sterilization; any condensate being drained away after which the steam is replaced with inert gas at pressure above atmospheric pressure.

When the vessel or tank has been filled to its ultimate height, there will remain at the top inert gas under pressure greater than atmospheric pressure. Leakage, if any, will therefore be from the inside out, and atmospheric air cannot enter. Provision is made for keeping this pressure constant. If part of the contents is withdrawn, the pressure of inert gas will still be kept above atmospheric pressure, the gas replacing the product which is removed.

FIG. 1. Thermovac Sterilpac drum-filling system. 1, Hot holding tank; 2, feed pump; 3, flash separator; fill pump; 5, retort; 6, condenser; and 7, condensate receptor.

The patent also mentions the use of low-pressure steam for sterilizing purposes. If steam is used, great care must be used to prevent imploding. An appreciable vacuum can be produced very rapidly when the steam condenses on the large metal surfaces available, which can result in serious implosion of the tank because tanks cannot economically be constructed to withstand much vacuum.

The processing of product in bulk containers, 55 to 125,000 gallons, was a complete success and continues to this day. This success is due to a number of factors:

1. product quality,
2. convenience of use by customer,
3. economics for both seller and buyer, and
4. fewer waste-disposal problems.

F.   COMMENTS REGARDING ASEPTIC PROCESSING

There are certain facts which must be discussed and emphasized in this dissertation on aseptic processing. When one installs an aseptic processing and aseptic packaging line, it is absolutely essential to have a very deep commitment to maintaining sterility within the unit. Without sterility, one has nothing—there are no "gray areas" in aseptic processing. The system is either sterile or not sterile.

1. *Product Sterility:* the system has to be designed so that absolutely no nonsterile product from the "hot side" can enter the "cold side." Once this happens, after a short lag time, all cool product will have bacterial contamination.

2. The *equipment layout* should be as simple as possible: short coupled with as few fittings as possible. All locations which may be points of entry for microorganisms must be protected with steam seals or other means of preventing entrance of microorganisms.

3. In the United States when low-acid products are aseptically processed (pH greater than 4.6), it is necessary for the operation to be under the supervision of a person who has attended a *Better Process Control School*. The schools are approved by the Food and Drug Administration (FDA), and personnel receive instruction on aseptic processing as well as other processing methods.

4. Equipment must be maintained at all times in *top operating* and *top sanitary* conditions. Failures in these areas create most of the problems which arise in aseptic processing systems.

5. *Microbiological auditing:* with so much at risk, microbiological auditing should be included in the testing procedures for aseptic packaging lines. Standard

plate counts or large Erlenmeyer flasks are used for this purpose. It is essential to use the proper media in which the likely spoilage organisms will grow, e.g., with tomato paste the spoilage organism almost invariably is *Lactobacillus,* and the medium of choice for *Lactobacillus* is orange serum agar. The real drawback to these methods is the time required for detection. After incubation at 37°C, detection can sometimes be made in 48 hr, but usually 72 hr are required and, unfortunately in that period, a great deal of production can be packed before the problem is discovered.

There are procedures now available which are faster, such as the work of Luster (1978) utilizing determination of diacetyl or acetyl methyl carbinol, products of the metabolism of spoilage organisms—*Lactobacillus* and yeasts. It is claimed that the method can detect microbial contamination within 4–12 hr.

Impedance microbiology is also now used to speed up results. As bacteria multiply in a medium, the metabolism of their growth creates an impedance to an alternating electric current conducted through the medium. This impedance can be measured and can be correlated to plate counts. Samples are monitored every 6 min for impedance, and as soon as impedance is detected the detection time is displayed on a screen. It is claimed that results are obtained in 4–48 hr. Heavy contamination will, of course, show up much sooner than light contamination.

Radiometric microbiology is another new method in which results are obtained as early as 5 hr.

Some processors use incubation of samples from each code for their microbiological auditing procedure. With some containers, this is very difficult (e.g., 55-gallon drum or 300-gallon bag-in-bin). The U.S. Food and Drug Administration recommends incubation tests of representative samples of each code for all low-acid, aseptically processed products.

6. *Heat exchangers:* aseptic systems as we know them today involve the use of heat exchangers for both heating and cooling the products. The choice of exchanger should be engineered to the characteristics of the product. For products such as juices and juice drinks, the plate-type heat exchanger does an excellent job of heating and cooling. Extra care must be taken to maintain all gaskets in good order, particularly on the cool side. Plate exchangers should not be used for thick products, and plate units are not satisfactory for products containing particulates and other coarse materials. These particles build up between the plates and prevent proper circulation of the product. Tabular heat exchangers can also be used for juices and juice drinks as well as for products which are somewhat thicker than juices. The tubular exchangers are more versatile than the plate exchangers with respect to the number of products which can be handled successfully. A more recent development of tubular heaters is a tube-within-a-tube exchanger, in which thick products (including tomato paste) are handled successfully. Scraped-surface heat exchangers are used for products containing particulates as well as for very thick products. Scraped-surface units

differ from plate and tubular units in that they use rotating blades. The units are normally 6 in. in diameter and are jacketed for heating or cooling. The blades are mounted concentrically along a shaft within the heat exchanger. Product is pumped through the exchanger and, at the same time, the shaft with the blades turns. The blades are free to move and the rotation of the shaft throws the blades against the heat-exchange surface. The blades are constantly removing and depositing product on the heat-exchange surface. This action prevents fouling of the exchanger surface. Steam-injection and steam-infusion heating systems are also used mainly for dairy products. This is the most rapid method of heating available.

7. *Pumps* are also essential in any aseptic system. Sometimes it is necessary to install a pump on the cool side of the system. If this is the case, this pump must be an aseptic pump with proper steam seals or other means of preventing microorganisms from entering the system.

Normally, one would use a centrifugal pump for juices and a positive displacement pump for thicker products. For low-acid products, it is necessary to use a pump which will accurately discharge a given volume of product. It may also be necessary to change the volume discharged from time to time. A variable-drive, positive-displacement pump is normally used for this purpose where the revolutions per minute of the pump can be changed as needed. The variable-speed device should be fitted with a lock, and only authorized persons permitted to make changes in a low-acid product line.

8. Problems may and do develop in aseptic systems to produce unsterile conditions. I have had personal experience with the following.

Stress cracks in welds: the weld will operate for years and then suddenly develops a stress crack allowing leakage of cooling water, product, or air which contaminates the system. The correction of stress cracks in welds is to produce a proper weld in the first place wherein stress in the weld is held to a minimum.

Stress cracks and pinholes develop in metal.

Dead-end pipelines: These result from improper design of the piping system, wherein a "dead-end pipeline" exists. It is impossible to properly sterilize a dead-end pipeline and, thus, it creates spoilage problems.

The *product holding tube* must be sloped upward. The FDA recommends at least 0.25 in./ft.

Improper sanitation: this is a situation where, between runs of a product, the product is not properly cleaned out of the system and, when the system is resterilized, complete sterility is not obtained because of the contamination of the remaining food product in the system. This can be a problem with very thick products, such as tomato paste, which are both difficult to clean from the system and difficult to sterilize because of their very slow rate of heat transfer.

Human error: this can and does occur. Improper assembling of an aseptic fitting and improper assembling of an aseptic seal are two examples.

III.   MIDDLE ERA: 1961–1981

A.   TETRA-PAK ASEPTIC PACKAGING MACHINE

The middle era of aseptic processing was initiated by the introduction of the first Tetra-Pak unit into commercial production in 1961. According to Sizer (1982), the package was developed by Ruben Rausing and utilized a unique tetrahedron-shaped package. Prior to 1961, the package had been in use principally for milk products. In 1961, the package was made aseptic by the use of hydrogen peroxide. This aseptic system initiated the tremendous growth phase of aseptic processing and maintains its preeminence today. The most popular system worldwide is the vertical form, fill, and seal Tetra-Pak unit (also known as Brik Pak Filler). Figure 2 shows a sketch of the unit, a very simple, yet ingenious aseptic filler. This machine utilizes a continuous web of printed laminated material on a reel. This laminate

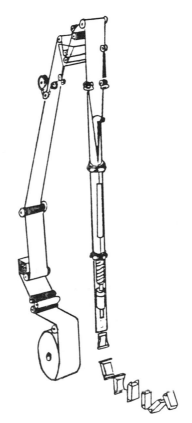

FIG. 2.   Diagram of aseptic Brik filler.

comprises polyethylene/printed paper/polyethylene/aluminum foil/polyethylene/polyethylene. The polyethylene provides the surface necessary to provide the seal as well as an inert surface in contact with the foodstuff. The aluminum foil gives the package barrier properties to both oxygen and light.

As shown in Fig. 2, the web is unwound and travels up the rear of the machine. A longitudinal sealing strip is welded to the edge of the web, after which the laminate goes to the hydrogen peroxide bath where it is coated with a thin layer of 35% hydrogen peroxide. Then, the web passes over the upper bending roller and starts down the front of the machine through forming rings which shape the web into a cylinder. The tube is next formed with a longitudinal seal. The product filling tube is at the center of the laminate tube and is surrounded by a radiant heater. The temperature is 500–600°F. The high temperature heats the internal polyethylene film surface to 110–120°C, which, in combination with the hydrogen peroxide present, sterilizes the polyethylene surface and then evaporates or decomposes any remaining hydrogen peroxide. Sterile product is introduced with a flow counter-current to the downward travel of the tube or web. Sterile air helps to maintain a sterile environment and removes any residue of hydrogen peroxide. The level of product in the tube is maintained about 2 feet above the level of the bottom transverse seal by controlled addition of product from the filling tube. Transverse seals are made at regular intervals through the product in the tube utilizing 8000 pounds of jaw pressure and induction heating. Packages are then cut, and the flaps are sealed to the side forming the characteristic shape of this carton.

The filling technique is the same regardless of product. Worldwide, the principal products have been milk and milk products, but many other aseptic products are produced on these fillers, including fruit juices, juice drinks, puddings, custards, and fruit-juice concentrates.

By sealing through the liquid or product in the tube laminate, Tetra-Pak produces a package with no headspace.

The key to the success of the Tetra-Pak aseptic packaging unit was the use of hydrogen peroxide plus heat for sterilizing the packaging material. Swartling and Lundgren (1968) reported on the sterilizing effect against *Bacillus subtilus* spores of hydrogen peroxide at different temperatures and concentrations as shown in Table V. With an initial spore count of $0.04/cm^2$, a count that is often found on commercial Tetra-Pak paper, a decimal reduction of 4 would be just sufficient. In this case, treatment of paper for about 10 sec with a 20% hydrogen peroxide solution at 90–95°C would meet this requirement. The number of nonsterile packages must not exceed 1 in 1000 packages.

von Bockelman and von Bockelman (1986) have studied the microbial counts on plastic food-contact surfaces and reported these to range from 0.3–10 microorganisms/100 cm^2. The microflora found on polyethylene food-contact surfaces

TABLE V

TIME (TO THE NEAREST SECOND) TO CAUSE REDUCTIONS OF 3–6 LOG CYCLES

Reduction in number of spores (logarithmic cycles)	Hydrogen peroxide concentration (%)					
	15			20		
	80°C[a]	90°C[b]	95°C[b]	80°C[a]	90°C[b]	95°C[b]
3	17	10	9	11	7	5
4	23	14	11	15	9	7
5	39	18	14	19	12	9
6	35	21	16	23	14	11

From Swartling and Lundgren (1968); © *Journal of Dairy Research*; reprinted by permission of Cambridge University Press.

[a] By experiment.

[b] By extrapolation.

of paperboard-based laminates averaged a total count of 2–5 microorganisms/100 cm² with 10.6% yeast, 20.6% molds, and 68.8% bacteria. A further differentiation of the bacterial flora (based on the total microbial count) showed the following: 44.4% micrococci, 3.1% bacterial spores, 3.7% streptococci, 1.2% *Pseudomonas*, 6.9% gram-positive rods, and 9.4% gram-negative rods. All of these were obtained immediately after producing the packaging material and did not account for further infection of the food-contact surface at the site of the commercial processor. The microbiological data on food-contact surfaces clearly indicate an airborne infection. von Bockelman and von Bockelman (1986) further state the failure of a sterilization process is mainly determined by the number of the most resistant organisms present—bacterial spores—and not by total count. Little is known about spore counts on packaging material food-contact surfaces. Consequently, calculation of minimum sterilization effects (decimal reductions) necessary are often based on the assumption that all microorganisms on food-contact surfaces are bacterial spores. Sterilization of such surfaces has been defined as a reduction of the microbial load from 10^4 to 10^0. To obtain a maximum spoilage rate of 5 in 10,000, 4 to 5 decimal reductions are considered necessary.

With this unique filling–packaging machine, Tetra-Pak provided the impetus for the tremendous growth we have seen in aseptic processing. In 1961, the year of the introduction of the Tetra-Pak unit, aseptic processing was alive but far from a dynamic industry. The volume was static, but since 1961, we have seen tremendous increases in volume. It is estimated that the 1986 volume was 26 billion units worldwide, and for the past several years, volume has been increasing at a rate of approximately 2 billion containers per year worldwide.

B.   READY-TO-EAT PUDDINGS

During the 1960s in the United States, aseptic processing maintained a very low profile in consumer and institutional products. The Dole system was the only system available, and products were limited to specialty sauces (such as white sauce, cheese sauce, and Hollandaise sauce), to special soups, and to a small volume of condensed milk and other milk products. The volume of aseptically processed products was either static or decreasing. In other countries, through the use of plastic containers and hydrogen peroxide for sterilizing the container, aseptic processing was surging ahead; but the use of H_2O_2 was not allowed in the United States. However in 1969, aseptically packed individual servings of ready-to-eat puddings were introduced in the United States. The reception of these products was overwhelming. The packers could not keep the product on the shelves. Volume increased at a rate of 50% per year for several years. Dole made available a filler–sterilizer capable of 300–600 cans/min for the individual serving size. The popularity of the individual serving size also created a demand for institutional-sized containers of ready-to-eat puddings as well. Many companies became involved in packing and selling aseptically processed, ready-to-eat puddings. The products had excellent flavor, color, and consistency because of the use of aseptic processing methods with well-formulated products. But suddenly, as with so many aseptic products, sales volume began a steady downward trend instead of increasing. In 1987 one finds most of the packers have discontinued the item, and only two producers remain with perhaps a few copackers.

C.   BAG-IN-BOX

About 1960, the Scholle Corporation introduced the bag-in-box concept for pasteurized, refrigerated milk to replace metal dairy cans for dispensing milk in restaurants, schools, hotels, etc. The package replaced all dairy cans. Some of the dairies felt the next step was to go to aseptic or ultrahigh temperature (UHT) milk to eliminate refrigeration. After they expressed their interest in an aseptic filler to the Scholle Corporation, Scholle, in 1968, introduced a filler capable of filling aseptically processed milk utilizing bag-in-box packaging.

The bag was saranex/polyethylene/polyethylene or saranex/saranex/polyethylene/polyethylene—the saranex was the oxygen and water vapor barrier in the package. The bags were heat sealed on the four outer edges, and each bag had a spout with a removable cap. The bags were presterilized with ethylene oxide and arrived at the dairy in sterile condition. The filler head was sterilized with saturated steam at 250°F for 30 min and then maintained sterile with the use of sterile air and chlorine mist. Millipore filters were used for sterilizing the air. The sterile air served to atomize the chlorine and keep positive air pressure within the filling head.

In the actual filling operation, an operator placed the bag up into the aseptic chamber where the cap was automatically removed; the fill tube was then inserted into the spout and a vacuum was drawn on the bag after which product flow began. A magnetic flow meter controlled the amount of product going into each bag. At the completion of the fill, a puff of nitrogen filled the small headspace in the spout. The fill tube was removed, and the cap was automatically replaced. The bag was rejected from the chamber and placed in a corrugated box, and the filler was ready for the next bag.

The important function in this operation is the design of the spout and the cap. It is absolutely essential that the cap maintain a hermetic seal at all times: during sterilization, after sterilization, prior to filling, after filling, and prior to use (which includes storage under various conditions and the shipping trauma). The cap was successful in fulfilling all of its functions.

According to Orbell (1980), the tests were successful from a technological standpoint. There was no spoilage; the product shipped well and had adequate shelf-life, but the tests were marketing failures. The American public did not like aseptic (UHT) milk. Similar results were obtained later on tests of UHT milk with smaller, consumer-sized packages. So the unit sat idle for several years.

During this period, bulk aseptic processing was increasing in volume, particularly in California with the 55-gallon drum pack. This activity was principally in tomato paste, but involved other products as well: tomato catsup, pizza sauce, and concentrated fruit purees (apricot, peach, pear, and apple). In 1971, a California canner approached the Scholle Corporation concerning the use of the Scholle filler for these products named above. Experimental packs were made of concentrated fruit purees in 6-gallon, bag-in-box containers in 1971. Two processors made commercial runs in 1972 and 1973 of products in 55-gallon bag-in-box containers. All of the bags used in these tests were sterilized with ethylene oxide. In 1974, the FDA ruled against the use of ethylene oxide for sterilizing bags which were to be used for food products. This proved to be only a temporary setback for bag-in-box. In 1975, Scholle Corporation introduced bags which were sterilized using gamma radiation, which is the method still in use today. Actually, the ban was fortuitous; with ethylene oxide, it was impossible to develop a bag with good barrier properties because of the necessity of having a film which would allow the ethylene oxide to permeate it. With gamma-radiation sterilization, barrier properties have no effect whatsoever on the sterilization. The result of this has been steady improvement in the barrier properties of the bags, and these barrier properties will continue to improve. A comparison of new and old films is in order and is shown in Table VI.

W. J. Scholle (unpublished data) also reports similar improvement in barrier

TABLE VI

NEW FILM VS. OLD FILM: RATE OF TRANSMISSION OF OXYGEN[a]

Film type	Pure O_2 transmission (100 in.^{2}/24 hr at 70°F)
Saranex/polyethylene: Old film	0.50
Saranex/saranex/polyethylene: Old film	0.23
Metallized polyester: New film	0.05
Metallized polyester/polyethylene: New film	0.05
Metallized polyester/metallized polyester/ polyethylene: New film	0.01

[a] After W. J. Scholle, unpublished data.

properties of the spout assemblies. At 70°F the old spout assemblies had an O_2 transmission rate of 0.9 cc pure oxygen/assembly/24 hr as compared to 0.5 cc pure oxygen/assembly/24 hr for new spout assemblies. It is now possible to seal off the spout assembly, which results in further improvement of the barrier properties of the package.

Products vary in shelf-life and transportation properties. The proper package will satisfy both requirements, and we now have more choices to engineer the proper package.

The list of products utilizing aseptic bag-in-box packaging is rather wide and includes tomato paste, tomato catsup, pizza sauce, apple juice, concentrated grape juice, orange-juice concentrate, peach-puree concentrate, pear-puree concentrate, pineapple-juice concentrate, apple slices, peach slices, various berries, crushed pineapple, and various tropical fruit purees. Well over 200 fillers for aseptic bag-in-box packaging have been installed worldwide, and the annual growth rate is 10–20 additional fillers. Fillers and bags are now available from other suppliers, but Scholle remains the principal source of bags and aseptic filling equipment.

The outer container is indispensable for bag-in-box packaging. The outer container provides rigidity, stackability, protection, and shipping strength for the bag. For 1–6 gallon sizes the outer container is a corrugated fiber box, the 55-gallon bag uses a steel or fiber drum, the 60-gallon bag uses a corrugated fiber box, and the 300-gallon bag uses a wooden bin with a fiber or plastic insert to protect the bag from the wood.

The first test pack of 300-gallon bag-in-bin was in 1976. The initiation of the 300-gallon bag has resulted in a consistent growth pattern in the United States, replacing 55-gallon drums in the same manner that 55-gallon drums replaced #10 cans. The product aseptic processing equipment that is used for 55-gallon drums can be used with no change for 300-gallon bag-in-bin operations. A number of operations are equipped with a valve in the product line to direct the product to either the bag filler or the drum filler. Tomato paste is the principal item used in 300-gallon bag-in-bin; however, concentrated fruit juices and particulate fruits are also packed in this container. Every year, new products appear in 300-gallon bins. The bin is a "knock-down" type and is returned for reuse. With some of the bins, 10 trips have been logged. Overseas, there has also been steady growth, principally utilizing a 55-gallon bag in a used metal drum, although there is also production of 60-gallon bags in corrugated boxes.

Nelson (1984) had this to say on bag-in-box:

Movement of partially processed product (i.e., concentrates) closer to consumer markets for final product manufacture (i.e., catsup) has created demands for economical ways of holding and moving this partially processed product. Initially, #10 cans were utilized to fill this remanufacturing need. However, costs and handling problems have caused the industry to search for alternative packaging. With the advent of aseptic processing, the aseptic drum has been used to meet remanufacturing demands; but, like the #10 can, it is being challenged by the need for more efficient and less costly methods of handling. Thus enters the Bag-In-Box technology.

There are a number of reasons for the steady growth of bag-in-box packaging, and these are reasons why bag-in-box packaging will continue to grow:

1. First and foremost is the much lower container cost.
2. Space savings for both empty and full containers.
3. Economics of use of a large container vs a greater number of small containers.
4. Freight savings on empty and full containers.
5. Adequate to superior shipping qualities.
6. Adequate shelf life.
7. Energy savings.
8. Waste-disposal savings.
9. The advantages of aseptic processing.

D. BULK TANKS

In the early 1970s, P. E. Nelson utilized bulk tanks for a number of products other than tomato paste, including crushed tomatoes and tomato puree. As a result of this activity a number of new bulk tank installations were made, principally in California, Indiana, New York, and Japan. The products processed and stored in these tanks included tomato puree, crushed tomatoes, apple juice, and grape juice. Tanks were usually of a 40,000 gallon capacity. Sterilization was accomplished by the use of iodophor solutions at 25 ppm I_2. The same solution used for the storage tanks was used for the tank trucks or tank cars that shipped the aseptic products.

IV. LATE ERA: 1981–1987

A. USE OF HYDROGEN PEROXIDE ALLOWED
AS A STERILIZING AGENT

In the United States in the late 1970s, bulk aseptic processing was in a growth mode. Consumer aseptic products were either static or declining in volume, whereas in Europe, the use of consumer aseptic products was growing at a rapid rate. The growth principally involved milk products, but other products were involved as well—juices, juice drinks, desserts, puddings, and sauces, to name a few. The Tetra-Pak machine was primarily used, but because of the tremendous size of the market, other manufacturers were in the market with filling machines. This tremendous growth was the result of the use of plastic packaging; whereas, in the United States only metal could be used for aseptic processing.

The advantages of plastic over metal for packaging are many—lower cost, lighter weight, less shelf and storage space, and the ability of containers to be formed just prior to filling. Most plastic containers will not stand up to the rigors of hot filling products at 190–205°F. To make use of the advantages of plastic packaging, products are normally filled into the container at about 90°F. These low filling temperatures require aseptic processing and aseptic packaging to achieve sterility. The aseptic packaging sterility can be obtained by the use of hydrogen peroxide.

The use of hydrogen peroxide for sterilization was not available in the United States until February 9, 1981, when the Food and Drug Administration ruled that 30–35% hydrogen peroxide could be used to sterilize polyethylene surfaces provided that no more than 0.1 ppm hydrogen peroxide remained on the surface just prior to filling.

From that point in time, aseptic processing in plastic containers has been in the forefront of food industry production, research, and marketing. By June of 1983, 110 aseptic fillers were in use in the United States with flexible plastic packaging. In 1983, 500 million aseptic packages were processed, and over 1 billion packages were processed in 1985. It has been estimated that up to 10 billion aseptic plastic containers will be produced in 1990. This is a tremendous achievement in converting a recent technical development into commercial usage. Juices and juice drinks make up the principle volume, but considerable volumes of dips, sauces, soups, gravies, and puddings are all in the mix. Milk is not included in this list. Unlike Europe, aseptically processed UHT milk is not successful in the U.S. marketplace.

The tremendous growth of aseptic processing has developed methods other than hydrogen peroxide for sterilizing the container, but the vast majority of installed systems utilize hydrogen peroxide as the container sterilant, and hydrogen peroxide has been the choice for container sterilization to be used for low-acid foods.

Stevenson and Shafer (1983) reported on bacterial spore resistance to hydrogen peroxide and indicated that at low concentrations, hydrogen peroxide solutions are bactericidal but not highly sporicidal. The sporicidal efficiency increases with increasing concentrations. To obtain rapid sporicidal activity, relatively high concentrations (e.g., 35%) are utilized in aseptic systems to sterilize the packaging material. Stevenson and Schafer go on to say that the temperature of hydrogen peroxide has a pronounced affect on the rate of spore destruction. At room temperature, hydrogen peroxide is not rapidly sporicidal. The Q^{10} value—the influence of a 10°C temperature rise—has been reported to be from 1.6 to 2.5. Since hydrogen peroxide is relatively stable at high temperatures, some researchers have utilized temperatures as high as 95°C or treatment with hydrogen peroxide followed by hot-air heating at 125°C.

According to Stevenson and Shafer (1983), Bayless and Waites reported a synergistic effect of simultaneous application of UV radiation and hydrogen peroxide. Best results were obtained with 0.5–1.0% concentration of hydrogen peroxide and UV irradiation at 254 mm. A U.S. patent by Peel and Waites (1981) utilizes this principle.

B. BROADENED USE OF HYDROGEN PEROXIDE AS A STERILIZING AGENT

The original regulation of the FDA allowed the use of only polyethylene with hydrogen peroxide. On April 1, 1985, the FDA issued new regulations allowing a wider use of plastic materials. This regulation is 21 CFR 178.1005 as of April 1, 1985.

On August 14, 1984, the FDA issued an additional regulation which allowed aseptic packagers to use concentrations of hydrogen peroxide lower than 30%, providing that the processes they employ continue to achieve commercial sterility. The new regulation recognizes the availability of systems that sterilize with lower levels of hydrogen peroxide and UV light or with heat. Hydrogen peroxide at 35% is still the maximum percentage of hydrogen peroxide allowable and the residual hydrogen peroxide level is still at a maximum of 0.1 ppm.

C. GREATLY EXPANDED CHOICE OF METHODS FOR STERILIZING ASEPTIC PACKAGES

Not too many years ago in aseptic processing, the industry was limited to cans as containers and the use of saturated steam or superheated steam as the sterilizing media for the cans. But in 1987, there are many choices for packaging sterilant and package type. The choice of packaging sterilant is H_2O_2 and hot air, H_2O_2 and UV, UV radiation, saturated steam, superheated steam, hot air, preirradiated bags, presterilization by extrusion heat, delamination of sterile roll in sterile chambers, presterilization by molding or extrusion heat, and electron beams. The choice of package type is paper–foil–film carton; plastic cups; aluminum cups; film pouches; stand-up foil pouches; composite cans; metallized plastic film bags; metal drums; paper, foil, gabletop, and plastic bottles; foil/film bags; and metal cans.

The machinery technology available also gives many choices: vertical form/fill/seal; web-fed preformed bags/fill/seal; deposit/fill/seal/preformed cups; convey/fill/seal; form/fill/seal; preformed sleeves/fill/seal; thermoform/fill/seal; preformed bags/fill/seal; and blow-mold/fill/seal.

Ito and Stevenson (1984) reviewed the sterilization of packaging materials using aseptic systems. They reiterated that

> To produce a commercially sterile product, an aseptic system must meet three basic requirements. The product must be sterile; the package or container in which the product will be placed must be sterile; and the environment in which the produce and package will be brought together must be sterile. For low acid foods, inherent in each of these requirements is the need to know that spores of *C[lostridium] botulinum*, if present, will be destroyed. The conditions necessary to meet these conditions are determined and confirmed by microbiological testing.
>
> In aseptic canning, sterilization of the packaging material and the product filling and closing systems are critical factors. Each of these systems must be tested separately to establish the process according to the regulation.

Package sterilization has been accomplished by using a number of different methods and combinations of methods. Some of these methods are given in Table VII (Ito and Stevenson, 1984). An anonymous contribution to *Food Engineering* (Anonymous, 1985) has an excellent synopsis of the many choices available in aseptic processing today as shown in Table VIII.

Finally, after years of stagnation, aseptic packaging of food products has become a stable, growing market and is fulfilling the dreams of Ball, Martin, and others. Growth at the present time is 20–30% per year, and growth will continue for many years involving both present products in production and an ever-expanding list of new products. The list of products now available from aseptic packaging is an imposing one: juices, juice drink products, juice concentrates, soups, sauces, milk, milk products, puddings, tomato paste, tomato catsup, pizza sauce, fruit-puree concentrates, tropical fruit purees, pineapple-juice concentrate, baby foods, applesauce, nutritional supplements, yogurt products, tofu, deciduous fruits, and berries. This list will grow, and the comments in Section V will explain why many products will soon be added to the list.

V. FUTURE ERA AND RESEARCH NEEDS

It should be noted that the information in this section comes from many conversations between the author and producers and users of aseptic products.

TABLE VII

METHODS FOR STERILIZING ASEPTIC PACKAGES[a]

Method	Application	Advantages/disadvantages
Superheated steam	Metal containers	High temperature at atmospheric pressure Microorganisms are more resistant than in saturated steam
Dry hot air	Metal or composite juice and beverage containers	High temperature at atmospheric pressure Microorganisms are more resistant than in saturated steam
Hot hydrogen peroxide	Plastic containers, laminated foil	Fast and efficient
Hydrogen peroxide/UV light combination	Plastic containers (preformed cartons)	UV increases effectiveness of hydrogen peroxide
Ethylene oxide	Glass and plastic containers	Cannot be used where chlorides are present or where residuals would remain
Heat from coextrusion process	Plastic containers	No chemicals used
Radiation	Heat-sensitive plastic containers	Can be used to sterilize heat-sensitive packaging materials; expensive; problems with location of radiation source

[a]After Ito and Stevenson (1984).

These comments represent the hopes and desires of these producers and users for the aseptic products of the future.

A. PACKAGING

Packaging has been the catalyst that has launched aseptic packaging and aseptic processing and will continue to take the lead position in pushing aseptic processing forward. There will be improved packages with respect to oxygen transmission. The plastic container will approach the can with respect to barrier properties. There will be improvements in film to decrease product interaction which affects flavor, such as the flavor absorbance from citrus products. Faster production speeds are needed. New packages, new sizes, and easy-open devices will all be a part of the new packages we can expect to see in the future. We may also see in-line sterilization of packaging utilizing electron-beam radiation as well as many other developments, some of which will be startling to all of us.

TABLE VIII
GUIDE TO ASEPTIC PACKAGING SYSTEMS[a]

Manufacturer or U.S. supplier	Package type/size range	Machinery technology	Sterilant	Production capacity
Asepak Corp., Corrington, OH	Plastic bags, pouches ($\frac{1}{2}$ pint–10 gal)	Web-fed preformed bags/ fill/seal	Presterilized bags via extrusion heat	Up to 10,000 gallons per min
Astec, Cedar Rapids, IA (Metal Box Ltd., U.K.)	Plastic cups (3–15 oz)	Deposit/fill/ seal/preformed cups	Hydrogen peroxide	40–160 per min
Benco, Boston, MA (Benco, Italy)	Plastic cups (up to 1 liter)	Thermoform/fill/ seal	Hydrogen peroxide	6,000–25,000 per hr
Ben Hill (Benz & Hilger, W. Germany)	Plastic cups, tubs	Deposit/fill/ seal, preformed cups	UV radiation	Up to 48 per min
Boise Cascade Co., Hazelwood, MO (James Dole Corp)	Composite cans (up to 46 oz)	Convey/fill/seal	Hot air	Up to 70 per min
Bosch Packaging Machinery, Piscataway, NJ (Hesser, W. Germany)	Stand-up foil pouches	Form/fill/seal	Hydrogen peroxide	5,000–10,000 per hr
Combibloc, Inc., Columbus, OH (PKL Jagenberg, W. Germany)	Paper/foil film cartons (200 ml–1 liter)	Preformed sleeves, fill/seal	Hydrogen peroxide	5,000–10,000 per hr
Continental Can Co., Stamford, CT (Erca, France)	Plastic cups (4 oz–2 liter)	Thermoform/fill/ seal	Delamination of roll stock in sterile chamber	8,000–50,000 per hr
DuPont (Canada), Massassagua, Ont. (Prepac, France)	Film pouch (4 oz–2 liter)	Vertical form/ fill/seal	Hydrogen peroxide	Up to 33 per min
FranRica Mfg. Co., Stockton, CA	Metallized plastic film bags (1–300 gal)	Preformed bags/ fill/seal	Preirradiated bags, steam	Varies with product, bag size

(continued)

TABLE VIII (*Continued*)

Manufacturer or U.S. supplier	Package type/size range	Machinery technology	Sterilant	Production capacity
FranRica Mfg. Co., Stockton, CA (Prodo-Pak Corp)	Foil/film bags (up to 10 liter)	Vertical form/fill/seal	Preirradiated films, steam	Up to 40 per min
FranRica Mfg. Co., Stockton, CA (Dai Nippon, Japan)	Plastic cups (4–8 oz)	Thermoform/fill/seal	Hydrogen peroxide	200+ per min
International Paper, New York, NY	Paper/foil/film cartons (200–250 mil)	Vertical form/fill/seal	Hydrogen peroxide, heat	3,650 per hr
Jagenberg, Inc., Enfield, CT (Plastimeme-canique, France)	Plastic cups (up to 1 liter)	Thermoform/fill/seal	Hydrogen peroxide	Up to 1,500 per min
Jagenberg, Inc., Enfield, CT (Gasti, W. Germany)	Plastic, aluminum cups (up to 8 oz)	Deposit/fill/seal/preformed cups	Hydrogen peroxide	Up to 300 per min
Jagenberg, Inc., Enfield CT (Gasti, W. Germany)	Plastic cups	Deposit/fill/seal/preformed cups	Saturated steam	Up to 300 per min
James Dole Corp., Redwood City, CA	Metal cans (2–128 oz)	Convey/fill/seal	Superheated steam or hot air	Up to 500 per min
Liqui-Box Corp., Worthington, OH	Plastic film/foil bags (1–300 gal)	Preformed bags, fill/seal	Preirradiated bags, steam	Varies with product, bag size
Liquipak International Inc., St. Paul, MN (Liquipak International, UK)	Paper/foil gable-top cartons 1/2 gal)	Preformed sleeves, fill/seal	Hydrogen peroxide, UV radiation, HEPA air	60 per min
Rampart/Mead Pkg., Williamsburg, VA; Atlanta, GA	Plastic cups (up to 10 oz)	Deposit/fill/seal preformed bags	Citric acid (high-acid foods only)	300 per min

(*continued*)

TABLE VIII (*Continued*)

Manufacturer or U.S. supplier	Package type/size range	Machinery technology	Sterilant	Production capacity
Rommelag, USA, Fords, NJ (Rommelag, W. Germany)	Plastic bottles (0.1–10 liter)	Blow-mold/fill/ seal	Molding heat, sterile air	Up to 24,000 per hr
Scholle Corp., Northlake, IL	Metallized film bags (3 liter– 330 gal)	Preformed bags, fill/seal	Preirradiated bags, chlorine, hydrogen peroxide	Varies with product/bag size
Serac, Inc., Addison, IL (Serac, France)	Plastic, glass bottles (to 5 liter), aerosol cans	Blow-mold/fill/ seal (plastic), convey/fill/ seal (cans)	Hydrogen peroxide, chlorinated water	Up to 20,000 per hr
Stoelting, Inc., Kiel, WI (Hamba, W. Germany)	Plastic cups (4– 32 oz)	Deposit/fill/seal, pre-formed cups	UV radiation, hydrogen peroxide, sterile air	Up to 300 per min
Tetra-Pak, Inc., Shelton, CT (Tetra-Pak, Rausing, Switzerland)	Paper/foil/film cartons (125 ml–1 liter)	Vertical form/ fill/seal	Hydrogen peroxide	Up to 200 per min
Thermoforming, USA, Columbus, OH (Thermoforming, Italy)	Plastic cups, fill/seal	Thermoform/fill/ seal	Hydrogen peroxide	Up to 200 per min
Verpa, Inc., Norwood, NJ (Verpa, W. Germany)	Plastic cups	Thermoform/fill/ seal	Electronic beam or UV radiation	Not available

[a]After Anonymous (1985).

B. PARTICULATE PRODUCTS

There is a need for particulate products in both high-acid products and low-acid products.

1. Particulate Fruits and Tomatoes

With respect to high-acid particulate products, there are two categories—diced tomatoes and fruits. With respect to diced tomatoes, many desire a crisp tomato dice with a minimum heat treatment to preserve as much of the natural flavor as possible. The tomato dice would be used on pizzas, in pizza sauce, in various tomato sauces (marinara, spaghetti, ravioli, etc.), and in many other areas where tomatoes are used. A number of attempts have been made to produce aseptically processed tomato dices, but efforts have been unsuccessful to date. Perhaps what is needed first is a successful aseptic dejuicing screen. It seems logical that the more liquid moved through the system, the less damage will be done to particulates within that system (providing the excess liquid can be removed prior to packaging). A number of years ago, a small quantity of aseptically diced tomatoes were produced annually by one tomato processor. This equipment is no longer in use, so the market is wide open.

Particulate fruits are used in yogurts, preserves, pies, deserts, and canned fruits. The fruits can be in the form of dices, purees, slices, tidbits, and halves. Unlike diced tomatoes, there is one successful producer of aseptic fruit particulate products who is doing a very commendable job and has spent many years developing this art and technique. The operation is described in Smittcamp *et al.* (1981). The comments on the results using aseptic processing with bag-in-box packaging are of interest.

High quality of fruit color and flavor is maintained by short time heating and immediate cooling. The entire product receives the necessary amount of heating and cooling in the scraped surface heat exchangers; product in the center of the package is the same temperature as product on the periphery. This is an all natural product with no added color or preservatives. Product can be handled without freezing at an energy savings of around $.02 per pound. Packaging costs are reduced by about 50% in comparison to 5 gallon plastic pails, 55 gallon drums and #10 cans. Energy costs for heating and cooling the product have dropped approximately 30% and an additional savings of 25% energy is obtained through the use of refrigerated storage (to preserve quality) versus frozen storage required before for all-natural products.

There are others working on particulate fruits and new breakthroughs may be possible. As stated previously, perhaps a successful aseptic dejuicing unit would aid in producing a satisfactory product, but for such a system, it is very important to aseptically dejuice in order to obtain an adequate drained weight of particulate fruit. The drained juice would be reused over and over again to be successful.

There are areas for the use of fruits where aseptically processed products could be immediately substituted if available. These areas are as follows.

a.   Pineapple Tidbits in Canned Fruit Cocktail.   Several hundred thousand cases of 6/10's are used yearly in the production of canned fruit cocktail in California. When tidbits can be successfully aseptically packaged into either a 55-gallon bag, in a fiber drum or a 300-gallon bag-in-bin, there are large savings in packaging costs, storage space required, shipping costs, ease of reuse, and waste disposal. In addition, there is a superior product because of its more natural flavor and crisper texture. I am confident that our researchers will find a way to give us this product in the not-too-distant future.

b.   Peaches and Apricots for Use in Preserves, Pies, and Yogurt.   These products now principally use frozen product in 55-gallon drums with a film liner. It requires 4–7 days to defrost the drums before processing the fruit. With aseptically processed fruits, on a moment's notice the fruit can be rolled into the processing area, and it is ready to be processed. This eliminates the expensive freezing and frozen storage costs, as well as the expensive frozen storage shipping costs because the products will be held at ambient temperatures. In many instances, there is better color.

c.   Berries for Use in Preserves and Ice Cream.   All of the comments that come into play under apricots and peaches are also relevant for berries. With aseptically processed berries, one also has the problem of color degradation of the product. This added problem may slow down the use of aseptic processing, but I believe the large savings which evolve from aseptic processing will create the pressure necessary to facilitate the research required to solve the problem.

d.   Sliced Apples for Pies and other Bakery Products.   Frozen apples are now used for these products and, although the frozen apple slices are excellent products, the cost advantages of aseptic processing vs the increasing cost of freezing, frozen storage, and frozen shipment creates the climate to provide the necessary research to produce aseptically processed apple slices.

2.   Low-Acid Particulate Products

Soups with 9-mm particulates are now available in England, and a great deal of work must be going on in the United States because there is constant news that such products will be shortly introduced. Low-acid particulate products, at the present time, are not products for everyone to be considering. The effort will require a great deal of test work to know that the spores of *Clostridium botulinum,* if present, are destroyed. One will have no guarantee that every particulate receives the necessary heat to destroy the *C. botulinum* spores. Effort, time, money, and good research will be the major parts of the equation to produce successful, aseptically processed low-acid particulate products. The successful application of this process will add many new products to the list of aseptically processed products, including soups, meat products (such as stews), chicken products (such as fricassee), cream-style corn, etc. The universe of products will be greater than now contemplated.

C.   CITRUS PRODUCTS

Aseptic packaging has a very small niche in this very large industry. This involves the use of both bulk sizes (bag-in-box) and consumer sizes. The industry is beginning to see more juice products on the market, but in general, these juice products do not have as good a flavor as their frozen counterparts—this one factor is holding back the aseptic industry in citrus. Some experts in the industry feel that citrus products cannot be successfully aseptically packaged to produce a marketable product. However, the advantages of flexible packaging, together with the cost savings of ambient or refrigerated storage vs frozen storage and the savings of ambient transportation vs frozen transportation, will fuel the necessary research projects to eventually solve the problem. A number of difficulties are creating the quality problems in citrus. Oxygen is a degrading factor and must be removed prior to packaging (probably as early in the process as possible). Once the product is put into the package free of oxygen, the package must prevent any further passage of oxygen into the product. We also have the problem of chemical reaction between the packaging film and product, as with polyethylene and orange juice. Finally, there is the temperature problem. If one wishes to store at ambient or refrigerated temperatures, the temperature profile of the product throughout the process should be kept as low as possible. For enzyme inactivation, evaporation, and sterilization, the temperature profile must be kept as low as possible. New techniques may evolve which will reduce the required heat for these unit processes. So solution of the problem involves both processing and packaging; for those who are successful, a vast market awaits.

D. BULK BAG-IN-BOX CONTAINERS

1. Low-Acid Foods

There has been a desire to package low-acid foods in larger size containers— bag-in-box. For several years, development of such a filler has been underway. Challenge tests to the filler with microorganisms have been completed successfully. The filler utilizes hydrogen peroxide to maintain sterility in the filling head and also to sterilize the exterior spout and spout area prior to filling. Work is now progressing to determine the proper dosage of radiation for the sterilization of bags to be used for low-acid foods. The tests utilized 3- and 5-gallon bags with 700 and 1000 square in. of surface, respectively. One-third of the wash was used for aerobic bioburden, one-third for anaerobic bioburden, and one-third for anaerobic bioburden plus spores; 81 bags were tested.

In low-acid food products, the spore count is the important factor. Of the tests for spores, 93% were negative, and 7% of the tests showed a spore count of 0.84 or less per 100 in.^{2} (W. J. Scholle, unpublished data).

Two low-acid fillers are in place in processing plants, and when the sterilization data for the bags becomes available, processes will be filled with the FDA for approval. Commercial production of low-acid products packaged in bag-in-box will be underway with FDA approval of the filed processes. Bag-in-box packaging lends itself very well to products containing particulates. One filler has a 1-in. clearance for particulates, and a second filler type has a 3-in. clearance for particulates; so, if and when low-acid particulate product processes are approved, bag-in-box is certain to be considered as one source of packaging.

2. Web-Fed Bags

A popular item for a number of years has been 3-gallon bag-in-box tomato catsup, and millions of containers are packed each year. Up to this time, there has been little or no other activity to replace #10 cans, but there is movement for further replacement of cans with the availability of a web-fed bag filler which automates the filling operation, thus increasing production rates; seven to ten 3- to 6-gallon bags can be produced per minute per filling head. Figure 3 shows the new web fed filler. A leading tomato paste buyer in England has notified his suppliers that he will no longer purchase tomato paste in 5 kg cans. All of the paste must be in 55-gallon bags in used drums. There is also pressure from fast-food outlets to eliminate cans. We will see increasing amounts of bag-in-box products replacing #10 cans of the same product.

3. Aseptic Unloading

Aseptic unloading is now available in 300- and 55-gallon bag sizes. It is necessary to install a second unloading spout for bags to be used in this manner. In the unloading process, the product is kept aseptic. The use of the unloader reduces handling of the product and, in many instances, reduces holding times. The first use is for yogurt, but as technologists gain familiarity with the concept and technique, additional uses will be found for aseptic unloading.

4. Fifty-Five-Gallon Bag-in-Fiber Drum

Worldwide, the use of 55-gallon bags in used metal drums has been popular for aseptically packed products and is a growing market, but this type of packaging is not used in the United States. The aseptic 55-gallon metal drum is the package used today in the United States for the 55-gallon size. A new fiber drum has been made available for use with 55-gallon bags. The advantages of the fiber drum are cheaper cost, less shipping weight, higher stacking (they can be stacked four high), outside storage capabilities, and, in many instances, reuse of the fiber drum. The industry will see increasing production of product in fiber drums for those customers who desire the 55-gallon size.

VI. CONCLUSION

In the time frame of food preservation techniques (drying, salting, smoking, canning, and freezing), aseptic packaging is indeed not very old—50 years. But

FIG. 3.   Scholle Auto-Fill 19A automatic feed aseptic bag-in-box filler.

in those 50 years aseptic packaging has made great progress. However, what has taken place in aseptic processing is only the tip of the iceberg. There is much, much more to come. Worldwide, there are many research centers capable of performing aseptic packaging research, and more of these centers are in the development stage. These research centers involve government, universities, and associations as well as industry, and many millions of dollars are spent yearly to allow talented personnel to work on many aseptic packaging projects. From these investments, there will surely be some striking results, and these research forces will make changes over the entire universe of aseptic processing as it is now known.

In the field, there will be new varieties, new cultural methods, improved transportation, and improved storage of raw product. With aseptic processing, a superior means of preserving color, flavor, texture, and nutritional values exists.

These properties will improve as improvements are made in processing equipment. Methods will be found to decrease oxygen retention in foodstuffs. New heat exchangers and new evaporators to minimize heat treatment are needed. Evaporators may be replaced by reverse osmosis, hyperfiltration, or freeze concentration.

In packaging, means will be found to further reduce oxygen transmission into aseptically packaged foodstuffs. The can will be approached with respect to barrier properties. The industry will have new packages and better production speeds. With respect to storage and distribution of the finished products, the industry will find new and better methods to improve the shelf life of products.

The industry is in the dynamic phase of the growth curve of aseptic packaging and there are still volumes to be written on the subject, but it still revolves around the original concept as defined in Section I.

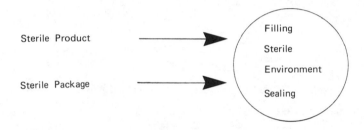

ACKNOWLEDGMENT

I am indebted to the National Food Processors Association Laboratory, Dublin, California, and the University of California Food Science Department, Davis, California, for allowing me the use of their library facilities.

REFERENCES

Anonymous 1985. Guide to aseptic packaging systems. *Food Eng.* **57**, 62–63.

Ball, C. O. 1936. Apparatus for and method of canning. U.S. Patent No. 2,029,303.

Ball, C. O., and Olson, F. C. W. 1957a. The HCF process. *In* "Sterilization in Food Technology," pp. 96–98. McGraw Hill, New York.

Ball, C. O., and Olson, F. C. W. 1957b. The Avoset process. *In* "Sterilization in Food Technology," pp. 99–100. McGraw Hill, New York.

Collier, C. P., and Townsend, C. T. 1956. The resistance of bacterial spores to superheated steam. *Food Technol.* **10**, pp. 477–481.

Dixon, M. S., Warshall, R. B., and Crerar, J. B. 1963. Food processing method and apparatus. U.S. Patent No. 3,096,161.

Havighorst, C. R. 1951. Aseptic canning in action. *Food Eng.* **23,** 72–73.

Ito, K. A., and Stevenson, K. E. 1984. Sterilization of packaging materials using aseptic systems. *Food Technol.* **38,**60–62.

Luster, C. 1978. A rapid and sensitive sterility monitoring technique for aseptically processed bulk tomato paste. *J. Food Sci.* **43,** 1046, 1048, 1062.

Martin, W. M. 1948. Flash process, aseptic fill, are used in new canning unit. *Food Ind.* 1069.

Martin, W. M. 1951. Continuous aseptic process. *Food Eng.* **23,** 67–70, 134–137.

Nelson, P. E. 1984. Outlook for aseptic bag-in-box packaging of products for remanufacture. *Food Technol.* **38,** 72–73.

Orbell, J. A. 1980. Aseptic bag-in-box packaging. *Food Technol.* **34,** 56–57.

Sizer, C. 1982. Aseptic system and European experience. *Proc. Annu. Short Course Food Ind., 22nd; Univ. Florida* pp. 93–100.

Smittcamp, R. E., Truxell, J. H., and Aobe, K. 1981. Aseptic-pack fruits retain color, flavor, save 30% processing energy. *Food Process.* **42,** 86–88.

Stevenson, K. E., and Shafer B. D. 1983. Bacterial spore resistance to hydrogen peroxide. *Food Technol.* **37,** 111–114.

Swartling, P., and Lundgren, B. 1968. The sterilizing effect against *Bacillus subtilus* spores of hydrogen peroxide at different temperatures and concentrations. *Dairy Res.* **35,** 423.

von Bockelman, B. A. H., and von Bockelman, I. L. I. 1986. Aseptic packaging of liquid food products—a literature review. Reprinted with permission from *Agric. Food Chem.* **34,** 384–392.

ADVANCES IN FOOD RESEARCH, VOL. 32

CONVECTIVE HEAT TRANSFER TO FLUID FOODS IN CANS

M. A. RAO

Department of Food Science and Technology
Cornell University
Geneva, New York 14456

R. C. ANANTHESWARAN

Department of Food Science
Pennsylvania State University
University Park, Pennsylvania 16802

39

I. INTRODUCTION

Canning is one of the most effective means of preserving a large part of our food supply. The canning industry developed significantly since the time Appert invented canning and is constantly on the march to innovative grounds (Jackson and Shinn, 1979). Each year in the United States, 36 billion pounds of food are processed in approximately 37 billion containers (Lopez, 1981). Processes are being developed to improve nutrient retention (Lund, 1977) and to use lesser amounts of energy (Carroad *et al.*, 1980). Extensive mathematical analyses of conduction heating of foods have been carried out by many researchers (Hayakawa, 1970, 1978; Manson *et al.*, 1970; Teixeira *et al.*, 1969a,b; Teixeira, 1978). Heat penetration studies on conduction heating of foods have been reviewed in texts such as those of Ball and Olson (1957), Stumbo (1973), and Pflug (1982). However, studies on convection heating of foods are more difficult and have not received as much attention. This contribution reviews the literature on convection heating of foods in cans.

A. HEATING OF FOODS IN CANS

Heat transfer is a fundamental unit operation in most of the processes in the chemical industry. Hence, it has been extensively studied in the literature. Numerous fundamental studies on heat transfer have been conducted in the areas of chemical and mechanical engineering. However, relatively few of the studies can be applied to foods due to the wide range and often unpredictable magnitudes of thermophysical properties of foods that, in turn, are a result of wide variation in composition. The net result is that theoretical prediction of the time–temperature data necessary for thermobacteriological applications is very difficult, and one must rely on experimental data.

The heating characteristics of food products in cans can be divided into three different types based on the shape of their heat penetration curve (Fig. 1): (1) conduction-heated products exhibit slower heating rates and longer lag times, (2) convection-heated food products exhibit faster heating rates and shorter lag times, and (3) some food products heat by convection initially and then heat by conduction, e.g., as a result of gelatinization of starch resulting in what is referred to as broken-heating curve.

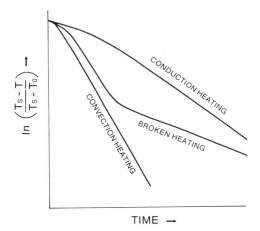

FIG. 1.   Types of heating curves for food products heated in containers.

During conduction, heat is transferred between adjacent molecules without appreciable displacement of the particles of the solid (Rohsenow and Hartnett, 1973). Energy is transferred from molecules with a higher level of energy to those (with which they are in contact) with a lower energy level. Canned food products that heat by conduction include canned meats, tightly packed vegetables or fruits, and solid pet foods.

During convection, heat is transferred by bulk motion of the fluid particles. This results in a mixing of the particles of different temperatures within a fluid. In natural convection, the motion of the particles results entirely from the differences in the density of the fluid, which arises out of the temperature differences within the fluid. In forced convection, the motion of the fluid is produced by external means. Food products heating by convection, either completely or in part, include single-strength fruit juices, fluid milk, vegetables packed in brine, fruits packed in syrup, and thin broths and soups. Heat transfer by convection always occurs in series with conduction heating through walls of containers and, in some cases, also through the solid portion of the food. In the latter situation, the ratio of conduction to convection is dependent on the type of the product and how tightly it is packed within the can.

Much work has been done to understand the time–temperature relationships for different types of foods heated by conduction. In comparison, there have been fewer experimental and analytical studies on convection heating of foods. The main reason is that heat transfer by convection is governed both by fluid motion and by temperature difference.

In convection heating of products, the rate of heat penetration into the can's contents can be increased by agitation of the can while it is being heated. Product movement within the container during agitation aids heat transfer to the product.

This facilitates the use of higher temperatures for sterilization, and the time required for processing is lowered. The accrued benefits are better quality of the final product and potential increase in the processing plant's capacity.

Most published studies have been based on Newtonian liquids. Because many of the processed foods are non-Newtonian in nature, there is a need to understand convection heat transfer in non-Newtonian liquids. Recently, a few studies have been reported (Anantheswaran and Rao, 1985b; Rao *et al.*, 1985) in which the non-Newtonian rheological properties have been taken into account. A better understanding of heat transfer to non-Newtonian liquids will aid in more accurate determination of processing times resulting in higher quality in thermally processed foods.

B.   TRANSPORT EQUATIONS FOR FLUIDS

In general, the problem of heat transfer to pure fluids with constant density, viscosity, and thermal conductivity can be set up in terms of the following three transport equations (Bird *et al.*, 1960).

$$\nabla \cdot \bar{V} = 0 \tag{1}$$

$$\rho \frac{D\bar{V}}{Dt} = \nabla p + \eta \nabla^2 \bar{V} + \rho \bar{g} \tag{2}$$

$$\rho c_p \frac{DT}{Dt} = k \nabla^2 T \tag{3}$$

Equation (1) is the equation of continuity, Eq. (2) is the equation of motion, and Eq. (3) is the equation of energy neglecting the viscous dissipation of energy within the fluid.

Equations (1)–(3) have been solved for many heat-transfer problems under restricted boundary conditions to obtain the time–temperature profiles within a fluid. Natural convection heat transfer to fluids from a vertical plate, heat transfer in fully developed laminar flow in pipes with a constant wall temperature (Graetz problem), and heat transfer to a falling liquid film are some of the typical problems for which analytical solutions have been worked out (Bird *et al.*, 1960).

All three equations can be also used for the case of forced convection heating of foods within cans. However, it is very difficult to obtain analytical or numerical solutions for the temperature within the can as a function of time and position in the can. This is due in part to the difficulty in postulating the boundary conditions for the fluid temperature and expressions for the velocity of the fluid within the can. Also, the physical and thermal properties of the fluid are functions of position and time. Therefore, it has become customary to study convection heat transfer to canned liquids either in terms of heat penetration parameters or in terms of dimensionless groups. However, efforts to solve the applicable equations for specific problems have begun, and these will be discussed later.

C. METHODOLOGIES FOR STUDYING CONVECTIVE HEAT TRANSFER TO FOODS

The energy balance for convection heating of a product in an enclosed container can be written as Eq. (4)

$$UA(T_s - T) = mc_p \frac{dT}{dt} \tag{4}$$

where T is the mass average temperature of the product within the can. The left-hand side of Eq. (4) represents the rate of heat that is being transferred to the product within the can, and the right-hand side represents the rate of accumulation of heat within the product in the can. U is the overall heat transfer coefficient and UA is the reciprocal of the total resistance to heat transfer. When steam is the heating medium, the major heat-transfer resistance is due to the product film on the inside of the can; therefore, U can be conveniently replaced by h_i, the heat-transfer coefficient of this film. If the heating medium is another fluid instead of steam, the resistance due to the film of the heating fluid will be significant, and the error due to neglecting it will be large.

On rearranging Eq. (4) and substituting h_i for U, Eq. 5 is developed.

$$h_i \, dt = \frac{mc_p}{A} \frac{dT}{(T_s - T)} \tag{5}$$

If the retort temperature (T_s) and the heat-transfer coefficient (h_i) are assumed to be constant over the entire process of heat transfer, then the Eq. 5 can be analytically integrated. An exponential function is obtained as the solution for the temperature within the can as a function of time [Eq. (6)].

$$\frac{T_s - T}{T_s - T_0} = \exp\left(-\frac{Ah_i}{mc_p}\right)t \tag{6}$$

In Eq. (6), the term on the left-hand side is the dimensionless temperature, ξ. If $\ln \xi$ is plotted against time, then the slope of the curve is the term inside the exponential function on the right-hand side of Eq. (6). From the slope, the heat-transfer coefficient h_i can be calculated. Equation (6) can be rearranged to give the temperature within the can [Eq. (7)].

$$T = T_s - (T_s - T_0) \exp\left(-\frac{Ah_i}{mc_p}t\right) \tag{7}$$

The temperature at the center of the can, in terms of the f value, may be written as shown in Eqs. (8) and (9) (Ball and Olson 1957).

$$T = T_s - (T_s - T_0) \, 10^{(-t/f)} \tag{8}$$

$$T = T_s - (T_s - T_0) \exp(-2.303 \, t/f) \tag{9}$$

Comparing Eqs. (7) and (9), a relationship between the traditional f value and h_i can be obtained [Eq. (10)].

$$f = 2.303 c_p m / A \, h_i \tag{10}$$

1. Methods of Determining Heat-Transfer Coefficients

Different methods of evaluating a representative heat-transfer coefficient for the heating cycle have been used in the literature. These methods can be used for either natural or forced convection heat transfer.

Lenz and Lund (1978) selected as the value of heat-transfer coefficient that value which minimized the sum of squares of the deviation between the actual temperature of the product and the temperature predicted by the solution to the energy balance equation [Eq. (4)].

Duquenoy (1980) first determined the overall heat-transfer coefficient between steam and the can's contents from the heat-penetration curve. The heat-transfer coefficient on the steam side was estimated from the heat-penetration data for a copper cylinder, which had nearly zero internal resistance, being heated in the retort. The heat-transfer resistance on the liquid side was calculated as the difference between the total heat-transfer resistance and that on the steam side.

Anantheswaran and Rao (1985a,b) and Rao et al. (1985) evaluated the instantaneous heat-transfer coefficients by numerically integrating the energy balance equation and calculated a time-average heat-transfer coefficient for each run. Naveh and Kopelman (1980) determined the heat-transfer coefficients from the slope of the $\ln \xi$ vs time graph for 10-sec intervals during the process, up to the time when the product temperature was 5°C below the retort temperature. An average heat-transfer coefficient for the entire process was then determined.

D. FLOW MODELS FOR FLUID FOODS

The heat-transfer rates to liquid foods are influenced by flow conditions, such as the geometry and the velocity of flow, as well as by the physical and thermal properties of the liquid. In fact, the correlation of heat-transfer data in terms of dimensionless groups in convection heat transfer requires knowledge of the pertinent physical and thermal properties. In many instances, properties such as the specific heat (c_p), density (ρ), and thermal conductivity (k) of liquid foods can either be assumed to be close to those of water or be determined relatively easily, such as in the case of density.

TABLE I

FOODS EXHIBITING NEWTONIAN FLOW BEHAVIOR[a]

Milk	Egg products
Total solids 8.4–29.1%	Whole egg (unfrozen)
Clear fruit juices	Stabilized egg white
Depectinized apple juice (15–75° Brix)	Plain yolk
Filtered orange juice	Sugared and salted yolk
Depectinized grape juice (15–50° Brix)	Sucrose solutions
Most honeys	Corn syrups

[a] Source: Rao (1986a).

One property that plays an important role in heat transfer to fluid foods is the viscosity (or the apparent viscosity in the case of non-Newtonian fluids). The viscosity function η can be used to classify the flow behavior of several foods. It is defined in Eq. (21).

$$\eta = \sigma_{21}/\dot{\gamma} \tag{11}$$

The viscosity of Newtonian foods is influenced only by temperature and composition; it is independent of the shear rate and previous shear history. Foods known to be Newtonian are listed in Table I.

Fluids which do not follow Newtonian behavior are called non-Newtonian fluids. The flow properties of non-Newtonian fluids are influenced by the shear rate. Instead of the Newtonian viscosity η, for non-Newtonian fluids the apparent viscosity η_a at a specified shear rate can be used. Here, η_a is defined as the ratio of the shear stress (σ_{21}) to the shear rate $(\dot{\gamma})$.

Because many fluid foods are non-Newtonian in nature and recent studies (Anantheswaran and Rao, 1985b; Rao et al., 1985) indicate that heat transfer to non-Newtonian fluids can be analyzed if the pertinent rheological parameters are known, their classification and the determination of their behavior will be described in brief. Detailed treatments on rheological behavior can be found elsewhere (Rao, 1986a; Whorlow, 1980).

1. Classification of Non-Newtonian Fluids

Non-Newtonian foods can be divided into two categories: *time independent* or *time dependent*. At a constant temperature, η_a for the former depends only on the shear rate; for the latter, η_a also depends on the duration of shear. Time-independent flow behavior can be divided into *shear-thinning (pseudoplastic)* and *shear-thickening (dilatant)* categories depending upon whether η_a decreases or increases with increase in shear rate, respectively. A large number of non-Newtonian fluid foods exhibit pseudoplastic behavior, and these foods are listed in Table II. Figure 2 illustrates the flow curves of Newtonian and *time-independent* non-Newtonian fluids.

TABLE II
FOODS EXHIBITING SHEAR-THINNING FLOW BEHAVIOR[a]

Concentrated fruit juices	Dairy cream
Undepectinized apple juice (50–65° Brix)	Thawed frozen whole egg
Passion fruit juice (16–33° Brix)	Unmixed egg white
Undepectinized grape juice (50–65° Brix)	Fruit and vegetable purees
Orange juice (50–65° Brix)	Gum solutions—high concentrations
Melted chocolate	French mustard
Salad dressings	Protein concentrates

[a] Adapted from Rao (1986a).

Shear-thickening foods are rarely encountered. Pryce-Jones (1953) observed shear-thickening behavior for honeys from *Eucalyptus ficifolia, Eucalyptus eugeniodes, Eucalyptus corymbosa,* and *Opuntia engelmanni.* Bagley and Christianson (1982) observed shear-thickening behavior for cooked starch suspensions. While these studies do indicate that shear thickening behavior can be found among foods, very often instrument artifacts and limited amount of data have been interpreted as indicators of shear-thickening behavior.

Non-Newtonian foods with time-dependent, flow properties are subdivided into *thixotropic* and *rheopectic* fluids. It the case of the former at a fixed shear rate, the viscosity decreases with time; for the latter, the viscosity increases with time. Thixotropic behavior has been noted for condensed milk (Higgs and Norrington, 1971), mayonnaise (Tiu and Boger, 1974; Figoni and Shoemaker, 1983), and egg white (Tung *et al.,* 1970). Rheopectic foods have not been reported thus far.

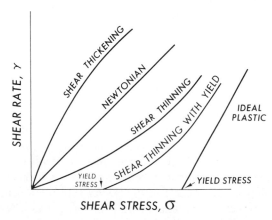

FIG. 2.   Flow curves for Newtonian and time-independent non-Newtonian fluids.

a.   Models for Time-Independent Flow Behavior.   The power-law model [Eq. (12)] has been employed extensively to describe the flow behavior of viscous foods over wide ranges of shear rates (Rao, 1986a; Vitali and Rao, 1984a,b):

$$\sigma_{21} = K\dot{\gamma}^n \tag{12}$$

where, K is the consistency index and n is the flow behavior index.

Holdsworth (1971) and Steffe *et al.* (1986) compiled magnitudes of the power-law parameters reported in the literature and they should be consulted for data on specific foods. Typical magnitudes of viscosities of Newtonian foods are 4.8 (Pa·sec) at 25°C for honey; at 30°C magnitudes are 0.0064 (Pa·sec) for whole egg, 0.0027 (Pa·sec) for stabilized egg white, and 0.40 (Pa·sec) for salted yolk. The flow behavior index can be found to vary from 1.0 for Newtonian foods to about 0.2 for highly shear-thinning pureed foods such as tomato concentrates. Magnitudes of the consistency index as high as 200 ($N \cdot sec^n/m^2$) have been reported for tomato concentrates (Rao *et al.*, 1981).

b.   Viscoelastic Fluids.   Some fluid foods exhibit viscous as well as elastic properties, and they are called viscoelastic foods. The techniques that are employed for measuring viscoelastic properties and their magnitudes for several foods have been compiled (Rao, 1986b; Kokini and Plutchok, 1987). Because of the complex nature of the experimental techniques, the relatively few studies that have been published deal with the role of composition and mathematical models for viscoelastic foods. It appears that not many studies have been conducted on the role of viscoelastic properties on heat transfer.

E.   MEASUREMENT OF FLOW PROPERTIES OF FLUID FOODS

1.   Introduction

Instruments for measuring the flow properties of fluid foods can be classified into the following categories (Rao, 1986a): (1) fundamental, (2) empirical, and (3) imitative. In fundamental tests, geometries of measuring systems whose flow fields are amenable to mathematical analysis are employed, and they yield rheological properties in terms of fundamental units of mass, length, and time. Empirical tests measure parameters that are not clearly defined, but the parameters have been found to be useful from past experience. Imitative tests measure properties under test conditions similar to those in practice.

2.   Fundamental Methods of Viscosity Measurement

The fundamental methods can be classified under the specific geometry employed: capillary, Couette (concentric cylinder), plate and cone, and parallel plate. Van Wazer *et al.* (1963) and Whorlow (1980) described many commercial instruments and their principles of operation. Walters (1975) has discussed in detail the underlying equations and assumptions. These references must be consulted for the instruments and the methods that can be employed in obtaining well-defined rheological parameters. Rao (1977) discussed the problems that can be encountered during the measurement of rheological properties of fluid foods.

3.   Empirical Methods of Viscosity Measurement

Instruments such as the Bostwick consistometer and the U.S. Department of Agricultre (USDA) Flow Sheet (Adams Consistometer) have been employed extensively in the quality control of pureed foods (Kramer and Twigg, 1970). With these devices, the distance covered by a food in a specific length of time (10 or 30 sec) is called the consistency. The major drawbacks of the Adams and Bostwick consistometers are (1) the consistency measured by the devices decreases with an increase in viscosity of a fluid, contrary to expectation, and (2) they are not equipped for adequate temperature control. Thus, these empirical devices, while adequate for quality control of pureed foods, will not provide rheological data suitable for use in dimensionless groups and in quantitative engineering applications.

3.   Imitative Methods of Viscosity Measurement

In addition to the consistometers, spindles whose flow field cannot be analyzed due to their complex geometries have been employed with rotational viscometers. These devices can provide the shear-rate–shear-stress data of a fluid in fundamental units when the experiments are performed such that developments in the area of mixing of fluids are utilized. Specifically, it is assumed that the shear rate is directly proportional to the rotational speed of the agitator and that the flow behavior of the fluid can be described by the power-law model [Eq. (12)]. Procedures to be followed for determining the proportionality constant and the power-law parameters have been described elsewhere (Rao, 1975; Rao and Cooley, 1984). This method is particularly well suited for systems containing large particles where fundamental methods using the concentric cylinder, plate and cone, and parallel plate systems cannot be used because of the narrow gap of the flow field.

F.   DIMENSIONAL ANALYSIS FOR CONVECTION HEAT TRANSFER

Dimensional analysis is based on the assumption that there are only five fundamental units: mass, length, time, temperature, and heat. Further, it is assumed that a quantity under consideration is a function of several known variables. For example, the heat-transfer coefficient in convection heat transfer in containers can be expected to depend on the characteristic dimension of the container, the physical and thermal properties of the fluid foods, and other factors such as the rotational speed of a retort. The pertinent dimensionless groups for an application can be determined by the application of Buckingham's Pi theorem, which states that the relationship among q quantities whose units may be expressed in terms of u fundamental units may be written as a function of $q - u$ dimensionless groups (Bird et al., 1960).

Additional information on the Pi theorem and on determining dimensionless groups can be found in texts by McAdams (1954) and Bird et al. (1960). One must consult these and the references contained in them in order to appreciate the power and meaning of dimensional analysis and dimensionless groups. Here, only a brief treatment of the subject is given in order to facilitate discussion of studies in which dimensionless groups have been employed.

1. Dimensionless Groups for Convection Heat Transfer

There are many dimensionless groups that are well known and that are used for correlating experimental heat transfer data. Among these are the Nusselt (Nu), Reynolds (Re), Prandtl (Pr), and Grashof (Gr) numbers. In addition, the ratio of viscosity at the wall, η_w, to the viscosity in the bulk fluid, η_b, is used to deal with situations where there are significant temperature gradients between the wall and the bulk fluid. It is useful to think of dimensionless groups as ratios of forces or effects in a system (Bird et al., 1960; Foust et al., 1980). For example, the Reynolds number can be expressed as the ratio of inertial forces to viscous forces, so that a low value of the Reynolds number means that viscous forces are large in comparison with inertial forces. Another dimensionless group frequently encountered in dimensionless correlations for convective heat transfer is the Prandtl number, and it is the ratio of molecular diffusivity of momentum to molecular diffusivity of heat.

Because the apparent viscosity of non-Newtonian fluids depends on the shear rate, it can be evaluated at a shear rate meaningful for a particular application. For example, in mixing systems the effective shear rate for a non-Newtonian fluid is evaluated from the viscosity of a Newtonian fluid that produces the same magnitude of torque (Rao and Cooley, 1984). For heat transfer to canned non-Newtonian fluids, Anantheswaran (1984) showed that the generalized Reynolds number developed by Metzner (1956) for flow in pipes can be adapted [Eq. (13)]:

$$Re' = \frac{D_r^2 N^{2-n} \rho}{8^{n-1} K [(3n + 1)/4n]^n} \tag{13}$$

One can, of course, use another characteristic dimension, such as the diameter of the can (Rao et al., 1985) in this equation. Further, the apparent viscosity (η_{aM})

in Re' can be used in place of the Newtonian viscosity in other dimensionless groups (Anantheswaran, 1984; Rao *et al.*, 1985):

$$\eta_{aM} = \frac{K8^{n-1}}{N^{1-n}} \left(\frac{3n+1}{4n} \right)^n \tag{14}$$

There are many options available for the characteristic dimension: the diameter of the container, the radius or the diameter of rotation, and, in the case of particulate systems, the dimension of a solid particle. For natural convection heat transfer in fluids free of particles, the diameter of the container, as opposed to the diameter of rotation, is a logical choice because the magnitude of the buoyancy force depends on the volume of liquid in the container.

II. HEAT TRANSFER BY NATURAL CONVECTION

Convection-heated foods, in the absence of any externally induced agitation, are heated by means of the natural convection currents produced within the food product. Upon being agitated, these foods heat up much more rapidly due to the presence of the forced convection currents. The studies dealing with velocity profiles, f and j parameters, and heat-transfer coefficients in natural convection heat transfer in cans are summarized in Table III.

A.   CONVECTION CURRENTS AND VELOCITY PROFILES

A knowledge and understanding of the flow patterns and velocity profiles are necessary to understand convection heating of products within cans.

Hiddink (1975) used the particle-streak method to observe flow patterns during heating of liquids in cans; here, small, glittering particles were suspended in the liquid and were illuminated by a flat, narrow slit of light against a dark background. This method, previously employed in flow visualization studies, yielded an overall picture of the flow patterns in the can.

For flow visualization studies, a special half-cylindrical brass container was used (Figs. 3 and 4). The flat front wall and the top cover were made of double-windowed pyrex glass. The compartment in between was also filled with liquid. Thus, the heat loss through the front wall was minimized, and the test container was made as close as possible to a complete container. Flow patterns were studied in 75% glycerol, water, silicone fluid F111/100 (medium viscosity), and silicone fluid F111/1000 (very high viscosity).

Temperature profiles were measured by means of iron-constantan thermocouples in a cylindrical copper container (Fig. 5). The container was heated in a retort by condensing steam. Cylindrical symmetry was assumed and the assumption was verified in a test with water.

TABLE III

SUMMARY OF STUDIES ON HEAT TRANSFER TO CANNED FOODS BY NATURAL CONVECTION

Reference	Products	Can sizes	Heat-transfer parameters	Comments
Jackson and Olson (1940)	Bentonite suspensions	307×409 603×700	f, j, temperature profiles	Headspace: 0–11/32 in.; retort temperature 93–132°C
McConell (1952)	Bentonite suspensions	307×409 401×411 603×700	f and j parameters	Retort temperature 116–121°C
Blaisdell (1963)	Water, aq. 50% sucrose solution	303×406	Wall–fluid heat-transfer coefficient, temperature profiles	—
Evans and Stefany (1966)	Water, methyl alcohol, n-butyl alcohol, and glycerine	Fabricated cans, L/D = 0.75–2.0		—
Stevens (1972)	Glycols	401×411 (2 1/2)	Temperature profiles	—
Jowitt and Mynott (1974)	Water and aq. 60% sucrose solution	300×410	Wall–fluid heat-transfer coefficient	—
Hiddink (1975)	Water, aq. 30–60% sucrose solutions, 75% glycerol, and silicone fluids	Fabricated cans, L/D = 0.25–2.0	Wall–fluid heat-transfer coefficient, temperature profiles	—
Sastry (1984)	Mushrooms in water	211×212	Fluid–particle heat-transfer coefficient	—

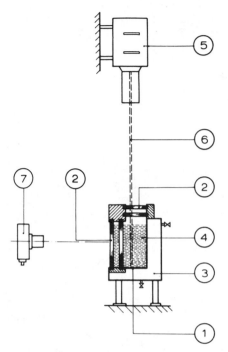

FIG. 3.   Schematic of apparatus for determining flow patterns during natural convection heating of fluids in containers (Hiddink, 1975). 1, Half-cylindrical container; 2, glass windows; 3, steam chamber; 4, liquid; 5, slide projector; 6, slit of light; 7, camera.

Figure 6 illustrates the flow patterns and temperature profiles based on several observations. At the onset of heating, the liquid near the wall was heated and the buoyancy forces drove the liquid upwards. This resulted in an upward boundary-layer flow at the wall. When the liquid reached the top, it spread over the free liquid surface and then slowly moved downwards. In the lower part of the container, however, the liquid circulated around in the form of eddies giving rise to liquid eruption. The height of the eddy region decreased with time, and an equilibrium height of 30% was reached after about 6 min in the case of 75% glycerol.

When foods of high water and low solids content are placed in a sugar syrup, a concentration gradient of the solids in the syrups occurs as the water rises to the top of the jar (Mulvaney et al., 1960). This gradient was found to be large enough to inhibit natural convection when these products were heated. The concentration gradients disappeared after several days of storage.

Nicholas et al. (1960a) studied convection in syrup-packed products. They postulated that there will be no convection unless the density of the liquid above any given point is higher than the density of the liquid below the same point.

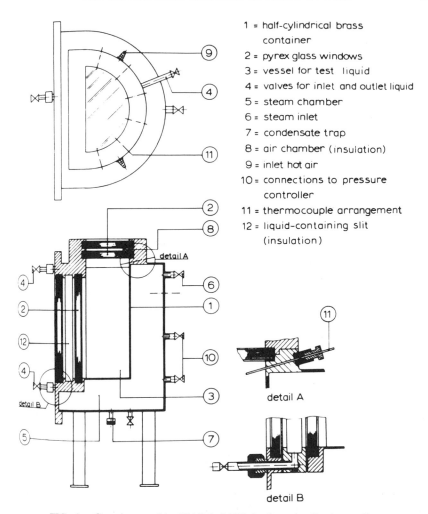

1 = half-cylindrical brass
    container
2 = pyrex glass windows
3 = vessel for test liquid
4 = valves for inlet and outlet liquid
5 = steam chamber
6 = steam inlet
7 = condensate trap
8 = air chamber (insulation)
9 = inlet hot air
10 = connections to pressure
     controller
11 = thermocouple arrangement
12 = liquid-containing slit
     (insulation)

detail A

detail B

FIG. 4.   Container used by Hiddink (1975) for flow visualization studies.

From the equation for the density of sucrose solutions as a function of concentration and temperature, they described mathematically the condition for no convection within sucrose solutions. They showed that a difference of 7% in sucrose concentration between two points will prohibit convection between these two points even if the heavier syrup is 60°C in temperature.

Nicholas *et al.* (1960b) also studied convection heating of water–syrup-layered systems which exhibit a built-in stratification. The jars containing water were found to heat up faster than the jars containing syrup. However, the jars containing both syrup and water were found to heat considerably slower. The

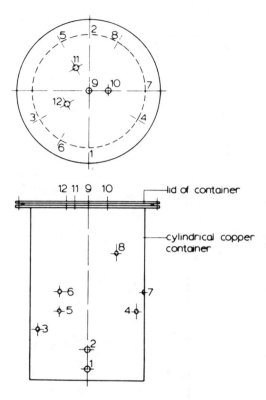

FIG. 5. Location of thermocouples in a can for temperature profiles in natural convection heating (Hiddink, 1975).

slowest heating point was found to be in the region just under the boundary between the water and the syrup within the jar. These studies indicated the role of ingredients on the rate of heat penetration and stressed the need, on the part of the commercial manufacturers, to strictly adhere to the formulation of the product.

B.   TEMPERATURE PROFILES

The convection currents generated within a closed container give rise to temperature profiles. Several studies have been reported on temperature profiles within liquids being heated by natural convection.

Blaisdell (1963) studied temperature profiles within a can using several thermocouples. The horizontal temperature profiles indicated an off-center cold point near the base of the container. Other cold points were also found to exist at stagnation points and at vortex centers.

Jowitt and Mynott (1974) determined the bulk temperature of liquids being heated by convection from the net thermal expansion of the liquid in an expan-

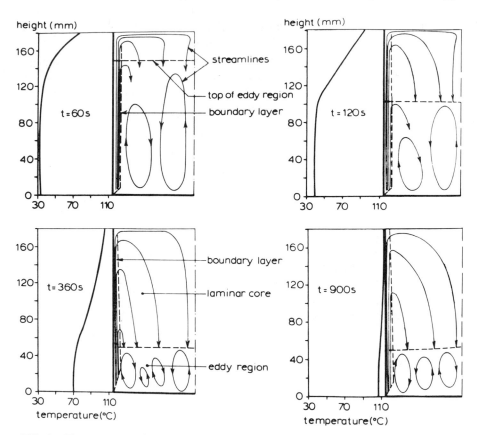

FIG. 6.   Flow patterns and temperature profiles in natural convection heating in a can (Hiddink, 1975).

sion tube attached to a specially designed can that was completely filled with the test liquid. In order to simulate the insulating effect of headspace, they soldered an inverted empty can to the top of the test can. Water and a 60% sucrose solution were the test fluids. The bulk temperature, at any instant, was found to be higher than the temperature at the geometric center of the can. The shape of the profiles, as a function of time, were similar for both the bulk temperature and the center temperature. They evaluated the heat-transfer coefficients based on Eq. (6) and found that the Nusselt number was independent of the Rayleigh number for most of the heating process. Toward the end of the heating process, the Nusselt number decreased with a decrease in the Rayleigh number.

Hiddink (1975) monitored the temperature profiles at various points within a can (Fig. 5) as a function of time. It was found that the side-wall heating produced a thermal stratification, whereby the hot liquid from the boundary layer rose up and spread on top of the cooler core. The heating of the bottom of the containers resulted in eddies, close to the bottom, which penetrated up to a certain height within the can. As heating proceeded, this height decreased and the stream lines for the flow of stratified layer shifted downwards. A change in the slope of the temperature profile was also seen at the top of this eddy region. The temperature profile was found to become more uniform with time. The radial temperature profiles were found to be flat, except in the vicinity of the wall. The bulk temperature was calculated by integrating the axial temperature profile, and it was found to coincide with the temperature at the geometric center.

Due to convection currents, the *slowest heating zone* (SHZ) within a convection-heating food lies below the geometric center of the can. It is mandatory that this cold point be determined experimentally before making any thermal process determination. For most convection heating products, the SHZ lies in the bottom part of the container.

Zechman (1983) studied the location of the slowest heating zone in (1) water, (2) 1% aqueous solutions of bentonite, cellulose gum, and xanthan gum, (3) paraffin oils, and (4) silicone fluids. Tests were conducted with water as the fluid in containers of 13 sizes ranging from 211 × 101.5 to 603 × 700; with the other fluids tests were conducted in 211 × 400 containers. The SHZ along the vertical axis was found, as expected, near the container bottom. Zechman (1983) found the SHZ to be 0.5 cm from the bottom of 211 × 400 containers, while the numerical computations of Datta and Teixeira (1986) indicated that the SHZ was in the bottom 15% of the height of the container. Semilogarithmic heating curves for the SHZ were not linear.

C. STUDIES ON HEAT-TRANSFER RATES IN NATURAL CONVECTION

Prescott and Underwood (1897) were the first to measure the rate of heat penetration into cans. They used maximum temperature thermometers sealed within cans that were heated by boiling water. A theoretical analysis of the time–temperature relationships during sterilization of canned foods, based on conduction theory, was first described by Thompson (1919) who regarded convection as an increase in conduction since it was occurring locally within the cans. On the basis of conduction theory, Eq. (15) was derived for the temperature at the center of the can:

$$T = T_s - T_0 A' \exp\{-\alpha[(2B_1/D)^2 + \pi^2/L^2]t\} \tag{15}$$

where A' is a constant that depends on the initial temperature distribution within the can. The theoretical model was verified by experimental determination of temperature as a function of time within canned foods.

Jones (1931) appears to be the first to utilize the film model to account for thermal resistance of a canned fluid food. The model assumed that heat transfer to the canned food takes place by conduction through a stagnant film of liquid on the inside surface of the can. The heat is then instantaneously absorbed by the region of violently agitated liquid adjacent to the surface of the can. Assuming a value of 0.6447 W/m·K for the thermal conductivity of the film and 0.09 cm for the thickness of the film, the heat-transfer coefficient for water was calculated by dividing the former by the latter. Substituting this value of the heat-transfer coefficient in Eq. (7), the predicted time–temperature curves for heating of water in cans were in good agreement with the experimental time–temperature curves.

Jackson and Olson (1940) studied heating rates and the mechanisms of heat transfer in cans containing bentonite suspensions of various concentrations from 1 to 3.5%. The retort temperature was found to have a significant effect on the form of the broken-heating curve observed in the bentonite suspensions. The time at which the break occurred was found to be inversely proportional to the retort temperature. The change from convection to conduction heating in such broken-heating products was explained in terms of a sol–gel transition within the product. Townsend *et al.* (1949) and Powers *et al.* (1952) found that the heating rates of bentonite in jars and cans were not significantly different with boiling water and steam as the heating media.

Blaisdell (1963) studied transient heating and cooling of food containers in the absence of any agitation and applied the concepts of dimensionless groups to interpret the results. Studies were conducted with water and a 50% sucrose solution in glass containers of different sizes. Convection was found to begin at the lateral surface, and a turbulent boundary layer was observed for large temperature differences. The time required to initiate convection was found to be a function of the Prandtl number, the Rayleigh number, the Nusselt number, and the Fourier modulus of the fluid and the container.

Evans and Stefany (1966) also studied transient heat transfer to liquids in cylindrical containers. They used water, methanol, *n*-butanol, and water–glycerine mixtures and spanned a range of Rayleigh numbers from 10^5 to 10^9. The experimental apparatus consisted of a cylinder that contained the process fluid and was heated by a water bath on the outside. The length/diameter (L/D) ratios were varied from 0.75 to 2.0. The water bath was held at a temperature of 50°C. They measured the mixed-mean temperature of the process liquid as a function of time and evaluated the instantaneous heat-transfer coefficients on the inside wall. The values of the physical and thermal properties of the liquids evaluated at the wall temperature were used in the dimensionless numbers. The heat-transfer coefficients were correlated with Eq. (16):

$$Nu = 0.55 \, Ra^{0.25} \tag{16}$$

The characteristic dimension in the Nusselt and Rayleigh numbers was the length of the can.

Using the center temperature within the can and the steam (heating medium) temperature, Hiddink (1975) determined the overall heat-transfer coefficient as the slope of the plot of ln ξ vs time, as per Eq. (7). Water, 30, 40, 50, and 60% sucrose solutions, 75% glycerol, and silicone fluids (F111/100 and F111/10000) were employed in the study. A dimensionless correlation, with the physical properties of the liquid at the steam temperature, was developed that had an R^2 of 99%:

$$Nu = 0.31 \ [(Gr)(Pr)]^{0.268} \tag{17}$$

The radius of the can was used as the characteristic dimension in the Nusselt and Grashof numbers. A weak dependency of the Nusselt number on L/D was detected, but this was not included in the correlation.

Zechman correlated heat-transfer data with an equation similar to that of Hiddink (1975), except that the characteristic dimension was assumed to be the ratio of the liquid volume to the surface area of the product in contact with the container (V_f/A_f), the constant was 0.69, and the exponent was 0.24. An important consideration with convection heating of foods is the calculation of the f value of one container from that of another. Therefore, an equation was proposed for calculating the f value for heating water in any sized container:

$$f = 3.34 \ \rho_0(c_p k)^{0.76} \ [\eta/(g\beta\Delta T\rho^2)]^{0.24}(V_f/A_f)^{1.28} \tag{18}$$

D. NUMERICAL SOLUTION FOR NATURAL CONVECTION HEATING

Stevens (1972) was the first to attempt a numerical solution of the governing equations for natural convection heating of Newtonian liquids in cans being heated in still retorts. The system of equations containing the energy conservation equation, the vorticity equation, and a stream function equation was numerically solved to obtain transient velocity and temperature fields within the field. However, limitations of computation time did not allow for a satisfactory solution of the governing equations. The calculated transient temperatures were compared with temperature measurements at selected points in a can containing ethylene glycol. While the trends in the calculated and experimental temperature profiles were similar, quantitative agreement between the two was poor.

Datta and Teixeira (1986) numerically solved the nondimensionalized transformed governing equations for natural convection heating of a fluid in a container of radius R and height Z on a CDC Cyber 170/730 computer. The transformations used and the system of non-dimensionalized partial differential equations and their boundary conditions are given in the following equations

$$\tau = \frac{\alpha t}{H^2}$$

$$z = Z/H, \qquad r = R/H$$

$$u = HU/\alpha, \qquad v = HV/\alpha, \qquad \omega = (H^2\Omega/\alpha)$$

$$\theta = \frac{T - T_0}{T_s - T_0}$$

$$\frac{\partial\theta}{\partial\tau} + \left\{\frac{\partial(u\theta)}{\partial z} + \frac{1}{r}\frac{\partial(rv\theta)}{\partial r}\right\} = \left\{\frac{\partial^2\theta}{\partial z_2} + \frac{1}{r}\frac{\partial}{\partial r}\left(r\frac{\partial\theta}{\partial r}\right)\right\} \tag{19}$$

$$\frac{\partial\omega}{\partial\tau} + \left\{\frac{\partial(u\omega)}{\partial z} + \frac{\partial(v\omega)}{\partial r}\right\} = -\{(Gr)(Pr)\}\frac{\partial\theta}{\partial r}$$

$$+ Pr\left\{\frac{\partial^2\omega}{\partial z^2} + \frac{\partial}{\partial r}\left(\frac{1}{r}\frac{\partial(r\omega)}{\partial r}\right)\right\} \tag{20}$$

$$-\omega = \frac{1}{r}\frac{\partial^2\psi}{\partial z_2} + \frac{\partial}{\partial r}\left(\frac{1}{r}\frac{\partial\psi}{\partial r}\right) \tag{21}$$

$$u = \frac{1}{r}\frac{\partial\psi}{\partial r} \tag{22a}$$

$$v = -\frac{1}{r}\frac{\partial\psi}{\partial z} \tag{22b}$$

The boundary conditions are

side wall: $r = R/H$, $0 \leq z \leq 1$, $\theta = 0$, $\psi = 0$, $u = 0$, $v = 0$; (23a)

center line: $r = 0$, $0 \leq z \leq 1$, $\dfrac{\partial\theta}{\partial r} = 0$, $\omega = 0$, $\psi = 0$, $\dfrac{\partial u}{\partial r} = 0$, $v = 0$; (23b)

bottom wall: $0 \leq r \leq R/H$, $z = 0$, $\theta = 0$, $\phi = 0$, $u = 0$, $v = 0$; (23c)

top wall: $0 \leq r \leq R/H$, $z = 1$, $\theta = 0$, $\psi = 0$, $u = 0$, $v = 0$, (23d)

The initial conditions are

$$0 \leq r \leq R/H, \ 0 \leq z \leq 1, \ \theta = 1, \ \omega = 0, \ \psi = 0, \ u = 0, \ v = 0 \tag{24}$$

Because of the iterative solution of the complex equations, approximately 10 hr of central processing unit (CPU) time was required to simulate 30 min of heating. Good agreement was found between the computed radial velocity profiles and the experimental data of Hiddink (1975). The study of Datta and Teixeira (1986) is an important step in the understanding of natural convection heat-transfer phenomena.

III. HEAT TRANSFER BY FORCED CONVECTION

Agitation of convection-heating foods can result in improved flavor, color, and texture of the food (Wilbur, 1949). Agitation also prevents separation of different ingredients in the product during thermal processing as in the case of water and syrup systems, which tend to stratify (Nicholas *et al.*, 1960b).

A. FACTORS AFFECTING FORCED CONVECTION HEAT TRANSFER

The headspace, fill of the container, solid–liquid ratio, consistency of the product, and speed of agitation were highlighted as the crucial factors to be standardized in agitated processing (Wilbur, 1949). In addition, the type of agitation imparted to a can in a retort is of utmost importance. These factors have to be taken into consideration for determining a process schedule using an agitated cooker.

Mansfield (1962) discussed heat penetration into canned foods processed in continuous agitation cookers and recommended agitation also for products that primarily heat by conduction, but are fluid enough to allow induced convection currents when processed under agitation; examples of such products are cream-style corn, soups, and spaghetti that have solid materials within sauces containing thickening agents.

Several studies have been conducted on the affect of agitation on heat penetration to canned products during thermal processing. Most of the previous studies dealt with the effect of agitation on the *f* and *j* values for heating and cooling of the product within the can. However, recent studies have focused on the heat-transfer coefficient. The studies on heat transfer to canned foods in agitated retorts are summarized in Table IV.

Different methods of agitating the containers are presently being utilized in the food processing industry. The degree of agitation of a can's contents depends on the type of rotation imparted to the can within the retort.

B. HEAT TRANSFER IN STERILMATIC AND ORBITORT RETORTS

The Sterilmatic is a continuous-pressure retort widely used in the food processing industry. The cans are carried on a reel within the retort. During the bottom one-third of the rotational cycle, the cans are rolled against the shell of the retort (Fig. 7). As the can rolls, the headspace travels along the cylindrical contours of the can, resulting in the agitation of the contents. The Steritort is a pilot scale model of the Sterilmatic. The Orbitort is another type of agitating retort in which the cans are held in place on the reel and are not allowed to roll. The motion of cans in an Orbitort is illustrated in Fig. 8. The normal reel speed for the operation of Orbitort is 35 rpm, which is higher than in a Steritort.

TABLE IV

SUMMARY OF STUDIES ON HEAT TRANSFER TO CANNED FOODS IN AGITATED RETORTS

References	Products	Can sizes	Type of retort or agitation[a]	Heat-transfer parameter
Roberts and Sognefest (1947)	Cut green beans, peas, diced beets and carrots, corn kernels, and lima beans	307 × 409	Axial rotation and EOE, 0–50 rpm and mixed vegetables	f parameter
Clifcorn et al. (1950)	Water, tomato pulp, peas, carrots, sliced beets, asparagus spears (cuts and tips), cabbage, mushroom soup, and evaporated milk	300 × 314, 404 × 700, 603 × 700	EOE, 0–200 rpm, radius of rotation: 0–7 in.	Come-up time for the foods
Conley et al. (1951)	Water, tomato puree, corn kernels, peas, and orange concentrate	307 × 409	EOE, 15–90 rpm, radius of rotation: 6 1/4–16 in.	Heating curve at the can's center
Pruthi et al. (1962)	Canned fruits, fruit juices, juice concentrates, and tomato puree, paste, and soup	202 × 214; headspace: 1/4–1/2 in.	Spin cooker, 0–400 rpm	Come-up time for the foods
Quast and Siozawa (1974)	Sucrose solutions, CMC, orange juice, banana puree, pineapple juice, passion fruit juice, peach nectar, and tomato	300 × 406, 401 × 411, 604 × 614; headspace: 3/16–13/16 in.	Spin cooker, 0–420 rpm	Overall heat transfer coefficient
Parchomchuk (1977)	Bentonite suspensions	303 × 700	EOE (27–144 rpm), circular oscillation (100–400 rpm)	Heating curve
Lenz and Lund (1978)	Water and sucrose solutions	303 × 406, 608 × 700	Steritort (0–8 rpm)	Wall–fluid heat-transfer coefficient
Lenz and Lund (1978)	Spheres (0.95, 2.1, and 3-cm diameters) in water and 60% sucrose solution	303 × 406, 608 × 700	Steritort (0–8 rpm)	Particle–fluid heat-transfer coefficient
Berry et al. (1979)	Cream-style corn of different consistencies	303 × 406, headspace: 1/8–11/32 in.	Steritort (5–11 rpm)	f_h

(continued)

TABLE IV (*Continued*)

References	Products	Can sizes	Type of retort or agitation[a]	Heat-transfer parameter
Berry and Bradshaw (1980)	Cream-of-celery soup	211 × 400, 404 × 700, 603 × 700	Orbitort (25–42 rpm)	F_0
Duquenoy (1980)	Water, ethylene glycol, toluene, aniline aq. sugar solutions, and ethanol and salt solutions	Fabricated cans, L/D = 0.94–2.03	EOE (2–40 rpm)	Wall–fluid heat-transfer coefficient
Naveh and Kopelman (1980)	Glucose solutions	Fabricated can, L/D = 1.16; headspace: 0–10.7%	EOE, axial rotation (20–120 rpm)	Wall–fluid heat-transfer coefficient
Berry and Dickerson (1981)	Whole kernel corn in brine and vacuum packed corn	303 × 406, 603 × 700, 607 × 306, 603 × 600 Effect of fill weight (headspace)	Steritort (1–15 rpm) and Orbitort (10–42 rpm)	f and j parameters
Berry and Bradshaw (1982)	Sliced mushroom	300 × 400, 603 × 700, effect of fill weight (headspace)	Steritort (0–9 rpm)	f and j parameters and F_0
Soule and Merson (1985)	Water and silicone oils	303 × 406, 401 × 411, 404 × 700	Axial rotation, 0–150 rpm	Wall–fluid heat-transfer coefficient
Anantheswaran and Rao (1985a,b)	Water, aq. sucrose solutions, glycerine, and guar gum solutions	Fabricated can, L/D = 0.73–1.37	EOE (0–37 rpm), radius of rotation: 0–15 cm	Wall–fluid heat-transfer coefficient
Berry and Kohnhorst (1985)	Milk based formulas	211 × 308, 300 × 407, 307 × 710	Steritort (3–11 rpm)	f and j parameters and F_0
Rao et al. (1985)	Water, glycerine, sugar, and guar gum solutions	303 × 406, 603 × 700	Steritort (2–8 rpm)	Wall–fluid heat-transfer coefficient

[a] EOE, end-over-end agitation.

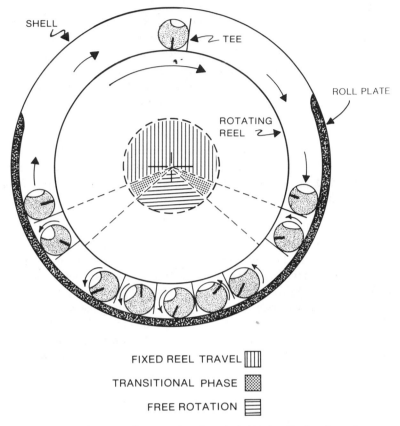

FIXED REEL TRAVEL ▦

TRANSITIONAL PHASE ▦

FREE ROTATION ▤

FIG. 7. Schematic of rotation of a can and motion of a bubble in a Sterilmatic continuous-pressure retort.

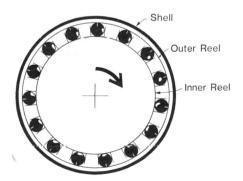

FIG. 8. Schematic of rotation of a can and motion of a bubble in an Orbitort.

Lenz and Lund (1978) developed a correlation to describe heat transfer to liquid foods agitated in a Food Machinery Corporation (FMC) Steritort. The variables studied were container size (303 × 406 and 608 × 700), fluid viscosity (distilled water and 60% sucrose solution), steam temperature (110 and 121°C), and the reel speed (2, 3.5, and 8 rpm). From the time–temperature data for the liquid, they estimated the convective heat-transfer coefficient at the inside wall of the can using a computer program. The program selected the value of heat-transfer coefficient for each run as that value which minimized the sum of squares of the deviation between the actual temperature of the liquid and the temperature predicted by the solution to Eq. (4) assuming an exponential temperature rise within the experimental retort. Based on their data they developed the correlation given in Eq. (25).

$$Nu = 115 + 15\,Re^{0.3}\,Pr^{0.08} \tag{25}$$

Because the convective heat-transfer coefficients were found to be independent of the container size used in their study, in their correlations they used the retort reel radius as the characteristic length of the system in the Reynolds and Nusselt numbers.

Berry and Bradshaw (1980) found that factors affecting the rate of heat penetration in condensed cream-of-celery soup processed in a Steritort were the size of headspace, the rotational speed of the can, and the consistency of the product. They also studied the heating characteristics of this product in an Orbitort and found that a headspace bubble of sufficient size was essential for effective agitation of the product. The fill weight was determined to be a critical parameter for this product, for whole kernel corn (Berry and Dickerson, 1981), and for sliced mushrooms (Berry and Bradshaw, 1982). In contrast to these foods containing particulates, for homogeneous-milk-based formulas the Steritort rotational speed had the greatest effect on heating and the headspace was not as critical (Berry and Kohnhorst, 1985).

Rao et al. (1985) studied heat transfer to canned liquids in a Steritort. Their test liquids consisted of water, glycerin, and aqueous sucrose solutions (30, 40, 50, and 60% w/v), as well as non-Newtonian aqueous guar gum solutions (0.3, 0.4, 0.5, and 0.75%). The wall heat-transfer coefficient to both Newtonian and non-Newtonian fluids was correlated by Eq. (26).

$$Nu_D = A[(Gr)(Pr)]^B + C[(Re_D)(Pr)(D/L)]^D \tag{26}$$

In Eq. (26), the constants A, B, C, and D were determined from experimental data. It was found that natural convection was very important in the heating of the Newtonian fluids. The coefficients A, B, C, and D for Newtonian fluids were 0.135, 0.323, 3.91×10^{-3}, and 1.369, respectively. The characteristic dimension for the pertinent dimensionless groups was the diameter of the can. For the non-Newtonian fluids, the generalized Reynolds number $(Re_D{'})$ was used in place of Re, and Pr and Gr were based on the apparent viscosity in $Re_D{'}$. The

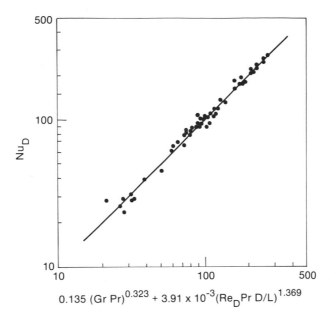

FIG. 9.   Dimensionless correlation for the wall heat-transfer coefficient of canned Newtonian fluids heated in a Steritort (Rao *et al.*, 1985).

magnitude of the coefficients A, B, C, and D for non-Newtonian guar gum solutions were 2.319, 0.218, 4.10×10^{-7}, and 1.836, respectively. The heat-transfer data in terms of the dimensionless numbers for the Newtonian and the non-Newtonian fluids are shown in Figs. 9 and 10, respectively.

C.   HEAT TRANSFER IN END-OVER-END (EOE) AGITATION

During EOE rotation, sealed cans are rotated around a circle in a vertical plane (Fig. 11), thereby creating a positive movement of the headspace bubble all through the rotating cycle. Since the headspace is moving along the length of the can and reverses direction every half a rotation, EOE rotation results in a random and, hence, complete mixing of the can contents.

The EOE method of rotating the can was proposed by Clifcorn *et al.* (1950), who found it to be superior to a reciprocating type of agitation with water as the test fluid in a 300×314 can with a 0.3-cm ($\frac{5}{16}$-in.) headspace. Further, EOE rotation was found to require less mechanical energy than axial rotation. The rotational speed required to minimize the come-up time was found to be lower when the radius of rotation was increased.

Clifcorn *et al.* (1950) found that the time for the can's contents to reach the temperature of the retort decreased with an increase in the speed of EOE rotation

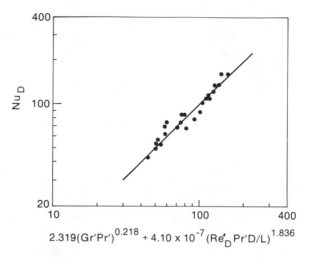

FIG. 10.   Dimensionless correlation for the wall heat-transfer coefficient of canned non-Newtonian fluids heated in a Steritort (Rao *et al.*, 1985).

and reached a minimum for a specific speed of rotation called the optimum speed of rotation. Beyond this optimum speed of rotation, there was no change in the heating rate of the can for a short interval in the speed of rotation, and any further increase reduced the heating rate. This decrease was due to the excess centrifugal forces acting on the can, which induced a static condition in part of the can's contents.

1.   Maximum Rotational Speed in EOE Agitation

In principle, the agitation of the can's contents will cease when the centrifugal force due to rotation is equal to the gravitational force acting on the can. Equat-

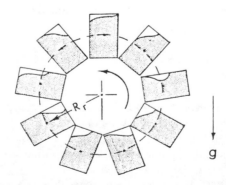

FIG. 11.   Illustration of end-over-end rotation of a can and motion of a bubble.

ing these two forces, the maximum speed of rotation (N) in relation to the radius of rotation (R_r, in meters) can be calculated from Eq. (27).

(mass $\times$ velocity^2)/radius = mass $\times$ gravitational acceleration
mass $(\pi 2R_r N)^2/(R_r)$ = mass (9.8 m/s^2)
$N = [9.8/(\pi^2 4R_r)]^{0.5}$
$$N = 0.498/R_r^{0.5} \tag{27}$$

In a typical commercial EOE agitating retort, the radius of the shell is 66 cm (Anonymous, 1983a) and, hence, the maximum speed of rotation should be less than 36.8 rpm to ensure that the centrifugal force is less than the gravitational force. Increased amounts of centrifugal force will retard the movement of the headspace bubble through the liquid within the can. This occurs because of the increasing tendency of the liquid within the can to stay away from the center of the can at higher speed of rotation. If the axis of EOE rotation was at the center of the can, the liquid will then be equally distributed between both ends of the can at high rotational speeds, resulting in the headspace bubble residing at the center of the can.

There has been a concern about cans located at different radial positions receiving different thermal processes within an EOE agitating retort, since the cans located further away have a higher tangential velocity associated with their position. Hence, there have been suggestions to also axially rotate the cage containing the cans. However, this will require more complex machine components and will also result in higher energy requirements for operating the retort.

2. Heat Penetration in EOE

Parchomchuk (1977) studied the effect of end-over-end rotation on the rate of heat penetration in 603 $\times$ 700 size cans containing 5% bentonite with a 0.5% headspace. The radius of rotation was 35 cm (14 in.), and the speed of rotation was varied from 27 to 144 rpm. The maximum rate of heat penetration was obtained at 40 rpm, whereas the speed of rotation for his retort, as per Eq. (27), is 50 rpm.

3. Heat-Transfer Correlations in EOE

Duquenoy (1980) used water, toluene, glycol, ethylene, aniline, sugar solutions, ethanol, and sodium chloride solutions at various concentrations from 10 to 80% by weight as model liquids. Length-to-diameter ratios of the cans employed ranged from 0.936 to 2.025. The heat-transfer data were correlated in terms of dimensionless numbers:

$$Nu = (17 \times 10^5) \, Re^{1.449} \, Pr^{1.19} \, W_e^{-0.551} \, (D/2L)^{0.932} \, (V_p/V_c)^{0.628} \tag{28}$$

In Eq. (28), the characteristic length in Nu and Re was the radius of the can, while in We it was half the height of the can. The heat-transfer coefficient on the product side was found to increase with the retort temperature.

Naveh and Kopelman (1980) evaluated the heat-transfer coefficients for an 84° Brix glucose syrup heated within cans and being rotated by EOE method in a Stork rotating autoclave. EOE rotation was found to result in a 2 to 3 times higher heating rate than with axial rotation. EOE rotation with an off-center axis of rotation resulted in a higher heat-transfer coefficient than EOE agitation with the axis at the center of the can. An increase in rotational speed increased the heat-transfer coefficient continuously during heating, and it approached an asymptotic value at about 40 rpm for cooling. The presence of a 2% headspace markedly increased the heat-transfer coefficient vs that with no headspace. Further increase in headspace volume, up to 10%, improved the heat-transfer coefficients only slightly.

Anantheswaran and Rao (1985a,b) studied heat penetration to model fluids in cans during EOE rotation. The rate of heat transfer was found to be independent of the size of the can and the radius of rotation in the range of 0–14.9 cm. Similar observation with respect to the radius of rotation was reported by National Food Processors Association using a commercial EOE agitating retort (Anonymous, 1983b). A headspace volume in the range of 3–9% was not found to significantly affect the rate of heat transfer; hence, they concluded that just the presence of a minimal headspace brings about sufficient agitation during rotation of the can. Based on their data, they developed a dimensionless correlation to predict the heat transfer coefficient [Eq. (29)]:

$$Nu = 2.9 \, Re^{0.436} \, Pr^{0.287} \tag{29}$$

They extended this study to non-Newtonian fluids consisting of various concentrations of guar gum solutions, and the correlation for non-Newtonian fluids were found to be very similar [Eq. (30)]:

$$Nu = 1.3 \, Re'^{0.485} \, Pr'^{0.367} \tag{30}$$

The generalized Reynolds number similar to that developed for pipe flow (Metzner, 1956) was found to be suitable in the correlation of their heat transfer data. In the case of highly viscous fluids, such as glycerin and 0.75% guar gum solution, the rate of heat transfer did not increase with EOE rotation of the can. Based on the temperature profile, they inferred that the core in such highly viscous fluids moves like a plug within the can, and the movement of the headspace bubble and the resulting agitation is restricted to the fluid near to the wall of the can. The dimensionless correlation for the Newtonian fluids is shown in Fig. 12. The correlation form for the non-Newtonian fluids was similar to that for the Newtonian fluids.

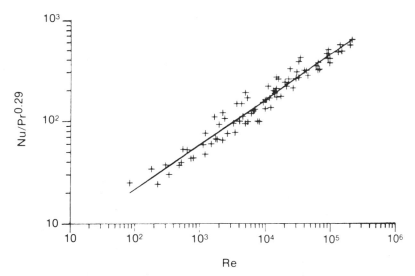

FIG. 12.   Dimensionless correlation for the wall heat-transfer coefficient of canned Newtonian fluids heated under end-over-end agitation (Anantheswaran and Rao, 1985a).

D.   HEAT TRANSFER IN SPIN COOKER AND AXIAL ROTATION

In a spin cooker, the cans are axially rotated as they travel through the length of the retort, and steam is used as the heating medium. Very high speeds of rotation, up to 500 rpm, are quite common in such axially agitating retorts. In the late 1930s, this process was introduced under the trade name of Thermo-Roto process (Berkness, 1939, 1940).

Pruthi *et al.* (1962) studied the effect of spin pasteurization of tropical canned fruit juices on the retention of some of the nutrients. In general, the retention of ascorbic acid during spin cooking was somewhat better than when still cookers were used. Further, there were only negligible losses of carotene during spin processing. The flavor, color, and texture of spin-processed products were judged to be superior to the corresponding still-heat-processed sets.

Quast and Siozawa (1974) studied heat transfer to cans in spin cookers. They used sucrose solutions of various concentrations as model liquids in their studies. The heat-transfer coefficients were evaluated from the slope of the plot of ln ξ time. In general, the heat-transfer coefficient was found to be similar for all can sizes. In the case of viscous solutions, the heat-transfer coefficient markedly increased with the amount of headspace. A dimensionless correlation, shown in Eq. (31), was developed to describe their data on heat transfer.

$$Nu_D = 0.55(Re)(Pr)^{0.33}(L/E)^{0.33} \qquad (31)$$

In Eq. (31), the characteristic length in Nu was the diameter of the can, and in Re it was the diameter of the roller. However, the rotational velocity used was that of the can wall.

Soule and Merson (1985) studied the effect of axial rotation on heat-transfer coefficients to Newtonian liquids with stem as the heating medium. They employed a single-can flame-sterilization simulator to obtain axial rotation of cans. Distilled water and silicone oil were used as model fluids. Commercial cans with L/D ratios of 1.11, 1.32, and 1.61 were used in the experiments. A headspace height of 1 cm and a closing vacuum of 50.8 cm (20 in.) of mercury were maintained within the can. The vacuum facilitated vaporization of the liquids readily at the retort temperature. The heat-transfer coefficients were evaluated from the slope of $\ln \xi$ vs time. The heat-transfer coefficients were found to be highly reproducible for experiments conducted under the same conditions, the reproducibility being within a limit of $\pm 2\%$. Soule and Merson (1985) also developed a correlation for heat-transfer rates, shown in Eq. (32), with an R^2 of 83%.

$$Nu_D = 0.434 Re_D^{0.571} Pr^{0.278} (L/D)^{0.356} (\eta/\eta_w)^{0.154} \qquad (32)$$

In Eq. (32), the characteristic dimension in Re and Nu was the diameter of the can.

E. HEAT TRANSFER IN FLAME STERILIZATION

Flame sterilization of axially rotating cans was originally developed in France (Beauvais *et al.*, 1961). The process uses a flame of combustible gases to heat the rotating can as illustrated schematically in Fig. 13. Since the flame temperatures are as high as 1,100°C, the process results in very short process times. Table V is a summary of studies of heat transfer in flame sterilization.

Paulus and Ojo (1974) investigated the temperature distribution inside and outside of the can as a function of flame temperature, distance of the burners,

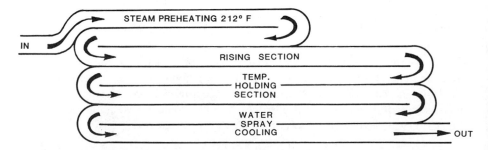

FIG. 13.   Schematic diagram of a flame sterilizer (Peralta Rodriguez and Merson, 1982).

TABLE V

SUMMARY OF HEAT-TRANSFER STUDIES DURING FLAME STERILIZATION

References	Products	Can sizes	Type of retort or agitation	Heat-transfer parameter
Paulus and Ojo (1974)	Water, bentonite–water mixtures	401 × 411 (2 1/2)	Flame sterilization, axial rotation: 0–60 rpm	Heating curves
Merson et al. (1981)	Clay suspensions and sugar solutions	303 × 406	Flame sterilization, axial rotation: 303 × 406	Wall–fluid heat-transfer coefficient
Peralta Rodriguez and Merson (1983)	Silicone oils	303 × 406	Flame sterilization, effect of spacing between can and burner 10–100 rpm	Wall–fluid heat-transfer coefficient
Teixeira Neto (1982)	Water, aq. sucrose solutions, and CMC solutions	0.5 kg can (303 × 406), headspace 0.24–0.71 cm	Flame sterilization, 50–200 rpm	Wall–fluid heat-transfer coefficient

rotational speed, and the properties of the can's contents. The temperature pro-files on the outside of the can were markedly affected by the flame temperature and the burner distance. The rotational speed decreased the temperature dif-ference between various points on the outside of the container. A lag phase was observed in the heating curve for the product at low rotational speeds. The temperature gradients were found to disappear at higher rotational speeds. The rate of heat transfer was found to improve up to a headspace volume of 200 cm³ in size 2½ cans, with greater volumes bringing about no further improvement. They stressed the need to optimize heat-transfer rates by considering all the factors that affect temperature distribution on the inside and the outside of the can.

Merson *et al.* (1981) monitored the temperature distribution within cans un-dergoing flame sterilization and found that it was uniform during axial rotation even with a pure liquid with no headspace, which is the worst-case condition. They used a film model and assumed bulk mixing in the interior of the can to describe internal heat transfer. They obtained a correlation for Nusselt number as shown in Eq. (33), which is a modified version of the model developed by Quast and Siozawa (1974) using a spin cooker.

$$Nu_D = 0.37 Re^{0.52} Pr^{0.33} (L/D)^{0.33} \qquad (33)$$

In Eq. (33), the characteristic length in Nu was the diameter of the can, and in Re it was the diameter of the roller. However, the rotational velocity was based on the diameter of the can and the rotational speed of the can.

Teixeira Neto (1982) studied heat transfer in a flame-sterilization simulator (Fig. 14) using sodium carboxymethylcellulose (CMC) as a model solution. He determined the overall heat-transfer coefficient (U) as a function of headspace, rotational speed of can, and product viscosity. The heat-transfer coefficient was calculated from the slope of ln ξ vs time, as described in Section I,C. The average of the specific heat of the can and its contents was used as the effective specific heat of the system in the heat-transfer calculations. The major heat-transfer resistance during flame sterilization and found to be on the flame side

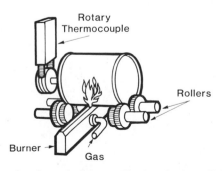

FIG. 14.   Illustration of a pilot-scale flame-sterilization simulator (Teixeira Neto, 1982).

due to the hot air on the outside of the can. He correlated his data by means of Eq. (34):

$$Nu_D = 0.433 \, Re_i^{0.56} \, Pr_i^{0.6} \, Re_e^{-0.68} \tag{34}$$

where, Re_i is the Reynolds number and Pr_i is the Prandtl number, both evaluated for the fluid within the can, and Re_e is the Reynolds number evaluated for the combustible gases on the outside of the can. The diameter of the can was the characteristic dimension in the Nusselt and the Reynolds numbers. All the properties in the above dimensionless numbers were evaluated at the average arithmetic temperature between 90 and 120°C, which represented the range of temperatures registered at the center of the cans during the flame heating cycle. Teixeira Neto noted that the film temperature exhibited a complex behavior as a function of the can rotational speed and other variables of the process. Because 90% of the heat-transfer resistance was on the flame side of the can, the product viscosity and headspace had no real effects on the overall rates of heat transfer. However, the rotational speed of the can did significantly affect the rates of heat transfer.

Peralta Rodriguez and Merson (1982) modeled heat transfer to liquids in cans during flame sterilization. They equated heat transfer to cans by convection and radiation to the rate of heat accumulation within the can. They integrated the resulting differential equation to obtain a solution that described the time–temperature history of the liquid food during the heating period [Eq. (35)].

$$\frac{T - T_s}{T_0 - T_s} = \exp\left(-\frac{AU}{mc_p}t\right) - \frac{A_c B (e_f F_{cf} T_f^4 - T_w^4)}{h_s(T_s - T_0)}\left[1 - \exp\left(-\frac{AU}{mc_p}t\right)\right] \tag{35}$$

In Eq. (35), T_s is the temperature of the combustion gases.

During experimental verification of this model using four silicone oils of various viscosities, it was found that the predicted values of the heating rates were consistently higher than the experimental values (Peralta Rodriguez and Merson, 1983). This was attributed to higher values of temperature driving force being used to calculate the predicted heating rate values. The experimental heating rate of the most viscous silicone oil was higher than the heating rate for the least viscous silicone oil used. This could be due to temperature profiles existing within the highly viscous liquids due to incomplete mixing. Hence, it was inferred that the center temperature, measured for calculating the rate of heat transfer, is not the representative temperature within the can during flame sterilization.

F. HEAT TRANSFER IN AN OSCILLATING CAN

Parchomchuk (1977) studied an oscillation method of agitation processing, where the can was rotated in a circular path such that its orientation remained fixed at all times. The products studied consisted of 3.25 and 5% bentonite, and the height of the headspace was varied from 0.63 cm (0.25 in.) to 1.25 cm (0.5 in.). The cans were oscillated at various speeds from 100 to 400 rpm. The rates of heat penetration were improved by increasing radius and speed of oscillation and the amount of heatspace. Orientation of the can, either horizontally or vertically, had no effect upon rate of heat transfer. On agitating a 603 × 700 size can of cream-style corn with a 1.25-cm (0.5-in.) headspace, average heating time was reduced from 6 hr for still cooking to 18.4 min for 0.75-in. radius circular oscillation at 175 rpm.

On comparing the nature of heat transfer in an oscillating can to that during EOE rotation of the can, Parchomchuk (1977) found that both of the methods of agitation were equally effective in improving heat transfer. However, oscillation method will require lesser amount of mechanical energy to agitate the can.

G.   EFFECT OF SURFACE ROUGHENERS IN CANS

One means of increasing the rate of heat transfer at a solid–fluid interface is to increase the intensity of turbulence of the boundary layer by means of baffles. The affect of rotation on heat transfer to fluids in containers with baffles was reported by Marquis et al. (1982). The stainless-steel containers were 8 cm² cylindrical cross section and 7.4 cm² square cross section and were rotated about their horizontal axis at speeds ranging from 0 to 20 rpm. In some of the cylindrical containers, they placed 2 to 8 steel rods of 0.2 cm in diameter lengthwise to increase the "roughness" of the walls and to induce agitation. Rotation and the surface rougheners increased slightly the heat-transfer rates. However, natural convection was the predominant mode of heat transfer even in the presence of surface rougheners. Similar results were obtained by Rao et al. (1985) with Newtonian fluids in #303 and #10 cans heated under agitation in a Steritort. Therefore, surface rougheners do not increase the heat-transfer rates within cans significantly.

IV.   HEAT TRANSFER BY CONVECTION IN THE PRESENCE OF PARTICULATE MATTER

Many of the food products processed in cans contain particulate matter. In this case, it can be assumed that heat is transferred first to the fluid and then from the fluid to the particle. During agitated processing, the presence of particulate matter will alter the flow patterns and possibly contribute to the mixing of the can's contents due to their motion.

A number of studies discussed previously under agitated retorts dealt with particulate systems (Berry and Bradshaw, 1980, 1982; Berry and Dickerson,

1981; Roberts and Sognefest, 1947). Studies taking the role of particulates in foods into consideration that were not discussed earlier will be covered.

Conley *et al*. (1951) studied the heating rates of #2 cans containing brine-packed whole-kernel corn and brine-packed peas under the influence of EOE rotation. They also conducted studies with water and tomato puree. The heating rates were considerably higher for all of these products when the cans were rotated.

Berry *et al*. (1979) found that the rate of heat penetration in cream-style corn processed in a Steritort is determined by the size of headspace, the rotational speed of the can, and the consistency of the product. The headspace was found to increase approximately 0.5 cm (0.2 in.) during processing in a 303 × 406 can. With a decrease in the headspace, the rate of heat penetration decreased and so did the sterilization value F_0. The agitation was more effective at higter reel speeds, and the sterilization value was larger at higher rotational speeds for the same process time. However, beyond a speed of 6.5 rpm, broken-heating phenomenon was consistently observed. The sterilizing value was found to be very sensitive to changes in fill weights as low as 5 g, especially at higher speeds of rotation. The rate of heat penetration was found to decrease with the increase in the total consistency. The consistency of cream-style corn was influenced by the viscosity of the cream, the amount of particulate matter or kernels, and the product temperature. It was concluded that the headspace was the most critical parameter for agitated processing in Steritort, and the use of accurate filling machines to control headspace in commercial operations was recommended.

Lenz and Lund (1979) studied heat transfer to systems containing spherical particles in a Steritort. They formulated and solved the energy balance equation for the entire can to predict the temperature within the can as a function of time. The heat-transfer coefficient at the fluid–particle interface was determined from the measurements of the fluid and the particle surface temperature using Newton's law of cooling. The magnitude was found to be a function of the fluid properties, rotational speed of the Steritort, and the ratio of particle diameter to container diameter. Magnitudes of the heat-transfer coefficient ranged between 185 and 2080 $W/m^2 \cdot K$. A correlation was developed for predicting the heat-transfer coefficient for the container-wall–fluid interface in the presence of spherical particles [Eq. (36)].

$$Nu = -33 + 53Re^{0.28}\, Pr^{0.14}\, [D_p/R_r(1-\epsilon)]^{0.16} \tag{36}$$

Hiddink (1975) found that the presence of solid particles reduced the convection heating rate in viscous fluids. He measured the temperature profiles within a container filled with water and viscous silicone fluids both with and without the presence of glass spheres. The smaller particles were able to suppress convection almost completely in the silicone fluids. In the case of water, the heat-transfer coefficient between the heating medium and the liquid within the can increased with increases in the diameter of spheres from 3 to 6 mm. On increasing the diameter to 18 mm, the heat-transfer coefficient decreased. This effect of particle size on the heat-transfer coefficient has been attributed to the alteration of the boundary-layer flow.

Effects of processing temperature and particle size on convective heat-transfer coefficients for canned mushrooms in still retorts was reported by Sastry (1984). The studies were conducted using metallic castings of mushrooms within 211 × 212 size cans containing water. The heat-transfer coefficients at the interface between the liquid and the particles were evaluated using the procedure described by Lenz and Lund (1978). There was no significant effect of processing temperature on the convective heat-transfer coefficient, but the heat-transfer coefficients were strongly influenced by the size of the particle. A dimensionless correlation, shown in Eq. (36), was developed to predict the heat transfer coefficient.

$$Nu = 0.01561[(Gr)(Pr)]^{0.529}, \qquad R^2 = 0.33 \qquad (37)$$

The Gr was evaluated with the major axis diameter of mushroom cap as the characteristic length. Time-dependent heat-transfer coefficients were also evaluated by numerically solving the energy balance equation. There was an increase in these heat-transfer coefficients with time followed by a slow decrease toward the end of heating.

V. ADDITIONAL RESEARCH NEEDS

With the exception of studies by Stevens (1972) and by Datta and Teixeira (1986) on natural convection, there have been very few theoretical studies on convection heating of liquids in cans. Theoretical studies are also needed on the influence of agitation and particulate matter on heat transfer. The theoretical studies must be verified with sound experimental measurements of the velocity and temperature profiles such as those of Hiddink (1975).

Because a large number of foods are non-Newtonian fluids, theoretical and experimental studies are needed that are applicable to non-Newtonian foods. For studying heat transfer to non-Newtonian fluids under agitation, the dependence of viscosity on the shear rate resulting from agitation must be taken into account. It is difficult to estimate the shear rate inside the container during the complicated patterns of agitation of fluids. Nevertheless, data on heat transfer to non-Newtonian liquids during agitation have been correlated successfully based on the generalized Reynolds number (Metzner, 1956), with the apparent viscosity in it replacing the Newtonian viscosity in Prandtl and Grashof numbers (Anantheswaran and Rao, 1985b; Rao et al., 1985).

The complex fluid flow and heat transfer during convection heating of foods in cans imposes restrictions on the generalization of the results. The factors affecting the pattern of convection currents are too numerous for the development of a complete theoretical analysis. However, for practical problems in the field of heat transfer, the approach of dimensionless correlation has proved to be quite helpful. Data on heat transfer have been correlated in terms of the pertinent dimensionless numbers that have been shown to be useful for design and scaling up operations.

The present study revealed that few studies have been conducted on heat transfer to particulate foods. Because the heat-transfer phenomena in the presence of particulates would be much more complex than when only liquids are present, analyses of experimental data using dimensionless groups would be a fruitful approach. The dimensionless numbers that have been employed in studies on heat transfer in packed and fluidized beds may be useful in correlating data with particulate systems (Fernandez, 1987). These can be supplemented by theoretical studies on simpler scenarios. One can apply similar strategies to understand heat-transfer phenomena in the many agitated retorts that are in commercial practice.

VI. NOMENCLATURE

A. VARIABLES AND CONSTANTS

A, Area (m²);

A, Constant in Eq. (15);

A_c, Absorptivity of can;

B, Boltzmann constant = 5.14×10^{-10}, (W/m²·K⁴);

B_1, First root of Bessel function of 0th order;

c_p, Heat capacity (J/kg K);

D, Diameter of can, particle (m);

D_{250}, Index of microbial destruction time at 121.1°C (250°F) to reduce the microbial population by 90% (min);

D_r, $2R_r$ = diameter of rotation (m);

E, Height of head space (m);

E_a, Activation energy of viscous flow (kJ/kg);

e_f, Emissivity of flame;

F_0, Equivalent sterilization time at 121.1°C (250°F) for z = 10°C (18°F) (min);

$F_{c\,f}$, View factor from can to flame;

f_1 Time required for one log-cycle reduction of the temperature difference between the heating medium and the temperature of the liquid (product) (sec);

g, Acceleration due to gravity (m/sec²);

h_i,   Heat-transfer coefficient inside container (W/m$^2\cdot$K);

h_s Heat-transfer coefficient outside container (W/m$^2\cdot$K);

H,   Height of can (m);

j,   A ratio term used to relate the actual initial temperature of the product to the intercept temperature;

K,   Consistency index in power-law model ($N\cdot$sec^n/m^2);

k,   Thermal conductivity (W/m$\cdot$K);

l,   Characteristic length (m);

L,   Length of can (m);

L/D,   Ratio of length to diameter;

M,   Percent moisture content;

m,   Mass of liquid (product) (kg);

N,   Speed of rotation (1/sec);

n,   Flow behavior index in power-law model;

p,   Fluid pressure (Pa);

R,   Gas constant 8314, (J/kg$\cdot$K);

R_r,   Radius of rotation of reel (m);

S,   Percentage of solids by weight;

T,   Absolute temperature (K);

$\bar{T}$,   Average temperature (K);

T_0,   Initial temperature (K);

T_f,   Flame temperature (K);

T_s,   Temperature of heating medium (K);

T_w,   Wall temperature (K);

t,   Time (sec);

u,   Nondimensional velocity $= HU/\alpha$;

U,   Overall heat-transfer coefficient, vertical velocity component (W/m$^2\cdot$K, m/sec);

v,   Nondimensional velocity $= HV/\alpha$;

V,   Velocity, radial velocity component (m/sec);

$\bar{V}$,   Mass average velocity vector (m/sec);

V_c,   Volume of can (m^3);

V_p,   Volume of liquid (product) (m^3);

Z,   Distance in vertical direction (m);

z value,   Change in temperature to change in the index of microbial destruction by a factor of ten ($^\circ$C);

α,   Thermal diffusivity $= k/c_p\rho$ (m^2/sec);

β,   Coefficient of thermal expansion of liquid (product) (1/K);

Δx,   Thickness of product film (m);

ϵ,   Fraction of container volume occupied by fluid;

η,   Dynamic viscosity of Newtonian liquid (Pa$\cdot$sec);

η_a,   Apparent viscosity (Pa$\cdot$sec);

η_{aM},   Metzner apparent viscosity $= \dfrac{K\,8^{n-1}}{N^{1-n}}\left(\dfrac{3n+1}{4n}\right)^n$ (Pa · sec);

$\dot{\gamma}$ Shear rate (sec^{-1})

Ω Angular velocity, vorticity (radians/sec; 1/sec);

ρ,   Density (kg/m^3);

σ,   Surface tension (N/m);

σ_{21},   Shear stress (N/m^2);

ξ,   Dimensionless temperature $= (T_s - T)/(T_s - T_o)$;

τ,   Nondimensional time $= \propto t/H^2$;

θ, $(T - T_0)/(T_s - T_0)$;

ψ,   Nondimensional stream function $= \psi/H\alpha$;

Ψ_i Stream function defined as $U = \dfrac{1}{r}\dfrac{\partial \Psi}{\partial Z}, V = -\dfrac{1}{r}\dfrac{\partial \Psi}{\partial Z}$ (m^3/sec);

ω,   Nondimensional vorticity $= (H^2\Omega/\propto)$;

Ω,   Vorticity (1/sec).

B. SUBSCRIPTS

O,   Initial value;

b,   Evaluated at bulk temperature;

i,   Instantaneous value;

p,   Value of particle;

w,   Evaluated at wall temperature.

C. DIMENSIONLESS GROUPS

Gr,   Grashof number $= \dfrac{l^3 g\beta\Delta T\rho^2}{\eta^2}$;

Gr, $\dfrac{l^3\,g\,\Delta T\,\rho^2\,N^{2-2n}}{K^2\,8^{2n-2}(3n+1/4n)^{2n}} =$ Generalized Grashof number;

Pr', $\dfrac{c_p\,K\,8^{n-1}}{k\,N^{1-n}}\left(\dfrac{3n+1}{4n}\right)^n =$ Generalized Prandtl number;

Re', $\dfrac{D_r^2\,N^{2-n}\rho}{8^{n-1}\,K\,(3n+1/4n)^n} =$ Generalized rotational Reynolds number;

Nu, $h_i l/k =$ Nusselt[1] number;

Nu_D, $h_i D/k =$ Nusselt number based on diameter of can;

[1]Nusselt numbers based on various characteristic dimensions have been defined in the text.

Ra,	Gr Pr = Rayleigh number;
Re,	D_r^2 N ρ/η = rotational Reynolds[2] number based on diameter of rotation;
Re_D,	D^2 N ρ/η = rotational Reynolds[2] number based on diameter of can;
Pr,	$c_p\eta/k$ = Prandtl number;
St,	h_i/c_pG = Stanton number;
We,	$\Omega^2L^2\pi$ D$/\sigma$ = Weber number, Ω is angular velocity.

D. MATHEMATICAL OPERATIONS

D/Dt,	$\partial/\partial t + \nabla\cdot\bar{V}$ = substantial derivative;
d/dt,	derivative with respect to time;
$\delta/\delta t$,	partial derivative with respect to time;
exp x,	e^x = exponential function of x;
ln x,	logarithm of x to the base e;
$\log_{10} x$,	logarithm of x to the base 10;
∇,	*del* or *nabla* operator = $\partial/\partial x + \partial/\partial y + \partial/\partial z$.

REFERENCES

Anantheswaran, R. C. 1984. Heat penetration to model fluid foods in cans during end-over-end rotation. Ph.D. thesis, Cornell University, Ithaca.

Anantheswaran, R. C., and Rao, M. A. 1985a. Heat transfer to model non-Newtonian liquid foods in cans during EOE rotation. *J. Food Eng.* **4**, 21–35.

Anantheswaran, R. C., and Rao, M. A. 1985b. Heat transfer to model non-Newtonian liquid foods in cans during EOE rotation. *J. Food Eng.* **4**, 1–19.

Anonymous. 1983a. Technical data for Rotomat. Stock America, Inc., Milwaukee, Wisconsin.

Anonymous. 1983b. Process design for Rotomats. *Natl. Food Process. Assoc. Annual Rep.* pp. 36–37.

Bagley, E. B., and Christianson, D. D. 1982. Swelling capacity of starch and its relationship to suspension viscosity-effect of cooking time, temperature and concentration. *J. Text. Stud.* **13**, 115–126.

Ball, C. O., and Olson, F. C. W. 1957. "Sterilization in Food Technology." McGraw-Hill, New York.

Beauvais, M., Thomas, G., and Cheftel, H. 1961. A new method of heat-processing canned foods. *Food Technol.* **15**, 5–9.

Berkness, R. 1939. High speed processing and cooling of juices by the Thermo-Roto process. *Fruit Prod. J.* **18**, 356–357.

Berkness, R. 1940. Thermo-Roto high speed processing and cooling. *Fruit Prod. J.* **19**, 172–174, 185.

Berry, M. R., and Bradshaw, J. G. 1980. Heating characteristics of condensed cream of celery soup in a Steritort: Heat penetration and spore count reduction. *J. Food Sci.* **45**, 869–874, 879.

[2]Reynolds numbers with different characteristic dimensions and velocities have been defined in the text.

Berry, M. R., and Bradshaw, J. G. 1982. Heat penetration for sliced mushrooms in brine processed in still retort and agitating retorts with comparisons to spore count reduction. *J. Food Sci.* **47**, 1698–1704.

Berry, M. R., and Dickerson, R. W. 1981. Heating characteristics of whole kernel corn processed in Steritort. *J. Food Sci.* **46**, 889–895.

Berry, M. R., and Kohnhorst, A. L. 1985. Heating characteristics of homogenous milk-based formulas in cans processed in an agitating retort. *J. Food Sci.* **50**, 209–214, 253.

Berry, M. R., Savage, R. A., and Pflug, I. J. 1979. Heating characteristics of cream-style corn processed in a Steritort: effects of head space, reel speed and consistency. *J Food Sci.* **44**, 831–836.

Bird, R. B., Stewart, W. E., and Lightfoot, E. N. 1960. "Transport Phenomena." Wiley, New York.

Blaisdell, J. L. 1963. Natural convection heating of liquids in unagitated food containers. Ph.D. thesis, Michigan State University, East Lansing.

Carroad, P. A., Leonard, S. J., Heil, J. R., Wolcott, T. K., and Merson, R. L. 1980. High vacuum flame sterilization: Process concept and energy use analysis. *J. Food Sci.* **45**, 696–699.

Clifcorn, L. E., Peterson, G. T., Boyd, J. M., and O'Neil, J. H. 1950. A new principle for agitating in processing of canned foods. *Food Technol.* **4**, 450–460.

Conley, W., Lawrence, K., and Schuhmann, L. 1951. The application of EOE agitation to the heating and cooling of canned food products. *Food Technol.* **5**, 457–460.

Datta, A. K., and Teixeira, A. A. 1986. Numerical modeling of natural convection heating in canned liquid foods. *Winter Meet. Am. Soc. Agric. Eng., Chicago* Paper No. 86-6516.

Duquenoy, A. 1980. Heat transfer to canned liquids. *Proc. Int. Cong. Eng. Food, 2nd Eur. Food Symp. 8th, Helsinki* **1**, 483–489.

Evans, L. B., and Stefany, N. E. 1966. An experimental study of transient heat transfer to liquids in cylindrical enclosures. *Chem. Eng. Prog. Symp. Ser.* **62**, 209–215.

Fernandez, C. L. 1987. Heat transfer to two-phase systems processed in a Steritort. M. S. thesis, Cornell University, Ithaca.

Figoni, P. I., and Shoemaker, C. F. 1983. Characterization of time dependent properties of mayonnaise under steady shear. *J. Texture Stud.* **14**, 431–442.

Foust, A. S., Wenzel, L. A., Clump, C. W., Maus, L., and Andersen, B. 1980. "Principles of Unit Operations," 2nd Ed. Wiley, New York.

Hayakawa, K. 1970. Experimental formulas for accurate estimation of transient temperature of food and their application to thermal process evaluation. *Food Technol.* **24**, 80–99.

Hayakawa, K. 1978. A critical review of mathematical procedures for determining proper heat sterilization processes. *Food Technol.* **32 (3)**, 59–65.

Hiddink, J. 1975. Natural convection heating of liquids with reference to sterilization of canned food. Agric. Res. Rep. #839. Centre for Agric. Publ. Documentation, Wageningen, Netherlands.

Higgs, S. J., and Norrington, R. J. 1971. Rheological properties of selected foodstuffs. *Process Biochem.* **6**, 52–54.

Holdsworth, S. D. 1971. Applicability of rheological models to the interpretation of flow and processing behaviour of fluid food products. *J. Texture Stud.* **2**, 393–418.

Jackson, J. M., and Olson, F. C. W. 1940. Thermal processing of canned foods in tin containers. IV. Studies of the mechanisms of heat transfer within the container. *Food Res.* **5**, 409–421.

Jackson, J. M., and Shinn, B. M. 1979. "Fundamentals of Food Canning Technology," AVI Publ., Westport, Connecticut.

Jones, D. E. A. 1931. Heat penetration by convection. *Food Process. Ind.* **1**, 63–65.

Jones, D. E. A. 1932. The cooling of food stuffs. *Food Process. Ind.* **1**, 214–216.

Jowitt, R., and Mynott, A. R. 1974. Some factors affecting natural convective heat transfer to canned foods. *In* "Einfluss der Rheologie," p. 153–164. Dechema-Monographien NR 1505–1536 Band 77. Verlag Chemie, Weinheim/Bergstrasse.

Kokini, J. L., and Plutchok, G. J. 1987. Viscoelastic properties of semisolid foods and their biopolymeric components. *Food Technol.* **41**, 89–95.

Kramer, A., and Twigg, B. A. 1970. "Quality Control for the Food Industry," Vol. 1. AVI Publ., Westport, Connecticut.

Lenz, M. K., and Lund, D. B. 1978. The lethality–Fourier number method: Heating rate variations and lethality confidence intervals for forced-convection heated foods in containers. *J. Food Process Eng.* **2**, 227–271.

Lopez, A. 1981. "A Complete Course in Canning," Book I. The Canning Trade, Baltimore.

Lund, D. B. 1977. Design of thermal processes for maximizing nutrient retention. *Food Technol.* **31**, 71–78.

McAdams, W. H. 1954. "Heat Transmission," McGraw-Hill, New York.

McConnell, J. E. W. 1952. Effect of a drop in temperature upon the lethality of processes for convection heating products. *Food Technol.* **6**, 76–78.

Mansfield, T. 1962. Factors involved in heat penetration studies of canned foods processed in continuous agitating cookers. *Proc. Int. Congr. Food Sci. Technol., 1st, Sept. 18–21, London* **4**, 235–244.

Manson, J. E., Zahradnik, J. W., and Stumbo, C. R. 1970. Evaluation of lethality and nutrient retention of conduction heating foods in rectangular containers. *Food Technol.* **24**, 109–113.

Marquis, F., Bertsch, A. J., and Cerf, O. 1982. Sterilization of liquids in bottles with a horizontal axis. Influence of rotational frequency on heat transfer. *Lait* **62**, 220–233.

Merson, R. L., Leonard, S. J., Mejia, E., and Heil, J. 1981. Temperature distributions and liquid-side heat transfer coefficients in model liquid foods in cans undergoing flame sterilization heating. *J. Food Process Eng.* **4**, 85–98.

Metzner, A. B. 1956. Non-Newtonian technology: Fluid mechanics, mixing, and heat transfer. *Adv. Chem. Eng.* **1**, 78–153.

Mulvaney, T. R., Nicholas, R. C., and Pflug, I. J. 1960. Product-induced stratification of covering syrups. *Food Technol.* **14**, 207–211.

Naveh, D., and Kopelman, I. J. 1980. Effect of some processing parameters on the heat transfer coefficients in a rotating autoclave. *J. Food Process. Preserv.* **4**, 67–77.

Nelson, P. 1932. Importance of agitation discussed. *Canning Age* **13**, 341, 344.

Nicholas, R. C., Pflug, I. J., and Mulvaney, T. R. 1960a. Convection in syrup packed products. *Food Technol.* **14**, 205–207.

Nicholas, R. C., Pflug, I. J., and Mulvaney, T. R. 1960b. Convection heating studies of water–syrup layered systems. *Food Technol.* **14**, 212–214.

Parchomchuk, P. 1977. A simplified method of processing of canned foods. *J. Food Sci.* **42**, 265–268.

Paulus, K., and Ojo, A. 1974. Heat transfer during flame sterilization. *Proc. Int. Congr. Food Sci. Technol., 4th* **4**, 443–448.

Peralta Rodriguez, R. D., and Merson, R. L. 1982. Heat transfer and chemical kinetics during flame sterilization. *AIChE Symp. Ser.* **78**, 58–67.

Peralta Rodriguez, R. D., and Merson, R. L. 1983. Experimental verification of a heat transfer model for simulated liquid foods undergoing flame sterilization. *J. Food Sci.* **48**, 726–733.

Pflug, I. J. 1982. "Syllabus for an Introductory Course in the Microbiology and Engineering of Sterilization Processes." Environmental Sterilization Lab., Minneapolis, Minnesota.

Powers, J. J., Pratt, D. E., and Norris, W. 1952. Comparative heating rates of bentonite suspensions in jars processed in boiling water and in steam at atmospheric pressure. *Food Technol.* **6**, 246–250.

Prescott, S. C., and Underwood, U. L. 1897. Micro-organisms and sterilizing processes in the canning industry. *Technol.* **10**, 183–199.

Pruthi, J. S., Satyanarayana Rao, N. S., Susheela, R., and Satyanarayana Rao, B. A. 1962. Studies on the spin-pasteurization of some important tropical canned fruit products. *Proc. Int. Congr. Food Sci. Technol., 1st* **4**, 253–270.

Pryce-Jones, J. 1953. The rheology of honey. *In* "Foodstuffs: Their Plasticity, Fluidity and Consistency" (G. W. Scott-Blair, ed), pp. 148–176. North Holland Publ., Amsterdam.

Quast, D. G., and Siozawa, Y. Y. 1974. Heat transfer rates during axially rotated cans. *Proc. Int. Congr. Food Sci. Technol., 4th* **4**, 458–468.

Rao, M. A. 1975. Measurement of flow properties of food suspensions with a mixer. *J. Texture Stud.* **6**, 533–539.

Rao, M. A. 1977. Rheology of liquid foods—a review. *J. Texture Stud.* **8**, 135–168.

Rao, M. A. 1986a. Rheological properties of liquid foods. *In* "Engineering Properties of Foods" (M. A. Rao and S. S. H. Rizvi, eds.), pp. 1–47. Dekker, New York.

Rao, M. A. 1986b. Viscoelastic properties of fluid and semi solid foods. *In* "Physical and Chemical Properties of Food" (M. Okos, ed.), pp. 14–34. American Society of Agricultural Engineers, St. Joseph, Minnesota.

Rao, M. A., and Cooley, H. J. 1984. Determination of effective shear rates of complex geometries in rotational viscometers. *J. Texture Stud.* **15**, 327–335.

Rao, M. A., Bourne, M. C., and Cooley, H. J. 1981. Flow properties of tomato concentrates. *J. Texture Stud.* **12**, 521–538.

Rao, M. A., Cooley, H. J., Anantheswaran, R. C., and Ennis, R. E. 1985. Convective heat transfer to canned liquid foods in a Steritort. *J. Food Sci.* **50**, 150–154.

Roberts, H. L., and Sognefest, P. 1947. Agitating processes for quality improvement in vacuum-packed vegetables. *Canner* **104**, 20–24.

Rohsenow, W. M., and Hartnett, J. P. 1973. "Handbook of Heat Transfer." McGraw-Hill, New York.

Sastry, S. K. 1984. Convective heat transfer coefficients for canned mushrooms processed in still retorts. *Winter Meet. Am. Soc. Agric. Eng., New Orleans* Paper #84-6517.

Soule, C. L., and Merson, R. L. 1985. Heat transfer cofficients to Newtonian liquids in axially rotated cans. *J. Food Process Eng.* **8**, 33–46.

Steffe, J. F., Mohamed, I. O., and Ford, E. W. 1986. Rheological properties of fluid foods: Data compilation. *In* "Physical and Chemical Properties of Food" (M. Okos, ed.), pp. 1–13. American Society of Agricultural Engineers, St. Joseph, Minnesota.

Stevens, P. M. 1972. Lethality calculations, including effects of product-movement for convection heating and broken heating food in still-cook retorts. Ph.D thesis, University of Massachusetts, Amherst.

Stumbo, C. R. 1973. "Thermobacteriology in Food Processing." Academic Press, New York.

Teixeira, A. A. 1978. Conduction heating considerations in thermal processing of canned foods. *Annu. Meet. Am. Soc. Mech. Eng. San Francisco* Paper #78-WA/HT-55.

Teixeira, A. A., Dixon, J. R., Zahradnik, J. W., and Zinsmeister, G. E. 1969a. Computer determination of spore survival distributions in thermally processed conduction heated foods. *Food Technol.* **23**, 78–80.

Teixeira, A. A., Dixon, J. R., Zahradnik, J. W., and Zinsmeister, G. E. 1969b. Computer optimization of nutrient retention in the thermal processing of conduction-heating foods. *Food Technol.* **23**, 137–142.

Teixeira Neto, R. O. 1982. Heat transfer to liquid foods during flame-sterilization. *J. Food Sci.* **47**, 476–481.

Thompson, G. E. 1919. Temperature–time relation in canned foods during sterilization. *Ind. Eng. Chem.* **11**, 657–664.

Tiu, C., and Boger, D. V. 1974. Complete rheological characterization of time-dependent food products. *J. Texture Stud.* **5**, 329–338.

Townsend, C. T., Reed, J. M., McConnell, J., Powers, M. J., Esselsen, W. B., Somers, I. I.,

Dwyer, J. J., and Ball, C. O. 1949. Comparative heat penetration studies on jars and cans. *Food Technol.* **3,** 213–226.

Tung, M. A., Richards, J. F., Morrison, B. C., and Watson, E. L. 1970. Rheology of fresh, aged and gamma-irradiated egg white. *J. Food Sci.* **35,** 872–874.

Van Wazer, J. R., Lyons, J. W., Kim, K. Y., and Colwell, R. E. 1963. "Viscosity and Flow Measurement: A Laboratory Handbook of Rheology" Wiley (Interscience), New York.

Vitali, A. A., and Rao, M. A. 1984a. Flow properties of low-pulp concentrated orange juice: Serum viscosity and effect of pulp content. *J. Food Sci.* **49,** 876–881.

Vitali, A. A., and Rao, M. A. 1984b. Flow properties of low-pulp concentrated orange juice: Effect of temperature and concentration. *J. Food Sci.* **49,** 882–888.

Walters, K. 1975. "Rheometry." Chapman & Hall, London.

Whorlow, R. W. 1980. "Rheological Techniques." Wiley, New York.

Wilbur, P. C. 1949. Process determination in agitating pressure cookers. *Canner* **108,** 13, 26–28.

Zechman, L. G. 1983. Natural convection heating of liquids in metal containers. M.S. thesis, University of Minnesota, Minneapolis.

SELENIUM IN FOODS

GERALD F. COMBS, JR.

Division of Nutritional Sciences
Cornell University
Ithaca, New York 14853

I.   INTRODUCTION

In the three decades since the recognition of its nutritional essentiality (Schwartz and Foltz, 1957; Patterson *et al.*, 1957; Schwarz *et al.*, 1957), the element selenium (Se) has attracted the growing interest of the biomedical community. While the element was first appreciated for its practical value in preventing nutritional myopathies and vascular disorders in livestock, the discovery of its biochemical function as an essential component of the peroxide-metabolizing enzyme glutathione peroxidase (Rotruck *et al.*, 1973) has led to an appreciation of Se as an important factor in metabolic defense against oxidative stress (see Combs and Mercurio, 1986). Then, both after the identification of cardiomyopathy (Tan, 1982; Yang *et al.*, 1982; Ge *et al.*, 1983) and osteoarthropathy (Li *et al.*, 1982) associated with severe endemic Se deficiency in China and after reports of ecological correlations of low apparent Se status with increased mortality due to cancer (Shamberger and Frost, 1969; Schrauzer *et al.*, 1977), Se has

85

assumed putative roles in chronic diseases, most notably carcinogenesis and cardiovascular disease (see Combs and Combs, 1986).

Attendant to the growing interest in these potential roles of Se in human health has been interest in the assessment of nutritional Se status. This has included the estimation of dietary intakes of Se and the evaluation of the Se contents of diets and their constituent foods. Although scores of reports on the Se contents of foods have been published, most have concerned only a few selected foods. Only recently have extensive numbers of these reports been collated for the purpose of summarizing the available information concerning the Se contents of the many kinds of foods that people eat around the world (Combs and Combs, 1986). The reader is referred to that volume for actual data and references to original reports; the present discussion will focus on the main features of this base of information with particular attention to several issues pertinent to its use in assessing nutritional Se status.

II. RESEARCH ON SELENIUM IN FOODS

A. ANALYTICAL METHODS FOR THE ANALYSIS OF SELENIUM IN FOODS

Because the amounts of the element normally found in foods can be quite low, e.g., 10–300 ppb, methods for the analysis of Se in foods must offer low limits of detection. Thus, many of the methods (colorimetry, electrolytic deposition, atomic emission spectrometry, and X-ray fluorescence spectrophotometry) that can be useful for industrial and/or biomedical purposes, but have relatively high limits of detection, are not suitable for the analysis of Se in most foods. Other methods, however, have been used successfully; these include derivatization and fluorometry, atomic absorption spectrophotometry, neutron activation analysis, proton-induced X-ray emission measurement, and a double isotope dilution method. Of these, the method most suitable for the analysis of Se in foods is the fluorometric procedure using 2,3-diaminonapthalene (DAN) (Watkinson, 1966; Olson et al., 1975; Brown and Watkinson, 1977).

The DAN method offers very good sensitivity with a detection limit of 2–5 ppb in the hands of a careful technician. The procedure involves oxidation of the Se in the sample to Se^{4+} and Se^{6+}, and then reducing any Se^{6+} to Se^{4+}. The latter species is then reacted with DAN to form benzopiazselenol, which fluoresces intensely at 520 nm when excited at 390 nm and can be quantitated on that basis. The procedure is relatively low cost, the only major instrumentation required being a good quality fluorimeter or fluorescence spectrophotometer. However, the digestion step can be rather laborious.

The DAN method is subject to two problems. The first involves the loss of sample Se during the acid-digestion step; this is particularly important in samples containing large amounts of organic matter, such as high-fat foods (eggs, some meats, etc.). Such samples can easily char during acid digestion, particularly if sulfuric acid is used as the oxidant. In such cases the sample Se, which is present in foods mostly as Se^{2-}, may not be oxidized quantitatively to Se^{4+} and/or Se^{6+}, and volatile reduced Se compounds (probably H_2Se) may be lost from the reaction mixture. This loss can be avoided, however, both by maintaining strongly oxidizing conditions during sample digestion through the use of both nitric and perchloric acids and by using low heat to raise gradually the temperature of the mixture to 210°C. When the nitric–perchloric acid digestion is controlled and carefully attended, it produces results that compare favorably to the direct oxidation in oxygen (Watkinson, 1966).

The second problem with the DAN method involves interfering fluorescence due to degradation products of the DAN reagent. This problem can be easily avoided by stabilizing the DAN request with HCl and extracting it with hexane prior to use (Wilkie and Young, 1970) or by recrystallizing DAN from water in the presence of sodium sulfite and activated charcoal before preparing the reagent (Cukor and Lott, 1965).

Although conventional atomic absorption spectrophotometry does not have the sensitivity or precision required for the analysis of Se in foods, two variant methods, which are sensitive to 15–25 ppb, have been employed. The first involves hydride generation of sample Se with quantitative detection by flame atomic absorption spectrophotometry (Lloyd et al., 1982). This method has been automated and is suitable for aqueous matrix samples, but complex samples (such as foods) require initial acid digestion. In addition, it suffers from potential interferences due to other elements that can form hydrides (e.g., Cu, As, and Sb); of these, the most serious interference may be due to Cu, necessitating its removal using HCl, thiourea, etc. Electrothermal atomic absorption spectrophotometry (Kumpalainen et al., 1983a) gives better sensitivity, but also requires wet digestion of food samples. Although many interferences can be avoided by employing the high-temperature oxidation and atomization offered by this technique, the use of this method for food analysis has problems with background interferences, particularly from P and Fe. These problems may be reduced by the use of Ni and Pd matrix modifiers and with Zeeman effect background correction; however, like the hydride generation method, such steps do not result in sensitivity approaching the fluorometric procedure.

Selenium can also be measured in foods by instrumental neutron activation analysis. The greatest sensitivity (~20 ppb) allowed by this method is achieved by measuring ^{75}Se (Noda et al., 1983); however, the production and subsequent measurement of this isotope require lengthy irradiation (100 hr), and long periods of postirradiation holding (60 days) before counting. Greater economy with increased sample throughput has been achieved at the expense of sensitivity by the use of the short-lived (17.38 sec half-life) isotope ^{77}Se (Morris *et al.*, 1981). When using this isotope, samples can be irradiated (5 sec), decayed (15 sec) and counted (25 sec) very quickly in an automated system. The utility of the "fast" method is limited by its relatively low sensitivity (limit of detection ~50 ppb), rendering it unsuitable for accurately measuring the low amounts of Se in many foods.

The measurement of Se by proton-induced X-ray emission offers the potential advantage of simultaneous elemental analysis with reasonably good sensitivity for Se (~10 ppb) (Hyvoneu-Dabek *et al.*, 1984), although it has not been employed widely. This method involves proton bombardment of the sample, which causes the loss of inner shell electrons. As these are replaced by outer shell electrons, X-rays are emitted with energies corresponding to the differences between electron shells. These may be identified and measured.

A procedure for determining Se by double isotope dilution has been developed which has a reported sensitivity of ~1 ppb (Reamer and Veillon, 1983). This method involves adding a known amount of ^{82}Se as an internal standard and digesting the sample in nitric–phosphoric acid with HCl used to reduce any Se^{6+} to Se^{4+}. The Se^{4+} is then reacted with 4-nitro-*o*-phenylenediamine to form 5-nitropiazselenol, and the nitropiazselenonium ion cluster is determined by combined gas–liquid chromatography/mass spectrometry. The amount of native Se in the sample can be calculated from the measured isotope ratios using the ^{80}Se naturally present in the sample. This method appears to be suitable for measuring Se in foods.

A 12-site interlaboratory comparison of the more widely used methods for the measurement of Se in clinical materials (Thomassen *et al.*, 1987) found significant differences among the mean Se concentrations reported for a sample of lyophilized human serum analyzed by acid-digestion/DAN–fluorometry, electrothermal AAS, acid-digestion/hydride-generation AAS, or acid-digestion/ isotope dilution mass spectrometry. Slightly higher values were obtained by the fluorometric procedure. The four methods compared very favorably for the analysis of pooled lyophilized urine samples. However, only the fluorometric method showed homogeneity of variance among laboratories.

B. CHEMICAL SPECIATION OF SELENIUM IN FOODS

The predominant amount of Se naturally present in foods appears to be in the reduced state (i.e., Se^{2-}); however, little information is available concerning the chemical forms in which the Se occurs in most foods. Early work by Franke (1934) showed that the Se in seleniferous wheat and corn is predominately protein bound. Subsequent studies by Peterson and Butler (1962) and Olson *et al.* (1970) confirmed this and indicated that half or more of the Se in wheat occurs in the form of the Se analog of the amino acid methionine, i.e., selenomethionine. These papers are frequently cited to support the conclusion that most of the Se present in foods of plant origin occurs as selenomethionine. It should be remembered that, for technical reasons, these studies employed plant materials that contained several times more Se than is typical in these and other types of plant-derived foods. Therefore, while this conclusion may be correct for at least some seleniferous wheats, it is unclear if it is also correct for other widely diverse plant-derived foods.

Studies of the chemical forms of Se in animal tissues indicate that, in these materials as well, Se is essentially all protein bound. Hawkes *et al.* (1983) have found that, of several identifiable Se-containing proteins in the rat, Se is present in each only as the Se amino acid selenocysteine.

Therefore, the limited information currently available indicates that Se in food occurs in proteins probably chiefly as Se analogs of amino acids. In plant-derived foods, the major form may be selenomethionine, but in animal products it appears to be selenocysteine. This means that the utilization of food Se (i.e., its apparent bioavailability) may be affected by the digestibility of food protein and by the methionine and/or cysteine contents of the diet.

C. GEOGRAPHIC VARIATION IN THE SELENIUM CONTENT OF FOODS

Due to the intimate relationship between plants and animals in food chains, the Se content of foods from both plant and animal origins tends to be greatly influenced by the local soil Se environment. Much of the variation in the Se content of foods results from large-scale geographical differences in the amounts and availabilities (to plants) of Se in soils. Several regions of the world have soils that contain low amounts (i.e., less than 0.5 ppm) of Se. These include Denmark, eastern Finland, New Zealand, and a long belt extending from northeast to south central China (including parts of the provinces of Heilongjiang, Jilin, Liaoning, Hebei, Shanxi, Shaanxi, Sichuan, and Zhejiang as well as Inner Mongolia). These regions have historical problems involving Se deficiency in livestock and, in China, more recently recognized problems of diseases associated with Se deficiency in humans (see Combs and Combs, 1986). Less severe, yet still problematic in livestock, deficiencies of Se occur in parts of Canada (eastern British Columbia, western Alberta, northern Ontario, southeastern Quebec, and the Atlantic provinces), western Australia, and in several parts of the United States (Pacific northwest, northeast, southeastern seaboard).

The most important determinant of the availability of Se from soil to plants is its aqueous solubility. The amounts of water-soluble Se in soils vary considerably and do not correlate with total soil Se (Olson *et al.*, 1942); water-soluble Se tends to be greatest in alkaline soils due to the enhanced solubilities in those environments of soluble selenates and microbially produced organic Se compounds. Selenium-deficient soils can be fortified with the element (1) by the use of Se-enriched fertilizers (Gissel-Nielsen, 1971), such as are now used in Finland, (2) by top-dressing with selenate pellets, as is used in New Zealand (Watkinson, 1987), or (3) by the application of fly ash, which tends to be rich in Se, as a liming agent (Barrows and Swader, 1978). Therefore, the uptake of Se into food plants can vary tremendously among soils from different locations.

Soils rich in Se are found in parts of the United States (the northern Great Plains and parts of the southwest), in parts of Ireland (counties Limerick, Mead, and Tipperary), in a few small mountainous locations in China (Enshi County and Xuan County, Hebei Province; Ziyang County, Shaanxi Province), and in parts of Colombia, Venezuela, and Israel. Soils in these areas are typically alkaline and dry; they may average 4–5 ppm Se, with some places having 10–20 times that amount. Much of the Se in such alkaline seleniferous soils occurs in oxidized, water-soluble states (e.g., selenates), which can be accumulated by plants to levels great enough to be toxic to animals. Seleniferous soils that are acidic and moist typically contain very little water-soluble Se; therefore, while such soils may contain as much as 15 ppm, the low availability of the element to plants does not result in high-level accumulation. Such soils are found in Hawaii and Puerto Rico.

The geobotanical distribution of Se in North America and China has been delineated using the Se content of forage crops produced in those regions. This type of work was first conducted on a large scale by Kubota et al. (1967); their map of Se distribution has been expanded to include more recent data from Canada (Subcommittee on Selenium, NAS, 1983) (Fig. 1). Liu et al. (1987) conducted the same type of survey and produced a map of the Se distribution for most of the Chinese mainland. These maps are extremely useful in understanding the regional differences that are observed in the incidence of Se-deficiency-related (and, to a lesser extent, Se-excess-related) problems of livestock, as well as the variation in the Se status of human populations. In both cases, most variation results from regional differences in the Se content of foods and/or feedstuffs.

Geographic variation in the Se content of plant-derived foods is readily seen in comparisons of similar foods from different countries. For example, whole wheat grain may contain as much as 2 ppm Se if produced in South Dakota, but as little as 0.11 ppm Se if produced in New Zealand and only 0.005 ppm Se if produced in Shaanxi Province, China. Although regional differences in the Se contents of foods produced in the United States are not nearly as great, they can be significant nevertheless (Table I).

The interregional shipment of many foods may be expected to have an ameliorating effect on the impact on human populations of regional differences in the Se content of individual foods. This effect is certainly to be expected in large countries with highly developed national food distribution networks, such as the

LOW—APPROXIMATELY 80% OF ALL FORAGE AND GRAIN CONTAIN <0.10 PPM SELENIUM
VARIABLE—APPROXIMATELY 50% CONTAIN >0.10 PPM SELENIUM (INCLUDES ALASKA)
ADEQUATE—80% OF ALL FORAGES AND GRAIN CONTAIN >0.10 PPM SELENIUM (INCLUDES HAWAII)

FIG. 1. Geographic distribution of Se in food and forage plants in the United States and Canada (Subcommittee on Selenium, NAS, 1983).

United States; but even in this country, regional differences in nutritional Se status (as indicated by blood Se levels) are seen (see Combs and Combs, 1986). In large developing countries without extensive food distribution networks and, thus, with far greater dependence on locally produced foods, regional differences in food Se levels are likely to result in much greater regional differences in dietary Se intake and in nutritional Se status.

D. SELENIUM IN PLANT-DERIVED FOODS

The Se content of a wide variety of foods of plant origin has been determined, for the most part, by the DAN fluorometric procedure described in Section III,A. However, the geographic base from which the analyzed foods have been selected is not extensive. Thus, current knowledge of the Se content of plant-derived foods (such as that of animal-derived foods) is restricted to samplings from only a small number of countries; for most of the world, little or no information is available. Much of the data presently available has come from studies in countries (e.g., New Zealand, Finland) or areas (e.g., parts of the United States and China) in which interest in the Se content of food supplies was stimulated by local experiences with endemic Se-deficiency disorders of livestock. Most of these data come from North America and Europe.

Despite the incomplete nature of current information concerning the Se con-

TABLE I

GEOGRAPHIC VARIATION IN THE Se CONTENT (PPM) OF SELECTED FOODS
PRODUCED IN THE UNITED STATES[a]

State	Soft wheat[b]	Soybeans[c]	Lamb muscle[d]	Cow's milk[e]
Arkansas		0.16		
Colorado			0.28	
Florida		<0.07		
Idaho	0.06			0.13
Illinois	0.05		0.16	
Iowa		0.28		
Minnesota			0.28	
Missouri	0.12			
Montana				0.018–0.044
New York				0.012–0.015
North Carolina		<0.07		
Ohio	0.04–0.09			
Oregon				0.014
South Dakota		0.44		0.047
Tennessee	0.03–0.08			
Washington	0.07			
West Virginia			0.09	
Wyoming			0.70	

[a] After Combs and Combs (1986).
[b] Dry-measure (DM) basis, Lorenz (1978).
[c] DM basis, Wauchope (1978).
[d] DM basis, Paulson et al. (1968).
[e] Fresh-weight (FW) basis, Shamberger and Willis (1971).

tent of world food supplies, the available data demonstrate the important geographic variations described previously. On a global basis, foods with the lowest Se content occur in the low-Se belt in China, particularly in provinces of Heilongjiang, Shaanxi, and Sichuan where cereals may contain only 0.01 ppm Se. The highest naturally occurring levels of Se in foods, e.g., several parts per million in cereals, have also been reported in China, although these occur in only a few remote areas of that country. Most other parts of the world for which information exists have much more moderate food Se levels, e.g., 0.02–0.05 ppm in cereals.

The Se content of foods of plant origin can vary within a particular geographic region according to specific climatic conditions during the growing season which may affect rate of plant growth, maturity at harvest, and crop yield. Therefore, annual variations are seen in the Se content of such foods as the cereal grains, with grains produced in high-yield seasons having somewhat lower Se levels than those produced in low-yield seasons. This effect was shown by Varo et al.

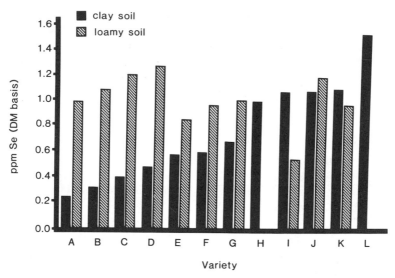

FIG. 2. Varietal differences in the Se content of soybeans grown on two soil types (after Wauchope, 1978).

(1980), who found that the Se content of wheat, rye, barley, and oats produced in Finland was low in 1975, a year with particularly favorable growing and harvesting conditions. The combination of favorable conditions that year resulted in the production of mature grain with relatively high starch but low Se content. The Se content (and other minerals) was only about two-thirds of that of the previous year, 1974, in which only average yields were realized. In general, grains produced in Finland in 1973, a year of relatively low yields, had still higher Se content.

Varietal differences in some food plants species can affect their Se content. For example, Wauchope (1978) found differences in the Se content of 18 varieties of soybeans that were grown either in Ames, Iowa, or in Stoneville, Mississippi. The Se content of the 6 varieties that were grown in Iowa varied by 600% (i.e., 0.08–0.48 ppm, air-dry weight); those of the 12 varieties that were grown in Mississippi varied by ~550% when they were grown in a clay soil, but only by ~145% when they were grown in a loamy soil in adjacent plots (Fig. 2). This interactive effect of plant variety and soil type shows that varietal differences in the Se content of foods of plant origin can vary between different geographic regions according to the local agronomic conditions.

The processing of cereal grains and oil seeds can produce food products with a Se content less than that of the parent materials. For example, the content of Se in soy protein isolates is almost twice that of the whole soybean (Ferretti and Levander, 1976). In cereal grains, the germ and outer layers of the kernel are generally richer in Se than the endosperm. Therefore, milled products based on germ or bran tend to contain higher levels of Se than the parent whole grains, whereas products based primarily on endosperm (wheat flour, corn flour, polished rice) tend to contain lower levels of Se than their parent grains (Ferretti and Levander, 1974). However, because differences in Se content of the different parts of the kernel tend to be small, the losses of Se due to the milling of cereal grains are generally of only low magnitude. For example, Ferretti and Levander (1974) found that the Se content of wheat flour, white corn flour, yellow corn flour, and polished rice was approximately 87, 86, 79, and 92%, respectively, of the corresponding whole grain. The Se content of wheat flours is affected by the blend of wheat milling fractions used to make them. For example, Lorenz (1978) found that wheat flour milled in several locations showed highly variable apparent losses in Se content due to milling (i.e., from −5% to 86%). Although Lorenz (1978) concluded that the Se content of flour decreased as the extraction percentage of the patent decreased, his data actually show that the apparent decreases were *not* related either to the extraction percentage of the patent or to the Se content of the whole grain. The apparent loss of Se was greatest for soft red winter wheat (31%) and Ontario soft winter wheat (42%) in comparison to the other wheats studied, e.g., hard red winter wheat (19%) and hard red spring wheat (16%).

Of the cooking techniques that have been examined in this regard (i.e., boiling, baking, broiling), most do not appear to cause appreciable losses of Se from plant-derived foods (Higgs *et al.*, 1972). However, the high-temperature drying of breakfast cereals and the boiling of asparagus and mushrooms (both of which are relatively high in Se) have been found to result in significant losses (presumably, as volatile forms) of Se.

In view of the expected variation due to geographic location of production, specific environmental conditions affecting crop yield, specific variety or cultivar, degree and manner of processing, and specific cooking techniques, the Se content of plant-derived foods is difficult to predict with great accuracy. The extensive collation of the published values for the Se content of foods by Combs and Combs (1986) shows this variation and indicates the numerous cases where no data are available for common foods. Those data have been used as the basis for developing Table II, which presents the range of reported Se content, as well as the present author's estimates of typical values, for several broad classes of plant-derived foods available in several countries. This table is intended for use in comparing the Se content of different general types of foods of plant origin, in comparing the Se content of plant-derived foods from several countries, and in approximating the typical Se intake of residents of those countries.

Of the foods of plant origin, cereal products tend to have the greatest amounts of Se, comparing favorably to meats in this respect. Within the same geographic region the range of Se content of whole grains tends to be small (e.g., 50%), but

TABLE II

TYPICAL Se CONTENT AND RANGE OF REPORTED VALUES (PPM, FRESH WEIGHT BASIS) OF Se IN
PLANT-DERIVED FOODS IN VARIOUS COUNTRIES[a]

Country	Cereal products	Vegetables	Fruits	Nuts and seeds
United States				
Low Se	0.300 (0.02–1.11)	0.010 (0.001–0.99)	0.004 (0.001–0.006)	0.190 (0.02–1.03)
Moderate Se	0.330 (0.03–0.66)	0.040 (0.001–0.517)	0.006 (0.002–0.013)	0.190 (0.03–29.6)
High Se	0.560 (0.02–21.3)	0.070 (0.003–1.18)	0.006 (0.002–0.011)	0.200 (0.03–29.6)
Canada	0.400 (0.01–1.35)	0.023 (0.001–0.119)	0.005 (0.001–0.023)	0.200[c]
England	0.110 (0.02–0.53)	0.010 (0.01–0.09)	0.005[b]	0.150 (0.01–0.53)
West Germany	0.290 (0.03–0.88)	0.020 (0.004–0.098)	0.010 (0.010–0.041)	0.200[b]
Finland	0.020 (0.005–0.115)	0.002 (0.001–0.002)	0.002 (0.002–0.030)	0.025 (0.02–0.03)
New Zealand	0.035 (0.004–0.086)	0.003 (0.001–0.021)	0.003 (0.001–0.004)	0.100[c]
China (PRC)				
Se deficient	0.010 (0.005–0.020)	0.010 (0.003–0.022)	0.001[c]	0.050[c]
Moderate Se	0.050 (0.017–0.106)	0.050 (0.002–0.089)	0.005[c]	0.200[c]
Seleniferous	3.880 (1.06–6.9)	5.680 (0.34–45.7)	—[c]	—[c]
Japan	0.070 (0.02–0.87)	0.015 (0.002–0.030)	0.004[b]	0.150[c]
Venezuela	0.340 (0.132–0.506)	0.030 (0.002–2.978)	0.020 (0.005–0.064)	0.400[c]

[a] Adapted from Combs and Combs (1986).

[b] Insufficient data to estimate range.

[c] No published data; "typical" value is author's estimate.

processed cereal products, particularly those containing brans, can vary considerably as already mentioned. The second-best plant sources of Se for humans are nuts and seeds. Some of these can contain rather high levels of Se, e.g., Brazil nuts have been found to contain as much as 50 ppm of the element. Vegetables and fruits tend to be much lower in Se content due, in part, to the high moisture contents of many of these types of foods in the forms in which they are normally consumed. Notable exceptions are mushrooms and texturized soy-protein products, which tend to be relatively rich in Se.

E.   SELENIUM IN ANIMAL-DERIVED FOODS

The Se content of foods of animal origin depends, in large part, on the Se intake of the livestock from which they are derived. Therefore, to the extent that the livestock diets reflect the Se status of locally produced feedstuffs, animal products will also show the regional variation in Se content described previously. Food animals raised in regions with low Se feeds will generally deposit relatively low concentrations of the mineral in their edible tissues and products (e.g., milk, eggs), while animals raised with relatively high Se feedstuffs will produce foods of much greater Se content.

The need of livestock for adequate amounts of Se for the prevention of a variety of debilitating deficiency syndromes is well recognized. Therefore, Se (usually as inorganic selenites) is used as a nutritional supplement in animal agriculture in many parts of the world. This practice, which has become widespread in North America, Europe, and New Zealand only within the last 10–15 years, has had the effect of ameliorating what might otherwise be strong geographic variation in the Se content of several animal-derived food products over many different parts of the world.

Dietary supplements of Se generally increase the Se content of animal meats, milk, and eggs over those levels produced using unsupplemented diets. This relationship, however, is direct but not linear. Within the ranges of normal Se intakes, muscle meats from most species tend to plateau in the range of 0.3–0.4 ppm Se (fresh-weight basis) (see Table III). Organ meats usually accumulate greater concentrations of Se; for example, the livers of several species have been found to contain about four times as much Se as skeletal muscle, and the kidneys of steers, lambs, and swine have been found to contain 10–16 times the amounts found in muscle. Poultry appear not to accumulate such great renal concentrations of Se; kidneys from young broiler chickens and turkey poults average only about 5 and 1.5 times, respectively, the amounts found in muscle. Because of the accumulation of Se in liver and kidney of most species, foods made from those organs tend to be rich sources of Se.

The Se content of most fish and shellfish products tends to be substantially greater than that of red meats and poultry. However, some of these products may also contain relatively high amounts of heavy metals, the presence of which is associated with reduced biological availability of Se.

The typical Se content of dairy products and eggs in several countries is presented in Table IV. For most foods of these types, few analytical values have been reported. Almost all Se in milk is associated with protein; therefore, the fluid milk products tend to have low concentrations of Se by virtue of their low solids contents. The Se content of processed milk products of lower moisture content is, however, much greater. The Se content of (chicken) eggs is markedly affected by the Se intake of laying hens at levels up to ~0.3 ppm; thus, it tends to show regional variation corresponding to geobotanical Se status. Egg yolk generally has at least three times the Se concentration of egg albumen, accounting for ~65% of the total amount of Se in the edible contents of whole eggs. Separated yolk and albumen fractions typically have ~200 and ~60%, respectively, of the Se concentration of whole eggs.

Although many cooking techniques do not appear to cause appreciable losses of Se from animal-derived foods (Higgs et al., 1972), those that result in the loss of fats (which are low in Se) from meats may be expected to increase the Se content of the cooked food. Such effects, of course, would be expected to be greatest in high-fat meat products. The extent to which specific methods of cooking affect the amounts or biological availability of Se in foods derived from

TABLE III

TYPICAL Se CONTENT (PPM, FRESH WEIGHT BASIS) OF MEATS IN VARIOUS COUNTRIES[a]

Country	Red muscle meats	Organ meats	Processed meats	Poultry	Fish	Shellfish
United States						
Low Se	0.195 (0.23–0.36)	1.070 (0.18–4.17)	0.150 (0.082–0.22)	0.100 (0.038–0.156)	0.665 (0.12–1.93)	0.650 (0.49–1.88)
Moderate Se	0.210 (0.058–0.27)	1.020 (0.43–1.90)	0.150[c]	0.120 (0.039–0.150)	0.665[b]	0.650 (0.59–0.66)
High Se	0.370 (0.24–0.76)	1.335 (0.62–3.26)	0.375 (0.19–0.76)	0.410 (0.38–0.71)	0.665 (0.19–1.15)	0.650[b]
Canada	0.275 (0.03–0.31)	1.220 (0.36–3.22)	0.365[c]	0.150[b]	0.275 (0.046–1.57)	1.00 (0.97–1.61)
England	0.120 (0.01–0.14)	0.600 (0.20–2.46)	0.300[c]	0.120[c]	0.120 (0.10–0.61)	0.320[c]
West Germany	0.210 (0.13–0.28)	0.500 (0.09–0.95)	0.250[c]	0.150[c]	0.425 (0.24–0.53)	0.320[c]
Finland	0.050 (0.01–0.07)	0.480 (0.06–1.71)	0.065 (0.02–0.17)	0.075 (0.05–0.10)	0.325 (0.18–0.98)	0.380 (0.21–0.56)
New Zealand	0.030 (0.01–0.04)	0.075 (0.05–2.03)	0.030[b]	0.075[c]	0.040 (0.034–0.31)	0.380 (0.06–0.46)
China (PRC)						
Se deficient	0.025[c]	0.075[c]	—[c]	0.050[c]	0.150[c]	—[c]
Moderate Se	0.100[c]	0.480[c]	—[c]	0.100[c]	0.400[b]	—[c]
Seleniferous	—[c]	—[c]	—[c]	—[c]	—[c]	—[c]
Japan	0.120 (0.08–0.16)	—[c]	0.120[b]	0.180[b]	0.350 (0.09–1.36)	0.180[b]
Venezuela	0.500 (0.171–0.833)	0.600 (0.36–0.833)	—[c]	0.700[b]	0.535 (0.32–0.93)	0.200[c]

[a] Adapted from Combs and Combs (1986).

[b] Insufficient data to estimate range.

[c] No published data; "typical" value is author's estimate.

TABLE IV

TYPICAL Se CONTENT AND RANGE OF REPORTED VALUES (PPM, FRESH WEIGHT BASIS) OF Se
IN DAIRY PRODUCTS AND EGGS IN VARIOUS COUNTRIES[a]

Country	Milk	Cheeses	Butter, cream, ice cream	Eggs
United States				
Low Se	0.010 (0.005–0.276)	0.085 (0.034–0.132)	0.006[b]	0.060[b]
Moderate Se	0.030 (0.01–0.241)	0.100 (0.052–0.105)	0.006[b]	0.100[b]
High Se	0.055 (0.046–0.069)	0.300 (0.070–0.76)	0.016[b]	0.450[b]
Canada	0.010[b]	0.060[b]	0.005[b]	0.060[b]
England	0.010[b]	0.085[b]	0.010[c]	0.150[c]
West Germany	0.010[b]	0.100[b]	0.002 (0.002–0.005)	0.180[b]
Finland	0.005 (0.002–0.020)	0.025 (0.01–0.04)	0.002[c]	0.135 (0.11–0.18)
New Zealand	0.004 (0.003–0.010)	0.025[c]		0.240 (0.24–0.98)
China (PRC)				
Se deficient	0.002[c]	—[c]	—[c]	0.050[c]
Moderate Se	0.020[c]	—[c]	—[c]	0.160[c]
Seleniferous	—[c]	—[c]	—[c]	—[c]
Japan	0.030[b]	0.030[c]	0.030[c]	0.240[b]
Venezuela	0.115[b]	0.400 (0.382–0.425)	0.010[c]	1.520[b]

[a] Adapted from Combs and Combs (1986).
[b] Insufficient data to estimate range.
[c] No published data; "typical" value is author's estimate.

animals (or plants) is largely conjectural at the present time, as very little research relevant to these issues has been conducted.

F. SELENIUM IN LIQUID FORMULA FOODS

The Se content of liquid formula diets, such as infant formulas and parenteral feeding solutions, varies according to both the particular combination of ingredients used and the Se content of those ingredients. For example, the Se content of infant formulas based on casein or meat as the major protein source is substantially greater (e.g., 0.052–.0098 ppm Se) than that of formulas based on either milk (e.g., 0.005–0.024 ppm Se) or soy protein (0.006–0.024 ppm Se) (Zabel *et al.*, 1978). Those of the latter type tend to have similar Se levels; because these levels have tended to be lower than those of human milk in countries such as the United States [the Se concentration of human milk in the United States is typically 20 ppm (fresh-weight basis) (see Combs and Combs, 1986)], there has been some interest in this country in fortifying these types of formulas with Se. Recent studies (Combs and Litov, 1987) demonstrated that fortification with sodium selenite can be effective in increasing the levels of biologically available Se in whey-predominant or soy-based infant formulas.

Parenteral nutrition fluids, particularly those based on amino acid mixtures rather than protein hydrolysates, can be very low in Se content if they are not supplemented with the element. Zabel *et al.* (1978) found that amino acid–based total parenteral feeding solutions then available in the United States provided less than 5 μg Se/1000 kcal, whereas solutions based on casein hydrolysates provided 16–95 μg Se/1000 kcal. Similar findings have been reported in New Zealand (van Rij *et al.*, 1979) and Sweden (Jacobson and Wester, 1977). Thus, it is not surprising that several investigators have found that maintenance of patients on parenteral formulas for extended periods can result in very low Se status (Fleming *et al.*, 1984; Jacobson and Wester, 1977; Van Rij *et al.*, 1979; Baker *et al.*, 1983). To assure adequacy of Se status, Levander (1984) has recommended that feeding solutions intended for total parenteral nutrition should provide 25–30 μg Se/person/day.

G. BIOAVAILABILITY OF SELENIUM IN FOODS

Schwarz and Foltz (1957) first observed that the utilization of dietary Se by the rat varied greatly according to the chemical form in which Se was fed. Since that report, many researchers have found that not only the chemical form of Se but also other dietary factors can influence the nutritional utilization of the element. The utilization of dietary Se is actually the net result of several physiological and metabolic processes that convert a portion of ingested food Se into the metabolically active form(s) necessary for normal physiological function.

Selenium in ingested food may be lost in several ways en route to its conversion to critical Se protein(s) and, perhaps, low-molecular-weight metabolites. These losses result from inefficiencies in digestion and/or absorption from the digestive tract. Thus, Se compounds that are insoluble in the lumenal environment of the small intestine, as well as Se-containing proteins that are poorly digested, will pass through the digestive tract and be eliminated with the feces. Because the normal enterohepatic circulation of absorbed Se is probably very small, fecal Se usually represents the nonabsorbable fraction of food Se. In general, the apparent absorption by humans of Se in foods, inorganic compounds, and Se amino acids is good, i.e., ~70% (Thomson and Stewart, 1973; Stewart *et al.*, 1978; Swanson *et al.*, 1983; Sirichakwal *et al.*, 1987). However, not all absorbed Se is physiologically active. A portion may be methylated and excreted through the lungs or kidneys. Another portion, which exists as (or can be metabolized nondescriminately to) analogs of the sulfur-containing amino acids, may be incorporated into tissue proteins, most of which do not depend on the presence of Se rather than S for their physiological function. While such Se-containing proteins may have nutritional significance as long-term stores of Se, the immediate nutritional role of Se appears to involve only one protein, the Se-dependent glutathione peroxidase (SeGSHpx). Therefore, the appropriate measure of the nutritional utilization of food Se involves the response either of SeGSHpx or of specific Se-deficiency syndromes, all of which appear to involve SeGSHpx deficiencies.

Thus, the biological utilization of food Se is the integrated response of several physiologic and metabolic processes of varying complexity. The term *bio-availability* (i.e., biological availability) is used in this context to denote the quantitative description of the utilization of Se. While this concept is useful in facilitating the evaluation of the adequacy of Se in particular menus and dietary patterns because estimates of the bioavailability of Se in foods are derived experimentally using any of several response criteria, these values must be considered in the context of the biological response(s) upon which they are based.

Three approaches, each relying on a different type of biological response, have been used to estimate the bioavailability of Se in foods. [For an extensively documented review of this topic, the reader is referred to Combs and Combs (1986) which served as the basis of the present discussion.] The first involves the evaluation of the relative efficacy of known amounts of Se in reducing the incidence and/or severity of a particular Se-deficiency syndrome in an experimental animal species (e.g., hepatic necrosis in the vitamin E- and Se-deficient rat, exudative diathesis in the vitamin E- and Se-deficient chick, myopathies in vitamin E- and Se-deficient lambs, calves, or turkey poults, and acinar pancreatic degeneration in the Se-deficient chick). The second approach involves the evaluation of the relative efficacy of known amounts of Se in supporting normal Se accumulation in various tissues. This approach can be taken with any species, including those that do not show discrete pathological signs of nutritional Se deficiency; it can employ readily obtained tissues such as blood plasma, cells, or platelets and is, therefore, applicable to studies with human subjects. The third approach is the functional assay, which involves the evaluation of the relative efficacy of known amounts of Se in supporting the activities of SeGSHpx of various tissues. This, like the Se accumulation approach, can be used with any species that can first be depleted of Se and, with the use of blood plasma or platelets, produces depleted results that are also applicable to studies in low Se human populations. With any approach to the estimation of the bioavailability of Se in foods and/or particular Se compounds, it has been traditional to employ sodium selenite, which is generally highly available, as a reference standard; Se bioavailability is expressed in terms of responses relative to this standard, which is assigned arbitrarily the value of 100%.

Different approaches to the determination of the bioavailability of Se in foods, feedstuffs, and specific Se compounds have produced different quantitative estimates. When different approaches have been taken with the same sources of Se, the most consistent estimates have resulted from (1) the prevention of hepatic necrosis vs. the support of tissue SeGSHpx in the rat, (2) the prevention of pancreatic atrophy vs. the accumulation of tissue Se in the chick, and (3) the prevention of exudative diathesis vs the accumulation of tissue Se in the chick. A notable exception is for the Se-enriched yeast products, which have shown remarkable consistency of bioavailability estimates by several different approaches [e.g., 106% by prevention of exudative diathesis (Cantor et al., 1975), 116% by accumulation of tissue Se (Vinson and Bose, 1987), 107% by support of plasma SeGSHpx (Combs et al., 1984), and 134% by support of platelet SeGSHpx (Levander et al., 1983)]. Discrepant estimates of Se bioavailability may indicate that Se is utilized differently between and, perhaps, within species for various physiological purposes, i.e., Se may be utilized with different efficiencies in supporting normal liver function in the rat, normal capillary permeability or pancreatic exocrine function in the chick, or SeGSHpx activities in the various organs and different species. It is possible that a particular form of Se may be very useful in preventing one Se-deficiency syndrome, but may be much less useful in preventing another.

Despite the lack of consistency in the present information concerning the bioavailability of Se in foods, the following generalizations can be made:

1. The reduced (and insoluble) inorganic forms of Se have very low bioavailabilities.
2. The common Se-containing amino acids (i.e., selenomethionine and selenocysteine), as well as Se in most plant-derived foods, have reasonably good bioavailabilities (i.e., approaching that of sodium selenite).
3. The Se in most animal-derived foods has low to moderate bioavailabilities.

In addition, it is clear that a number of other food- and diet-related factors can influence significantly the bioavailability of dietary Se.

The factors known to affect the bioavailability of dietary Se are listed in Table V. These include several that can enhance the apparent bioavailability of dietary Se: antioxidants (vitamin E, vitamin C, synthetic antioxidants), high levels of vitamin A, nutritionally adequate levels of methionine and/or total protein, and restricted growth rate (e.g., via food restriction). Other factors are known to impair the apparent bioavailability of dietary Se: heavy metals (Hg, As, Cd), nutritional deficiencies of vitamins B_2, B_6, and E as well as of methionine, high levels of sulfur, and several mercaptans. The reader interested in a critical review of this area with citations to the primary references is referred to Combs and Combs (1986).

Abundant data indicate that the chemical form of Se is a primary determinant of the bioavailability of Se in foods. But in spite of a fairly large body of analytical data concerning the Se content of foods, there remains very little known about the actual chemical forms in which that Se is present. Additionally, although it is clear that several other dietary factors can also affect the bioavailability of Se, present understanding of these interrelationships is not complete enough for the prediction (with reasonable accuracy) of the amounts of

TABLE V

FACTORS AFFECTING THE BIOAVAILABILITY OF
DIETARY Se

Chemical form of Se	Highly available forms
	Selenates
	Selenites
	Se amino acids
	Poorly available forms
	Selenides
Food sources	Highly available sources
	Se-enriched yeast
	Wheat
	Moderately available sources
	Most plant materials
	Poorly available sources
	Most meat and fish products
	Soybean
Other dietary factors	Availability enhancers
	Restricted food intake
	Methionine/protein
	Vitamin E
	Vitamin A (high levels)
	Antioxidants
	Availability decreasers
	Heavy metals
	Pyridoxine deficiency
	Riboflavin deficiency
	Vitamin E deficiency
	Methionine deficiency
	High dietary sulfur

biologically active Se in complex diets. Therefore, while it is possible to estimate from food intake data the typical Se intakes for at least some populations, it is not possible at present to assess meaningfully from the same data the nutritional value of those intakes.

H.   SELENIUM IN HUMAN DIETS

Differences in geography, agronomic practices, food availability and preferences, and methods of food preparation result in differences in the dietary contents of Se among human populations. Because many of these differences are difficult to quantify, the evaluations of Se intake that have been attempted for specific human population groups have not been precise. It is possible, however, to make some general comparisons of populations on the basis of the Se content of available food supplies by using the average Se concentration determined within specific major classes of foods in different locales presented in Tables II–IV. The typical Se content of the major classes of foods presented in these tables is, for the most part, based upon actual analyses of foods. Where analytical values were not available and where it appeared reasonable to do so, typical values have been estimated by the author; these values are so identified.

Several investigators have estimated the average per capita daily Se intake of adult Americans (Schroeder *et al.*, 1970; Watkinson, 1974; United States Food and Drug Administration, 1975; Mahaffey *et al.*, 1975; Ganapathy *et al.*, 1978; Olson *et al.*, 1978; Schrauzer and White, 1978; Welsh *et al.*, 1981). These estimates contradict the popular notion that regional geobotanical differences in Se status within the United States are overcome by interregional food shipment. Instead, they indicate that the Se intake of residents of different regions is highly variable (e.g., 60–216 μg Se/person/day) but, nevertheless, shows regional variation (e.g., low Se areas, 60–198 μg Se/person/day; moderate Se areas, 81–168 μg Se/person/day; high Se areas, 191–216 μg Se/person/day). It is noteworthy, too, that residents in the parts of the United States with the lowest geobotanical Se status (e.g., northeast, southeastern seaboard, Pacific northwest) have an estimated Se intake approximately 2- to 5-fold greater than that of residents of Finland (e.g., 30–60 μg Se/person/day) (Varo and Koivistoinen, 1980, 1981; Kumpalainen *et al.*, 1983b) or New Zealand (e.g., 28–70 μg Se/person/day) (Thomson and Robinson, 1980; Watkinson, 1981), and 10- to 20-fold greater than that of residents of the Keshan disease-endemic area of China (e.g., 7–11 μg Se/person/day) (Yang, 1987).

The most important sources of Se in the diets for most people are cereals, meats, and fish (Combs and Combs, 1986; Lane *et al.*, 1983; Schubert *et al.*, 1987: Snook *et al.*, 1987). This is shown by the relative contributions of each class of food to the total Se intake of residents of several countries as presented in Table VI, which summarizes the estimates of several authors. In general, meats and fish appear to contribute around 40–50% of the total intake of the element regardless of its level. The Se contributions of cereals, in contrast, appear to vary with the total Se intake. Whereas cereals may be expected to provide from about one-quarter to two-thirds of the dietary Se in countries with total Se intake greater than about 40 μg/person/day, they appear to contribute only one-tenth to one-quarter of the total dietary Se in countries with intakes lower than that level (e.g., Finland, New Zealand). Dairy products and eggs contribute relatively small amounts (i.e., up to 12 μg/person/day) of Se to the total intake in most parts of the United States. Vegetables and fruits, which are uniformly low in Se, would be expected to provide only small amounts (less than 5% of the total intake) of Se in most American diets.

Differences in patterns of food consumption, whether general due to cultural influences or specific due to personal preferences and food availability, can

TABLE VI

CONTRIBUTIONS OF THE MAJOR CLASSES OF FOODS TO THE Se INTAKE
(μg Se/PERSON/DAY) OF ADULTS IN SEVERAL COUNTRIES[a]

Country	Cereals	Vegetables and fruits	Meats and fish	Dairy and eggs	Total intakes
United States					
Moderate-Se area[b]	45 (34%)	5 (4%)	69 (52%)	13 (10%)	132
High-Se area[c]	57 (26%)	10 (5%)	101 (47%)	48 (22%)	216
Canada[d]	90 (66%)	6 (4%)	28 (21%)	12 (9%)	136
England[e]	30 (50%)	3 (5%)	23 (37%)	5 (8%)	60
Finland[f]	3 (10%)	1 (4%)	19 (63%)	7 (23%)	30
New Zealand[g]	4 (14%)	1 (4%)	12 (43%)	11 (39%)	28
Japan[h]	24 (27%)	6 (7%)	46 (52%)	12 (14%)	88
Venezuela[i]	88 (27%)	15 (5%)	153 (47%)	70 (21%)	326

[a] Numbers in parentheses show the percentage of the total intake contributed by each class of foods.

[b] From U.S. Food and Drug Administration (1975) and Schrauzer and White (1978).

[c] From Olson et al. (1978).

[d] From Thompson et al. (1975).

[e] From Thorn et al. (1978).

[f] From Varo and Koivistoinen (1980).

[g] From Thomson and Robinson (1980) and Watkinson (1981).

[h] From Sakurai and Tsuchiya (1975).

[i] From Mondragon and Jaffee (1976).

significantly affect Se intake. In a study of the Se intake of Maryland residents, Welsh et al. (1981) found great individual variation in free-living subjects of the study. Although the mean daily intake of Se by 22 subjects was 81 μg/person, ~17% of a duplicate plate sampling of 132 diets selected by those subjects was found to provide less than 50 μg Se/person/day, whereas total of 54% of the diets provided more than 150 μg Se/person/day.

Because meats are the major source of Se in average mixed diets, individual patterns of meat consumption can be important determinants of the amount of Se consumed by an individual. Combs and Combs (1986) illustrated this point by comparing the Se intake expected from the same food supply by two different patterns of food consumption: a relatively high-meat (290 g of meat and fish per day) American-type diet (based on the survey data of Mahaffey et al., 1975) and a relatively low-meat (119 g of meat and fish per day), Japanese-type diet (based on the pattern reported by Sakurai and Tsuchiya, 1975). The latter pattern was rich in cereals, while the former contained more dairy products, eggs, and total food in addition to meats and fish. The comparison showed that the low-meat, high-cereal pattern of food consumption provided 7–54% less Se than did the high-meat pattern and that the difference between the two patterns was greatest when calculated based on food supplies from areas with low Se cereal grains (e.g., Finland, New Zealand, China, Japan). Thus, it is not surprising that vegetarians have been found to consume only one-half to two-thirds as much Se as persons using meat-containing diets (Robinson, 1976; Abdulla *et al.*, 1981, 1984).

Although the quantitative dietary Se needs of Americans are not firmly established, it has been suggested that daily intakes of 50–60 μg Se/adult should be adequate for almost all Americans (National Academy of Sciences, 1980; Combs and Combs, 1986). Because studies indicate that most Americans consume substantially more than that amount, concern for preventing Se deficiency in this population should be centered on those groups living in geographic areas of relatively low Se status and those people whose food habits are likely to provide only small amounts of the element (e.g., vegetarians). For the purposes of addressing questions of Se and health in these and other groups, it is unfortunate that presently available food Se analyses are restricted to a relatively few geographic areas of the United States. The usefulness of "national" values of food Se contents is very limited, particularly for many types of food that are not widely distributed on a national basis. Further, it does not permit the detection of suboptimal Se intake that, due to specific combinations of geobotanical, socioeconomic, and personal lifestyle factors, may occur locally. Although nation-based food Se data may not be relevant to local food Se status, they can be useful in evaluating the Se adequacy, in a general sense, of national food supplies.

III. RESEARCH NEEDS

The evaluation of the nutritional adequacy of food supplies with respect to Se presently involves many important but unanswered questions. Answering these questions will require research in three main areas:

1. Improved characterization of Se in core foods of local or regional food supplies;
2. Improved understanding of factors affecting the bioavailability of Se from meals; and
3. Improved understanding of health hazards associated with both low and high intakes of Se.

The results of research to date indicate that, in a given food supply, some foods are more important than others in providing Se. Therefore, while it may be of some interest to know the Se content of specific foods, it will be of far greater value to public health to develop a more complete understanding of the amounts and nature of Se in those foods that provide most of the dietary Se for specific populations or population subgroups. In so doing, it will be most effective to approach the problem from the perspective of "core foods" for Se, i.e., to identify lists of foods most likely, by virtue of Se content and frequency of consumption, to provide important amounts of Se to individuals in specific areas. Core foods for Se would be expected to include meats, fish, cereal products, and, perhaps, some dairy and egg products; they would not include most vegetables and fruits. Core foods must be identified relative to the specific dietary habits of particular populations or subgroups to which they relate. For example, rice may be a core food in southern China but not in many parts of the United States. Core foods should also include those potentially significant sources of Se that are produced and consumed locally, such as many types of meats and dairy products.

Important initial work in the identification of core foods for Se has been conducted by Schubert *et al.* (1987). Employing data from the U.S. Department of Agriculture (USDA) 1977–78 Nationwide Food Consumption Survey and published values for the Se contents of American foods, which were screened according to reliability of analytical results, they found that 5 foods (beef, white bread, pork, chicken, and eggs) contributed 50% of the total Se in "typical" American diets. They further estimated that 80% of total dietary Se was provided by a core of only 22 foods. While core foods in specific geographic regions may be expected to vary somewhat from that list due to differences in consumption patterns and Se content of available foods, this work will provide direction in the identification of core foods for Se within different geobotanical and cultural regions.

With the identification of regionally referenced lists of core foods for Se, analyses of the Se content will be needed to assess the degrees of variation both within and between regions. It can be expected that certain core foods will have relatively similar Se content between different geographic regions of the United States; for these foods, Se values based on nationally sampled composites will be adequate. Foods in this category may include some wheat products (many of which are made from grains blended from different sources) and poultry meat (most of the nation's broilers are produced by a small number of companies using similar dietary formulations with similar Se levels). At the same time, it can be expected that other core foods will have highly variable Se contents between regions; for these foods, Se values based on locally sampled composites will be required. Foods in this category might include some meat products, especially pork (due to the highly nonuniform ways in which cattle and swine are fed).

Because knowledge of the amount of total Se in a food or meal provides only part of the information required to evaluate its adequacy with respect to Se, it is necessary to improve present understanding of those factors which affect the bioavailability of food Se. The first area of needed research pertinent to this question concerns the identification of the chemical forms of Se in foods. Here, the core food approach should be used to direct research efforts toward the speciation of Se in foods that are important in providing the element in human diets. These research activities must be pursued in conjunction with additional studies to elucidate the actual contributions, over both short and long terms, of the Se amino acids and, perhaps, other forms of Se that may be found in core foods. This is needed because it is necessary to understand the relative metabolic utility of selenocysteine and selenomethionine in practical circumstances before the evaluation of either form of Se in a food or diet can be made. In addition, further work should be conducted to evaluate the stability and nutritional efficacy of inorganic Se salts as supplements to formula (e.g., infant formulas and perenteral feeding solutions) and engineered (e.g., texturized soy protein products) foods most of which have been found to be naturally low in Se.

In addition, more studies are needed to identify the other dietary factors with known potential for increasing or decreasing the utilization of dietary Se that can act as determinants of the bioavailability of Se in human diets. For example, ascorbic acid has been shown to improve the utilization of sodium selenite in chicks (Combs and Pesti, 1976; Cupp et al., 1987), but because it is also known to reduce selenite to the nutritionally unavailable elemental state (Ganther, 1979), it is possible that the ingestion of high levels of vitamin C might reduce rather than enhance the bioavailability of selenite. Robinson et al. (1985) found that both effects on selenite utilization can occur in humans when ascorbic acid is consumed. First, the retention of oral selenite was substantially reduced when it was administered in solution with 1 g of ascorbic acid before breakfast. However, when selenite was given with 200 ml of orange juice (containing 60 mg ascorbic acid) at breakfast, the apparent absorption and urinary output of the element appeared to be improved. Recent studies by Martin et al. (1987) indicate that ascorbic acid status in humans can affect the metabolism of dietary selenite both at the level of the gastrointestinal tract and at a systemic level. Research is needed to delineate those conditions in which the bioavailability of the most nutritionally important forms of Se are effected by ascorbic acid and/or other dietary factors.

Despite the wealth of information from animal experimentation concerning the mode of action of Se in metabolism and the role of the element in nutrition and health, relatively little information is available concerning the amounts of Se required by or toxic to humans. This quantitative information is highly relevant to the evaluation of the Se adequacy of food supplies: research is needed to fill the gaps. The dietary needs of humans for Se have been estimated by the National Academy of Sciences (1980), Levander (1982, 1983), Combs and Combs (1986), and Yang (1987). The estimate of the National Academy of Sciences (1980) as discussed by Levander (1982) (i.e., the lower end of the "safe and adequate range") was merely a rough extrapolation from the quantitative requirements of animals that was adjusted for differences in food intake between humans and animals. This approach has been criticized (Combs and

Combs, 1986); nevertheless, it yields an estimate of human Se needs similar to those estimated on the basis of maintenance of optimal plasma activities of Se-dependent glutathione peroxidase (i.e., ~50 μg Se/day for a 70-kg man). However, this estimate is at least twice the level of Se intake that is associated with prevention of Se-responsive Keshan disease in China; therefore, its value as a criterion of dietary Se adequacy is not clear. Additional studies are needed to establish which of the available parameter(s) of Se status are valid for assessing dietary Se needs and to estimate quantitatively those needs in humans.

The level of Se that may be hazardous to humans is even less clear. Information presently available concerning the toxicology of Se is incomplete, but is of increasing importance in view of the growing interest in the putative role of Se compounds as cancer chemopreventative agents (Clark and Combs, 1986). Present data are few but suggest that the earliest signs in humans exposed by oral routes are dermatological and gastrointestinal in nature. However, the maximum safe level of oral intake, an important consideration both in evaluating high Se foods and oral Se supplements and in guiding the possible Se supplementation of formulated foods, has no concensus. The upper limit of the ''safe and adequate range'' set by the National Academy of Sciences (i.e., 200 μg Se/day for an adult) is undoubtedly much lower than necessary to protect humans from selenosis [Combs and Combs (1986) have suggested that 750 μg Se/person/day is probably safe] however, more studies are needed to establish, on the basis of experimental results, such an upper safe level.

The elucidation of the questions raised here will require continued active and informed research in the areas of the food chemistry, metabolism, and toxicology of Se. Answering these questions will improve understanding of the importance of Se in health and nutrition as well as of the roles of specific foods and patterns of food intake on Se nutrition of humans. Then will it be possible to act in an informed manner to prevent and/or correct instances of Se deficiency and, perhaps, toxicity in humans at risk.

REFERENCES

Abdulla, M., Andersson, I., Asp, N. G., Berthelsen, K., Birkhed, D., Dencker, I., Johansson, C. G., Jagerstad, M., Kolar, K., Nair, B. M., Nilsson-Ehle, P., Norden, A., Rassner, S., Akesson, B., and Ockerman, P. A. 1981. Nutrient intake and health status of vegetarians. Chemical analyses of diets using the duplicate portion sampling technique. *Am. J. Clin. Nutr.* **34,** 2464.

Abdulla, M., Aly, K. O., Andersson, I., Asp, N. G., Birkhed, D., Dencker, I., Johansson, C. G., Jagerstad, M., Kolar, K., Nair, B. M., Nilsson-Ehle, P., Norden, A., Rassner, S., Svenson, S., Akesson, B., and Ockerman, P. A. 1984. Nutrient intake and health status of lactovegetarians: Chemical analyses of diets using the duplicate portion sampling technique. *Am. J. Clin. Nutr.* **40**, 325.

Baker, S. S., Lerman, R. H., Krey, S. H., Crocker, K. S., Hirsch, E. F., and Cohen, H. 1983. Selenium deficiency with total parenteral nutrition: Reversal of biochemical and functional abnormalities by selenium supplementation: A case report. *Am. J. Clin. Nutr.* **38**, 769.

Barrows, S. A., and Swader, F. N. 1978. Agricultural uses of flyash in the Northeast. Final Report to Empire State Electric Energy Research Corp., Cornell Univ., Ithaca, New York.

Brown, M. W., and Watkinson, J. H. 1977. An automated fluorometric method for the determination of nanogram quantities of selenium. *Anal. Chem.* **89**, 29.

Cantor, A. H., Langevin, M. L., Noguchi, T. N., and Scott, M. L. 1975. Efficacy of selenium in selenium compounds and feedstuffs for prevention of pancreatic fibrosis in chicks. *J. Nutr.* **105**, 106.

Clark, L. C., and Combs, Jr., G. F. 1986. Selenium compounds and the prevention of cancer: Research needs and public health implications. *J. Nutr.* **116**, 170.

Combs, Jr., G. F. and Combs, S. B. 1986. "The Role of Selenium in Nutrition." Academic Press, New York.

Combs, Jr., G. F., and Litov, R. E. 1987. Bioavailability of selenium in human milk and infant formulas determined by chick selenium-dependent glutathione peroxidase. *Fed. Proc., Fed. Am. Soc. Exp. Biol.* **46**, 1154 (Abstr. No. 4880).

Combs, Jr., G. F., and Mercurio, S. D. 1986. Selenium and oxidative injury. *In* "Nutritional Diseases: Research Directions in Comparative Pathobiology" (D. Scarpelli and G. Magaki, eds.), p. 347. Liss, New York.

Combs, G. F., Jr., and Pesti, G. M. 1976. Influence of ascorbic acid on selenium nutrition in the chick. *J. Nutr.* **106**, 958.

Combs, Jr., G. F., Su., Q., and Wu, K. Q. 1984. Use of the short-term glutathione peroxidase response in selenium-deficient chicks for assessment of bioavailability of dietary selenium. *Fed. Proc., Fed. Am. Soc. Exp. Biol.* **473** (Abstr. No. 1100).

Cukor, P., and Lott, P. F. 1965. The kinetics of reaction of selenium (IV) with 2,3-diaminonapthalene. *J. Phys. Chem.* **69**, 3232.

Cupp, M. S., Combs, Jr., G. F., and Corradino, R. A. 1987. Influence of ascorbic acid on the activity of glutathione peroxidase in the cultured chick duodenum. *Proc. Int. Symp. Selenium Biol. Med., 3rd* p. 360.

Ferretti, R. J., and Levander, O. A. 1974. Effect of milling and processing on the selenium content of grains and cereal products. *J. Agric. Food Chem.* **22**, 1049.

Ferretti, R. J., and Levander, O. A. 1976. Selenium content of soybean foods. *J. Agric. Food Chem.* **24**, 54.

Fleming, C. R., McCall, J. T., O'Brien, J. F., Forsman, R. W., Ilstrup, D. M., and Petz, J. 1984. Selenium status in patients receiving home parenteral nutrition. *J. Parent. Entomol Nutr.* **8**, 258.

Franke, K. W. 1934. A new toxicant occurring naturally in certain samples of plant foodstuffs. II. The occurrence of the toxicant in the protein fraction. *J. Nutr.* **8**, 609.

Ganapathy, S. N., Joyner, B. J., Sawyer, D. R., and Hafner, K. M. 1978. Selenium content of selected foods. *In* "Tace Element Metabolism in Man and Animals" (M. Kirchgessner, ed.), Vol. 3, p. 332. Technische Univ., Munich.

Ganther, H. E. 1979. Metabolism of hydrogen selenide and methylated selenides. *Adv. Nutr. Res.* **2**, 107.

Ge, K., Xue, A., Dai, J., and Wang, S. 1983. Keshan disease—an endemic cardiomyopathy in China. *Virchows Arch.* **401**, 1.

Gissel-Nielsen, G. 1971. Selenium content of some fertilizers and their influence on uptake of selenium in plants. *J. Agric. Food Chem.* **19**, 564.

Hawkes, W. C., Wilhelmsen, E. C., and Tappel, A. L. 1983. The biochemical forms and tissue and subcellular distribution of selenium in the rat. *Fed. Proc., Fed. Am. Soc. Exp. Biol.* **42,** 928 (Abstr. No. 3723).

Higgs, D. J., Morris, V. C., and Levander, O. A. 1972. Effect of cooking on selenium content of foods. *J. Agric Food Chem.* **20,** 678.

Hyvoneu-Dabek, M., Nikkineu-Vilkki, P., and Dabek, J. T. 1984. Selenium and other elements in human maternal and umbilical serum, as determined by proton-induced x-ray emission. *Anal. Chem.* **30,** 529.

Jacobson, S., and Wester, P. O. 1977. Balance of twenty elements during total parenteral nutrition in man. *Br. J. Nutr.* **37,** 107.

King, W. W. K., Michel, L., Wood, W. C., Malt, R. A., Baker, S. S., and Cohen, H. J. 1981. Reversal of selenium deficiency with oral selenium. *N. Engl. J. Med.* **304,** 1305.

Kubota, J., Allaway, W. H., Carter, D. L., Cary, E. E., and Lazar, V. A. 1967. Selenium in crops in the United States in relation to selenium-responsive diseases of animals. *J. Agric. Food Chem.* **15,** 448.

Kumpalainen, J., Raittila, A. M., Lehto, J., and Koivistoinen, P. 1983a. Electrothermal atomic absorption spectrometric determination of selenium in foods and diets. *J. Assoc. Offic. Anal. Chem.* **66,** 1129.

Kumpalainen, J., Vuori, E., Kuitunem, P., Makinen, S., and Kara, S. 1983b. Longitudinal study of the dietary selenium intake of exclusively breast-fed infants and their mothers in Finland. *Int. J. Vitam. Nutr. Res.* **53,** 420.

Lane, H. W., Taylor, B. J., Stool, E., Servance, D., and Warren, D. C. 1983. Selenium content of selected foods. *J. Am. Diet. Assoc.* **83,** 23.

Levander, O. A. 1982. Clinical consequences of low selenium intake and its relationship to vitamin E. *Ann. N.Y. Acad. Sci.* **393,** 70.

Levander, O. A. 1983. Recent developments in selenium nutrition. *Nutr. Uptake* **1,** 147.

Levander, O. A. 1984. The importance of selenium in total parenteral nutrition. *Bull. N.Y. Acad. Sci.* **60,** 144.

Levander, O. A., Alfthan, G., Arvilommi, H., Gref, C. G., Huttunen, J. K., Kataja, M., Koivistoinen, P., and Pikkarainen, J. 1983. Bioavailability of selenium to Finnish men as assessed by platelet glutathione peroxidase activity and other blood parameters. *Am. J. Clin. Nutr.* **37,** 887.

Li, J., Ren, S., and Cheng, D. 1982. A study of selenium associated with Kaschin–Beck disease in different environments in Shaanxi. *Acta Sci. Circumstant.* **2,** 1.

Liu, C. H., Lu, Z. H., Su, Q., and Duan, Y. Q. 1987. Regional selenium deficiency of feeds in China. *Proc. Int. Symp. Selenium Biol. Med. 3rd* p. 47.

Lloyd, B., Holt, P., and Delves, H. T. 1982. Determination of selenium in biological samples by hydride generation and atomic absorption spectrophotometry. *Analyst* **107,** 927.

Lorenz, K. 1978. Selenium in wheat and commercial wheat flours. *Cereal Chem.* **55,** 287.

Mahaffey, K. R., Corneliussen, P. E., Jelinek, C. E., and Fiorina, J. A. 1975. Heavy metal exposure from foods. *Environ. Health Perspect.* **12,** 63.

Martin, R. F., Young, V. R., Blumberg, J., and Janghorbani, M. 1987. Ascorbic acid–selenite interactions in humans studied with an oral dose of $^{74}SeO^{2-}$. *Am. J. Clin. Nutr.* (in press).

Mondragon, M. C., and Jaffee, W. G. 1976. Consumo de selenio en la cividad de Caracas en comparacion con el de otras cividades del mundo. *Arch. Latinam. Nutr.* **26,** 31.

Morris, J. S., McKown, D. M., Anderson, H. D., May, M., Primm, P., Cordts, M., Gebhardt, D., Crowson, S., and Spate, V. 1981. The determination of selenium in samples having medical and nutritional interest using a fast instrumental neutron activation analysis procedure. *In* "Selenium in Biology and Medicine" (J. E. Spallholz, J. L. Martin, and H. E. Ganther, eds.), p. 438. AVI Publ., Westport, Connecticut.

National Academy of Sciences, Food and Nutrition Board. 1980. "Recommended Dietary Allowances," 9th Rev. Ed. National Academy Press, Washington, D.C.

Noda, K., Taniguchi, H., Suzuki, S., and Hirai, S. 1983. Comparison of the selenium contents of vegetables of the genus *Allivon* measure by fluorometry and neutron activation analysis. *Agric. Biol. Chem.* **47,** 613.

Olson, O. E., Whitehead, E. I., and Moxon, A. I. 1942. Occurrence of soluble selenium and its availability to plants. *Soil Sci.* **545,** 47.

Olson, O. E., Novacek, E. J., Whitehead, E. I., and Palmer, I. S. 1970. Investigation on selenium in wheat. Phytochemistry **9,** 1181.

Olson, O. E., Palmer, I. S., and Cary, E. E. 1975. Modification of the official fluorometric method for selenium in plants. *J. Assoc. Offic. Anal. Chem.* **58,** 117.

Olson, O. E., Palmer, I. S., and Howe, S. M. 1978. Selenium in foods consumed by South Dakotans. *Proc. S. Dakota Acad. Sci.* **2,** 113.

Patterson, E. L., Milstrey, R., and Stokstad, E. L. R. 1957. Effect of selenium in preventing exudative diathesis in chicks. *Proc. Soc. Exp. Biol. Med.* **95,** 617.

Paulson, G. D., Broderick, G. A., Bauman, C. A., and Pope, A. L. 1968. Effect of feeding sheep selenium fortifies trace mineralized salt: Effect of tocopherol. *J. Anim. Sci.* **27,** 195.

Peterson, P. J., and Butler, G. W. 1962. The uptake and assimilation of selenite by higher plants. *Aust. J. Biol. Sci.* **15,** 126.

Reamer, D. C., and Veillon, C. 1983. A double isotope dilution method for using stable selenium isotopes in metabolic tracer studies: Analysis by gas chromatography/mass spectrometry (GC/MS). *J. Nutr.* **113,** 786.

Robinson, M. F. 1976. The moonstone: More about selenium. *J. Hum. Nutr.* **30,** 79.

Robinson, M. F., Thomson, C. D., and Huemmer, P. K. 1985. Effect of megadose of ascorbic acid, a meal and orange juice on the absorption of selenium as sodium selenite. *N. Zealand Med. J.* **98,** 627.

Rotruck, J. T., Pope, A. L., Ganther, H. E., Swanson, A. B., Hafeman, D. G., and Hoekstra, W. G. 1973. Selenium: Biochemical role as a component of glutathione peroxidase. *Science* **179,** 588.

Sakurai, H., and Tsuchiya, K. 1975. A tentative recommendation for maximum daily intake of selenium. *Environ. Physiol. Biochem.* **5,** 107.

Schrauzer, G. N., and White, D. A. 1978. Selenium in human nutrition. Dietary intakes and effects of supplementation. *Bioinorg. Chem.* **8,** 303.

Schrauzer, G. N., White, D. A., and Schneider, C. J. 1977. Cancer mortality correlation studies. III. Statistical association with dietary selenium intakes. *Bioinorg. Chem.* **7,** 23.

Schroeder, H. A., Frost, D. V., and Valassa, J. J. 1970. Essential trace elements in man: Selenium. *J. Chronic Dis.* **23,** 227.

Schubert, A., Holden, J. M., and Wolf, W. R. 1987. Selenium content of a core group of foods based on a critical evaluation of published analytical data. *J. Am. Diet. Assoc.* **87,** 285.

Schwarz, K., and Foltz, C. M. 1957. Selenium as an integral part of factor 3 against dietary liver degeneration. *J. Am. Chem. Soc.* **79,** 3293.

Schwarz, K., Bieri, J. G., Briggs, G. M., and Scott, M. L. 1957. Prevention of exudative diathesis in chicks by factor 3 and selenium. *Proc. Soc. Exp. Biol. Med.* **95,** 621.

Shamberger, R. J., and Frost, D. V. 1969. Possible protective effect of selenium against human cancer. *Can. Med. Assoc. J.* **104,** 82.

Shamberger, R. T., and Willis, C. E. 1971. Selenium distribution and human cancer mortality. *CRC Crit. Rev. Clin. Lab. Sci.* p. 211.

Sirichakwal, P. P., Young, V. R., and Janghorbani, M. 1987. Absorption and urine excretion of selenium from doubly labeled eggs. *Proc. Int. Symp. Selenium Biol. Med., 3rd* p. 500.

Snook, J. T., Kinsey, D., Palmquist, D. L., DeLany, J. P., Vivian, V. M., and Moxon, A. L. 1987. Selenium content of foods purchased or produced in Ohio. *J. Am. Diet. Assoc.* **87,** 744.

Stewart, R. D. H., Griffiths, N. M., Thomson, C. D., and Robinson, M. F. 1978. Quantitative selenium metabolism in normal New Zealand women. *Br. J. Nutr.* **40,** 45.

Subcommittee on Selenium, Committee on Animal Nutrition, Board on Agriculture, National Research Council. 1983. "Selenium in Nutrition," Rev. Ed. National Academy Press, Washington, D.C.

Swanson, C. A., Reamer, D. C., Veillon, C., King, J. C., and Levander, O. A. 1983. Quantitative and qualitative aspects of selenium utilization in pregnant and nonpregnant women: An application of stable isotope methodology. *Am. J. Clin. Nutr.* **38,** 169.

Tan, J. A. 1982. The Keshan disease in China: A study of ecological chemico-geography, *Natl. Geogr. J. Ind.* **28,** 15.

Thomassen, Y., Ihnat, M., Veillon, C., and Wolynet, M. S. 1987. IUPAC interlaboratory trail for the determination of selenium in clinical material. *Proc. Int. Symp. Selenium Biol. Med., 3rd* p. 571.

Thompson, J. N., Erdody, P., and Smith, D. C. 1975. Selenium content of food consumed by Canadians. *J. Nutr.* **105,** 274.

Thomson, C. D., and Robinson, M. F. 1980. Selenium in health and disease with emphasis on those aspects peculiar to New Zealand. *Am. J. Clin. Nutr.* **33,** 303.

Thomson, C. D., and Stewart, D. R. H. 1973. Metabolic studies of [75Se]selenomethionine and [75Se]selenite in the rat. *Br. J. Nutr.* **30,** 139.

Thomson, C. D., and Stewart, D. R. H. 1978. The metabolism of [75Se]selenite in young women. *Br. J. Nutr.* **32,** 47.

Thorn, J., Robertson, J., Buss, D. H., and Bunton, N. G. 1978. Trace nutrients. Selenium in British food. *Br. J. Nutr.* **39,** 391.

United States Food and Drug Administration. 1975. *Bureau of Foods compliance program evaluation report: Total diet, studies of fiscal year 1974.* U.S. Govt. Printing Office, Washington, D.C.

van Rij, A., Thomson, C. D., McKenzie, J. M., and Robinson, M. F. 1979. Selenium deficiency in total parenteral nutrition. *Am. J. Clin. Nutr.* **32,** 2076.

Varo, P., and Koivistoinen, P. 1980. Mineral element composition of Finnish foods. XII. General discussion and nutritional evaluation. *Acta Agric. Scand.* **22,** 165.

Varo, P., and Koivistoinen, P. 1981. Annual variations in the average selenium intake in Finland: Cereal products and milk as sources of selenium in 1979/80. *Int. J. Vitam. Nutr. Res.* **51,** 62.

Varo, P., Nuurtamo, M., Saari, E., and Koivistoinen, P. 1980. Mineral element composition of Finnish foods. III. Flours and bakery products. *Acta Agric. Scand. Suppl.* **22,** 37.

Vinson, J. A., and Bose, P. 1987. Relative bioavailability of inorganic and natural selenium. *Proc. Int. Symp. Selenium Biol., 3rd* p. 445.

Watkinson, J. H. 1966. Fluorometric determination of selenium in biological materials with 2,3-diaminonapthalene. *Anal. Chem.* **32,** 981.

Watkinson, J. H. 1974. The selenium status of New Zealander. *N. Zealand Med. J.* **80,** 202.

Watkinson, J. H. 1981. Changes in blood selenium in New Zealand adults with the importation of Australian wheat. *Am. J. Clin. Nutr.* **34,** 836.

Watkinson, J. H. 1987. Annual topdressing of pasture with selenate pellets to prevent selenium deficiency in grazing stock: Research and farming practices in New Zealand. *Proc. Int. Symp. Selenium Biol. Med., 3rd* p. 783.

Wauchope, R. D. 1978. Selenium and arsenic levels in soybeans from different production regions of the United States. *J. Agric. Food Chem.* **26,** 266.

Welsh, S. O., Holden, J. M., Wolf, W. R., and Levander, O. A. 1981. Selenium in self-selected diets of Maryland residents. *J. Am. Diet. Assoc.* **79,** 277.

Wilkie, J. B., and Young, M. 1970. Improvement in the 2,3-diaminonapthalene reagent for micro-fluorescent determination of selenium in biological materials. *Agric. Food Chem.* **18,** 944.

Yang, G. Q. 1987. Research on Se-related problems in human health in China. *Proc. Int. Symp. Selenium Biol. Med., 3rd* p. 9.

Yang, G. Q., Wang, G. Y., Yin, T. A., Sun, S. Z., Zhou, R. H., Man, R. E., Zhai, F. Y., Guo, S. H., Wang, H. Z., and You, D. Q. 1982. Relationship between distribution of Keshan disease and selenium status. *Acta Nutr. Sin.* **3,** 199.

Zabel, N. Z., Harland, J., Gormican, A. T., and Ganther, H. E. 1978. Selenium contents of commercial formula diets. *Am. J. Clin. Nutr.* **31,** 850.

CHEMISTRY OF MAILLARD REACTIONS: RECENT STUDIES ON THE BROWNING REACTION MECHANISM AND THE DEVELOPMENT OF ANTIOXIDANTS AND MUTAGENS

MITSUO NAMIKI

Department of Food Science and Technology
Nagoya University
Nagoya, Japan 464

I. INTRODUCTION

The interaction between amino and carbonyl compounds resulting in complex changes in biological and food systems, called the "amino–carbonyl reaction," has exerted a strong influence on human existence throughout the ages as evidenced in, among other phenomena, the formation of humus on the earth's surface and the browning and flavor changes associated with the processing and cooking of foods. Although unaware of this reaction prior to its discovery, in 1912, by Louis-Camille Maillard, its importance was nonetheless felt, most often in the enhancement of food flavor by heating treatment (i.e., cooking) and sometimes in inferior food quality (e.g., browning).

As mentioned by Maillard (1912b), Ling (1908) first noted the enhancing effects of heating at 120–140°C on the flavor and browning of malt. Maillard's discovery of the amino–carbonyl reaction was made in the course of his studies on the synthesis of peptides under physiological conditions (Maillard, 1911), and he succeeded in synthesizing glycine peptides by heating a glycerol system where aldose instead of alcohol was used in the amino acid reaction. As a result, Maillard found marked development of color and flavoring (Maillard, 1912a; cf. Kawamura, 1983).

Since that time these reactions, often called Maillard reactions, continue to be a significant focus of attention in the chemistry of foods. During the past 75 years, numerous works have been published on the Maillard reactions. As summarized and reviewed by Hodge (1953), the interest of researchers was at first limited to the browning and flavoring of foods. Later, studies on the effects of the reactions on nutritional and physiological properties, as well as changes in the physicochemical properties of proteins and antixoidative activity, began to increase in number. Recent studies of these reactions have widened to include problems of food safety (e.g., mutagen formation), the chemistry of proteins *in vivo,* and diabetic and geriatric studies.

Why are the amino–carbonyl reactions so important in food and biological systems and the subject of growing scientific interest?

Regarding food quality, let us suppose a synthetic and nutritionally complete food is prepared by mixing polysaccharides (e.g., starch), pure proteins, lipids, vitamins, and minerals. Such a food containing no low-molecular-weight compounds may be adequate for feeding experimental animals but utterly tasteless to humans. The kind of food we wish to have in our daily diet usually contains large amounts of low-molecular-weight compounds (such as amino acids, sugars, and fatty acids). Not only do these components make food taste good but, as a result of amino–carbonyl reactions, they are also the source of appetizing smells and colors when the food is properly cooked, processed, or stored. Throughout the long history of food culture, humans have acquired various techniques for selecting and combining materials and processing conditions to control these reactions.

Fermented Oriental foods, notably soy sauce and *miso* (bean paste)—which are composed of amino acids, peptides, proteins, and sugars whose complex interactions during processing result in fine flavors and colors—are good examples.

It is interesting to note that research on the Maillard reaction in Japan has been conducted, for the most part, with emphasis on the coloring and flavoring which occur in soy protein foods, a major source of protein in the Japanese diet; the Maillard reaction is thus very desirable in making food more appetizing. In America and Europe, however, research has focused on the undesirable effects of coloring as a result of the Maillard reaction in dairy products, a major source of protein in the Western diet.

The following chemical aspects also underscore the importance of the amino–carbonyl reactions in food and biological systems. Despite the great abundance and complexity of possible biological compositions, the main constituents of all biological systems, as well as those of foods (which are, after all, derived from biological materials and consumed with or without some kind of processing), are only of three types: proteins, polysaccharides, and lipids. The functional groups of their structural units—amino acids, monosaccharides, fatty acids, and alcohols—are limited to the following four groups: —COOH, —OH, —NH$_2$, and —CHO. These groups are directly responsible for the formation of polymeric biological constituents by one-step reversible condensation reactions mediated by enzymes. This reversibility is apparent in the enzymatic polymerization of amino acids, which goes as far as to form, for example, proteins as the final product. However, the combination of —CHO and —NH$_2$ is quite different (see Fig. 1). Although the first step of the nonenzymatic reaction between these groups is reversible (formation and decomposition of glycosyl–amino products), its products undergo Amadori rearrangement to form ketosyl–amino products, which undergo complex irreversible reactions involving dehydration, rearrangement, scission, and so on to yield decomposed and polymerized products including flavor constituents and melanoidins. The physicochemical and physiological functions of proteins are naturally affected by these reactions. This irreversibility and complexity involving the two functional groups —CHO and —NH$_2$ are unique features of the initial stage of the Maillard reaction and distinct from the combinations formed by the other functional groups.

Given the importance and complexity of the reaction, numerous articles have appeared over the years; more than 500 directly related to the Maillard reaction are listed in *Chemical Abstracts* for the past 10 years, and more can be found that deal indirectly with the reaction in food systems.

In response to this growing interest, the First International Symposium on the Maillard Reaction was held in 1979 in Sweden under the auspices of the International Union of Food Science and Technology (IUFST) and other organizations. The proceedings of the first (1979, Sweden), second (1982, United States), and third (1985, Japan) symposia have been published [Eriksson, ed. (1981), Waller

Functional groups

-COOH, -OH, -NH₂, -CHO(-CO) : (-SH, -PO₃H, etc.)

Reactions between functional groups

(Enzymatic)

RCOOH + R'-NH₂ ⇌ RCONHR'   Peptide, Protein

RCOOH + R'-OH ⇌ RCOOR'   Fat

RCHO + R'-OH ⇌ R-OR'   Glycoside

(R-OH)   Polysaccharide

(Nonenzymatic)

RCHO + R'-NH₂ ⇌ RCH=NR' ⟶ Amadori product
                                  ↘ Scission products
                                         ↓
                                  Maillard reaction
                                  products

FIG. 1.   Reactions between main functional groups in food and biological constituents.

and Feather, eds. (1983), and Fujimaki *et al.*, eds. (1986), respectively). Many reviews have also appeared, two of them, concerning mainly the chemistry of nonenzymatic browning, in this series (Reynolds, 1963, 1965). The most recent review, also in this series, treats the Maillard reaction as related to the development of flavor (Danehy, 1985).

As can be seen in Table I, the Maillard reaction covers a broad spectrum reaching into a number of various fields. In this article, however, no attempt is made to cover the advances in all of these diverse albeit related fields. Only chemical studies on quality changes in foods effected by the amino-carbonyl reactions, particularly the browning reaction mechanism and the formation of antioxidants and mutagens, are reviewed. Nutritional aspects and physicochemical quality changes involving proteins are not discussed.

Flavor formation is, of course, an important part of the chemistry of the amino–carbonyl reaction. Since there are several articles which list the vast number of volatile flavor compounds generated by the Maillard reaction (Hurrell, 1982; Maga, 1982; Shibamoto, 1983a; Fors, 1983) and relatively little work has been done on the study of the mechanism of flavor formation by Maillard reactions in foods since the reviews by Hodge (1967) and Hodge *et al.* (1972), discussion of the chemistry of flavor formation is excluded from this article.

TABLE I

MAILLARD REACTION IN FOOD AND BIOLOGICAL SYSTEMS

Reactant

Amino acid, peptide, protein, amine, ammonia + Reducing sugar, carbonyl compounds (from oxidation of fatty acid, ascorbic acid, and polyphenol)

Influencing factors

pH, temperature, moisture content, heavy metal ions, oxygen, light, sulfite and other constituents

Chemistry	Browning reaction mechanism, isolation and identification of intermediate products, structure and properties of melanoidin
Food technological aspects	Flavor development, physicochemical quality changes, antioxidant, control of browning
Nutritional aspects	Loss of amino acid (lysine, arginine etc.), loss of nutritive value, antinutritive properties, metal ion chelation
Toxicology	Mutagen formation, Antimutagenesis
In vivo	Diabetic diseases, aging, etc.

II. BROWNING REACTION MECHANISM

A. INTRODUCTION

As is well known, the rate of coloration, the color produced, and the product properties of the browning reaction (the most characteristic consequences of the Maillard reaction) are strongly dependent on the nature of the reactants and the reaction conditions, especially pH and temperature. For example, the browning rates of aldoses in general are higher than those of ketoses, those of pentoses are higher than those of hexoses, and two- and three-carbon sugar analogs brown very rapidly. Basic amino acids generally brown more easily than acidic amino acids in the following order: lysine $>$ β-alanine $>$ α-alanine $>$ glutamic acid. Alkaline pH and higher temperatures greatly enhance the reactions and result in changes in the product distribution.

Despite the number of chemical studies, these phenomena have not yet been explained in full due to the high reactivities of the reactants and products, the intertwining reaction routes, and the diversity of products. At present, attempts to establish an inclusive, general reaction mechanism would be largely futile, and separate explanations must be given for each individual reaction. However, the reviews by Hodge (1953, 1967) on the early stages of the formation of the precursors to the various browned matter present an extremely well-organized review of the subject and include numerous data. These works serve their purpose well as far as the processes of the initial stages are concerned. However, essentially no new findings have been added in the more than 30 years since the first review was written despite rapid developments in the research techniques necessary to isolate and identify the reaction products. Based on Hodge's generally accepted scheme (Fig. 2), an attempt is made here to describe step-by-step the new findings on each stage of the browning reaction.

Hodge divided his scheme of browning into three stages. (1) An initial stage (reactions A and B) involving the formation of glycosyl–amino products followed by an Amadori rearrangement. (2) An intermediate stage (reactions C, D, and E) involving dehydration and fragmentation of sugars, amino acid degradation, and others. (3) A final stage (reactions F and G) involving aldol condensation, polymerization, and the formation of heterocyclic nitrogen compounds and colored products.

According to the accepted view, the key step is the Amadori rearrangement (reaction B), which irreversibly produces ketosyl compounds that enolize and lead to the complex reactions in the intermediate stage. Until recently it was believed that this part of the reaction sequence was common to all Maillard reactions and that different individual reactions occurred in the later stages. Each stage will be described in the following sections.

B.   REACTIONS DURING THE INITIAL STAGE

The scheme proposed by Hodge for the initial stage of the Maillard reaction is shown in Fig. 3. The first step of the reaction is the simple condensation between the carbonyl group (as the aldehyde form of the reducing sugar) and the free amino group of amino acid, protein, or amine, to give an N-substituted glycosylamino compound followed by the reversible formation of the Schiff base derivatives (Fig. 3a). This condensation reaction is initiated by an attack of a nucleophilic amino nitrogen, with an unshared electron pair, on the carbonyl carbon. The reaction usually requires an acidic catalyst. Protonation of the carbonyl group should enhance its reactivity to the nucleophilic reagent. while protonation of the nitrogen of the amino group inhibits the attack on the carbonyl carbon. The favorable combination of the reactants is shown in Fig. 4. In this step, the maximum rate occurs when the product of the concentrations $[>C=O]$ $[RNH_2]$ is maximum. These concentrations vary in the opposite direction with pH,

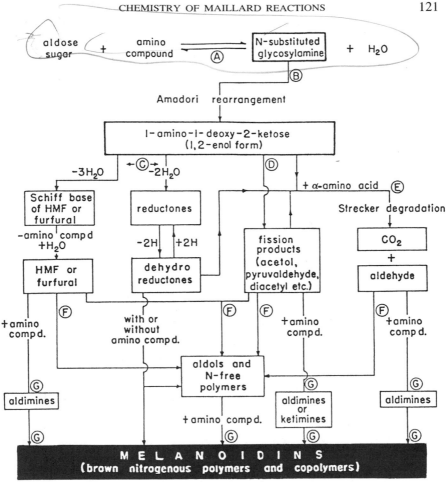

FIG. 2.   Review of Maillard reaction pathways (Hodge, 1953).

so the rate of condensation reaches maximum at a weakly acidic pH in the reaction involving aldose and amine.

The remaining steps for formation of the Schiff base usually occur faster than the first combination step. The increase in the nucleophilic strength of the amine increases the rate of the carbonyl–amine reaction, but has almost no effect on the equilibrium (Feeney *et al.*, 1975).

With aromatic aldehydes, the equilibrium is shifted in favor of Schiff base formation, but aliphatic aldehydes, which possess a hydrogen atom on the carbon adjacent to the carbonyl group, do not generally yield Schiff bases. In the case of sugar, the Schiff base may be an intermediate which rapidly cyclizes to the *N*-

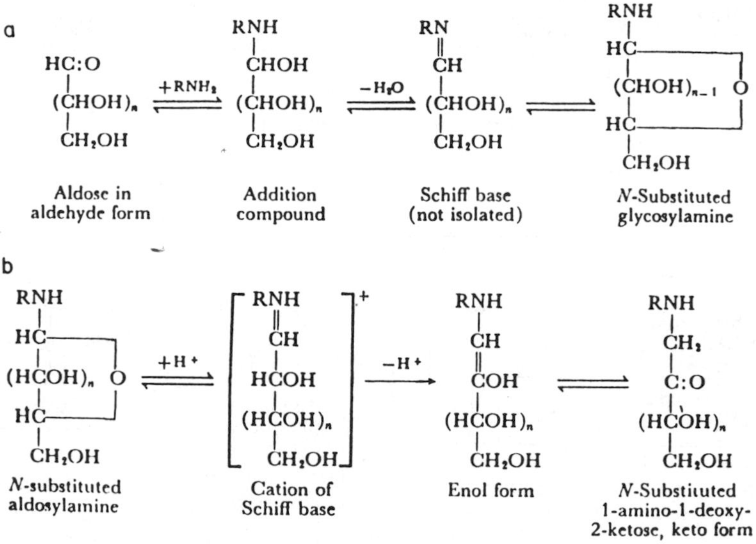

a

$$\begin{array}{ccccc}
\text{HC:O} & & \text{CHOH} & & \text{CH} \\
| & & | & & || \\
(\text{CHOH})_n & \xrightleftharpoons{+\text{RNH}_2} & (\text{CHOH})_n & \xrightleftharpoons{-\text{H}_2\text{O}} & (\text{CHOH})_n \\
| & & | & & | \\
\text{CH}_2\text{OH} & & \text{CH}_2\text{OH} & & \text{CH}_2\text{OH}
\end{array}$$

Aldose in aldehyde form   Addition compound   Schiff base (not isolated)   N-Substituted glycosylamine

$$\begin{array}{c}
\text{RNH} \\
| \\
\text{HC} \\
| \qquad\quad \\
(\text{CHOH})_{n-1} \quad \text{O} \\
| \\
\text{HC} \\
| \\
\text{CH}_2\text{OH}
\end{array}$$

b

$$\begin{array}{ccccc}
\text{RNH} & & \left[\begin{array}{c}\text{RNH} \\ || \\ \text{CH}\end{array}\right]^+ & & \text{RNH} \\
| & & & & | \\
\text{HC} & & & & \text{CH} \\
| \quad\;\; \text{O} & \xrightleftharpoons{+\text{H}^+} & \text{HCOH} & \xrightarrow{-\text{H}^+} & \text{COH} \\
\text{HC} & & (\text{HCOH})_n & & (\text{HCOH})_n \\
| & & | & & | \\
\text{CH}_2\text{OH} & & \text{CH}_2\text{OH} & & \text{CH}_2\text{OH}
\end{array}$$

N-substituted aldosylamine   Cation of Schiff base   Enol form

$$\begin{array}{c}
\text{RNH} \\
| \\
\text{CH}_2 \\
| \\
\text{C:O} \\
| \\
(\text{HCOH})_n \\
| \\
\text{CH}_2\text{OH}
\end{array}$$

N-Substituted 1-amino-1-deoxy-2-ketose, keto form

FIG. 3.   The initial stage of the Maillard reaction (Hodge, 1967).

substituted glycosylamine. Up to this step, the reaction is reversible because the glycosylamine can be hydrolyzed, in aqueous solution, into the parent compounds. The formation of the N-substituted glycosylamine is usually very fast and the product is unstable; especially in an aqueous system, it is susceptibile to reverse hydrolysis as well as to additional irreversible reactions (even at room temperature). The glycosylamines derived from amines show a certain stability, while those from amino acids are difficult to isolate because they are immediately converted into the Amadori products, N-substituted 1-amino-1-deoxy-2-ketoses. However, the isolation of the N-glycosylamino derivatives of amino acids is possible using an amino acid ester or metal salt.

This Amadori rearrangement of the N-substituted glycosylamines, the most

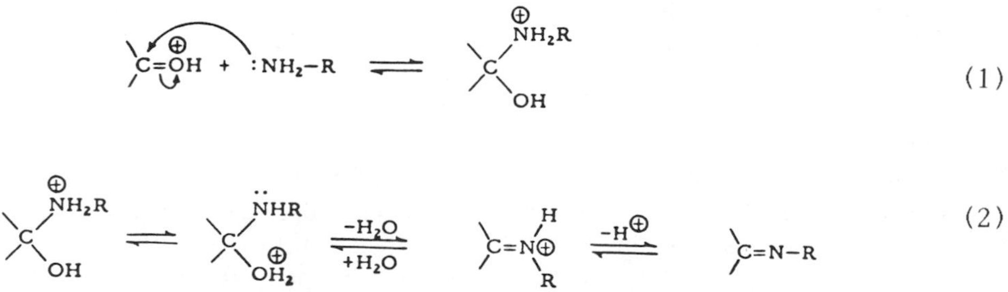

$$\begin{array}{c}
\overset{\oplus}{\underset{/}{\overset{\backslash}{C}}}=\overset{\oplus}{O}H \;+\; :NH_2-R \;\rightleftharpoons\; \overset{\overset{\oplus}{NH_2R}}{\underset{\;OH}{\overset{|}{\underset{/}{\overset{\backslash}{C}}}}}
\end{array} \tag{1}$$

$$\underset{\;OH}{\overset{\overset{\oplus}{NH_2R}}{\overset{|}{\underset{/}{\overset{\backslash}{C}}}}} \;\rightleftharpoons\; \underset{\overset{\oplus}{OH_2}}{\overset{\overset{..}{NHR}}{\overset{|}{\underset{/}{\overset{\backslash}{C}}}}} \;\underset{+\text{H}_2\text{O}}{\overset{-\text{H}_2\text{O}}{\rightleftharpoons}}\; \underset{/}{\overset{\backslash}{C}}=\overset{H}{\underset{R}{\overset{\oplus}{N}}} \;\overset{-\text{H}^{\oplus}}{\rightleftharpoons}\; \underset{/}{\overset{\backslash}{C}}=N-R \tag{2}$$

FIG. 4.   Condensation of carbonyl compounds with amino compounds.

important in the Maillard reaction, is believed to be the only reaction in the second step of the initial stage. The Amadori reaction is catalyzed by weak acids, where the protonation of the Schiff base and the subsequent protonic shift constitute the critical step; the amino acids serve as their own acid catalysts so the reaction is rapid even in the absence of added acid.

It should be noted here that the reactions in the initial stage of the Maillard reaction are all favored by acidic conditions and are apparently not compatible with the observed fact that neutral or alkaline conditions promote the browning reactions. A group of reactions involving the early scission of sugar molecules, which was recently reported by this author's group, may serve to at least complement the existing, widely recognized scheme. This is described in the following section.

C. SUGAR FRAGMENTATION DURING THE INITIAL STAGE AND A NEW BROWNING REACTION MECHANISM

1. Development of Novel Free Radicals during the Initial Stage

It is generally agreed that the Amadori compounds in the Maillard reaction mixture could exist as enaminol structures. The reducing power of the reaction mixture, probably attributable to such reductones, increases with browning (Kirigaya et al., 1968), and the browning products have been shown to possess antioxidative activity. A representative reductone, ascorbic acid, has been shown to have a free radical structure as the intermediate of its oxidation process by electron spin resonance (ESR) spectrometry, and it also acts as a kind of antioxidant (Bielski, 1982). On the other hand, the presence of fairly stable free radicals was observed in the amino–carbonyl reaction of ninhydrin with amino acids (Yuferov et al., 1970) as well as in the highly alkaline solutions of some reducing sugars (Lagercrantz, 1964). These facts suggest that the Maillard reactions may involve a free radical process or produce some kind of free radical product. However, no studies have indicated the presence of free radical in the Maillard reaction except for that of Mitsuda et al. (1965). They showed the presence of a stable free radical in the melanoidin from glucose and glycine heated for a long time by detection of a broad singlet ESR spectrum that may exist in the unsaturated structure of the polymerized product as is found in humus (Tollin et al., 1963; Steelink and Tollin, 1962).

In 1973, Namiki et al. found a novel free radical in a very early stage of the sugar–amino acid reaction mixtures. The free radical showed an ESR spectrum with a clear hyperfine structure and was apparently different from that observed in the melanoidin (Namiki and Hayashi, 1975, 1981, 1983; Namiki et al. 1977).

Figure 5 shows the results of reactions of D-glucose with α- or β-alanine. The important characteristics are as follows. (1) The ESR signal was detected soon after the reaction mixture was heated, and the relative intensity of signal in-

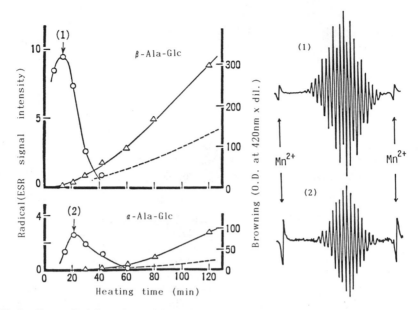

FIG. 5.   Free radical formation and browning in the reaction of D-glucose with α-alanine or β-
alanine or β-alanine, and ESR spectra of the reaction mixtures (Namiki and Hayashi, 1983). ○, ESR
signal with hyperfine structure; - - - -, ESR signal with broad line; △, browning. The hyperfine ESR
spectra at peaks (1) and (2) are shown on the right side.

creased rapidly very early in the reaction when the mixture was not yet significantly colored. (2) After reaching a maximum peak, the intensity of the ESR
signal decreased with heating time and was accompanied by a gradual increase in
browning, a disappearance of the hyperfine structure, and a gradual increase of
the broad singlet in the ESR spectra. (3) The intensity and speed of the ESR
signal with browning was stronger and faster for β-alanine than for α-alanine. (4)
The hyperfine structure of the ESR signal for these two systems apparently
differs in splitting number.

The development of similar ESR spectra was observed for almost all reaction
mixtures of sugar–amino compounds, indicating that the formation of a novel
free radical product is a normal process of the Maillard reaction and occurs at an
early stage. The results of the reactions of various sugars with α- and β-alanine
are summarized in Table II. The sugars and their related carbonyl compounds all
gave essentially the same types of ESR hyperfine structure, i.e., the hyperfine
structures split into 19 lines in the sugars with α-alanine systems, while those
with β-alanine systems split into 25 lines (except in the case of three-carbon
sugars—the spectra of three-carbon sugars were more complex and resembled
each other).

TABLE II

ESR SPECTRAL DATA ON FREE RADICALS AND BROWNING IN THE REACTION OF SUGAR
AND OTHER CARBONYL COMPOUNDS WITH α- AND β-ALANINE[a,b]

	ESR Spectra		
	Splitting line number	Intensity[c]	Browning[c]
α-Alanine			
D-Glucose	19	+	+
D-Fructose	19	±	+
D-Arabinose	19	+	++
D-Xylose	19	+	++
D-Ribose	19	+	++
Glycolaldehyde	19	+++	+++
β-Alanine			
D-Glucose	25	++	++
D-Fructose	25	±	++
D-Arabinose	25	++	+++
D-Xylose	25	++	+++
D-Ribose	25	++	+++
Glyceraldehyde	~35	+++	++++
Dihydroxyacetone	~35	+++	++++
Glycolaldehyde	25	++++	+++++
3-Deoxyglucosone	25	+	+++
5-Hydroxymethylfurfural			++
Furfural			+++
Glyoxal	25	++	+++
Crotonaldehyde			+++
Propionaldehyde			+

[a] Namiki and Hayashi (1983).
[b] Aqueous solutions (each 3 M) were heated in boiling water bath.
[c] +++, High; ++, moderate; +, low; ±, insignificant.

Carbonyl compounds that are highly reactive in the formation of a free radical are also effective in browning, while carbonyl compounds, such as furfural and crotonaldehyde, show high activity only for browning. This suggests that the presence of an enediol or a potential enediol grouping in the carbonyl compounds as a reducing sugar is necessary for the radical formation. Glycolaldehyde showed extremely high activity in both free radical formation and browning.

With the exception of certain compounds such as aniline, cysteine, and ethylamine, radical formation was observed only in the case of the primary amino compounds.

The radical formed even under weakly acidic conditions and, like browning, increased markedly with pH, although the radical product was rather stable under acidic conditions. Interestingly, the radical was produced without necessarily removing oxygen from the system. It appeared to be fairly stable within the reaction mixture, but it disappeared rapidly when air was bubbled through the system (Namiki and Hayashi, 1975).

2. Structure of Novel Free Radical Products

Based on many ESR experiments on the various amino compound–sugar systems, Hayashi et al. (1977) found that, as shown by α- and β-alanine, the difference in the hyperfine structure depends upon the difference in the number of protons on the α carbon of the amino compound and not upon the carbon number of the common sugar. They also found that all spectra have in common splittings that arise from interactions of the free radical with two equivalent nitrogen atoms and four equivalent protons in addition to an even number of equivalent protons with different splitting constants. These assignments led to the assumption that the radical products are N,N'-disubstituted pyrazine cation radical derivatives, as shown in Fig. 6.

This is strongly supported by the fact that the hyperfine structure, as well as g value of the ESR spectrum of the reaction mixture of ethylamine with D-glucose, was in good agreement with those of the ESR spectrum of the radical from synthesized N,N'-diet-hylpyrazine (Curphey and Prasad, 1972). Despite a vast number of pyrazine derivatives in the Maillard reaction products, the presence of such N,N'-disubstituted pyrazinium derivatives has rarely been demonstrated. This is probably due to their high instability, which makes them difficult to track.

Milic and others (Milic et al., 1980; Milic and Piletic, 1984) also conducted ESR studies on this kind of free radical developing at an early stage of the Maillard reaction in model systems of 2-, 3-, and 4-aminobutylic acids with D-glucose. The results of their ESR spectral analyses are consistent with the previously mentioned assignments of the free radical products. Their studies also included the investigation of the kinetics of the formation of the free radicals.

3. Formation Process of the Free Radical Products

The novel pyrazine derivatives have no substituents on the ring carbons, so the plausible formation mechanisms are limited to the following two pathways: (a) formation of a two-carbon enaminol compound by sugar fragmentation and subsequent dimerization, or (b) bimolecular condensation of the enaminol of the Amadori products followed by elimination of the substituted sugar residues.

Investigations of these possible pathways (Hayashi and Namiki, 1981; Namiki and Hayashi, 1983) indicated (1) that the free radical developed rapidly prior to (or simultaneously with) the formation of the Amadori product and then began to decrease while the Amadori product continued to increase and 3-deoxyosone was produced thereafter, and (2) that the glycosyl amino compound alone resulted in marked free radical formation while no free radical was formed from the

```
CHO              CH=NR        H-C≏N-R          H      glycol-
|        +RNH₂   |            |    H-OH        HC-NR  aldehyde
CHOH    ───────  CHOH    ───  H-C-OH    ─────  ‖      alkylimine
|        -H₂O    |            |                HC-OH  (enol type)
CHOH            CHOH         H-C⁺OH  NH₂-R     |
|               |                             CHO
R'              R'           R'               R'

sugar                    reverse-aldol reaction
                                                              ↘
                                                         ┌──────────┐
         conden-                                         │ Browning │
   (I)   sation                                          └──────────┘
                                                              ↑
  ⎧ HC-ṄR ⎫                                                   │
  ⎪   ‖   ⎪        R              R                   R
  ⎪ HC-OH ⎪     H   N   H      H   N   H           H   N⁺  H
  ⎨  ↓↑ H ⎬  ─   │‖¨│     ─    │(·+)│     ─         │   │
  ⎪ H₂C-ṄR⎪     H   N   H      H   N   H           H   N⁺  H
  ⎩ HC=O  ⎭        R              R                   R

  (2)          dialkyl-         dialkyl-            dialkyl-
               dihydro-         pyrazine           pyrazinium
               pyrazine         radical            compound

   H
  HC-NR  ←──  HC=NR  ←──   HC=NR  ←──  HC=N-R  ----→  HC=O
    ‖         |      oxi-   |    +RNH₂  |     -2RNH₂  |
  HC=O       H₂C-OH dation HC=O  -H₂O  HC=N-R +2H₂O  HC=O
                                   2

              glycol-          glyoxal       glyoxal       glyoxal
              aldehyde         mono-         di-
              alkylimine       alkylimine    alkylimine
```

FIG. 6. A possible pathway for formation of the free radical product, sugar fragmentation products, and browning in the reaction of sugar with amino compounds (Namiki and Hayashi, 1983; Hayashi *et al.*, 1986a).

Amadori product alone or with amine or sugar. In addition, as mentioned previously, glycolaldehyde showed especially high activity in both free radical formation and browning. These results indicate that the novel free radical is produced before the Amadori rearrangement and possibly via the pathway (a). This is quite interesting since the occurrence of changes such as fragmentation prior to Amadori rearrangement had never been considered in the Maillard reaction mechanism and required substantiation.

4. Sugar Fragmentation at an Early Stage of the Maillard Reaction

The proposed scheme of radical formation involves sugar fragmentation to give a very reactive enaminol compound for browning. Sugar fragmentation and the role of fragmentary low-molecular-weight carbonyl compounds in browning have been noted by Hodge (1953):

The fission products of the sugars very conceivable in their potential for browning. Fragments which retain the α-hydroxycarbonyl grouping will undergo browning alone in aqueous solutions;

and, in the presence of amino compounds, the browning is greatly accelerated. The most highly
reactive compounds are glycolaldehyde, glyceraldehyde, pyruvaldehyde, dihydroxyacetone, acetoin,
and diacetyl. . . . [Ep. 935]

He proposed the formation of pyruvaldehyde and other carbonyl compounds
from 1-deoxyglucosone, the product (through 2,3-enolization) of the Amadori
compound, and also postulated that cleavage would occur at the C-2/C-3 position of the sugar to give two-carbon carbonyl products by a reverse aldol mechanism (Hodge, 1953). However, the formation of such carbonyl compounds at an
early stage of the Maillard reaction was not chemically demonstrated, and their
role in browning, especially concerning two-carbon products at a very early stage
of the Maillard reaction, was not clarified.

Hayashi and Namiki (1980) demonstrated the production of a two-carbon
fragmentary product at an early stage of the Maillard reaction by isolating and
identifying glyoxal and its diimine derivatives in glucose–alkylamine mixtures
by thin-layer chromatograpy (TLC), gas–liquid chromatography (GLC), mass
spectroscopy (MS), and nuclear magnetic resonance (NMR) analyses. Quantitative measurements indicated that the production of the two-carbon sugar
fragmentation product increased after the production of the glycosyl amino compound, and that this was followed by free radical formation and subsequent
browning. Formation of the four-carbon product, the residual of hexose fragmentation, was also demonstrated to occur almost in parallel with the two-carbon
product formation (Namiki and Hayashi, 1983).

It should be noted here that glyoxal was known to be an artifact on the TLC
from glyoxal diimine in the reaction mixture, and neityer compound is the direct
precursor of the pyrazine radical because glyoxal showed only weak activity in
radical formation with amines and glyoxal diimine itself is inactive. However,
when ascorbic acid was added at an early stage (prior to free radical formation
and browning) to the glucose–alkylamine reaction mixture, an intense ESR
spectrum of the pyrazine radical appeared instantaneously, together with marked
browning (Hayashi *et al.*, 1985a). The same fact was also observed when ascorbic acid was added to the glyoxal dialkylimine solution. The initial two-carbon
fragmentary product of sugar, the precursor of the free radical formation and
browning, is assumed to be glycolaldehyde monoimine or its enaminol. The
N,N'-disubstituted pyrazinium salt was shown to be highly unstable in aqueous
systems and produced instantaneous browning. Possible pathways for the formation of the novel free radical, browning, and the production of glyoxal diimine
derivatives were proposed as shown in Fig. 6 (Namiki and Hayashi, 1983;
Hayashi *et al.*, 1985a).

It should be noted that the evidence indicating the formation of the fragmentary products at an early stage of the Maillard reaction was obtained mainly in
glucose–alkylamine systems. Systems employing alkylamines usually react fast-

er and more intensely to give the free radical product and to produce browning than do ordinary amino acids; this may be due to the tendency of amine-catalyzed reverse aldol condensation reactions to give higher amounts of intermediate fragmentary products, which results in more intense browning as well as in a higher yield of glyoxaldiimine, especially in ethanol reaction systems (Hayashi *et al.* 1985a). The formation of glyoxal diimine derivatives was also observed in the reactions of glucose and amino acids, e.g., glycine, lysine, arginine, and β-alanine, although in amounts smaller than amine derivatives (Hayashi *et al.*, 1985a).

As early as 1962 Kitaoka and Onodera reported sugar fragmentation into one- and two-carbon products in the reaction of 1,2-diamino–sugar derivatives and suggested its occurrence at an early stage browning of the Maillard reaction. However, they started from diaminated sugar derivatives formed by further amine addition of Amadori products and differs from the sugar fragmentation described previously.

5. Formation of Three-Carbon and Other Sugar Fragmentary Products

Strictly speaking, the discussion which follows may be better placed under the intermediate rather than the initial stage of the Maillard reaction. However, while the evidence is far from complete, there exists a good possibility that the formation of the C_3 compound occurs in the early stage.

As mentioned previously, Hodge (1967) proposed the formation of fragmentary products such as methylglyoxal and diacetyl from 1-deoxyglucosone, which is formed from the Amadori product through 2,3-enolization and deamination, although no clear evidence has been presented on this process.

Recently, Hayase and Kato (1986) investigated the formation of low-molecular-weight products of the glucose–*n*-butylamine reaction system by GLC analyses. The results showed that at pH 4.0 the ether extractable products are mainly heterocyclic compounds which are assumed to be formed from the Amadori product through 1,2-enolization. On the other hand, large amounts of low-molecular-weight fragmentation products, such as *N*-butylformamide and *N*-butylacetamide were produced very rapidly and abundantly at pH 11.4 while no heterocyclic compounds were produced. The reaction at pH 6.5 already showed a tendency to increase the fragmentation products. Hayase and Kato proposed that these low-molecular-weight amides are formed from glyoxal and diacetyl, respectively, and that diacetyl is formed through the scission of the C-2/C-3 and C-4/C-5 bonds of glucose after 2,3-enolization of the Amadori product. Production of *N*-butylformamide was observed as the first and most abundant product in the GLC, especially at a pH above 6.5. If, indeed, this indicates the formation of glyoxal or other two-carbon products at an early stage of the Maillard reaction, it is very interesting in light of the results obtained by Namiki and Hayashi (1983).

Diacetyl was detected as a main product in the headspace gas analysis of the reaction at pH 6.7. Formation of the acetamide derivative did not appear to occur via diacetyl, but from the C_6 compound or methylglyoxal. In any case, the results are interesting because diacetyl and glyoxal are known to be active intermediates in browning and, moreover, active cross-linking agents in the polymerization of proteins by the Maillard reaction (Cho *et al.*, 1986).

Meanwhile, Hayashi and others (Hayashi *et al.*, 1986a; Hayashi and Namiki, 1986b) directly observed the formation of C_3 compound in the sugar–amine reaction by isolation and identification of the diimine derivative of methylglyoxal. This was noted at a very early stage of the reaction, closely following the formation of two-carbon product and together with the Amadori product. Heating of glucose alone at pH 9.3 did not produce a detectable amount of methylglyoxal, indicating that the fragmentation occurred by the Maillard reaction. In this case, the reaction of the Amadori product with *n*-butylamine rapidly produced the C_3 compound in a manner similar to that of the glucose–*n*-butylamine system. A clear difference was observed between the reaction of glucose with *n*-butylamine and *t*-butylamine, especially in the production of the C_3 compound, which was significantly suppressed and delayed in the latter case, probably due to the bulky structure of *t*-butylamine. These results are difficult to explain from the scheme proposed by Hodge, in which the C_3 is formed by the scission of 1-deoxyosone, and suggest the presence of a new pathway of sugar fragmentation to give C_3 imine by a reverse aldol-type reaction of the additionally aminated Amadori product. C_3 carbonyl compound formation in the *n*-butylamine system may occur mainly via a newly proposed pathway, while that in the *t*-butylamine system may possibly occur according to the scheme of Hodge.

6. Role of Sugar Fragmentation Products in Browning Reaction

It has been demonstrated previously that sugar fragmentation producing the C_2 and C_3 carbonyl compounds or their imine derivatives occurs at an early stage of the Maillard reaction. In order to evaluate the role of sugar fragmentation in browning, it is necessary to quantify the yields as well as the browning abilities of the main fragmentation products. However, little research has been done on these aspects of the Maillard reaction, perhaps because until recently sugar fragmentation at an early stage of the reaction was not taken into account. Moreover, it is often difficult to measure accurately the amounts of active intermediates in the complicated processes of the reaction, especially glycoaldehyde in alkaline solution.

Recently, Hayashi and Namiki (1986a) quantified C_2 and C_3 carbonyl products in a glucose–β-alanine reaction mixture by the *o*-phenylenediamine method using GLC and showed that the production of these products was greatly influenced by pH: production was negligible at acidic pH, observable at neutral pH,

TABLE III

RELATIVE BROWNING ACTIVITY OF CARBONYL
COMPOUNDS
IN THE MAILLARD REACTION WITH β-ALANINE[a]

Sugar and analogous carbonyl compounds

Sugar or carbonyl compounds	Reaction temperature (°C)	Browning activity (1/min)	Relative value
Glucose	95	0.019	1
Fructose	95	0.014	0.74
Xylose	95	0.166	8.74
Xylose	80	0.037	
Methylglyoxal	80	2.77	654.3
Glyceraldehyde	80	8.33	1967
Glyoxal	80	0.515	121.6
Glycolaldehyde	80	8.93	2109

Main intermediate products

Materials[b]	Browning activity (1/min)	Relative value
Glucose + β-Ala	0.028	1
Glucosylamine	0.138	4.93
Amadori product	0.023	0.821
Amadori product + β-Ala	0.072	2.57
Glucosone + β-Ala	0.666	23.7
3-Deoxyglucosone + β-Ala	3.85	137.5

[a] Hayashi and Namiki (1986a).
[b] Mixtures (1 M each) were heated for 20 min in a boiling water bath.

and increased greatly at alkaline pH (although the yields were very low compared to that of the Amadori product). The production of these fragmentation products increased rapidly very early in the reaction, and then decreased when browning and Amadori product formation started to decrease rapidly.

The fragmentation products of C_2 and C_3 carbonyl compounds are assumed to be glycolaldehyde, glyoxal, glyceraldehyde, methylglyoxal, etc., or their imine derivatives. These are well known to be very active compounds in Maillard browning, but no quantitative evaluation has been done on their browning ability. Hayashi and Namiki (1986a) evaluated their browning activity and compared it with that of xylose and glucose at 80 and 95°C respectively. As shown in Table III, low-molecular-weight carbonyl compounds showed extremely high browning ability, i.e., the relative values of glycolaldehyde and glyceraldehyde are about 2000 times greater than that of glucose. The high values of the fragmentation products, despite their low yields in the reaction, correspond to the browning observed at the early stage of the Maillard reaction. In other words, the browning observed at the early stages of the Maillard reaction with pH at and above neutral may be caused mainly by the fragmentation pathways.

D. REACTIONS DURING THE INTERMEDIATE STAGE

What is called the "intermediate stage" in Hodge's scheme (1967) of the Maillard reaction involves a series of reactions which starts with the Amadori rearrangement products (i.e., 1-amino-1-deoxy-2-ketose derivatives produced from glycosyl amino compounds in the initial stage) to produce melanoidins. Compared to the relative simplicity of the first stage, the facts accumulated by the numerous studies on the second stage are chaotic and await systematization via some universally recognized dominant pathway(s) of melanoidin formation. Obviously, this situation has arisen because the high reactivities of almost every product in this stage result in complex paths, all of which, in turn, lead to a complex mass of colored polymers called melanoidins. We know very little of the chemistry of melanoidins despite the advanced analytical techniques currently available.

A number of studies on the products of this stage, especially the precursors of pigments, overlap to a large extent with studies on the production of flavors and antioxidants as well with those on protein modification as a result of the reactions. In this review, the emphasis is mainly on the formation of colored products.

1. Amadori Rearrangement Products

Amadori products, the key intermediate in Maillard reactions, are obtained from glycosylamino products (Gottschalk, 1952) and sugar–amino compound model systems (Abrams et al., 1955; Finot and Mauron, 1969), and the Amadori products from aromatic amines and sugars are especially easy to isolate in a pure and stable state (Baltes and Franke, 1978). Amadori products are also isolated from treated foods, e.g., freeze-dried fruits (Anet and Reynolds, 1957), liver extracts (Heyns and Paulsen, 1959), and soy sauce (Hashiba, 1978).

Recently, due to their very important effects on the physical, nutritive, and physiological properties of proteins, a number of studies have been done on Amadori product formation by sugar–protein reactions in food and biological systems. Major studies include Adrian (1974), Bayns et al. (1986), Erbersdobler (1986), Mauron (1981), Mester et al. (1981), and Monnier and Cerami (1983). However, these will not be discussed in this review.

Numerous studies on the features of Amadori rearrangement and product isolation have been thoroughly reviewed elsewhere (e.g., Reynolds, 1963, 1965) and will not be discussed here.

Recent analytical techniques have produced more detailed information on the nature of Amadori products. High-performance liquid chromatography (HPLC) has became a popular tool for analyzing Amadori products (Moll and Gross, 1981; Moll *et al.*, 1982) because of its rapidity and simplicity. Structural analyses by high-resolution NMR have shown that Amadori rearrangement products exist in the β-pyranose form at pH greater than 7 and favor the β-furanose form at pH 3 (Altena *et al.*, 1981). The equilibrium of N-(1-deoxy-D-fructos-1-yl)-L-amino acids in D_2O was shown by ^{1}H- and ^{13}C-NMR to be ~64% β-pyranose, 15% α-furanose, ~15% β-furanose, and ~6% α-pyranose forms (Röper *et al.*, 1983).

Amadori products are fairly stable and are weak in browning activity even in the presence of amino compounds. The main processes giving colored and flavor products from Amadori products are as follows (Fig. 7) (Hodge, 1967): formation of labile enolized intermediates, 1,2-enolization followed by elimination of the hydroxy group at C-3 and deamination at C-1 yielding 3-deoxyhexosone, the reactive dicarbonyl product itself, and later furfural as well as the reactive carbonyl compound.

On the other hand, 2,3-enolization of the Amadori products followed by elimination of the amino group from C-1 gives the 1-deoxydicarbonyl intermediate, which further reacts to produce reactive fission carbonyl products such as methylglyoxal, diacetyl, and others (Hodge, 1967). In most of the studies on the Maillard reaction, browning and flavor are considered to be caused by additional reactions of these active intermediates with amino compounds.

However, several cases have been reported in which the Amadori products yielded colored products without undergoing conversion to deoxyosones or other compounds. Hashiba (1976, 1978) reported oxidative coloration of Amadori products, focusing on the coloration of soy sauce. Although Kato (1963) reported oxidative degradation of N-glucosides, model experiments show that oxygen does not interfere in the Maillard reactions.

In actual foods—miso, sake, soy sauce, wine, etc.—the browning effected by oxygen is of practical importance. Hashiba *et al.* (1981) confirmed that Maillard reactions, rather than polyphenol oxidation, are responsible for this kind of browning and isolated several Amadori products as key intermediates. These products produce intense red color on contact with oxygen, especially in the presence of Fe ions. Hashiba (1986) observed that the addition of Fe^{2+} ions increased the absorption at 550 nm of glucose–glycine melanoidin as well as of the Amadori product from that system, and that addition of EDTA had the opposite effect. Apparently, the Fe^{2+} ion is involved not only as a catalyst but in the coloration itself. Pigment isolated from the reaction of a fructose–glycine Amadori product with Fe^{2+} and air (or H_2O_2) was identified as 2-hy-

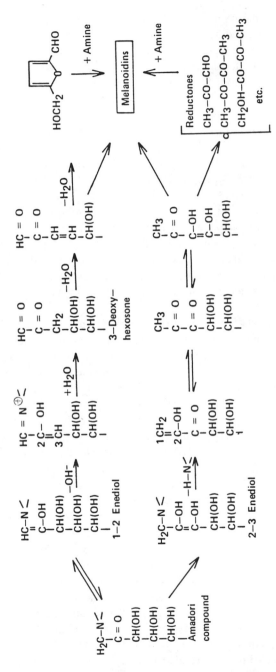

FIG. 7. Reactions at the intermediate stage (Hodge, 1967); enolization and degradation of Amadori compounds.

droxymethyl-3,5-dihydroxy-1-(4-pyridone)acetic acid, (Fig. 8, 1) and was assumed to be formed by cyclization of the Amadori product, resulting in the pigment by 1 : 1 chelation with the Fe^{2+} ion. The Fe^{3+} ion also produced a colored product with this pigment. Maltol behaved similarly toward Fe ions, but 4-hydroxy-2,5-dimethyl-1,3(2H)-furanone chelated only with the Fe^{2+} ion. Hashiba concluded that the oxidation of Amadori products is involved in the coloration of soy sauce and that the presence of similar structures may be responsible for the coloration and metal chelating activity of melanoidin.

Many nitrogen-containing heterocyclic products have been isolated from sugar–ammonia caramel products, some of which are pyridine and pyrazine derivatives presumed to originate from Amadori products. For example, Tsuchida et al. (1973, 1975) isolated a number of polyhydroxy alkylated pyridines, pyrazines, and pyrroles from weakly acidic sugar–ammonia systems with or without sulfite by GLC and ion-exchange chromatography (Fig. 8, 2–8). The formation of the β-hydroxypyridines (4 and 5) by the reaction of furfural and amino compounds had already been shown by Aso (1939). Deoxyfructosazine [(2-D-arabino-tetrahydroxybutyl)-5-(D-erythro-trihydroxybutyl)pyrazine] (Kuhn et al., 1961) and its 6-isomer (Fig. 8, 2 and 3) were present in this reaction mixture in approximately a 1 : 1 ratio. These pyrazine derivatives were considered to be condensation products of Amadori products with 3-deoxyosone and ammonia. They also isolated and identified many new polyhydroxy heterocyclic compounds (Tsuchida et al., 1986). With caramelization in the presence of sulfite, the variety of products decreased, and the main product was deoxyfructosazine. Furan derivatives with cyclized side chains have also been isolated (Tsuchida et al., 1986). Many nitrogen-containing heterocyclic products from cyclization, including sugar fragments (e.g., methylglyoxal), are found in the products of caramel formation under alkali conditions (Tsuchida et al., 1976).

2. Enolization and Degradation of Amadori Products

In the intermediate stage of Hodge's scheme, 1,2-enolization is considered to be favored under acidic conditions, and 3-deoxyosones (Anet, 1960; Kato, 1960), furfural, and hydroxymethylfurfural (Anet, 1962, 1964) are the main products which have been isolated and identified from acidic sugar–amino acid reaction mixtures as well as in actual food systems. These intermediate products are also known to be produced by acidic decomposition of sugars and caramelization (Feather and Harris, 1973). On the other hand, 1-deoxyosones, the main 2,3-enolization Amadori products, have not yet been isolated from food systems and are presumably produced only by the Maillard reaction (Ledl et al., 1986a).

Detailed examination of these processes was carried out by Feather and co-workers (1969; 1970; 1981) using isotope incorporation (D_2O, T_3O) and NMR.

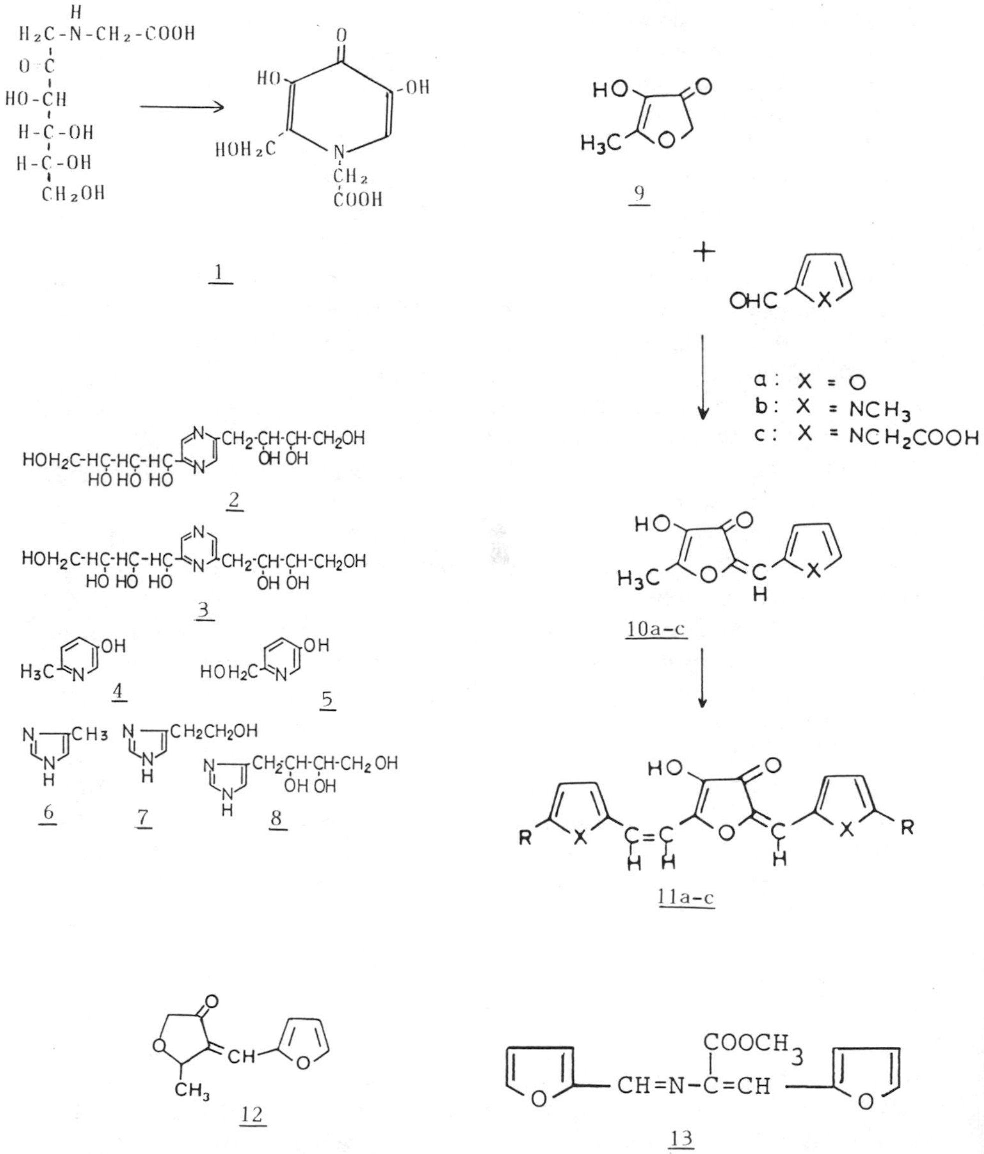

FIG. 8.   Some active intermediates and colored precursors of melanoidin. **1**, Hashiba (1986); **2–8**, Tsuchida *et al.*, (1975); **9**, Severin and Seilmeir (1968) and Feather (1981); **10a–c** and **11a–c**, Ledl and Severin (1981); **12**, Nursten and O'Reilly (1983); **13**, Obretenov and Arginov (1986).

The study of the decomposition of sugars in 3 N HCl using furfural as the marker showed that deuterium is not incorporated into the furfural ring, suggesting that the formation of the furan ring is fairly straightforward from 1,2-enolization without intervening keto–enol equilibria in the process. In contrast, examination of the decomposition of the Amadori products using aromatic N-substituents of different basicities and under different acidities of the medium (with acetic acid or HCl) showed (1) that the Amadori products produce hydroxymethylfurfural in higher yields than do the sugars and (2) that deuterium is incorporated into the furan ring (especially with acetic acid). This suggests the ease of 1,2-enolization and the presence of intervening keto–enol equilibria in the case of Amadori products. It was shown also that 1,2-enolization occurs more easily when the nitrogen atom of the Amadori compound is nearly completely protonized in acidic media.

Feather *et al.* also studied 2,3-enolization using 4-hydroxy-5-methyl-3(2H)-furanone (**9**) as the marker; this has been isolated from cooked beef flavor and is produced by the reaction of amines with xylose (Severin and Seilmeier, 1968) and with ribose (Peer *et al.*, 1968). It has been confirmed that this compound is derived from 1-deoxyosone by 2,3-enolization of the Amadori product according to evidence of incorporation of the ^{14}C-1 atom of the labeled Amadori product into its methyl group and by NMR studies (Hicks and Feather, 1975). In heating Amadori products formed from N-substituted aromatic amines with different basicities, Feather (1981) also showed that furfural production in a strongly acidic medium increased with the basicity of subsituted amines, and a slight amount of methylfuranone was detected with only weakly basic Amadori products. On the other hand, no furfural and only methylfuranone production was observed at pH 7.0 in all Amadori derivatives. These results indicate that the formation of furfural is favored by strong acidity because the nitrogen atom protonized completely and only weakly basic Amadori products produced furfural in acidic media, while under less acidic or neutral conditions, the amino group is only partially protonized and tends to result in 2,3-enolization followed by the formation of methylfuranone.

3. Colored Intermediates and Precursors of Melanoidin

Given this background, we will now consider how the pigments are formed from their precursors. Concerning the additional reactions of the products of 1,2-enolization, it became known early on that the reactions of furfural with amino compounds produce pyrrole and pyridine derivatives (Aso, 1939, 1940). Several other products of the same type also became known (Pachmeyer *et al.*, 1986). Exhaustive studies of colored intermediates and melanoidin precursors by Severin, Ledle, and others continue to be conducted. Their achievements include the isolation of colored furanone derivatives as an intermediate (Fig. 8, **10a–c**) from pentose–methylamine (or glycine) model systems (Krönig and Severin, 1972). These intermediates are considered to be the condensation products of furfural or the respective pyrrole derivatives with a furanone derivative (9) isolated earlier from the glucose–methylamine–acetic acid system (Severin and Seilmeier, 1968), and a number of their analogs have been synthesized (Ledl and Severin, 1978). Another colored condensate (11a–c) of furfural with 10a–c was obtained by increasing the content of primary amine (Ledl and Severin, 1981). The same products have been obtained by HPLC fractionation of petroleum ether extract of a xylose–glycine reaction mixture by Nursten and O'Reilly (1983, 1986b); they have also isolated a colored product assumed to be a condensate of furfural with methylfuranone at the 4-hydroxy position of the latter (Fig. 8; 12).

Colored products from furfural, e.g., N-furilidene-β-furyl-α,β-dehydroalanine methyl ester (13), have been obtained by Obretenov and Arginov (1986) by reaction with glycine methyl ester in ether.

Ledle et al. (1983) also isolated colored products having furanone and β-pyranone moieties (Fig. 9a, 16 and 18). Since these were formed by the reaction of 3-deoxyosone and furfural, they were considered to be the condensate of furfural and β-pyranone (14), the product of its ring opening and ring closure to furanone, the product of further addition of furfural, etc. The analogous colored pyrrolinone derivatives (19) were also obtained by the reaction of furfural and methylamine (Ledl et al., 1986) (Fig. 9a).

As for the colored products from the intermediates of the reaction path from 1-deoxyosone produced by 2,3-enolization, Ledl and Fritsch (1984) isolated a pyrrolinone-type reductone (Fig. 9b, 25) as a key intermediate in melanoidin formation, which they considered to have formed from 1-deoxyosone of monosaccharide via acetylformin (24) and condensation with primary amine as glycine ester (Fig. 9b). The actual contents of 25 were 60 and 100 ppm in the glucose–glycine reaction mixture (after 3 hr at 80°C and 15 min at 130°C, respectively), and 40 ppm in colored malt. They also obtained a β-pyranone intermediate (14) from disaccharide, e.g., lactose, believed to originate from 1,5-deoxy intermediates. The presence of two reaction paths of disaccharides, one via the 1,5-deoxy intermediates and the other via 1,6-deoxy intermediates, has been surmised (Ledl et al., 1986).

The formation of pyrroles and pyridinols in Maillard reactions, e.g., from a glucose–glycine system (Nyhammer et al., 1983) or a fructose–alanine system (Shaw and Berry, 1977), is known. This has been attributed to a hypothetical path from the Amadori products via formation of osones, Strecker degradation with (for example) glycine to form deoxyenaminols, and ring closure (Olsson et al., 1981a). (Fig. 10a). However, Nyhammer et al. (1983) presented contradictory results in their study using [^{13}C]glucose. They demonstrated that compounds 28 and 29 form more easily from 3-deoxyosone (26) than from glucose and is favored by a lower reaction pH. On the other hand, the formation of

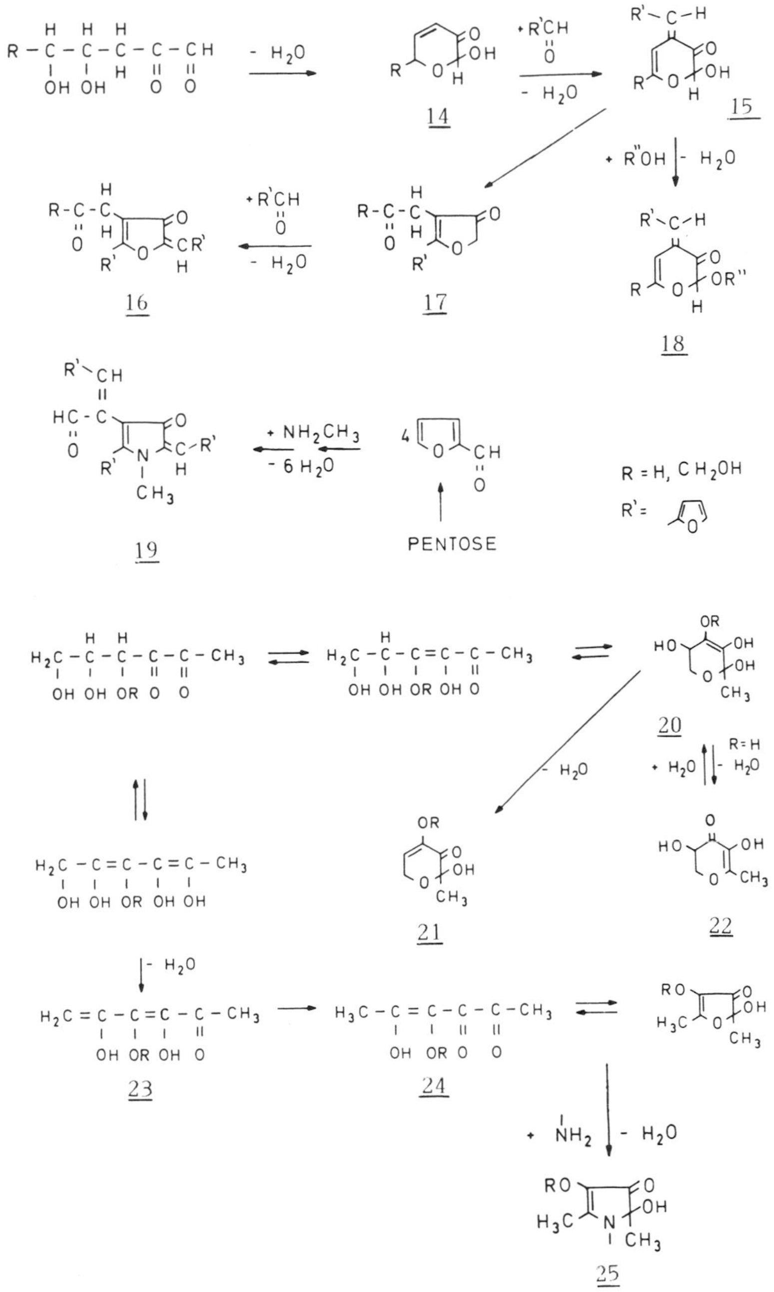

FIG. 9. Formation pathways of intermediates and colored precursors of melanoidin (Ledl *et al.*, 1986a). a, from 3-deoxyosone; b, from 1-deoxyosone.

a

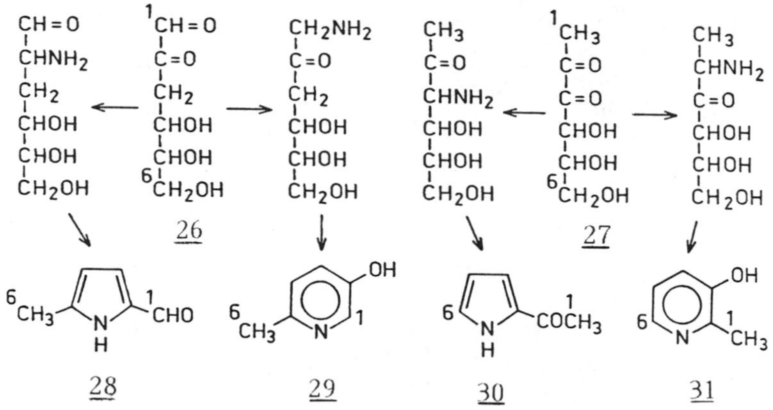

$$
\begin{array}{cccccc}
CH=O & {}^{1}CH=O & CH_2NH_2 & CH_3 & {}^{1}CH_3 & CH_3 \\
CHNH_2 & C=O & C=O & C=O & C=O & CHNH_2 \\
CH_2 & CH_2 & CH_2 & CHNH_2 & C=O & C=O \\
CHOH & CHOH & CHOH & CHOH & CHOH & CHOH \\
CHOH & CHOH & CHOH & CHOH & CHOH & CHOH \\
CH_2OH & {}^{6}CH_2OH & CH_2OH & CH_2OH & {}^{6}CH_2OH & CH_2OH
\end{array}
$$

$$\underline{26} \qquad \underline{27}$$

28   29   30   31

b

$$
\begin{array}{cccc}
CHO & CH=N-CH_2-C-O^- & CHNH_2 & CH=NH \\
H-C-OH & H-C-OH\ \ O & CH & CH \\
HO-C-H & HO-C-H & HO-C-H & CH \\
H-C-OH & H-C-OH & H-C-OH & H-C-OH \\
H-C-OH & H-C-OH & H-C-OH & H-C-OH \\
CH_2OH & CH_2OH & CH_2OH & CH_2OH
\end{array}
$$

$$
\begin{array}{cc}
CH_2NH_2 & CH_2NH_2 \\
CH & CH \\
CH & CH \\
C=O & C=O \\
H-C-OH & C=O \\
CH_2OH & CH_3
\end{array}
$$

30

31

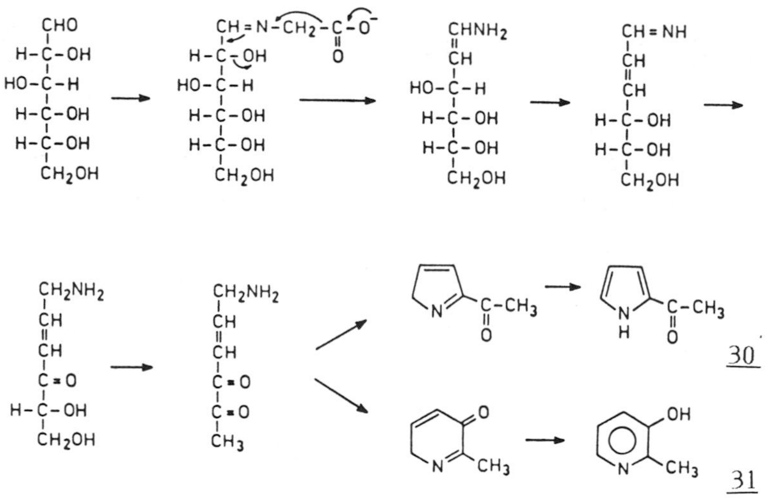

FIG. 10. Proposed pathways of the formation of 2-acetylpyrroles and 3-pyridinols from D-glucose and glycine. a, Olsson *et al.* (1981a); b, Nyhammer *et al.* (1983).

compounds **30** and **31** is hindered by low pH and did not form from 3-deoxyyosone. The reaction of D-[1-^{13}C]glucose with glycine yielded ^{13}CHO-**28**, 5-^{13}C-**30**, 2-^{13}C-**29**, and 6-^{13}C-**31**. A conceivable alternate origin of **30** and **31** as 1-deoxyosone (**27**) was, however, not supported by the ^{13}C study. The results indicated overlooked reaction route(s) and that 2-deoxy sugars may be a possible origin of compound **31**, but no explanation was given concerning the origin of **30** (Fig. 10b).

4. Reactions of Sugar Fragmentary Products

As mentioned previously, Hayase and Kato (1986) examined low-molecular-weight products in an ether extract of a glucose–butylamine (or glucose–glycine) Maillard reaction mixture. They found considerable amounts of N-butylfor-mamide and N-butylacetaminde as well as 2,3-dihydro-3,5-dihydroxy-6-meth-yl-4H-pyran-4-one and pyrrole derivatives in the neutral and alkaline reaction mixtures; the products from the acidic reaction mixture were mainly N-butyl-2-formyl-5-(hydroxmethyl)pyrrole and contained hydroxymethylfuran. The assumed origins of the products were Amadori products for hydroxymethylfuran (through 1,2-enolization), 1-deoxyosone or diacetyl for the acetamide derivatives (through 2,3-enolization), and 3-deoxyosone for the formamide derivative. However, the results for the formamide derivatives seem to suggest some processes other than 1,2-enolization because of the very small quantities obtained from the acidic reaction mixture as opposed to the rapid formation of large amounts in neutral and alkaline reaction mixtures.

Ledl (1982) obtained a pyrrole derivative as the main product of the reaction of furfural with hydroxyacetone (a simplified sugar model) and methylamine. Among complex products of a similar reaction using piperidinum acetate, a cyclic dihydroxypentenone, a colored furan derivative, an amino reductone, and a reductic acid were isolated.

The carbonyl compounds, which are fragmented products of sugars (hexoses, pentoses) such as methylglyoxal, diacetyl, and others, are obtained directly from sugar by caramelization, from Amadori products through 2,3-enolization and 1-deoxyosone formation (Hodge, 1967), and from additional amination of Amadori products (Hayashi and Namiki, 1986a). Many studies have been done on the browning reactions of these products with amino compounds, mainly on the Strecker degradation of amino acids by these products leading to flavor formation. Recent results of Hayashi *et al.* (1986a) have been described previously. Takagi and Morita (1986) also examined the browning activities of low-molecular-weight carbonyl compounds with lysine, which revealed the order glycolaldehyde > glyceraldehyde > dihydroxyacetone > methylglyoxal >> glyoxal.

Piloty and Baltes (1979a,b) reported that the reactivity of amino acids with diacetyl at pH 4 and 100°C is greater for basic or hydroxylated amino acids (e.g., arginine, histidine, lysine, and threonine) than for others; they also isolated and identified oxazolines, pyrazines, and pyrroles from the reaction mixtures.

There are a number of reports on the reactions of active carbonyl compounds from sugar fragmentation, especially diacetyl and methylglyoxal, with amino acids (e.g., Maga, 1982; Piloty and Baltes, 1979b); they focus mainly on the formation of the flavor components as aldehydes and heterocyclic compounds by Strecker degradation.

To summarize, the main products of the intermediate stage of Maillard reactions are heterocyclic compounds produced from osones (by 1,2- and 1,3-enolization in Hodge's scheme), furfurals, and carbonyl fragmentation products produced by mutual reactions and, especially, by reactions with amino compounds. Many of these products have been obtained as flavors, precursors to flavors, and pyrolysis products from sugars. Although some of them are colored and may be regarded as intermediates of melanoidin formation, we know very little about the melanoidin formation itself. Does it occur as the straightforward polymerization of a single or mixed species? What role do these products actually play in melanoidin formation? In seeking the answers to these questions, it must be kept in mind that no matter how small the quantity of a product isolated from the reaction mixture, it may be important in melanoidin formation. In other words, the more reactive the product, the more difficult it is to isolate and identify.

E. NONSUGAR MAILLARD BROWNING REACTION

Certain nonsugar carbonyl compounds of foods (e.g., products of ascorbic acid, polyphenols, and unsaturated fatty acids) are known also to take part in the Maillard reaction with amino compounds and are involved in browning and other reactions.

Reactions involving oxidized products of polyphenols and unsaturated fatty acids mainly involve proteins, so they are not included in the following discussion. For recent studies on reactions involving these compounds the reader is referred to Suyama and Adachi (1986) for fatty acid products and to Igarashi and Yasui (1985) regarding polyphenols. Coloration attributed with ascorbic acid oxidized products is the main subject of discussion in this section.

1. Ascorbic Acid and Oxidized Products

Ascorbic acid (AsA), besides being a nutritionally important food component, is widely used as a meat coloring agent, as an antioxidant, as a baking additive, etc. (Counsell and Horning, 1980; Bauernfeind, 1982). While these uses originate mainly from its nature as a reductone with an enediol structure, the high reactivity of AsA and its decomposition and oxidation products often cause problems in food processing, for example, by discoloration and other effects, mainly as a result of reaction with amino compounds.

a. Nonoxidative Decomposition of AsA. The mode of decomposition of AsA is mainly oxidative, but nonoxidative AsA decomposition also occurs. AsA is most stable at pH 6, when anaerobically decomposed at pH 2, 4, or 6. Furfural, by decomposition of the undissociated form of AsA, is the main product of the reaction under strongly acidic conditions (Herbert *et al.*, 1933; Huelin *et al.*, 1971). Since 3-deoxypentosulose (3-DP) was also identified as the another carbonyl decomposition product, 3-DP or its enol form may be an intermediate to furfural, although details are not known (Kurata and Sakurai, 1967a). The formation of reductic acid, 2,5-dihydro-2-furoic acid, and others are also reported, but their origins are not known (Coggiola, 1963). Although furfural and 3-DP are highly reactive products, the role of nonoxidative decomposition of AsA in browning reaction is considered relatively small (Kurata *et al.*, 1967).

b. Oxidative Decomposition of AsA. The most important factors in the oxidative decomposition of AsA are pH and the presence of metal ions; decomposition is rapid in an alkaline medium and is much slower at a pH less than 7 in the absence of metal catalysts, e.g., Cu ions (Seib and Tolbert, 1982). Oxidation starts with a one-electron withdrawal from an AsA anion that produces the ascorbate anion radical, which disproportionates to dehydroascorbic acid (DHA) and AsA (Yamazaki *et al.*, 1959; Bielski, 1982). DHA, which exists in a hydrated form in aqueous solutions, produces 2,3-diketo-L-gulonic acid (DKG) by ring opening, which is very slow at pH 2.4 and proceeds faster with increasing pH (Terada and Ohmura, 1966). The decomposition of inherently unstable DKG produces 2-furoic acid and 3-hydroxy-2-pyrone through decarboxylation and dehydration (Kurata and Sakurai, 1967b). The enol form of DKG also decomposes to 3-keto-4-deoxypentosulose (KDP) by dehydration and decarboxylation (Kurata and Fujimaki, 1976). A highly unstable DKG δ-lactone having a 3,4-enediol structure has recently been isolated and found to be very susceptible to browning; this compound is considered to be an important intermediate in the oxidative browning of AsA (Ohtsuka *et al.*, 1986).

Besides the browning of AsA by the interaction of various decomposed carbonyl compounds, the reaction of carbonyl products (notably α-dicarbonyl compounds) with amino compounds leads to the active formation of pigments and flavors. The activity and variety of the reactions of DHA with amino compounds, e.g., Strecker degradation with α-amino acids, makes DHA an interesting subject of investigation.

2. Dehydroascorbic Acid–Amino Acid Reactions

a. Formation of Red Pigment. Initially, the reaction of DHA with α-amino acids in aqueous media rapidly produces a conspicuous red pigment, which is then followed by browning (Koppanyi *et al.*, 1945; Kurata *et al.*, 1973a,b). This pigment was found to be related to the coloration that occurs during the processing and storage of dried vegetables and other foods and is also considered to be an intermediate of the browning reaction (Nakabayashi and Shibata, 1967;

Ranganna and Setty, 1968). Since the reactions of DHA with most α-amino acids give the same kind of red pigment and liberate carbon dioxide and aldehydes, these reactions occur through typical Strecker degradations. The lactone ring in DHA seems to be a requisite for pigment formation because DKG does not form the pigment (Kurata *et al.*, 1973a). Kurata *et al.* (1973b) successfully obtained this unstable pigment in a pure crystalline form by oxidation of L-scorbamic acid (SCA), a DHA–amino acid reaction product, and elucidated its structure as 2,2′-nitrilodi-2(2)-deoxy-L-ascorbic acid ammonium salt (NDA), which is formed by the condensation of SCA with oxidized SCA (dehydro-SCA) (Fig. 11). The hypothesis that the red pigments were pyrazine or dihydropyrazine derivatives was thus proved wrong (Lecocq, 1951). The murexide-type structure of red pigment was confirmed by detailed NMR and ESR studies and the calculation of π-electron densities or spin densities of the chromophore system using Hückel's molecular orbital method (Kurata *et al.*, 1986).

   b. Formation of Free Radical Species by DHA–Amino Acid Reactions. Namiki *et al.* (1974) and Yano *et al.* (1974) found strong ESR signals with the formation of NDA in the reactions of DHA and α-amino acids in water or in an ethanol mixture. Analysis of hyperfine structures of the signals showed two components, A and C, in the signal of the aqueous reaction mixture and two components, A and B, in the signal of the ethanolic reaction mixture. Surprisingly, thin-layer chromatography yielded a blue spot indicating the radical species A (R—A) and a yellow spot indicating component C (R—C) close to that of NDA. The blue spot of R—A changed to the red spot of NDA with oxidation in air (Yano *et al.*, 1976a). Increasing the pH of reaction mixture of DHA with amino acid to a neutral or weakly alkaline pH dramatically increased R—A, suggesting the presence of a precursor (Yano *et al.*, 1978b). Hayashi and Namiki (1979) and Hayashi *et al.* (1981) succeeded in isolating this product and identified it as tris(2-deoxy-2-L-ascorbyl)amine, having a 3-fold symmetric structure around one nitrogen atom originating from the amino acid. Tsuji *et al.* (1980) examined the processes using electrochemical methods and confirmed that the dianion of the product produces R—A by eliminating one electron; the product additional one-electron oxidation produced a labile oxidized form which liberates a deoxy-AsA molecule and produces the red pigment NDA. R—C was found to be a one-electron reduction product of NDA (Yano *et al.*, 1976a; Kurata and Fujimaki, 1974). Production of these radical species was enhanced by the addition of AsA. These products do not appear to play important roles in browning reactions (Hayashi *et al.*, 1983b).

   c. Browning Reactions. Hayashi *et al.* (1983a) also found considerable amounts of a yellow pigment on the developed chromatogram of a DHA–amino acid reaction mixture; analysis showed the presence of two nitrogen atoms,

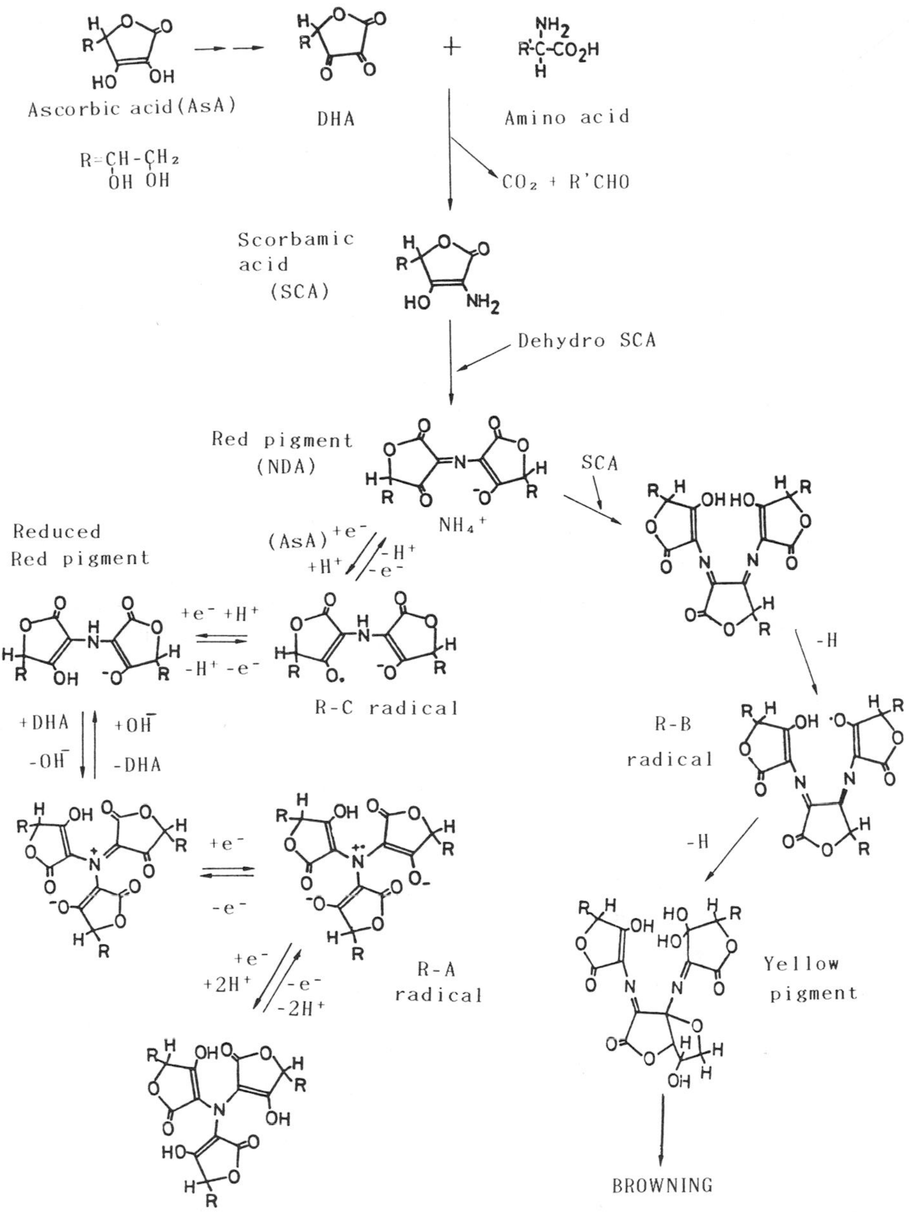

FIG. 11. A possible pathway for formation of colored products, free radical products, and browning in the reaction of dehydroascorbic acid (DHA) and amino acid (Kurata *et al.*, 1973b; Hayashi *et al.*, 1983b).

cyclic DHA, hydrated DHA, and AsA moieties. The reactions of SCA with NDA or DHA produced large amounts of this pigment, which was thus assumed to be a condensation product of SCA with NDA. Heating the yellow pigment or its mixture with DHA in an aqueous solution produced pronounced browning, which suggests a browning reaction scheme involving the DHA–amino acid system via NDA and yellow pigment. One-electron reduction of this pigment produced a stable free radical species identified with the formerly observed radical component B.

From these experimental results, Hayashi *et al.* (1983b) proposed a whole scheme for the formation processes of the colored products, the free radical products, and browning in the reaction of DHA–amino acid system as shown in Fig. 11. The pathway involves complicated mutual redox reactions between starting materials, intermediates, and the products. This reaction system was also shown to produce a purple pigment (Hayashi *et al.*, 1984) and new antioxidative products (Namiki *et al.*, 1982a,b).

d. DHA–Alkylamine Reaction Systems. Paralleling the DHA–amino acid reactions, the reactions of DHA with alkylamines produce red pigments and free radical species. Since the Strecker degradation cannot take place in these cases, the presumed products are red pigments having a substituted nitrogen atom and corresponding free radicals. Yano *et al.* (1976b, 1978a) and Hayashi *et al.* (1978) isolated and deduced the structures of several products from DHA–methylamine and other systems.

An interesting finding is related to the DHA–alkylamine reaction of DHA with casein, serum albumin, and egg albumin under freeze-dried conditions at room temperature or 60°C (Namiki *et al.*, 1986; Hayashi *et al.*, 1986b). It was shown that NDA, the same red pigment as produced from DHA and α-amino acid, was also formed by this reaction. Studies including protein analyses and experiments using hexylamine and other model compounds confirmed that DHA reacts with the ε-amino group of lysine in proteins, resulting in deamination to give NDA and, at the same time, the formation of a carbonyl group, which leads to the polymerization of protein. The reactions of DHA with proteins in the presence of water produced rapid browning; no NDA was obtained, but deamination of this type is considered to play an important role in browning.

F.   CHEMISTRY OF MELANOIDINS

In the final stage of the Maillard reaction, colored intermediates and other reactive precursor products (such as enaminol products, low-molecular-weight sugar analogs, and unsaturated carbonyl products) proceed to condense and polymerize to form brown polymers, or melanoidins, under acceleration by an amine catalyst. As mentioned previously, the formation of intermediates differs greatly by reactant and reaction conditions, and a variety of intermediate products are known to form even under fixed reactant and reaction conditions; so the browned products naturally differ in chemical structures and properties at least in degree of polymerization, depending on preparation conditions. It is wishful thinking to assume a single structure for a product of a Maillard reaction; even the most advanced separation and analytical methods currently available cannot be expected to clarify their structures completely. Nevertheless, continuous efforts are being made to determine the structures of representative melanoidin products, e.g., those prepared from glucose–glycine heated for a long time and then dialyzed. HPLC and GLC for separation, infrared (IR), NMR, MS, and ESR spectrometry for structural analysis, and refractive index (RI) and other advanced techniques are now available to accomplish what ionophoresis and elemental analysis did in the past, but the accumulated data are limited and, so far, only partial structures of the melanoidin products have been determined.

A general formula, "sugar + amino acid $- 2 \sim 3$ H_2O," has been proposed for melanoidins based on the consideration that the main pathway of melanoidin formation involves the reactions of amino compounds with deoxyosones, furfural, and other fragmentation products which accompany the dehydration reaction (Wolform *et al.*, 1953; Kato and Tsuchida, 1981).

However, the evolution of carbon dioxide during melanoidin formation has been demonstrated, and it was noted that decarboxylation by Strecker degradation of α-amino acids is responsible for this evolution. This was supported by studies using ^{14}C-1-labeled amino acid (Stadtman *et al.*, 1952; Wolform *et al.*, 1953). Sugars can also be a source of carbon dioxide (Stadtman *et al.*, 1952).

Liberation of aldehydes by Strecker degradation is also conceivable, as reported by Feather and Hung (1985, 1986) on melanoidins derived from D-glucose-1- and -6-^{14}C, glycine-1- and -2-^{14}C, or methionine-1- and -[^{14}C]methyl. The fastest loss of carbon dioxide occurs by Strecker degradation, but loss of ^{14}C-2 in glycine was also found to occur. The remaining numbers of carbon atoms were glucose-6-C > glucose-1-C > glycine-1-C > glycine-2-C after a 16-hr reaction, suggesting liberation of carbon dioxide and aldehydes. ^{13}C-NMR results also support liberation of carbon dioxide and aldehyde. However, the remaining amounts of ^{14}C during the reaction (at 8, 16, and 24 hr) were not always constant, except in the glucose–methionine reaction system, suggesting the involvement of dehydration and rearrangement reactions after polymer formation. ^{13}C analyses of melanoidins from glucose and L-alanine-enriched ^{13}C-1 or ^{13}C-2 indicated that both ^{13}C-labeled carbons of L-alanine are incorporated into the polymer and C-1 and C-2 of L-alanine remain as a carboxyl carbon and a substituted amino carbon, so the source of the liberated carbon dioxide may not be limited to the carboxyl group of the α-amino acid.

The study of xylose–glycine reactions by Benzing-Purdie and Ratcliff (1986), utilizing cross-polarized–magnetic angle spinning (CP-MAS) ^{13}C- and ^{15}N-

NMR, partly simulated soil humus formation at relatively low temperatures (22, 68°C). As the reaction progressed, ^{13}C-NMR absorption corresponding to the aromatic, heteroaromatic, and heteroaliphatic C=C, C=O, and C=N bonds (120 ~ 160 ppm) increased while the absorption corresponding to the ester (or amide) C=O group decreased. ^{15}N CP-MAS NMR also showed a decrease of amide nitrogen and an increase of tertiary nitrogen atoms of pyrroles and indoles in melanoidin. In general, the sugar species and amino acid species did not have a significant affect on the spectra, but the use of ammonia or urea as the nitrogen component produced some differences (Benzing-Purdie et al., 1983).

Nursten and O'Reilly (1986a) studied the petroleum ether and ethyl acetate-soluble fractions, which amounted to 0.1 wt% of the materials, of xylose–glycine melanoidin by HPLC. Over 100 fractions absorbing at 450 nm were found; these were divided into four classes by the peak characteristics. The largest number of fractions was found to absorb at 260 nm. A significant number of the fractions fluorescenced by irradiation at 254 or 360 nm, and the authors considered them to be intermediates of the browning reaction. Even though some of the fractions were identified with furan derivatives as the colored intermediates by Ledl (1982; see Section III,D), his data serve mainly to highlight the extreme complexity of the melanoidin structure.

Formation of stable free radical species in melanoidin was first reported by Mitsuda et al. (1965) and was based on broad singlet ESR signals. Namiki and Hayashi (1973) found a new free radical species producing hyperfine ESR signals in the initial stage of melanoidin formation, as mentioned in Section II,C. Following this work, Wu et al. (1986) examined the ESR of melanoidin fractions. Melanoidins prepared from glucose with glycine, glutamic acid, and lysine (at pH 9.0, 120°C, 15 ~ 240 min) showed hyperfine ESR signals in their 90% ethanol-insoluble fractions. Glucose–glycine and glucose–glutamic acid melanoidins gave broad singlets and almost no hyperfine structure, but the glucose–lysine melanoidin retained some part of the signal with 33-line hyperfine structures (Namiki and Hayachi, 1983) after a 4-hr reaction. The main low-molecular-weight fraction of this melanoidin showed 9-line hyperfine structures by Sephadex G-50 gel chromatography.

The structure of melanoidin was considered to consist mainly of a repeating aromatized moiety because of its dark brown color. However, ^{13}C-NMR studies by Kato and Tsuchida (1981) on pyrolysate and oxidized products of melanoidin from glucose–glycine, in addition to those by Olsson et al. (1981) on melanoidin from glucose–glycine, indicate that the spectrum of melanoidin is fairly simple, similar to that of Amadori products, and almost devoid of aromatic and olefinic carbon atoms. Kato and Tsuchida (1981) proposed that the structure of melanoidin has a repeating unit involving conjugated carbon double bonds and tertiary nitrogen (Fig. 12).

Recent studies by Kato et al. (1986), using GLC analysis of the ether-soluble

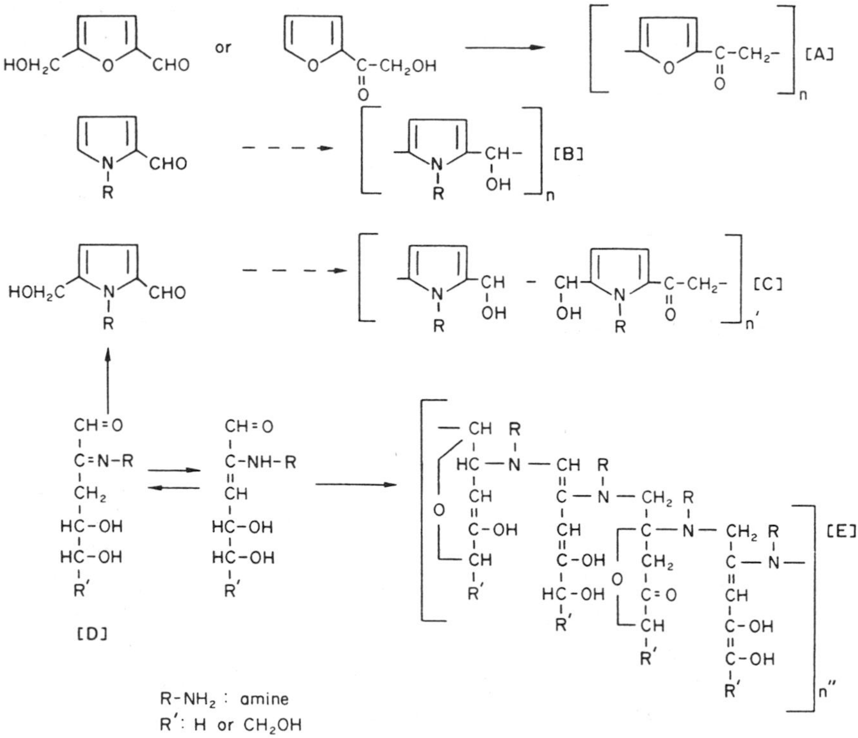

FIG. 12. Possible repeating units of polymeric brown products and their precursors (Kato and Tsuchida, 1981).

fractions of colorless ozonolysate or alkaline hydrogen peroxide decomposition products of melanoidin from glucose–glycine, suggested MeCO<, HOCH₂CH<, HOCH₂COH<, EtCHOHCH₂<, EtCHOHCOH<, Me₂COH-CH<, and Me₂COHCOH< as groups forming partial structures of melanoidin. The water-soluble fraction of the ozonolysate contained 5.7% glycine, and incorporation of glycine in melanoidin was suggested by ^{13}C-NMR of melanoidin from C-2-labeled glycine. ^{13}CNMR of melanoidin from C-1-labeled glucose showed the possibility of glucose C-1 incorporation as methyl, saturated and unsaturated carbons, and aliphatic and aromatic carbons. The presence of a saturated aliphatic carbon chain stable against ozonolysis, in addition to aliphic and aromatic unsaturated C=C bonds and C=O bonds in melanoidin, has been suggested by comparison of ^{13}C CP-MAS NMR and ^{13}C-NMR spectra before and after ozonolysis. These results support the chemical structure of melanoidin proposed previously (Kato and Tsuchida, 1981). The proposed scheme of melanoidin supports the presence of reductone (enaminol) structures, which have been considered to play important roles in antioxidative activity as well as in the metal chelating activity of melanoidin (see Section III). It was also recently known that melanoidin inactivates some mutagens, perhaps because of its reducing activity and inclusion power (see Section IV).

So far, the application of modern analytical methods has succeeded only in accumulating data on the partial structures of melanoidins. Further investigations must continue to seek characteristic partial structures as well as variations in the reaction products using related starting materials and reaction conditions.

III. ANTIOXIDANTS AND THE MAILLARD REACTION

A. INTRODUCTION

Fatty acids (especially polyunsaturated fatty acids) in foods are very susceptible to oxidation by oxygen in air, which results in the formation of hydroperoxides by a free radical chain reaction. The hydroperoxides are subjected to further reactions giving various secondary products, such as volatile carbonyl compounds, polymerized products, and some active oxygen radical species. These processes result in the development of rancid flavor and other deteriorative changes in food quality that limit the storage life of many food products and materials. The lipid peroxidation processes are very complicated and involve numerous factors, which requires the use of various techniques suited to the characteristics of each food to prevent lipid peroxidation. The most effective methods are tight packaging with removal of oxygen gas and the use of antioxidants. Recent developments in packaging materials and oxygen-removal techniques have shown remarkable progress and contributed greatly to protecting food against microbial as well as oxidative deterioration. In many cases, however, it is desirable for the food to possess antioxidative properties, which necessitates effective antioxidants. The most widely utilized antioxidants are phenolic compounds, such as butylated hydroxyanisol (BHA) and butylated hydroxytoluene (BHT), but these synthetic compounds are currently in disfavor because of the potential hazards associated with their use (Ito *et al.*, 1983a,b). The use of natural antioxidants, such as tocopherols, is increasing, although they are not as effective BHA and BHT.

On the other hand, much attention has recently focused on dietary antioxidants, such as vitamins E and C, as preventive agents against biological damage caused by active oxygen free radical species, especially damage to DNA and other important cell constituents which may possibly induce mutagenesis, carcinogenesis, and aging.

Given these circumstances, past and recent findings that the stability of foods increases when Maillard reactions occur within the food system are encouraging and, currently, the subject of much attention.

There are numerous examples of this kind of stabilization. Findley *et al.* (1946) reported increased antioxidative stability of powdered milk by treatment at 88–93°C for 20 sec before drying. This stabilization was considered to be due to the Maillard reaction that occurred during the treatment (Patton, 1955). The antioxidative action of the Maillard reaction products (MRPs) themselves (i.e., that of the MRP of glucose–glycine or glutamic acid system upon margarine oxidation) was first demonstrated by Franke and Iwainsky (1954) and Iwainsky and Franke (1956). Griffith and Johnson (1957) showed that using glucose instead of sucrose in cookie dough enhances the browning and antioxidative stability. Yamaguchi *et al.* (1964) observed increased stability with the addition of glucose and amino acids (especially valine, glycine, and lysine) to cookie dough in addition to the stabilizing effect of acetone extract on cookies baked after the addition of glucose and lysine. Improvement of antioxidative stability by heat treatment was observed by Anderson and co-workers (1963) in cereals such as wheat, corn, and oats.

These findings demonstrate the effectiveness of MRPs in the prevention of lipid peroxidation in foods. The Maillard reaction is very common in food processing and storage, especially in protein-rich foods subjected to heat treatment, so we have made use of this kind of process-induced antioxidants without fully understanding what is involved.

B. REACTION CONDITIONS FOR INDUCTION OF ANTIOXIDATIVE ACTIVITY

In MRPs from reducing sugars and amino compounds, the presence of an amino compound is required to induce antioxidative activity. This is evident from the fact that neither sugars nor their pyrolytic products (caramel) alone show activity, while there are many studies on the antioxidative activity of the compounds of secondary and tertiary liner or cyclic amines and amino acids or peptides, e.g., Marcuse (1962), Harris and Olcott (1966), Matsushita and Ibuki (1965), and Karel *et al.* (1966). However, the antioxidative activity of amino compounds reacting without sugar is far weaker than that induced by the Maillard reaction with sugars.

D-Glucose is used as the reactant carbonyl compound in most model Maillard reaction systems because it is the most common and abundant reducing sugar present in food and biological systems. However, as mentioned previously, pentoses are generally more susceptible to browning than hexoses, and, parallel to browning, xylose induces more potent antioxidative activity than does glucose in sugar–amino acid systems (Kirigaya *et al.*, 1968; Lingnert and Eriksson, 1980a). Low-molecular-weight sugars and some dicarbonyl compounds, such as methylglyoxal, glyceraldehyde (Hayashi *et al.*, 1986a), and dehydroascorbic acid (Namiki *et al.*, 1982b), are known to be far more reactive in inducing the Maillard browning than are hexoses, such as glucose. The MRPs from dihydroxyacetone with methionine and leucine (Itoh *et al.* 1975) and from methylglyoxal with leucine and isoleucine (Kawashima *et al.,* 1977) prepared in corn oil at 175°C exhibit more potent antioxidative activity than those from xylose or glucose. Dehydroascorbic acid with tryptophan heated in ethanol for 30 min resulted in intense browning along with the induction of potent antioxidative activity. These two activities were negligible when glucose was used instead of dehydroascorbic acid (Namiki *et al.,* 1982b).

Among the amino acids, on the other hand, MRPs from arginine, histidine, β-alanine, and cysteine with glucose showed stronger activities than MRPs from other amino acids (Kirigaya *et al.,* 1969). Tomita (1971a,b) studied the antioxidative activities of MRPs from several amino acids with glucose and demonstrated the superiority of MRPs from tryptophan over the others. Lingnert and Eriksson (1980a,b) examined the antioxidative activities of MRPs from glucose, fructose, or xylose with arginine, cysteine, glutamic acid, histidine, lysine, or valine using polarographic and gas chromatographic techniques. They observed potent activities in the MRPs from histidine and lysine with any sugar and in those from arginine with xylose, while MRPs from glutamic acid with each sugar showed no activity. They concluded that MRPs from basic amino acids produce higher activities than those from glutamic acid, valine, and cysteine. The arginine–xylose system produced especially strong activity.

Other reaction conditions (including pH, reaction temperature and time, molar ratio of the reactants and their concentrations, water activity, atmosphere, and the reaction medium) also greatly affect the induction of antioxidative activity. In general, higher media pH and higher amino compound/sugar molar ratios enhance the production of undialyzable melanoidins, the inclusion of nitrogen in MRPs, and the induction of antioxidative activity (Kirigaya *et al.,* 1969). Essentially the same tendencies in the effects of pH, molar ratio, and reactant concentration on the induction of antioxidative activity were reported for MRPs from glucose with various amino acids (Tomita, 1971a) and for MRPs from histidine–glucose (Lingnert and Eriksson, 1980a). Tomita (1971b) also noted the effect of buffer solution as a medium, and phosphate buffer more effectively enhanced the antioxidative activity from tryptophan–glucose than veronal or borate buffer. The optimum conditions are 0.1 M phosphate buffer and an initial pH of 9.0.

Maillard browning is shown to be most effective at intermediate water activity (a_w), e.g., 0.44–0.53 for whey powder (Saltmach *et al.,* 1981) and 0.60–0.70 for milk powder (Loncin, 1968). However, Eichner (1981) indicated that the lower water activity in the glucose–lysine–avicel freeze-dried system favors the production of antioxidative browning intermediates, which were assumed to be hydroperoxide-reducing Amadori products. That is, in the low-a_w system, the formation of visible browning is suppressed while colorless reducing intermediates are still being formed.

Nonparallelism between browning and antioxidative activity during the heating process has, at times, been observed. Antioxidative activity in the glucose–histidine system does not necessarily parallel the formation of undialyzable brown products; it is known that the antioxidative activity increases with the browning in the first stage but decreases with further heating after reaching a maximum (Lingnert and Eriksson, 1981). Park and Kim (1983) studied antioxidative activity in ethanol extracts of the glucose–glycine reaction mixture. The activity was found at an early stage of browning in products which were almost colorless but showed intense fluorescence; the activity remained unchanged with prolonged heating.

These results suggest that the relationship between heating and antioxidative activity is not a simple one, and the manifestation of the activity appears to be a complicated process (although melanoidins themselves are known to be antioxidative).

C. STRUCTURE–ANTIOXIDATIVE ACTIVITY RELATIONSHIP

The antioxidative activity observed in Maillard reaction mixtures is assumed to be present mainly in melanoidins, but since our knowledge of their structural aspects is limited to some of their partial structures, a structure–activity investigation of melanoidins is, at present, beyond reach. From what we know about the MRPs, the first possible candidates for active principles come from the reductone group. The key intermediate of the early stage of the Maillard reaction is the Amadori rearrangement product, which is a kind of amino reductone. Moreover, an increase in the consumption of Tillman's reagent as browning progresses has been reported (Kirigaya et al., 1968), which suggests the presence of reductone or amino reductone structures in melanoidin. Isolation and identification of amino reductones as an important intermediate product to melanoidin formation has been made (Ledl et al., 1986a,b).

The reductones are commonly considered to be an effective antioxidant due to their reducing activity and metal chelating ability; the experimental results, however, sometimes indicate an enhancement of lipid oxidation but not necessarily of the antioxidant (Yamaguchi, 1969). This contradiction was shown to be dependent upon the experimental conditions, especially on the moisture content of the system, in an experiment on ascorbic acid, a typical reductone, and a hydrogen donor (Ueda et al., 1986); whereas ascorbic acid is an antioxidative in a nonaqueous or low-moisture-content system, it is inactive (or may even act as an oxidation promotor) in an oil–water system.

Compared to the enediol-like reductones, amino reductones are more effective and more likely to be stable. Evans et al. (1958) showed the strong antioxidative activity of amino reductones prepared from secondary amines with aldohexose, and Obata et al. (1971) and Itoh et al. (1975) indicated that amino reductones from triose reductone with glycine, methionine, and valine have superior antioxidative activities than the original triose reductone, ascorbic acid, and reductic acid. Eichner (1981) suggested that reductone-like products, probably 1,2-enaminols formed by the Amadori rearrangement, may be responsible for the antioxidative activity of MRPs, which is assumed to be caused by the reduction of hydroperoxides to inactive products. Thus, the contribution of the enaminol structure in MRPs to antioxidative activity seems highly probable, but does not appear to depend on its reducing activity, as indicated by the results of the ozonolysis of melanoidins described shortly. In any case, the effect of reductone in MRPs remains inconclusive.

The metal chelating ability of reductone is assumed to contribute to the antioxidative activity, since Cu, Fe, and other heavy metal ions play an important role in promoting lipid peroxidation. The metal chelate does not always act as an inhibitor, but it sometimes promotes oxidation as exemplified by the copper–ascorbate system, possibly due to the production of some active oxygen species in the presence of oxygen (Martell, 1982).

Melanoidins are known to have high metal binding activity (Johnson et al., 1983), which is also assumed to be due to the reductone moiety. Yamaguchi and Fujimaki (1974b) observed that the antioxidative activity of tocopherol decreased in the presence of a small amount of copper ion, while that of melanoidin was not significantly affected. This suggests that the MRPs have some metal inactivating activity which may contribute synergistically to the antioxidative activity of melanoidins.

Several studies have been conducted to elucidate the chemical structure, by fractionation and chemical modification, of melanoidin as it relates to antioxidative activity. Yamaguchi et al. (1981) examined the activities of Sephadex gel chromatographic fractions of MRP from xylose–glycine (1 : 1). The first chromatography, G-15, gave two reducing peaks, and only the higher molecular weight fractions showed antioxidative activity. Further fractionations (G-50, G-100), and paper and thin-layer chromatography gave a markedly antioxidative fraction, with a molecular weight of around 4500 that gave a single spot by paper chromatography, but was not a purified substance. The antioxidative activity, however, was found widely distributed in other fractions by gel chromatography.

Lingnert and Eriksson (1983) attempted to characterize the antioxidative products of MRP from histidine and glucose. Upon dialysis through membranes with a nominal molecular weight cutoff of 1000, antioxidative compounds were concentrated in the retentate. Further purification using isoelectric precipitation and preparative electrophoresis gave somewhat more active fractions but did not yield a special fraction having intense activity, while some correlations were found between ESR signal intensity and the antioxidative activity of the fractions.

These results, even though interesting in themselves, are not sufficient to draw any conclusion about the nature of the antioxidative activity of melanoidins. However, a recent study of ozonolysis of antioxidative melanoidins (Yamaguchi,

1986) suggests a direction for future investigation: ozonolysis discolored the melanoidin and decreased its reducing capacity to a constant level but, interestingly, had no significant effect on the antioxidative activity. Sephadex G-25 fractionation of the ozonolyzed product gave a degraded, low-molecular-weight, nearly colorless fraction having higher antioxidative activity. IR examination showed a disappearance of C=C bonds and an increase of C=O groups, which agrees with the results of Kim *et al.* (1985). These ozonolysis products also showed synergistic activity with tocopherol. Although it is not yet clear if the initial activity in the melanoidin remained intact or the activity was an artifact of ozonolysis, this finding suggests that unsaturated melanoidins may not be essential for manifestation of the activity.

To elucidate chemical structure of the antioxidative principle of amino–carbonyl reaction products, Namiki *et al.* (1982b) investigated the reaction mixture of dehydroascorbic acid with tryptophan. This system demonstrated far stronger antioxidative activity than glucose–glycine; the reaction was conducted in refluxing ethanol to prevent production of unseparable high-molecular-weight melanoidin. From active HPLC fractions of butanol extracted from the reaction mixture, one of main active principles was isolated in crystalline form and identified as being a new equimolar condensation compound consisting of tryptophan and dehydroascorbic acid. (Namiki *et al.*, 1982a).

D.   APPLICATION

Apart from the chemical nature of the active principles, there is no doubt about the effectiveness of MRPs in practical food processing. Yamaguchi *et al.* (1964, 1967a,b) found that the antioxidative stability of lard in cookies was increased greatly by adding glucose and certain amino acids (especially valine, glycine, and lysine) to the dough. An observation has also been made that the addition of a histidine and glucose mixture to cookie dough before baking showed more effective antioxidation than the addition of MRPs prepared from the same mixture (Lingnert, 1980; Lingnert and Eriksson, 1981) and that the increase in activity paralleled browning. Regarding the oxidative stability of sausage during frozen storage, the development of rancid flavor was found to be effectively retarded by the addition of MRPs from glucose and histidine, but no effect was obtained by the addition of a histidine–glucose mixture (Lingnert and Lundgren, 1980). The inconsistency in these two cases may be due to insufficient heating in the latter. Enhancement of antioxidative activity of spray-dried whole milk was also observed by preheating with the addition of histidine and glucose, although it was accompanied by a decrease in the lysine content and some coloration (Lingnert and Hall, 1986).

The search for economical and effective MRP materials for practical food processing includes a study by Obretenov *et al.* (1986), who tested, using lard as the substrate, the antioxidative effectiveness of the reaction products of acid-hydrolyzed bovine blood or sunflower groat with hydrolyzed staroh and found that the former product is more effective, perhaps due to the higher content of sulfur-containing, chain-branched, basic amino acids. The best results were obtained when a 2 : 1 amino material–carbohydrate mixture was heated for 20 hr at 100°C.

Utilization of MRPs for food preservation may sometimes cause problems because of their inherent color. The decoloration of MRPs by ozonolysis without a significant decrease in the antioxidative activity (Yamaguchi, 1986) may provide a simple solution. While ozonolysis by itself is impractical for use in food processing from the standpoint of food safety, it may be possible to develop an acceptable method of biological oxidation based on the process.

Synergistic effect with other antioxidants, especially those of natural origin, is very important for preventing undesirable coloration with melanoidin. Yamaguchi and Fujimaki (1974a,b) demonstrated that MRP from xylose with ammonia and purified by gel chromatography showed marked synergistic effect in a model system with β-, γ-, and δ-tocopherol, but not with α-tocopherol. In margarine, the effect was stronger with the addition of citric acid and, in combination with 0.005–0.01% tocopherol and 0.0025% melanoidin [below its coloring level (0.005%)], inhibits autoxidation very effectively.

In any event, antioxidation is a very important factor in food processing and preservation, and the fact that it can be induced in food by intercomponent reactions is not only valuable information for food production and storage but also a very interesting problem in basic food chemistry. Although considerable information has been obtained with regard to conditions for inducing the activity, little is known about the chemical properties of the active principles involved, except that a complex MRP structure involving nitrogen appears to be responsible for the antioxidative activity. In order to fully utilize the antioxidative activity of MRPs, much more information on controlling the Maillard reaction in food processing, as well as on the chemical properties of melanoidins, is needed.

IV. MUTAGEN FORMATION

The development of simple and reproducible mutagenicity tests (Kada et al., 1972[1]; Ames et al., 1975[2]) resulted in the detection of numerous mutagenic

[1]The Rec-assay system is a method used to detect DNA-damaging substances by comparing the growth of DNA recombination-proficient (H17 rec +) and -deficient (M45 rec −) strain of Bacillus subtilis on a medium on which a paper disk containing test sample has been placed (Kada et al., 1972).

[2]The Ames test is a microbial assay method using mutants of Salmonella typhimurium LT2 to detect gene mutagens by counting revertant colonies having a histidine requirement to prototrophy after treatment with mutagens. The TA98 strain, specific for frameshift-type mutagens, and the TA100 strain, for base-pair substitution-type mutagens, are the most commonly used strains. The S9 mix, rat liver cell homogenates, is used to metabolically activate the test sample. (Ames et al., 1975).

substances in various foods and in the environment. Although mutagens are not always carcinogenic, nearly all known carcinogens are mutagenic (McCann *et al.*, 1975; Sugimura *et al.*, 1976). Since epidemiological research has revealed that the major causes of human cancer occur via the oral route (Wynder and Gori, 1977; Weisburger *et al.*, 1980; Doll and Peto, 1981; Ames, 1984), studies on the presence and the formation of mutagens in food are of extreme importance.

A. PYROLYSATE MUTAGENS

Besides the mutagens which occur naturally in foods (such as bracken and cycad) and those due to contamination by chemicals or mycotoxin-producing molds, mutagens produced by chemical reactions of food constituents during storage, processing, and cooking are of equal importance. *N*-nitrosoamines are the best known of this kind (Gough, 1978), but recent findings of mutagenic pyrolytic products found in broiled fish and meat, for example, have been the cause of general alarm. The study of these pyrolytic products was initiated by the discovery of mutagens other than benzo[*a*]pyrene, which was formerly believed to be the major mutagen in smoke condensate of broiled fish (Masuda *et al.*, 1966; Sugimura *et al.*, 1977a) and in cigarette smoke (Kier *et al.*, 1974; Hutton and Hackney, 1975; Sugimura *et al.*, 1976; Mizusaki *et al.*, 1977). Matsumoto *et al.* (1977), in a study on tobacco smoke, baked various amino acids at 300–800°C and found, by the Ames test (using TA98 with S9 mixture), that the tar produced from tryptophan was essentially highly mutagenic and, in a study of indol derivatives, revealed the importance of 3-position side chains for the manifestation of pyrolytic mutagenicity. The mutagenicity of smoke extracts from broiled sardine and beef was shown by the Ames method (TA98, S9 mix) (Nagao *et al.*, 1977a), as was that of the scorched part of grilled beef (Commoner *et al.*, 1978). The strong mutagenicity of pyrolysates of proteins (e.g., lysozyme) and tryptophan and the nonmutagenicity of pyrolysates of DNA, RNA, starch, and vegetables were noted by Nagao *et al.* (1977b). Strongly mutagenic products Trp P-1 and P-2 were isolated from pyrolysate of tryptophan at temperatures over 300°C (Sugimura *et al.*, 1977b) as well as Glu P-1 and P-2 (Yamamoto *et al.*, 1977) (Table IV). Tryptophan-containing especially, proteins and, peptides produced stronger mutagenic pyrolysates than did proteins not containing tryptophan, and the main mutagens in tobacco smoke were found to be the pyrolysates of tobacco proteins (Matsumoto *et al.*, 1978). The main mutagens in soybean protein pyrolysate were identified as α-carboline and methyl-α-carboline (Yoshida *et al.*, 1978).

These studies investigated mainly pyrolytic tarry products (of tryptophan or a protein alone) obtained in smoke at high temperatures of over 300°C, conditions which are not encountered in day-to-day cooking. However, in time it was discovered that mutagenicity also resulted in ordinary cooking conditions, e.g., broiled, semifried fish and grilled hamburger, with the formation of extraor-

TABLE IV
MUTAGENS ISOLATED FROM PYROLYSATES[a]

Chemical name	Abbreviation	Structure	Source of isolation
3-Amino-1,4-dimethyl-5*H*-pyrido[4,3-b]indole	Trp-P-1		Tryptophan pyrolysate
3-Amino-1-methyl-5*H*-pyrido[4,3-b]indole	Trp-P-2		Tryptophan pyrolysate
2-Amino-6-methyldipyrido-[1,2-α:3′,2′-d]imidazole	Glu-P-1		Glutamic acid pyrolysate
2-Aminodipyrido[1,2-α:3′,2′-d]carbazole	Glu-P-2		Glutamic acid pyrolysate
3,4-Cyclopentenopyrido-[3,2-α]imidazole	Lys-P-1		Lysine pyrolysate
4-Amino-6-methyl-1*H*-2,5,10,10b-tetraazafluoranthene	Orn-P-1		Ornithine pyrolysate
2-Amino-5-phenylpyridine	Phe-P-1		Phenylalanine pyrolysate
2-Amino-9*H*-pyrido-[2,3-b]indole	AαC		Soybean globulin pyrolysate
2-Amino-3-methyl-9*H*-pyrido[2,3-b]indole	MeAαC		Soybean globulin pyrolysate
2-Amino-3-methylimidazo-[4,5-f]quinoline	IQ		Broiled sardine
2-Amino-3,4-dimethyl-imidazo[4,5-f]quinoline	MeIQ		Broiled sardine
2-Amino-3,8-dimethylimidazo[4,5-f]quinoxaline	MeIQx		Fried beef

[a] Nagao *et al.* (1983).

dinarily high mutagenic products 2-amino-3-methylimidazo[4,5-f]quinoline (IQ) and 2-amino-3,4-dimethylimidazo[4,5-f]quinoline (MeIQ) from broiled fish (Kasai *et al.*, 1980a,b) and 2-amino-3,8-dimethylimidazo[4,5-f]quinoxaline (MeIQx) from broiled beef; these mutagens were isolated and identified as such by Kasai *et al.* (1981a,b). The results of various studies on the formation of mutagens fluctuated, and mutagenicity varied greatly depending on cooking conditions such as temperature, time, and moisture content (Spingarn and Weinburger, 1979; Pariza *et al.*, 1979; Dolara *et al.*, 1979); in the beginning it was not known that the Maillard reactions are involved in mutagen formation.

Significantly, Yoshida and Okamoto (1980a,b) reported the development of mutagenicity when glucose was added to mixed amino acids before pyrolysis at 150°C, while no activity was noted for mixtures of glucose with albumin or adenine, or in the case of albumin or adenine each by itself. Noteworthy was the remarkably strong mutagenicity in pyrolysates of the mixtures of creatine with amino acids (especially cystine, threonine, phenylalanine. and methionine), glucose, or fatty acids, even though pyrolysis of creatin and the other materials by themselves did not produce mutagenicity (Yoshida and Okamoto, 1980c; Yoshida and Fukuhara, 1982).

Jägerstad *et al.* (1983) found stronger mutagenicity in pyrolysates of beef with high sugar content than with low sugar content and reported that the addition of sugars increases the mutagenicity of pyrolysates; thus, they pointed out the importance of the presence of both sugar and amino compounds. It was as a result of these reports that the relationship between Maillard reactions and mutagenicity came to receive considerable attention (Barnes *et al.*, 1983).

Heating creatine–glucose–glycine or alanine systems in diethylene a glycol–water system at 130°C for 2 hr induced mutagenicity (Ames test, TA98 with S9 mix), which led to a proposal regarding the route of formation of the imidazoquinoline mutagens in fried beef (Jägerstad *et al.*, 1983) (Fig. 13). There is some question concerning the formation of the imidazoquinoline mutagens, especially in pyrolysates of the model system. Formation of IQ was first discovered in broiled fish in Japan. The discovery was widely reported, becoming a source of concern throughout the nation. Since it was found in broiled fish, it was believed that IQ would also be found in grilled beef, a major part of the diet in the West. This turned out not to be the case, however, since fried or grilled beef indicated only slight amounts of IQ; rather, the main mutagen in beef is MeIQx (see Table V). This is another case where dietary customs gave rise to different findings. Jägerstad *et al.* (1984) isolated MeIQx (but not IQ) from a heated mixture of creatine–glucose–glycine using HPLC. Negishi *et al.* (1984) isolated another new mutagen from same reaction mixture. Recently, Nyhammer *et al.* (1986) determined, by HPLC, the presence of MeIQx and a small amount of IQ in a heated mixture of creatine–fructose–glycine, as well as the presence of 4,8-DiMeIQx and a slight amount of MeIQx in a mixture of creatine–fructose–DL-

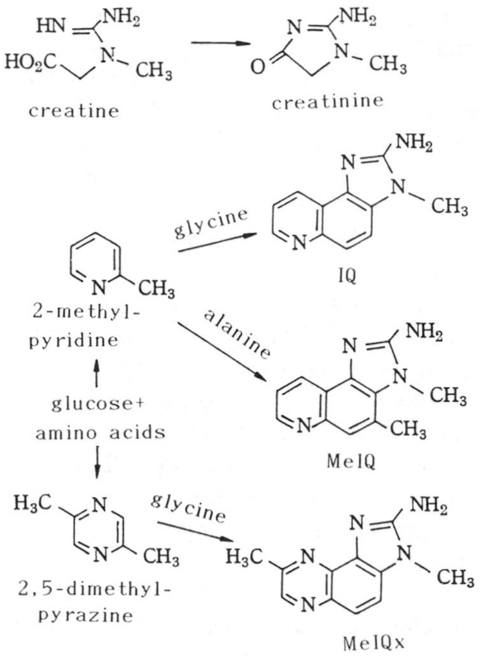

FIG. 13. Suggested route for the formation of the imidazoquinoline mutagens (Jägerstad *et al.*, 1983).

alanine heated at 140°C for 2 hr. IQ was also isolated from a heated mixture of creatine and proline (Yoshida *et al.*, 1984). Jägerstad *et al.* (1983) also observed that the addition of 2-methylpyridine in the creatine–glucose–glycine system enhanced the induction of mutegenicity.

Although the formation mechanism is yet to be clarified, these results clearly indicate involvement of the Maillard reactions in the formation of imidazoquinoline mutagens found in broiled fish and beef. The essential point of the formation seems to be the creatine–sugar–amino acid combination, and creatine is believed to be the key component that provides the imidazole ring to the IQ analogs, which are considered to be the active site of the mutagens.

Effective adsorption with "blue cotton" (cotton bearing copper–phthalocyanine) for IQ analogs in food and environmental systems (Hayatsu *et al.*, 1983) and HPLC analysis (Wakabayashi *et al.*, 1986) have been developed, enabling detection of very small amount of IQ and MeIQ. Employing HPLC, Wakabayashi *et al.* (1986) reported contents of MeIQx in broiled beef (0.5 ng/g), broiled chicken (2.1 ng/g) and fried ground beef (0.3 ng/g), as well as IQ in bacteriological-grade beef extract (41.6 ng/g).

IQ and MeIQ have been shown to be carcinogenic in mice (Ohgaki *et al.*,

TABLE V

EXAMPLES OF QUANTITATIVE ANALYSES FOR MUTAGENS IN COOKED FOODS[a]

Food material	Method of cooking	Methods of identification and quantification	Mutagens in cooked material (ng/g)	
Sun-dried sardine	Naked flame	GC/MS with MID	Trp P-1	13.3
			Trp P-2	13.1
Sun-dried sardine	Naked flame	GC/MS with MID by addition of CD_3-substituted MeIQ	IQ	158
			MeIQ	72
Beef	Electric hot plate	GC/MS with MID	IQ	0.59
			MeIQx	2.4
Beef	Naked flame	Identified by fluorescence and MF, quantified by GC/MS	Trp P-1	53[b]
Chicken	Naked flame	Fluorescence	AαC	180
			MeAαC	15
Sun-dried cuttlefish	Naked flame	Identified by UV, quantified by MF	Glu P-2	280[c]

[a] Nagao et al. (1983).
[b] ng/g of raw beef.
[c] ng/g of sun-dried material.

1984, 1985), and IQ to be carcinogenic in rat (Takayama et al., 1984), but their carcinogenicity was revealed not to be as strong as first supposed from their extremely strong mutagenicity as determined by the Ames test (with TA98 and S9 mix). The amounts of these mutagens in ordinary food as shown in some examples are known to be very small, and it is difficult to evaluate whether or not they constitute significant carcinogenicity with respect to human cancer. It should also be noted that mutagen formation in Maillard reactions has been observed only in water-poor model systems at high temperatures (above 130°C), and IQ and other mutagens are not formed in water-rich cooking conditions.

B. MUTAGENS OF AQUEOUS MAILLARD REACTIONS

The toxicity of melanoidins, which are produced in aqueous systems by browning reactions at lower temperatures (below 100°C) has been discussed (Lang and Baessler, 1971; Lee et al., 1981). Are they mutagenic? Caramel prepared from sugars alone or with ammonia and used in various beverages and liquors was first investigated for mutagenicity by Aeschbacher et al. (1981) using the Ames test, and no mutagenicity was observed in food caramel obtained

TABLE VI

MUTAGEN FORMATION IN AQUEOUS MAILLARD REACTION[a]

		Activity			
		TA100		TA98	
Group	Kinds of browned solutions with Glc	−S9	+S9	−S9	+S9
A	Lys · HCl, Leu, Ser, Thr, Met, Gln, Pro	+	Decrease	−	−
B	Arg, Gly, Ala, Val, Ile	+	Decrease	−	Increase
C	CySH	+	Increase	+	Increase
D	Phe	+	Increase	−	−
E	Trp, (Cys)$_2$, Tyr, Asp, Asn, Glu	−	−	−	−

[a] Shinohara et al. (1983).
[b] +, Positive mutagenic activity; −, no detectable mutagenic activity.

by heating pure sugar. No mutagenicity was noted in hydroxymethylfurfural (HMF) or in a plant protein hydrolysate. Recently, Scheutwinkel and von der Hude (1985) also reported no mutagenicity of commercially available caramel colors in Ames tests using four strains with or without S9 mix.

Omura and his group (Shinohara et al., 1980, 1983; Omura et al., 1983) examined the mutagenicity of browned aqueous mixtures of glucose with amino acids at 100°C using the Ames test and Rec-assay. The results showed varying mutagenicity depending mainly upon the kind of amino acid, the reaction conditions (especially pH), and the test systems used. As shown in Table VI, for the reaction systems using glucose–amino acid, the Ames test gave mutagenicity data that divided the amino acids into five groups which behaved differently according to the test bacterial strain (TA98 or TA100) and to the presence or absence of S9 mix. Among the amino acids, tryptophan, glutamic acid, and aspartic acid showed no mutagenicity despite the strong mutagenicity observed in pyrolysis of the first two. Mutagenicity was shown for lysine only with TA100 and without S9; for arginine, with TA100 and TA98 with S9, and for cysteine, with TA100 without S9. Their results also showed dependence of mutagenicity on sugar species, which in turn depend on the amino acid used.

The reaction between glucose and glutamic acid, arginine, or cysteine showed weak mutagenicity in Rec-assay and tests on pupal oocytes of silkworms (Yamashita et al., 1981).

Powrie et al. (1981) demonstrated that the Maillard reaction in the mixtures of glucose with various amino acids (especially lysine and arginine) without S9 mix induced significant increases in the chromosomal aberration test using Chinese hamster ovary (CHO) cells; mitotic recombination and mutation was induced in Saccharomyces cereviseae. The activities depended heavily on initial pH of the Maillard reaction and were stronger at pH 10 than at pH 7.

These results indicate the complexity of determining mutagenicity in Maillard reaction mixtures, with different test methods often giving contradictory results.

Concerning the mutagenic principle of Maillard reaction mixtures, Omura *et al.* (1983) isolated 5-hydroxymethylfurfural (HMF) from a glucose–phenylalanine system, HMF and a pyrrole derivative from a glucose–lysine system, and a thiazolidine derivative from a glucose–cysteine system. This was the first time that HMF, well known as an important intermediate of browning and flavor formation, was shown to be mutagenic.

According to Shinohara's detailed study on the formation of furan derivatives (Shinohara *et al.*, 1986), larger amounts of HMF are produced by lysine and arginine reactions with arabinose, xylose, or glucose (all at pH 7.0) than in reactions of phenylalanine, glutamic acid, lysine, and arginine with fructose at pH 2.0. In these cases, the amounts of HMF formed did not parallel the degree of browning; the highest degree of browning occurred in alkaline media with lysine and glycine without the formation of HMF. Some organic acids, e.g., oxalic acid and tartaric acid, promoted the formation of furan derivatives. Although the mutagenicity of HMF, shown by TA100 with S9 mix, is much weaker than that of IQ and its analogs, it is a cause for some concern because it is easily produced by Maillard reactions. Its carcinogenicity, however, is not known.

Shibamoto and co-workers examined the mutagenicity of Maillard reaction model systems of maltol-NH$_3$ (Shibamoto, 1980), L-rhamnose-NH$_3$-H$_2$S (Toda *et al.*, 1981), and cysteamine glucose (Mihara and Shibamoto, 1980) and detected mutagenicity by Ames test in the fractions containing pyrazine, pyrrole, and thiazolidine derivatives; the mutagenic principles were not identified (Shibamoto, 1982).

There are some other mutagenic products in foods which may be related to the Maillard reaction. Nagao *et al.* (1979) investigated the mutagenicity of coffee and claimed methylglyoxal (~10 μg/ml in regular coffee) to be its mutagenic component (TA100 without S9 mix) and warned of the potential hazards of coffee (Kasai *et al.*, 1982). Aeschbacher *et al.* (1980a,b), on the other hand, refuted this claim, stating that coffee showed only weak mutagenic activity toward TA100 in the Ames test which, moreover, disappeared with the addition of S9 mix. It should be kept in mind that coffee possesses bactericidal activity, a fact which casts some doubt on results obtained using the Ames test.

Methylglyoxal was proposed to be an important fragmentation product of the Amadori product in the Maillard reaction by Hodge (1967); this was recently confirmed by Hayashi and Namiki (1986a,b). Methylglyoxal is present in many foods, e.g., caramel (Hodge *et al.*, 1963; Severin *et al.*, 1984), bread (Wiseblatt and Kohn, 1960), and broiled potato (Kajita and Senda, 1972). Recently, Hayashi and Shibamoto (1985) noted a much higher content of methylglyoxal than previously found in coffee and root beer using a newly developed analytical method (Hayashi *et al.*, 1985b).

Methylglyoxal is known to be a very reactive compound and is assumed to be an important active carcinogenic carbonyl compound *in vivo* (Szent-Györgyi, 1980), but whether methylglyoxal in food is related to human cancer remains to be elucidated.

C. NITROSO MUTAGENS

N-nitrosoamines, the most hazardous of the carcinogens produced by the interaction of food components, are produced mainly from secondary amines and nitrous acid. Since the Maillard reaction produces a number of secondary amines including the Amadori products, the possibility of mutagen formation cannot be ignored. At the same time, it is also possible that the reductive products of the reaction exhibit desmutagenic action (Kada *et al.*, 1982) on the formation of *N*-nitroso compounds, as has been evidenced for ascorbic acid, a representative reductone (Mirvish *et al.*, 1972; Mirvish, 1981); reducton-like properties of Maillard products have been noted previously.

Several reports concerning the Maillard reaction–nitrous acid complex system have been published (Couglin *et al.*, 1979). Heyns *et al.* (1974, 1979) described the formation of nitrosated Amadori compounds, and Russel (1983) showed formation of positive dose–response mutagenicity of a nitrosated fructose–tryptophan mixture for both TA98 and TA100 strains without S9 mix in the Ames test. Shibamoto has reviewed Maillard nitrite reactions (1983a) and focused on the mutagenicity of nitroso derivatives of thiazolines, which are important meat flavor components (Fujimaki *et al.*, 1969) produced by the Maillard reaction (Sakaguchi and Shibamoto, 1979; Mihara and Shibamoto, 1980; Sekizawa and Shibamoto, 1981).

Although the mutagenicity of soy sauce was once the subject of some public concern, it was later disproved (MacDonald and Dueck, 1976; Nagahara *et al.*, 1986). However, mutagenicity was found to develop when nitrite was added to soy sauce (Lin *et al.*, 1979), a phenomenon which was not considered to be caused by nitrosamines (Shibamoto, 1983b).

Wakabayashi *et al.* (1983) also investigated the production of mutagens in the nitrite–soy sauce system and isolated β-carboline derivatives and Tyramine as precursors of the induced mutagen principle in the mixture (Ochiai *et al.*, 1984). The carbolines, considered to be a product of the reaction of tryptophan with methylglyoxal, furfural, or hydroxymethylfurfural, probably produce nitroso mutagens by reaction with nitrite.

Kinae *et al.* (1986) demonstrated the induction of significant mutagenicity upon addition of nitrite to a very slightly mutagenic reaction product of tryptophan with carbohydrates and other compounds, especially carbonyl compounds such as triose reductone, diacetyl, and furfural. Mutagenicity has been attributed to the formation of β-carboline compounds by condensation and cyclization followed by *N*-nitrosation by nitrite, although the final products have not yet been identified.

At the time these findings were reported, they became cause for general alarm throughout Japan concerning the safety of soy sauce and other foods. However, mutagenicity under practical conditions was, for the mosr part, disproved because of the enormous difference in nitrite concentration levels found in soy sauce and the experimental model systems, as well as because of evidence of the presence of reaction inhibitors in soy sauce (Nagahara *et al.*, 1986; Shibamoto 1983b).

Yen and Lee (1986) investigated mutagenicity of a browned casein–glucose system with or without nitrite by the Ames test (TA 100, 102, and 104 with S9 mix). The ether extracts showed mutagenicity in the nitrite-treated casein–glucose mixtures, especially in the browned casein–glucose mixture, but no activity was observed in the ether extracts of casein–glucose, browned casein–glucose, or nitrite–casein systems, nor was any activity observed in the water extract of samples of any test strain. Amino acid analysis showed a marked decrease in lysine content, especially in nitrite-treated systems.

D. ANTIMUTAGENESIS

The formation of these mutagens in foods naturally presents serious problems regarding safety. However, it must also be noted that, because studies on food mutagenicity are still in an early stage, in many cases it is not well understood whether or not mutagens are actually formed and/or function in actual food processing and living systems as they do in model systems. Inactivation of mutagens in food by other components has also been demonstrated. e.g., the inactivation of Trp P-1 by vegetable juices, especially cabbage, broccoli, and burdock (Kada *et al.*, 1978; Morita *et al.*, 1978; Inoue *et al.*, 1981) and also by BHA and others (Barnes *et al.*, 1983). The enzyme peroxidase in horseradish (Yamada *et al.*, 1979) and saliva (Nishioka *et al.*, 1981) has also been found to inactivate mutagens. Unlike peroxidase or other enzymes, the mechanism of inactivation in the case of burdock appears to be adsorption by some polymer (Morita *et al.*, 1984, 1985). The elimination of mutagenicity has been observed with the addition of nitrite (Yoshida and Matsumoto, 1978) (Tsuda *et al.*, 1980) and chlorine (Tsuda *et al.*, 1983), both of which appear to inactivate the active site by some kind of simple chemical reaction. The term *desmutagen*, proposed by Kada *et al.* (1982) for substances possessing such action, represents this concept well. Chan *et al.* (1982) reported the desmutagenic effects of a lysine–fructose reaction mixture and caramelized sucrose on pyrolysate mutagens, although the effective components have not yet been characterized. Kim *et al.* (1986) examined the effect of the addition of fractionated glucose–glycine melanoidin (molecular weights <1000, 1000–5000, and >5000) on the muta-

genicity of Trp P-1, Trp P-2, Glu P-1, Glu P-2, IQ, etc. and confirmed desmutagenic action that grew stronger with increasing molecular weight and paralleled the reducing power and antioxidative activity. Sodium borohydride
reduction lowered desmutagenic activity, and the inactivation of the pyrolysates
by humic acid has also been reported (Sato *et al.*, 1986, 1987). The desmutagenic effect of melanoidin, as well as that of humic acid, may be the result of the
adsorptive activity of mutagens, as has been observed in the case of a desmutagenic lignanlike fraction of burdock (Morita *et al.*, 1984). Desmutagenic
activity against pyrolysate mutagens by low-molecular-weight carbonyl compounds (such as diacetyl and glyceraldehyde, which are assumed to be fragmentation products of the Maillard reaction) has also been reported (Kim *et al.*,
1986); this is thought to be due to an amino–carbonyl reaction between these
carbonyl compounds and an amino group of the pyrolysate mutagens.

While these substances possess desmutagenic activity, compounds also exist
which, although not mutagenic themselves, appear to promote mutagenicity.
β-Carboline compounds from soybean protein pyrolysate are an example of this
type (Nagao *et al.*, 1977c).

Although it may not be directly involved in the mutagenicity of Maillard
reaction products, some Amadori products have been found to induce site-specif-
ic DNA breaks on some phages (Komano *et al.*, 1986; Kashimura *et al.*, 1986).
The effect depends on the Cu^{2+} ion and is inhibited by radical scavengers,
suggesting the involvement of active oxygen radicals.

The involvement of the Maillard reaction and its products in the formation and
elimination of mutagens is gradually being elucidated by studies which are being
conducted mainly in Japan. The mutagenicity of pyrolysates once caused grave
concern but, given the evidence of their low levels in actual food, their inactivation by other food components, and their own weak carcinogenicity, it now
seems that their actual involvement in carcinogenesis is less serious than first
thought. The actual role of pyrolysate mutagens in carcinogenesis should be
carefully examined taking into account both the overall process of food preparation and intake involving the desmutagenic actions.

V. TRENDS IN CONTINUING RESEARCH

As mentioned at the beginning, among the interactions of food and biological
constituents, Maillard reactions are unique, important, and involve many problems in numerous fields of food science and technology. The present view covers
only recent developments concerning the browning reaction mechanism and the
antioxidative and mutagenic activities of Maillard products, dealing mainly with
problems concerning low-molecular-weight compounds. In addition to browning
and other organoleptic aspects, Maillard reactions involving proteins are, of

course, very important for food quality, especially from the nutritive and physiological viewpoints. However, these topics are treated in a number of other studies and have not been included in this limited review. This final section deals with relevant problems which require further investigation.

A.   BROWNING REACTION MECHANISM

The mechanism for the Maillard reaction proposed by Hodge in 1953 has been accepted widely as the most appropriate description for the production of melanoidin, the browning polymer. The mechanism involves Amadori rearrangement as a key step to give major intermediates for browning polymers. However, the browning is known to be influenced greatly by reactants, pH, and other conditions, so it seems reasonable to assume the existence of different pathways that depend mainly on the pH and the reactant. In this respect, the new browning reaction mechanism described in Section II,C is noteworthy since it is the first which emphasizes the importance of sugar fragmentation occurring prior to Amadori rearrangement. Experimental results showed that the occurrence of such sugar fragmentation is negligible under acidic conditions, and the browning probably proceeds according to Hodge's proposal (although the rate of browning is slow). On the other hand, in systems above a weakly alkaline pH, the contribution of the sugar fragmentation to browning becomes dominant, especially in early browning. Thus, it seems important to elucidate the degree of the contribution of the sugar fragmentation pathways to browning in neutral or slightly acidic food systems, and also to browning in different reactant systems, e.g., lysine–glucose, glutamic acid–glucose, fructose–glycine, etc.

If the Maillard browning reactions proceed by additional reactions of furfural or osones with amino compounds in acidic conditions and by condensation of sugar fragmentation carbonyl compounds or their enaminols in alkaline conditions, the browning products which result will naturally be different in structure and chemical properties. Studies on precursor and colored products regarding these respects are needed.

The formation of C_2 fragmentary products of sugar before Amadori rearrangement has been elucidated by ESR spectral analysis and chromatographical isolation as well as by NMR and MS spectral identification. As for the C_3 fragmentary products, even though their production was recognized at an early stage of the reaction (closely after C_2 formation) it has not yet been clearly elucidated whether the C_3 formed directly from the Amadori product or from 1-deoxyosone according to Hodge's proposal. Moreover, a C_3 product was identified as methylglyoxal diimine derivative, but whether it is a direct fragmentary product or secondary product is not yet clear.

To elucidate the mechanism of a reaction as rapid and complicated as the Maillard reaction at neutral and higher pH, it is necessary to develop new and dynamic experimental techniques employing various new spectrometries to detect and analyze unstable intermediates and their changes in the reaction. Highly reactive intermediates to browning are sometimes difficult to isolate by the usual techniques and the yield is poor, while some products which are fairly stable and obtained in appreciable amounts sometimes turn out not to be the most important intermediates. The discovery of a free radical product in the early stage of the reaction leading to the elucidation of the presence of a new pathway to browning is an example of the application of such research methods.

Concerning the free radical products early in the Maillard reaction, an interesting question is why such free radicals are fairly stable in the reaction mixture. Perhaps they exist because of a balanced oxidation–reduction system. Another question concerns the kind of products involved, and the answer should be useful in further clarifying the browning mechanism.

B. REACTANTS

Recently, large amounts of isomerized sugar have been used in various foods and drinks. The behavior of fructose in the Maillard reaction is known to be considerably different from that of glucose, e.g., in the browning reaction rate and color tone. There are many studies on the Maillard reaction of fructose, and a reaction mechanism involving the Heyns rearrangement has been proposed. However, many problems concerning the reaction of fructose, especially in browning and the development of antioxidants and mutagens, remain.

As for carbonyl compounds other than reducing sugars in the Maillard reaction, this review discusses mainly oxidized ascorbic acid, but there are many interesting and important problems concerning the reactions of oxidized fatty acids and polyphenols.

On the other hand, differences in Maillard reactions that depend on the amino acids involved are well known, and there are many detailed studies on the formation of flavor products in special amino acid–sugar systems, e.g., proline (Tressl et al., 1986), threonine and serine (Baltes and Bochmann, 1986), and cysteine (Shibamoto et al., 1983a). However, not many studies have been done on development of browning, antioxidants, mutagens, etc., and further investigation is required concerning the products and the mechanism of formation by the Maillard reaction of special amino acid–sugar systems, such as lysine, histidine, arginine, tryptophan, and others. The fact that an ε-amino group is eliminated by DHA and other analogous carbonyl compounds (just as the α-amino group is eliminated by Strecker degradation) is very important regarding the nutritive and physicochemical properties of proteins. The kinds of carbonyl compounds involved and to what extent such deamination occurs in food system need further elucidation.

C. ANTIOXIDANTS

As mentioned in Section III, the antioxidative activity of melanoidin may result from multiple factors involving hydrogen or electron donating activity, metal chelating activity, and synergistic activity; it does not appear to be the result of a single and strongly active factor, but seems to involve many different activities. Thus, to elucidate the mechanism of the antioxidative activity, more detailed information on the structure and properties of melanoidin is required. Investigations to determine the Maillard reaction conditions for controlling antioxidative activity, and other properties such as flavor and color, are required. Antioxidative low-molecular-weight Maillard reaction products as observed in glucose–glycine (Park and Kim, 1983), DHA–tryptophan (Namiki et al., 1982a,b), and triose reductone–amino acid (Obata et al., 1971) systems also require examination.

Ozonolysis of melanoidin gave an almost colorless but still antioxidative melanoidin product. This is a very interesting finding and is important with respect to both the chemical study of melanoidin and the practical use of melanoidin as a food additive. Additional studies on the modification of melanoidin are needed on the formation of antioxidative products contributing to safety, color, flavor, solubility, and other important food quality factors.

D. MUTAGENS

Extremely strong mutagens, such as IQ and MeIQx, have been isolated and identified by the Ames test from broiled semidried fish and beef and demonstrated to be formed by Maillard reactions. It was found that creatine–amino acid–sugar systems are the most effective producers of these mutagens and also that their formation is greatly influenced by reaction conditions such as temperature and moisture content. Details concerning the effects of reaction conditions and the formation mechanism are, however, not yet known. Fortunately, additional studies showed that the carcinogenicity of the pyrolysate mutagens was not as strong as originally thought and that their yields in ordinary foods are very small. To prevent the production of the pyrolysate mutagens, it is necessary to elucidate these points as well as the effects of inactivating factors in food systems.

The mutagens are formed under low-moisture conditions. Concerning this and, moreover, the formation of antioxidants, flavors, and other changes in dried foods, more studies on Maillard reactions in low-moisture systems are needed.

Nitroso amino compounds have been noted as being strong carcinogens. As discussed, nitrite-Maillard reaction systems involve mutagen formation while, at the same time, involving desmutagenesis. The relevant reactions are very complicated, and thorough investigations employing reactant concentrations similar to those found in actual foods are required, as are studies on the effects of the presence of other food constituents.

In conclusion, the extremely complex Maillard reaction can perhaps be compared to a river which constantly flows and affects human life. The reactions and interactions are very complicated, and care must be taken not to isolate and focus too much on one aspect without taking into consideration all of the other relevant aspects. The dirt and debris which may be found on the banks do not present the total picture of the benefits and risks the river provides.

ACKNOWLEDGMENT

The author expresses gratitute to Dr. Keiichi Tsuji for his excellent advice concerning both the content and language of this review. Thanks are also due to Dr. Tateki Hayashi for helpful discussions.

REFERENCES

Abrams, A., Lowy, O. H., and Borsook, H. 1955. Preparation of 1-amino-1-deoxy-2-ketohexoses from aldohexoses and α-amino acids. *J. Am. Chem. Soc.* **77**, 4794–4796.

Adrian, J. 1974. Nutritional and physiological consequences of the Maillard reaction. *World Rev. Nutr. Diet.* **19**, 71–122.

Aeschbacher, H. U., and Wurzner, H. P. 1980a. An evaluation of instant and regular coffee in the Ames mutagen test. *Toxicol. Lett.* **5**, 139–45.

Aeschbacher, H. U., Chappuis, C., and Wurzner. 1980b. Mutagenicity testing of coffee: A study of problems encountered with the Ames *Salmonella* test system. *Food Cosmet. Toxicol.* **18**, 605–613.

Aeschbacher, H. U., Chappuis, CH., Manganel, M., and Aeschbach, R. 1981. Investigation of Maillard products in bacterial mutagenicity test systems. *Prog. Food Nutr. Sci.* **5**, 279–294.

Altena, J. H., van den Ouweland, G. A. M., Teunis, C. J., and Tjan, S. B. 1981. Analysis of the 220-MHz, P.M.R. spectra of some products of the Amadori and Hynes rearrangements. *Carbohyd. Res.* **92**, 37–49.

Ames, B. N. 1984. Cancer and diet. *Science* **224**, 668–670, 757–760.

Ames, B. N., McCann, J., and Yamazaki, E. 1975. Methods for detecting carcinogens and mutagens with the *Salmonella* mammalian-microsome mutagenicity test. *Mutat. Res.* **31**, 347–364.

Anderson, R. H., Moran, D. H., Huntley, T. E., and Holahan, J. L. 1963. Responses of cereals to antioxidants. *Food Technol.* **17**, 115–120.

Anet, F. E. L. J. 1960. Degradation of carbohydrates I. Isolation of 3-deoxy-hexosones. *Aust. J. Chem.* **13**, 396–403.

Anet, E. F. L. J. 1962. Formation of furan compounds from sugars. *Chem. Ind. (London)* **1962**, 262.

Anet, E. F. L. J. 1964. 3-Deoxyglucosones and the degradation of carbohydrates. *Adv. Carbohydr. Chem.* **19**, 181–218.

Anet, E. E. L. J., and Reynolds, T. M. 1957. Chemistry of non-enzymatic browning. I. Reactions between amino acids, organic acids, and sugars in freeze-dried appricots and peaches. *Aust. J. Chem.* **10**, 182–192.

Aso, K. 1939. Formation of 3-hydroxypyridines from the reaction of glucose and ammonium salts. *Nippon Nogeikagakukaishi.* **15**, 629–633.

Aso, K. 1940. Formation of 3-hydroxypyridines from the reaction of glucose and ammonium salts II. 2-hydroxymethyl-5-hydroxy-pyridine. *Nippon Nogeikagakukai-shi* **16**, 249–252.

Baltes, W., and Bochmann, G. 1986. Model reactions on roast aroma formation. The reaction of serine and threonine with sucrose. *Dev. Food Sci.* **13**, 245–255.

Baltes, W., and Franke, K. 1978. Modellreaktion. I. Nichtfluchtige Reaktionsprodukte der Umsetzung von D-glucose mit *p*-chloranilin. *Z. Lebensm. Unters. Forsch.* **167**, 403–409.

Barnes, W., Spingarn, N. E., Gravie-Gould, C., Vuolo, L. L., Wang, Y. Y., and Weisburger, J. H. 1983. Mutagens in cooked foods: Possible consequences of the Maillard reaction. *ACS Symp. Ser.* **215**, 486–506.

Bauernfeind, J. C. 1982. Ascorbic acid technology in agriculture, pharmaceutical, food, and industrial applications. *Adv. Chem. Ser.* **200**, 395–498.

Baynes, J. W., Ahmed, M. U., Fisher, C. I., Hull, C. J., Lehman, T. A., Watkins, N. G., and Thorpe, S. R. 1986, Studies on glycation of proteins and Maillard reactions of glycated proteins under physiological conditions. *Dev. Food Sci.* **13**, 421–431.

Benzing-Purdie, L., and Ripmeester, J. A. 1983. Melanoidin and soil organic matter; Evidence of strong similarities revealed by ^{13}C CP-MAS NMR. *Soil Sci. Soc. Am. J.* **47**, 56–61.

Benzing-Purdie, L., Ripmeester, J. A., and Preston, C. P. 1983. Elucidation of the nitrogen forms in melanoidins and humic acid by nitrogen-15 cross polarization–magnetic angle spinning nuclear magnetic resonance spectrometry. *J. Agric. Food Chem.* **31**, 913–5.

Benzing-Purdie, L. M., and Ratcliff, C. I. 1986. A study of the Maillard reaction by ^{13}C and ^{15}N CP-MAS NMR: Influence of time, temperature, and reactants on major products. *Dev. Food Sci.* **13**, 193–205.

Bielski, B. H. J. 1982. Chemistry of ascorbic radicals. *Adv. Chem. Ser.* **200**, 81–100.

Chan, R. I. M., Stich, H. F., Rosin, M. P., and Powrie, W. D. 1982. Antimutagenic activity of browning reaction products. *Cancer Lett.* **15**, 27–33.

Cho, R. K., Okitani, A., and Kato, H. 1986. Polymerization of acetylated lysozyme and impairment of their amino acid residues due to α-dicarbonyl and α-hydroxycarbonyl compounds. *Agric. Biol. Chem.* **50**, 1373–1380.

Coggiola, I. M. 1963. 2,5-Dihydro-2-furoic acid: A product of the anaerobic decomposition of ascorbic acid. *Nature (London)* **200**, 954–955.

Commoner, B., Vithayathil, A. J., Dolara, P., Nair, S., Madyastha, P., and Cuca, G. C. 1978. Formation of mutagens in beef and beef extract during cooking. *Science* **201**, 913–916.

Coughlin, J. R., Russel, G. F., Wei, C. I., and Hsieh, D. P. H. 1979. Formation of *N*-nitrosamine from Maillard browning reaction products in the presence of nitrite. *Toxicol. Appl. Pharmacol.* **48**, A45.

Counsell, J. N., and Horning, D. H. 1980. "Vitamin C (Ascorbic Acid)." Applied Science Publ.

Curphey, T. J., and Prasad, K. S. 1972. Diquaternary salts. I. Preparation and characterization of the diquaternary salts of some diazines and diazoles. *J. Org. Chem.* **37**, 2259–2266.

Danehy, J. P. 1985. Maillard reactions: Nonenzymatic browning in food systems with special reference to the development of flavor. *Adv. Food Res.* **30**, 77–138.

Dolara, P., Commoner, B., Vithayathil, A., Cuca, G., Tuley, E., Madyastha, P., Nair, S., and Kriebel, D. 1979. The effect temperature on the formation of mutagens in heated beef stock and cooked ground beef. *Mutat. Res.* **60**, 231–237.

Doll, R., and Peto, R. 1981. The causes of cancer: Quantitative estimate of avoidable risks of cancer in the United States today. *J. Natl. Cancer Inst.* **66**, 1191–1308.

Eichner, K. 1981. Antioxidative effect of Maillard reaction intermediates. *Prog, Food Nutr. Sci.* **5**, 441–451.

Erbersdobler, H. F. 1986. Twenty years of furosine. Better knowledge about significance of Maillard reaction in food and nutrition. *Dev. Food Sci.* **13**, 481–491.

Eriksson, C., ed. 1981. Maillard reactions in food. *Prog. Food Nutr. Sci.* **5**, ■■–■■.

Evans, C. D., Mosa, H. A., Cooney, P. M., and Hodge, J. E. 1958. Amino-hexose-reductones as antioxidants, I. Vegetable oils. *J. Am. Oil Chem. Soc.* **35**, 84–88.

Feather, M. S. 1970. The conversion of D-xylose and D-glucuronic acid to 2-furaldehyde. *Tetrahedron Lett.* 4143–4147.

Feather, M. S. 1981. Amine-assisted sugar dehydration reactions. *Prog. Food Nutr. Sci.* **5**, 37–45.

Feather, M. S., and Harris, J. F. 1973. Dehydration reactions of carbohydrates. *Adv. Carbohydr. Chem.* **28**, 161–224.

Feather, M. S., and Hung, R. D. 1985. Maillard polymer derived from D-glucose-1- and -6-^{14}C, glycone-1- and -2-^{14}C, and S-methyl-^{14}C methionine. *J. Carbohydr. Chem.* **4**, 363–368.

Feather, M. S., and Hung, R. D. 1986. Some studies on a Maillard polymer derived from L-alanine and D-glucose. *Dev. Food Sci.* **13**, 183–192.

Feather, M. S., and Russell K. R. 1969. Deuterium incorporation during the conversion of 1-amino-1-deoxy-D-fructose derivatives to 5-(hydroxymethyl)-2-furaldehyde. *J. Org. Chem.* **34**, 2650–2652.

Feeney, R. E., Blankenhorn, G., and Dixon, H. B. F. 1975. Carbonyl–amine reactions in protein chemistry. *Adv. Protein Chem.* **29**, 135–203.

Findley, J. D., Higginbottom, C., Smith, J. A. B., and Lea, C. H. 1946. The effect of the preheating temperature on the bacterial count and storage life of whole milk powder spray-dried by the Krause process. *J. Dairy Res.* **14**, 378–399.

Finot, P. A., and Mauron, J. 1969. Le blocage de la réaction de Maillard. I. Synthèse de *N*-(desoxy-1-D-fructosyl-1) et *N*-(desoxy-1-D-lactosyl-1)-L-lysines. *Helv. Chim. Acta.* **52**, 1488–95.

Fors, S. 1983. Sensory properties of volatile Maillard reaction products and related compounds: A literature review. *ACS Syme. Ser.* **215**, 185–286.

Franke, C., and Iwainsky, H. 1954. Zur antioxidativen Wirksamkeit der Melanoidine. *Dtsch. Lebensm. Rundsch.* **50**, 251–254.

Fujimaki, M., Kato, H., and Kurata, T. 1969. Pyrolysis of sulfur-containing amino acids. *Agric. Biol. Chem.* **33**, 1144–1151.

Fujimaki, M., Namiki, M., and Kato, H., eds. 1986. Amino–carbonyl reactions in food and biological systems. *Dev. Food Science* **13** (Elsevier).

Gottschalk, A. 1952. Some biochemically relevant properties of *N*-substituted fructosamines derived from *N*-glycosylamino acids and *N*-arylglucosylamines. *Biochem. J.* **52**, 455–460.

Griffith, T., and Johnson, J. A. 1957. Relation of the browning reaction to storage stability of sugar cookies. *Cereal Chem.* **34**, 159–169.

Harris, L. A., and Olcott, H. S. 1966. Reaction of aliphatic tertiary amines with hydroperoxides. *J. Am. Oil Chem. Soc.* **43**, 11–14.

Hashiba, H. 1976. Participation of Amadori rearrangement products and carbonyl compounds in oxygen-dependent browning of soy sauce. *J. Agric. Food Chem.* **24**, 70–73.

Hashiba, H. 1978. Isolation and identification of Amadori compounds from soy sauce. *Agric. Biol. Chem.* **42**, 763–768.

Hashiba, H. 1986. Oxidative browning of Amadori compounds. Color formation by iron with Maillard reaction products. *Dev. Food Sci.* **13**, 155–164.

Hashiba, H., Okuhara, A., and Iguchi, N. 1981. Oxygen-dependent browning of soy sauce and some brewed products. *Prog. Food Nutr. Sci.* **5**, 93–113.

Hayase, F., and Kato, H. 1986. Low-molecular Maillard reaction products and their formation mechanism. *Dev. Food Sci.* **13**, 39–48.

Hayashi, T., and Namiki, M. 1980. Formation of two carbon sugar fragment at an early stage of the browning reaction with amine. *Agric. Biol. Chem.* **44**, 2575–2580.

Hayashi, T., and Namiki, M. 1981. On the mechanism of free radical formation during browning reaction of sugar with amino compounds. *Agric. Biol. Chem.* **45**, 933–939.

Hayashi, T., and Namiki, M. 1986a. Role of sugar fragmentation in an early stage browning of amino–carbonyl reaction of sugar with amino acids. *Agric. Biol. Chem.* **50**, 1965–1970.

Hayashi, T., and Namiki, M. 1986b. Role of sugar fragmentation in the Maillard reaction. *Dev. Food Sci.* **13**, 29–38.

Hayashi, T., and Shibamoto, T. 1985. Analysis of methylglyoxal in foods and beverages. *J. Agric. Food Chem.* **33**, 1090–1093.

Hayashi, T., Ohta, Y., and Namiki, M. 1977. Electron spin resonance spectral study on the structure of the novel free radical products formed by the reactions of sugars with amino acids or amines. *J. Agric. Food Chem.* **25**, 1282–1287.

Hayashi, T., Hirata, T., Yano, M., and Namiki, M. 1978. Free radicals formed by the reaction of ninhydrin with alkylamines. *Agric. Biol. Chem.* **42**, 83–87.

Hayashi, T., and Namiki, M. 1979. Tri(2-deoxy-2-L-ascorbyl)amine: A novel compound related to a fairly stable free radical. *Tetrahedron Lett.* **46**, 4467–4470.

Hayashi, T., Manou, F., Namiki, M., and Tsuji, K. 1981. Structure and interrelation of the free radical species and its precursor produced by the reaction of dehydro-L-ascorbic acid and amino acids. *Agric. Biol. Chem.* **45**, 711–716.

Hayashi, T., Hoshi, Y., and Namiki, M. 1983a. On the yellow product and browning of the reaction of dehydroascorbic acid with amino acids. *Agric. Biol. Chem.* **47**, 1003–1007.

Hayashi, T., Namiki, M., and Tsuji, K. 1983b. Formation mechanism of the free radical product and its precursor by the reaction of dehydro-L-ascorbic acid with amino acid. *Agric. Biol. Chem.* **47**, 1955–1960.

Hayashi, T., Hoshi, Y., and Namiki, M. 1984. Purple pigment produced by the reaction of dehydro-L-ascorbic acid with phenylalanine. *Agric. Biol. Chem.* **48**, 2377–2378.

Hayashi, T., Mase, S., and Namiki, M. 1985a. Formation of the *N*,*N*'-dialkylpyrazine cation radical from glyoxal dialkylimine produced on reaction of a sugar with an amine or amino acid. *Agric. Biol. Chem.* **49**, 3131–3137.

Hayashi, T., Reece, C. A., and Shibamoto, T. 1985b. A new analytical method for volatile aldehyde. *ACS Symp. Ser.* **289**, 61–78.

Hayashi, T., Mase, S., and Namiki, M. 1986a. Formation of three-carbon sugar fragment at an early stage of the browning reaction of sugar with amines or amino acids. *Agric. Biol. Chem.* **50**, 1959–1964.

Hayashi, T., Terao, A., Ueda, S., and Namiki, M. 1986b. Red pigment formation by the reaction of oxidized ascorbic acid and protein in a food model system of low moisture content. *Agric. Biol. Chem.* **49**, 3139–3144.

Hayatsu, H., Oka, T., Wakata, A., Ohara, Y., Hayatsu, T., Kobayashi, H., and Arimoto, S. 1983. Adsorption of mutagens to cotton bearing covalently bound trisulfocopper-phthalocyanine. *Mutat. Res.* **119**, 233–238.

Herbert, R. W., Hirst, E. L., Percival, E. G. V., Reynolds, R. J. W., and Smith, F. 1933. Constitution of ascorbic acid. *J. Chem. Soc.* **1933**, 1270–1279.

Heyns, K., and Paulsen, H. 1959. Über "Fructose-aminosäuren" und "Glucose-aminosäuren" in Leberextrakten. *Liebigs Ann. Chem.* **622**, 160–174.

Heyns, K., Röper, H., und Koch, H. 1974. Zur Frage der Entstehung von Nitrosaminen bei der Reaktion von Monosacchariden mit Aminosäuren (Maillard reaktion) in Gegenwart von Natrium Nitrite. *Z. Lebensm. Unters. Forsch.* **154**, 193–200.

Heyns, K., Röper, S., Röper, H., and Meyer, B. 1979. *N*-nitroso sugar amino acids. *Angew. Chem. Int. Ed. Engl.* **18**, 878–380.

Hicks, K. B., and Feather, M. S. 1975. Studies on the mechanism of formation 4-hydroxy-5-methyl-3(2H)-furanone, a component of beef flavor, from Amadori products. J. Agric. Food. Chem. 23, 957–960.

Hodge, J. E. 1953. Chemistry of browning reaction in model systems. J. Agric. Food Chem. 1, 928–943.

Hodge, J. E. 1967. Origin of flavors in food. Nonenzymatic browning reactions. In "Chemistry and Physiology of Flavors" (H. W. Schulz, E. A. Day, and L. M. Libbey, eds.), pp. 465–491. AVI Publ., Westport, Connecticut.

Hodge, J. E., Fisher, B. E., and Nelson, E. C. 1963. Dicarbonyls, reductones and heterocyclics produced by reaction of reducing sugars with secondary amine salts. Proc. Amr. Soc. Brew. Chem. 84–88.

Hodge, J. E., Mills, F. D., and Fisher, B. E. 1972. Compounds of browning flavor derived from sugar–amine reactions. Cereal Sci. Today 17, 34–40.

Huelin, F. E., Coggiola, I. M., Sidhu, G. S., and Kennett, B. H. 1971. Anaerobic decomposition of ascorbic acid in the pH range of foods and in more acidic solution. J. Sci. Food Agric. 22, 540–542.

Hurrell, R. F. 1982. Maillard reaction in flavour. Dev. Food Sci. 3A, 399–437.

Hutton, J. J., and Hackney, C. 1975. Metabolism of cigarette smoke condensates by human and rat homogenates to form mutagens detectable by Salmonella typhimurium TA1538. Cancer Res. 35, 2461–2468.

Igarashi, K., and Yasui, T. 1985. Oxidation of free methionine and methionine residues in protein involved in the browning reaction of phenolic compounds. Agric. Biol. Chem. 49, 2309–2315.

Inoue, T., Morita, K., and Kada, T. 1981. Purification and properties of a plant desmutagenic factor for the mutagenic principle of tryptophan pyrolysate. Agric. Biol. Chem. 45, 345–353.

Ito, N., Fukushima, S., Hagiwara, A., Shibata, M., and Ogiso, T. 1983a. Carcinogenicity of butylated hydroxyanisole in F344 rats. J. Natl. Cancer Inst. 70, 343–352.

Ito, N., Fukushima, S., Imada, K., Sakata, T., and Masui, T. 1983b. Induction of papilloma in the forestomach of hamsters by butylated hydroxyanisole. Gann 74, 459–461.

Itoh, H., Kawashima, K., and Chibata, I. 1975. Antioxidant acitvity of browning products of triose sugar and amino acids. Agric. Biol. Chem. 39, 283–284.

Iwainsky, H., and Franke, C. 1956. Zur Antioxydativen wirkung der Melanoidine. Dtsch. Lebensm. Rundsch. 52, 129–133.

Jägerstad, M., Laser, A., Reutersward, R., Oste, R., Dahlqvist, A., Grivas, S., Olsson, K., and Nyhammer, T. 1983. Creatinine and Maillard reaction products as precursors of mutagen compounds formed in fried beef. ACS Symp. Ser. 215, 507–519.

Jägerstad, M., Olsson, K., Grivas, S., Negishi, C., Wakabayashi, K., Tsuda, M., Sato, S., and Sugimura, T. 1984. Formation of 2-amino-3,8-dimethylimidazo[4,5-f]quinoxaline in a model system by heating a mixture of creatine, glycine and glucose. Mutat. Res. 126, 239–244.

Johnson, P. E., Lykken, G., Mahalko, J., Milne, D., Inman, L., Garcia, W. J., and Inglett, G. E. 1983. The effect of browned and unbrowned corn products on absorption of xinc, iron, and copper in humans. ACS Symp. Ser. 215, 3349–3360.

Kada, T., Tuchikawa, K., and Sadaie, Y. 1972. In vitro and host-mediated "rec-assay" procedures for screening chemical mutagens; and phloxine, a mutagenic red dye detected. Mutat. Res. 16, 165–174.

Kada, T., Morita, K., and Inoue, T. 1978. Anti-mutagenic action of vegetable factor(s) on the mutagenic principle of tryptophan pyrolysate. Mutat. Res. 53, 351–353.

Kada, T., Inoue, T., and Namiki, M. 1982. Environmental desmutagens and antimutagens. In "Environmental Mutagenesis, Carcinogenesis, and Plant Biology" (E. J. Klekowski, Jr., ed.), Vol. 1, pp. 133–51.

Kajita, T., and Senda, M. 1972. Simutaneous determination of L-ascorbic acid, triose reductone and their related compounds in foods by polarographic method. *Nippon Nogeikagakukai-shi* **46**, 137–145.

Karel, M., Tannenbaum, S. R., Wallancee, D. H., and Maloney, H. 1966. Autoxidation of methyl linoleate in freeze-dried model systems III. Effect of added amino acids. *J. Food Sci.* **31**, 892–896.

Kasai, H., Yamaizumi, Z., Wakabayashi, K., Nagao, M., Sugimura, T., Yokoyama, S., Miyazawa, T., Springer, N. E., Weisburger, J. H., and Nishimura, S. 1980a. Potent novel mutagens produced by broiling fish under normal conditions. *Proc. Jpn. Acad.* **56B**, 278–283.

Kasai, H., Yamaizumi, Z., Wakabayashi, K., Nagao, M., Sugimura, T., Yokoyama, S., Miyazawa, T., and Nishimura, S. 1980b. Structure and chemical synthesis of Me-IQ, a potent mutagen isolated from broiled fish. *Chem. Lett.* 1391–1394.

Kasai, H., Yamaizumi, Z., Shimoi, T., Yokoyama, S., Miyazawa, T., Wakabayashi, K., Nagao, M., Sugimura, T., and Nishimura, S. 1981a. Structure of a potent mutagen isolated from fried beef. *Chem. Lett.* 485–488.

Kasai, H., Shimoi, T., Sugimura, T., and Nishimura, S. 1981b. Synthesis of 2-amino-3,8-dimethylimidazol[4,5-f] quinoxaline (Me-IQx), a potent mutagen isolated from fried beef. *Chem. Lett.* 675–678.

Kasai, H., Kumeno, K., Yamaizumi, Z., Nishimura, S., Nagao, M., Fujita, Y., Sugimura, T., Nukaya, H., and Kosuge, T. 1982. Mutagenicity of methylglyoxal in coffee. *Gann* **73**, 681–683.

Kashimura, N., Morita, J., Sato, I., Kumazawa, Z., Nishikawa, S., Ito, S., Koma, Y., and Komada, M. 1986. DNA cleavage reaction and in vitro virus-inactivating action of partially substituted reducing sugar. *Dev. Food Sci.* **13**, 401–410.

Kato, H. 1960. Isolation and characterization of new carbonyl compounds, 3-deoxyosones formed from N-glycosides and their significance for browning reaction. *Agric. Biol. Chem.* **24**, 1–12.

Kato, H. 1963. Identification of D-glucosone formed by oxidative browning degradation of N-glucoside. *Agric. Biol. Chem.* **27**, 461–466.

Kato, H., and Fujimaki, M. 1968. Formation of N-substituted pyrrole-2-aldehydes in the browning reaction between D-xylose and amino compounds. *J. Food Sci.* **33**, 445–449.

Kato, H., and Tsuchida, H. 1981. Estimation of melanoidin structure by pyrolysis and oxidation. *Prog. Food Nutr. Sci.* **5**, 147–156.

Kato, H., Kim, S. B., and Hayase, F. 1986. Estimation of the partial chemical structures of melanoidins by oxidative degradation and ^{13}C CP-MAS NMR. *Dev. Food Sci* **13**, 215–223.

Kawamura, S. 1983. Seventy years of the Maillard reaction. *ACS Symp. Ser.* **215**, 3–18.

Kawashima, K., Itoh, H., and Chibata, I. 1977. Antioxidant activity of browning products prepared from low molecular carbonyl compounds and amino acids. *J. Agric. Food. Chem.* **25**, 202–3.

Kier, L. D., Yamazaki, E., and Ames, B. N. 1974. Detection of mutagenic activity in cigarette smoke condensate. *Proc. Natl. Acad. Sci. U.S.A.* **71**, 4159–4163.

Kim, S. B., Hayase, F., and Kato, H. 1985. Decolorization and degradation products of melanoidins on ozonolysis. *Agric. Biol. Chem.* **49**, 785–792.

Kim, S. B., Hayase, F., and Kato, H. 1986. Desmutagenic effects of melanoidins against amino acid and protein pyrolyzates. *Dev. Food Sci.* **13**, 383–392.

Kinae, N., Yamashita, M., Takahashi, M., Ooishi, H., Tomita, I., and Kanamori, H. 1986. Isolation of β-carboline derivatives from Maillard reaction mixtures that are mutagenic after nitrite treatment. *Dev. Food Sci.* **13**, 343–352.

Kirigaya, N., Kato, H., and Fujimaki, M. 1968. Studies on antioxidant activity of nonenzymatic browning reaction products. Part I. Relations of color intensity and reductones with antioxidant activity of browning reaction products. *Agric. Biol. Chem.* **32**, 287–290.

Kirigaya, N., Kato, H., and Fujimaki, M. 1969. Studies on antioxidant activity of nonenzymatic browning reaction products. Part II. Antioxidant activity of nondialylyzable browning reaction products. *Nippon Nogei Kagaku Kaishi* **43**, 484–491.

Kitaoka, S., and Onodera, K. 1962. Oxidative cleavages of 1,2-Diaminosugars and their significance in the amino–carbonyl reactions. *Agric. Biol. Chem.* **26**, 572–580.

Komano, T., Nanjou, S., Ueda, K., and Fujii, S. 1986. Sequence-specific alkali-labile damage induced in DNA by D-isoglucosamine. *Dev. Food Sci.* **13**, 393–400.

Koppanyi, T., Vivino, A. E., and Veitch, Jr., F. P. 1945. A reaction of ascorbic acid with α-amino acids. *Science* **101**, 541–542.

Kort, M. J. 1970. Reactions of free sugars with aqueous ammonia. *Adv. Carbohydr. Chem. Biochem.* **25**, 143–153.

Krönig, U., and Severin, Th. 1972. Formation of pyrrole derivatives from pentoses and alkylammonium salts. *Chem. Mikrobiol. Tech. Lebensm.* **2**, 49.

Kuhn, R., Kruger, G., Haas, H. J., and Seeliger, A. 1961. Pyrazinbildung aus aminozuckern. *Ann. Dtsch. Chem. Ges.* **644**, 122–127.

Kurata, T., and Fujimaki, M. 1974. Monodehydro-2,2'-iminodi-2(2')-deoxy-L-ascorbic acid, a radical product from the reaction of dehydro-L-ascorbic acid with α-amino acid. *Agric. Biol. Chem.* **38**, 1981–1988.

Kurata, T., and Fujimaki, M. 1976. Formation of 3-keto-4-deoxypentosone and 3-hydroxy-2-pyrone by degradation of dehydro-L-ascorbic acid. *Agric. Biol. Chem.* **40**, 1287–1291.

Kurata, T., and Sakurai, Y. 1967a. Degradation of L-ascorbic acid and mechanism of non-enzymic browning reaction. Part II. Non-oxidative degradation of L-ascorbic acid including the formation of 3-deoxy-L-pentosone. *Agric. Biol. Chem.* **31**, 170–176.

Kurata, T., and Sakurai, Y. 1967b. Degradation of L-ascorbic acid and mechanism of non-enzymic browning reaction. Part III. Oxidative degradation of L-ascorbic acid (degradation of dehydro-L-ascorbic acid). *Agric. Biol. Chem.* **31**, 177–184.

Kurata, T., Wakabayashi, H., and Sakurai, Y. 1967. Degradation of L-ascorbic acid and mechanism of non-enzymic browning reaction. Part I. Browning reactivities of L-ascorbic acid and dehydro-L-ascorbic acid. *Agric. Biol. Chem.* **31**, 101–105.

Kurata, T., Fujimaki, M., and Sakurai, Y. 1973a. Red pigment produced by the reaction of dehydro-L-ascorbic acid with α-amino acid. *Agric. Biol. Chem.* **37**, 1471–1477.

Kurata, T., Fujimaki, M., and Sakurai, Y. 1973b. Red pigment produced by the oxidation of L-scorbamic acid. *J. Agric. Food Chem.* **21**, 676–680.

Kurata, T., Imai, T., and Arakawa, N. 1986. The structure of red pigment having murexide type chromophore. *Dev. Food Sci.* **13**, 67–75.

Lagercrantz, C. 1964. Formation of stable free radicals in alkaline solutions of some monosaccharides. *Acta Chem. Scand.* **18**, 1321–1324.

Lang, K., and Baessler, K. H. 1971. Formation of toxic substances by heat sterilization of food. *Wiss. Veroefftent. Dtsch. Ges. Ernaehr.* **21**, 90–96.

Lecocq, J. 1951. Tetronic acid-formation of pyrazine derivatives from α-amino-γ-methyltetronic acid. *Bull. Soc. Chim. Fr.*, 183–187.

Ledl, F. 1982. Untersuchung zur Bildung fäbiger Produkte bei Braunungsreaktionen: Umsetzung von Hydroxyaceton mit Furfurol. *Z. Legensm. Unters. Forsch.* **175**, 203–207.

Ledl, F., and Fritsch, G. 1984. Bildung von Pyrrolinonreduktonen beim Erhitzen von Hexosen mit Aminosären. *Z. Lebens. Unters. Forsch.* **178**, 41–44.

Ledl, F., and Severin, T. H. 1978. Browning reactions of pentoses with amines. *Z. Lebensm. Unters. Forsch.* **167**, 410.

Ledl, F., and Severin, T. H. 1981. Investigation of a xylose– and glucose–methylammonium acetate reaction mixture. *Prog. Food Nutr. Sci.* **5**, 65–69.

Ledl, F., Hiebl, J., and Severin, Th. 1983. Bildung fäbiger β-Pyranone aus Pentosen and Hexosen. *Z. Lebensm. Unters. Forsch.* **177**, 353–355.

Ledl, F., Fritsch, G., Hiebl, J., Pachmayr, O., and Severin. Th. 1986a. Degradation of Maillard products. *Dev. Food Sci.* **13**, 173–182.

Ledl, F., Ellrich, G., and Klostermeyer, H. 1986b. Nachweiss und Identifizierung einer neuen Maillard-Verbindung in erhitzter Milch. *Z. Lebensm. Unters. Forsch.* **182**, 19–24.

Lee, T. C., Kimiagar, M., Pintauro, S. J., and Chichester, C. O. 1981. Physiological and safety aspects of Maillard browning of foods. *Prog. Food Nutr. Sci.* **5**, 243–256.

Lin, J. Y., Wang, H. I., and Yen, Y.-C. 1979. The mutagenicity of soy bean sauce. *Food Cosmet. Toxicol.* **21**, 329–331.

Ling, A. R. 1908. Malting. *J. Inst. Brew.* **14**, 494–521.

Lingnert, H. 1980. Antioxidative Maillard reaction products. III. Application in cookies. *J. Food Proc. Preserv.* **4**, 219–233.

Lingnert, H., and Eriksson, C. E. 1980a. Antioxidative Maillard reaction products. I. Products from sugars and free amino acids. *J. Food Process. Preserv.* **4**, 161–172.

Lingnert, H., and Eriksson, C. E. 1980b. Antioxidative Maillard reaction products. II. Products from sugars and peptides or protein hydrolysates. *J. Food Process. Preserv.* **4**, 173–181.

Lingnert, H., and Eriksson, C. E. 1981. Antioxidative effect of Maillard reaction products. *Prog. Food. Nutr. Sci.* **5**, 453–566.

Lingnert, H., and Eriksson, C. E. 1983. Characterization of antioxidive Maillard reaction products from histidine and glucose. *ACS Symp. Ser.* **215**, 335–345.

Lingnert, H., and Hall, G. 1986. Formation of antioxidative Maillard reaction products during food processing. *Dev. Food Sci.* **13**, 273–279.

Lingnert, H., and Lundgren, B. 1980. Antioxidative Maillard reaction products IV. Application in sausage. *J. Food Proc. Preserv.* **4**, 235–246.

Loncin, M., Bimbenet, J. J., and Lengen, J. 1968. Influence or the activity of water on the spoilage of foodstuffs. *J. Food Technol.* **3**, 131–142.

McCann, J., Choi, E., Yamazaki, E., and Ames, B. N. 1975. Detection of carcinogens as mutagens in the Salmonella/microsome test: Assay of 300 chemicals. *Proc. Natl. Acad. Sci. U.S.A.* **72**, 5135–5139.

MacDonald, W. C., and Dueck, J. W. 1976. Long-term effect of shoyu (Japanese soy sauce) on the gastric mucosa of the rat. *J. Natl. Cancer Inst.* **56**, 1143–1147.

Maga, J. A. 1982. Pyrazines in flavour. *Adv. Food Sci.* **3A**, 283–323.

Maillard, L. C. 1911. Condensation des acides amines en presence de la glycerine: Cycloglycylglycine et polypeptides. *C.R. Hebd. Seances Acad. Sci.* **153**, 1078–1080.

Maillard, L. C. 1912a. Action des acides amines sur les sucres: Formation des melanoidines par voie methodique. *C.R. Hebd. Seances Acad. Sci.* **154**, 66–68.

Maillard, L. C. 1912b. Formation d'humus et de combustibles mineraux sans intervention de l'oxygène atmosphérique des microorganismes, des hautes températures, ou des fortes pressions. *C.R. Hebd. Seances Acad. Sci.* **155**, 1554–1556.

Marcuse, R. 1962. Effect of some amino acids on the oxidation of linoleic acid and its methyl ester. *J. Am. Oil Chem. Soc.* **39**, 97 103.

Martell, A. E. 1982. Chelates of ascorbic acid. Formation and catalytic properties. *Adv. Chem. Ser.* **200**, 153–178.

Masuda, Y., Mori, K., and Kuratsune, M. 1966. Polycyclic aromatic hydrocarbons in common Japanese foods. I. Broiled fish, roasted barley, shoyu, and caramel. *Gann* **57**, 133–142.

Matsumoto, T., Yoshida, D., Mizusaki, S., and Okamoto, H. 1977. Mutagenic activity of amino acid pyrolysates in *Salmonella typhimurium* TA 98. *Mutat. Res.* **48**, 279–286.

Matsumoto, T., Yoshida, D., Mizusaki, S., and Okamoto, H. 1978. Mutagenicities of the pyroly-
   zates of peptides and proteins. *Mutat. Res.* **56**, 281–288.
Matsushita, S., and Ibuki, F. 1965. Antioxidant and prooxidant abilities of some biological sub-
   stances and physiologically active substances on the oxidation of unsaturated fatty acids. *Agric.
   Biol. Chem.* **29**, 792–795.
Mauron, J. 1981. The Maillard reaction in food: A critical review from the nutritional standpoint.
   Prog. Food Nutr. Sci. **5**, 5–35.
Mester, L., Szabados, M., Mester, M., and Yadav, N. 1981. Maillard type carbonyl–amine reac-
   tions in vivo and their physiological effects. *Prog. Food Nutr. Sci.* **5**, 295–314.
Mihara, S., and Shibamoto, T. 1980. Mutagenicity of products obtained from cysteamine–glucose
   browning model systems. *J. Agric. Food Chem.* **28**, 62–66.
Milic, B. L. J., and Piletic, M. 1984. The mechanism of pyrrole, pyrazine and pyridine formation in
   non-enzymatic browning reaction. *Food Chem.* **13**, 165–180.
Milic, B. L. J., Piletic, M. V., Grujic-Injac, B., and Cembic, S. M. 1980. Kinetic behaviour of free
   radical formation in the nonenzymatic browning reaction. *J. Food Process. Preserv.* **4**, 13–26.
Mirvish, S. S. 1981. Inhibition of the formation of carcinogenic *N*-nitroso compounds by ascorbic
   acid and other compounds. *In* "Cancer: Achievements, Challenges, and Prospects for the
   1980s" (J. H. Burchenal and H. F. Oettgen, eds), pp. 557–587.
Mirvish, S. S., Laurence, W., Michael, E., and Philippe, S. 1972. Ascorbate–nitrite reaction.
   Possible means of blocking the formation of carcinogenic *N*-nitroso compound. *Science* **177**,
   65–68.
Mitsuda, H., Yasumoto, K., and Yokoyama, K. 1965. Studies on the free radical in amino–carbonyl
   reaction. *Agric. Biol. Chem.* **29**, 751–756.
Mizusaki, S., Okamoto, H., Akiyama, A., and Fukuhara, Y. 1977. Relation between chemical
   constituents of tobacco and mutagenic activity of cigarette smoke condensate. *Mutat. Res.* **48**,
   319–326.
Moll, N., and Gross, B. 1981. Isolation and purification of Amadori compounds by semi-preparative
   reversed phase high-performance liquid chromatography. *J. Chromatogr.* **206**, 186–191.
Moll, N., Gross, B., Vinh, T., and Moll, M. 1982. A full automated high-performance liquid
   chromatographic procedure for isolation and purification of Amadori compounds. *J. Agric.
   Food Chem.* **30**, 782–786.
Monnier, V. M., and Cerami, A. 1983. Nonenzymatic glycosylation and browning of proteins in
   vivo. *ACS Symp. Ser.* **215**, 431–449.
Morita, K., Hara, M., and Kada, T. 1978. Studies on natural desmutagens: Screening for vegetable
   and fruit factors active in inactivation of mutagenic pyrolysis products from amino acids. *Agric.
   Biol. Chem.* **43**, 1235–1238.
Morita, K., Kada, T., and Namiki, M. 1984. A desmutagenic factor isolated from burdock (*Arctium
   lappa* Linne). *Mutat. Res.* **129**, 25–31.
Morita, K., Yamada, H., Iwamoto, S., Satomura, M., and Suzuki, A. 1982. Purification and
   properties of desmutagenic factor from broccoli for mutagenic principle of tryptophan pyrolysates. *J. Food Safety* **4**, 139–150.
Morita, K., Nishijima, Y., and Kada, T. 1985. Chemical nature of a desmutagenic factor from
   burdock (*Arctium lappa* Linne). *Agric. Biol. Chem.* **49**, 925–932.
Nagahara, A., Ohshima, K., and Nasuno, S. 1986. Mutagenicity on Maillard reaction products in
   soy sauce. *Dev. Food Sci.* **13**, 373–382.
Nagao, M., Honda, M., Seino, U., Yahagi, T., and Sugimura, T. 1977a. Mutagenicities of smoke
   condensates and the charred surface of fish and meat. *Cancer Lett.* **2**, 221–226.
Nagao, M., Honda, M., Seino, Y., Yahagi, T., Kawachi, T., and Sugimura, T. 1977b. Mutagenicities of protein pyrolysates. *Cancer Lett.* **2**, 335–340.
Nagao, M., Yahagi, T., Kawachi, T., Sugumura, T., Kosuge, T., Tsuji, K., Wakabayashi, K.,

Mizusaki, S., and Matsumoto, T. 1977c. Comutagenic action of norharman and harman. *Proc. Jpn. Acad.* **53,** 95–98.

Nagao, M., Takahashi, Y., Yamanaka, H., and Sugimura, T. 1979. Mutagens in coffee and tea. *Mutat. Res.* **68,** 101–106.

Nagao, M., Sato, S., and Sugimura, T. 1983. Mutagens produced by heating foods. *ACS Symp. Ser.* **215,** 521–536.

Nakabayashi, T., and Shibata, A. 1967. Formation of red color by dehydrated food in the presence of ascorbic acid. *Nippon Shokuhin Kogyo Gakkaishi.* **14,** 11–14.

Namiki, M., and Hayashi, T. 1975. Development of novel free radicals during the amino–carbonyl reaction of sugars with amino acids. *J. Agric. Food Chem.* **23,** 487–491.

Namiki, M., and Hayashi, T. 1981. Formation of novel free radical products in an early stage of Maillard reaction. *Prog. Food Nutr. Sci.* **5,** 81–91.

Namiki, M., and Hayashi, T. 1983. A new mechanism of the Maillard reaction involving sugar fragmentation and free radical formation. *ACS Symp. Ser.* **215,** 21–46.

Namiki, M., Hayashi, T., and Kawakishi, S. 1973. Free radicals developed in the amino–carbonyl reaction of sugars with amino acids. *Agric. Biol. Chem.* **37,** 2935–2937.

Namiki, M., Yano, M., and Hayashi, T. 1974. Free radical product by the reaction of dehydroascorbic acid with amino acids. *Chem. Lett.* 125–128.

Namiki, M., Hayashi, T., and Ohta, Y. 1977. Novel free radicals formed by the amino–carbonyl reactions of sugars with amino acids, amines, and proteins. *Adv. Exp. Med. Biol.* **86d,** 471–501.

Namiki, M., Hayashi, T., and Shigeta, A. 1982a. Isolation of antioxidant product from the reaction mixture of dehydroascorbic acid with tryptophan and its identification. *Agric. Biol. Chem.* **46,** 1207–1212.

Namiki, M., Shigeta, A., and Hayashi, T. 1982b. Antioxidant effect of the reaction mixture of dehydroascorbic acid with tryptophan. *Agric. Biol. Chem.* **46,** 1199–1206.

Namiki, M., Terao, A., Ueda, S., and Hayashi, T. 1986. Deamination of lysine in protein by reaction with oxidized ascorbic acid or active carbonyl compounds produced by Maillard reaction. *Dev. Food Sci.* **13,** 105–114.

Negishi, C., Wakabayashi, K., Tsuda, M., Sato, S., Sugimura, T., Saito, H., Maeda, M., and Jägerstad, M. 1984. Formation of 2-amino-3,7,8-trimethyl-imidazo[4,5-f]quinoline, a new mutagen, by heating a mixture of creatine, glucose and glycine. *Mutat. Res. Lett.* **140,** 55–59.

Nishioka, H., Nishi, K., and Kyokame, K. 1981. Human saliva inactivates mutagenicity of carcinogens. *Mutat. Res.* **85,** 323–323.

Nursten, H. E., and O'Reilly, R. 1983. Colored compounds formed by the interaction of glycine and xylose. *ACS Symp. Ser.* **215,** 103–121.

Nursten, H. E., and O'Reilly, R. 1986a. The complexity of the Maillard reaction as shown by a xylose–glycine model system. *Dev. Food Sci.* **13,** 17–28.

Nursten, H. E., and O'Reilly, R. 1986b. Coloured compounds formed by the interaction of glycine and xylose. *Food Chem.* **20,** 45–60.

Nyhammar, T., Olsson, K., and Pernemalm, P. A. 1983. Strecker degradation products from (1-^{13}C)-D-Glucose and glycine. *ACS Symp. Ser.* **215,** 71–82.

Nyhammer, T., Grivas, S., Olsson, K., and Jägerstad, M. 1986. Isolation and identification of beef mutagens (IQ compounds) from heated model systems of creatine, fructose and glycine or alanine. *Dev. Food Sci.* **13,** 323–334.

Obata, H., Sato, E., and Tokuyama, T. 1971. Antioxidative effect of reductones on vegetable oils, *Nippon Nogei Kaggakukai-shi* **45,** 489–493.

Obretenov, T., and Argirov, O. 1986. Investigation of the interaction between furfural and glycine methyl ester as a model of Maillard reaction. *Dev. Food Sci.* **13,** 225–232.

Obretenov, T., Ivanov, S., and Peeva, D. 1986. Antioxidative activity of Maillard reaction products obtained from hydrolysates. *Dev. Food Sci.* **13**, 281–290.

Ochiai, M., Wakabayashi, K., Nagao, M., and Sugimura, T. 1984. Tyramine is a major mutagen precursor in soy sauce, being convertible to a mutagen by nitrite. *Gann* **75**, 1–3.

Ohgaki, H., Kusama, K., Matsukura, N., Marino, K., Hasegawa, H., Sato, S., Takayama, S., and Sugimura, T. 1984. Carcinogenicity in mice of a mutagenic compound 2-amino-3-methylimidazo[4,5-f]quinoline, from broiled sardine, cooked beef, and beef extract. *Carcinogenesis* **5**, 921–924.

Ohgaki, H., Hasegawa, H., Kato, T., Suenaga, M., Ubutaka, M., Sato, S., Takayama, S., and Sugimura, T. 1985. Induction of tumors in the forestomach and liver of mice by feeding 2-amino-3,4-dimethylimidazo[4,5-f]quinoline (MeIQ). *Proc. Jpn. Acad.* **61B**, 137–139.

Ohtsuka, M., Kurata, T., and Arakawa, N. 1986. Isolation and characterization of a degradation product derived from 2,3-diketo-L-gulonic acid. *Dev. Food Sci.* **13**, 77–84.

Olsson, K., APernemalm, P., and Theander, O. 1981. Reaction products and mechanism in some simple model systems. *Prog. Food Nutr. Sci.* **5**, 47–55.

Omura, II., Jaha, N., Shinohara, K., and Murakami, H. 1983. Formation of mutagens by the Maillard reactions. *ACS Symp. Ser.* **215**, 537–563.

Pachmeyer, O., Ledl, F., and Secerin, T. 1986. Formation of 1-alkyl-3-oxypyrridinum betaines from sugars XXI. Studies on the Maillard reaction. *Z. Lebensm. Unters. Forsch.* **182**, 294–297.

Pariza, M. W., Ashoor, S. H., Chu, F. S., and Lund, D. B. 1979. Effects of temperature and time on mutagen formation in pan-fried hamburger. *Cancer Lett.* **7**, 63–69.

Park, C. K., and Kim, D. H. 1983. Relationship between fluorescence and antioxidant activity of ethanol extracts of a Maillard browning mixture. *J. Am. Oil Chem. Soc.* **60**, 98–102.

Patton, S. 1955. Browning and associated changes in milk and its products: A review. *J. Dairy Sci.* **38**, 457–478.

Peer, H. G., van den Ouweland, G. A. M., and de Groot, C. N. 1968. The reaction of aldopentoses and secondary amine salts, a convenient method of preparing 4-hydroxy-5-methyl-2,3-dihydrofuran-3-one. *Rec. Trav. Chim. Pay-Bas* **87**, 1011–1016.

Piloty, M., and Baltes, W. 1979a. Untersuchungen zur Reaktion von Aminosäuren mit α-Dicarbonylverbindungen. I. Reaktivitaet von Aminosäeuren bei Reaktion mit α-Dicarbonylverbindungen. *Z. Lebensm. Unters. Forsch.* **168**, 368–373.

Piloty, M., and Baltes, W. 1979b. Untersuchungen zur Reaktion von Aminosauren mit α-Dicarbonylverbindungen. II. Fluechtige Reaktionsprodukte bei der Umsetzung von Aminosaeuren mit Diacetyl (2,3-butandion). *Z. Lebensm. Unters. Forsch.* **168**, 374–380.

Powrie, W. D., Wu, C. H., Rosin, M. P., and Stich, H. F. 1981. Clastogenic and mutagenic activities of Maillard reaction model systems. *J. Food Sci.* **46**, 1433–1438.

Ranganna, S., and Setty, L. 1968. Nonenzymatic discoloration in dried cabbage. Ascorbic acid–amino acid interactions. *J. Agric. Food Chem.* **16**, 529–533.

Reynolds, T. H. 1963. Chemistry of nonenzymic browning. I. The reaction between aldoses and amines. *Adv. Food Res.* **12**, 1–52.

Reynolds, T. H. 1965. Chemistry of nonenzymic browning. II. *Adv. Food Res.* **14**, 167–283.

Röper, H., Röper, S., and Heyns, K. 1983. N.M.R. spectroscopy of *N*-(1-deoxy-D-fructos-1-yl)-L-amino acids ("Fructose-amino acids"). *Carbohydr. Res.* **116**, 183–195.

Russel, G. F. 1983. Nitrite interactions in model Maillard browning systems. *ACS Symp. Ser.* **215**, 83–90.

Sakaguchi, M., and Shibamoto, T., 1979. Isolation of *N*-nitroso-2-methylthiazolidine from a cysteamine–sodium nitrite model system. *Agric. Biol. Chem.* **43**, 667–669.

Saltmach, M., Vagnini-Ferrari, M., and Labuza, T. P. 1981. Theoretical basis and application of kinetics to browning in spray-dried whey food systems. *Prog. Food Nutr. Sci.* **5**, 331–344.

Sato, T., Ose, Y., and Nagase, H. 1986. Desmutagenic effect of humic acid. *Mutat. Res.* **162**, 173–178.

Sato, T., Ose, Y., Nagase, H., and Hayase, K. 1987. Mechanism of the desmutagenic effect of humic acid. *Mutat. Res.* **176**, 199–204.

Scheutwinkel-Reich, M., and von der Hude, W. 1985. Untersuchung zur Mutagenität von Zükercouleuren. *Z. Lebesm. Unters. Forsch.* **181**, 455–457.

Seib, P. A., and Tolbert, B. M. 1982. Ascorbic acid: Chemistry, metabolism and uses. *Adv. Chem. Ser. 200,* American Chemical Society.

Sekizawa, J., and Shibamoto, T. 1980. Mutagenicity of 2-alkyl-nitrosothiazolidine. *J. Agric. Food Chem.* **28**, 781–783.

Severin, T. H., and Seilmeier, W. 1968. Studien zur Maillard-Reaktion III, Unwandlung von Glukose unter dem Einfluss von Methylammoniumacetat. *Z. Lebensm. Unters. Forsch.* **137**, 4–6.

Severin, T., Hiebl, J., und Pop-Ginsbach, H. 1984. Untersuchung zur Maillard-Reaktion. XX. Nachweis von Glycernaldehyd, Dihydroxyaceton und anderen hydrophilen Zuckerabbauprodukten in Caramellisierungsgemischen. *Z. Lebensm. Unters. Forsch.* **178**, 284–287.

Shaw, P. F., and Berry, R. E. 1977. Hexose–amino acid degradation studies involving formation of pyrrols, furans, and other low molecular weight peoducts. *J. Agric. Food Chem.* **25**, 641–644.

Shibamoto, T. 1980. Mutagenicity of 1,5-(or 7)-dimethyl-2,3,6,7-tetrahydro-1H,5H-biscyclopentapyrazine, obtained from a cyclotene/NH$_3$ browning model system. *J. Agric. Food Chem.* **28**, 883–884.

Shibamoto, T. 1982. Occurrence of mutagenic products in browning model systems. *Food Technol.* **36**, 59–62.

Shibamoto, T. 1983a. Heterocyclic compounds in browning and browning/nitrite model systems: Occurrence, formation mechanisms, flavor characteristics and mutagenic activity. In "Instrumental Analysis of Foods," Vol. 1, pp. 229–278.

Shibamoto, T. 1983b. Possible mutagenic constituents in nitrite-treated soy sauce. *Food Cosmet. Toxicol.* **21**, 745–747.

Shinohara, K., Wu, R.-T., Jahan, N., Tanaka, M., Morinaga, N., Murakami, H., and Omura, H. 1980. Mutagenicity of the browning mixtures by amino–carbonyl reactions on *Salmonella tyhimurium* TA 100. *Agric. Biol. Chem.* **44**, 671–672.

Shinohara, K., Jaha, N., Tanaka, M., Yamamoto, K., Wu, R.-T., Murakami, H., and Omura, H. 1983. Formation of mutagens by amino–carbonyl reactions. *Mutat. Res.* **122**, 279–286.

Shinohara, K., Kim. E.-H., and Omura, H. 1986. Furans as the mutagens formed by amino–carbonyl reactions. *Dev. Food Sci.* **13**, 353–362.

Spingarn, N. E., and Weisburger, J. H. 1979. Formation of mutagens in cooked foods. I. *Cancer Lett.* **7**, 259–264.

Spingarn, N. E., Sloncum, L. A., and Weisburger, J. H. 1980. Formation of mutagens in cooked foods. II. *Cancer Lett.* **9**, 7–12.

Stadtman, F. H., Chichester, C. O., and Rooney, C. S. 1952. Carbon dioxide production in the browning reaction. *J. Am. Chem. Soc.* **74**, 3194–3196.

Steelink, C., and Tollin, G. 1962. Stable free radicals in soil humic acid. *Biochim. Biophys. Acta* **59**, 25–34.

Sugimura, T., Sato, S., Nagao, M., Yahagi, T., Matsushima, T., Seino, Y., Takeuchi, M., and Kawachi, T. 1976. Overlapping of carcinogens and mutagens. *Proc. Int. Symp. Princes Takamatsu Cancer Res. Found., 6th* 191–215.

Sugimura, T., Nagao, M., Kawachi, T., Honda, M., Yahagi, T., Scino, Y., Matsushima, T., Shirai, A., Sawamura, M., Sato, S., Matsumoto, H., and Matsukura, N. 1977a. Mutagen-carcinogens in food with special reference to highly mutagenic pyrolytic products in broiled foods. *In* "Origins of Human Cancer" (J. D. Watson and H. Hoatt, eds.), pp. 1561–77. Cold Spring Harbor Laboratory, Cold Spring Harbor, New York.

Sugimura, T., Kawachi, T., Nagao, M., Yahagi, T., Seino, Y., Okamoto, T., Shodo, K., Kosuge, T., Tsuji, K., Wakabayashi, K., Iitaka, Y., and Itai, A. 1977b. Mutagenic principle(s) in tryptophan and phenylalanine pyrolysis products. *Proc. Jpn. Acad.* **53,** 58–61.

Suyama, K., and Adachi, S. 1986. Quaternary pyridinum salts formed by amino–carbonyl reaction and their thermal elimination reaction involving carbocation formation. *Dev. Food Sci.* **13,** 95–103.

Szent-Györgyi, A. 1980. The living state and cancer. *Physiol. Chem. Phys.* **12,** 99–110.

Takagi, M., and Morita, N. 1986. Lysine-catalyzed Maillard browning of sugar-related compounds smaller than tetrose, in neutral and alkaline solutions. *Dev. Food Sci.* **13,** 49–57.

Takayama, S., Nakatsuru, Y., Masuda, M., Ohgaki, H., Sato, S., and Sugimura, T. 1984. Demonstration of carcinogenicity in F344 rats of 2-amino-3-methyl-imidazo[4,5-f]quinoline from broiled sardine, fried beef and beef extract. *Gann* **75,** 467.

Terada, K., and Ohmura, T. 1966. Stability of dehydroascorbate in vitro I. *Nippon Nogeikagaku Kaishi* **40,** 196–200.

Toda, H., Sekizawa, J., and Shibamoto, T. 1981. Mutagenicity of the L-rhamnose–ammonia–hydrogen sulfide browning reaction mixture. *J. Agric. Food Chem.* **29,** 381–384.

Tollin, G., Reid, T., and Steelink, C. 1963. Structure of humic acid IV. Electron paramagnetic resonance studies. *Biochim. Biophys. Acta* **66,** 444–447.

Tomita, Y. 1971a. Studies on antioxidant activity of amino–carbonyl reaction products I. Antioxidant activity of amino acids and browning solutions of amino acid with glucose. *Kagoshima Daigaku Nogakubu Gakujutsu Hokoku.* **21,** 153–160.

Tomita, Y. 1971b. Antioxidant activity of amino–carbonyl reaction products II. Effect of reaction conditions of trypotophan and glucose on the antioxidant activity of the reaction system. *Kagoshima Daigaku Nogakubu Hokoku.* **21,** 161–170.

Tressl, R., Helak, B., Martin, N., and Rewicki, D. 1986. Formation of proline specific Maillard products. *Dev. Food Sci.* **13,** 235–244.

Tsuchida, H., Komoto, M., Kato, H., and Fujimaki, M. 1973. Formation of deoxyfractosazine and its 6-isomer on the browning reaction between glucose and ammonia in weakly acidic medium. *Agric. Biol. Chem.* **37,** 2571–2578.

Tsuchida, H., Komoto, M., Kato, H., and Fujimaki, M. 1975. Isolation of deoxyfructosazine and its 6-isomer from the nondialyzable melanoidin hydrolyzate. *Agric. Biol. Chem.* **39,** 1143–1148.

Tsuchida, H., Komoto, M., Kato, H., and Fujimaki, M. 1976. Differences in formation of pyrazine derivatives from glucose–ammonia reaction between in weakly acidic medium and in strongly alkaline medium. *Nippon Nogeikagakukai-shi* **50,** 187–189.

Tsuchida, H., Morinaka, K., Fujii, S., Komoto, M., and Mizuno, S. 1986. Identification of novel non-volatile pyrazines in commercial caramel colors. *Dev. Food Sci.* **13,** 85–94.

Tsuda, M., Takahashi, Y., Nagao, M., Hirayama, T., and Sugimura, T. 1980. Inactivation of mutagens from pyrolysates of tryptophan and glutamic acid by nitrite in acidic solution. *Mutat. Res.* **78,** 331–339.

Tsuda, M., Wakabayashi, K., Hirayama, T., Kawachi, T., and Sugimura, T. 1983. Inactivation of potent pyrolysate mutagens by chlorinated tap water. *Mutat. Res.* **119,** 27–34.

Tsuji, K., Hayashi, T., and Namiki, M. 1980. Redix reaction of tris(2-deoxy-2-L-ascorbyl)-amine. Formation of a persisting free radical species in water. *Electrochim. Acta* **25,** 605–611.

Ueda, S., Hayashi, T., and Namiki, M. 1986. Effect of ascorbic acid on lipid autoxidation in a model system. *Agric. Biol. Chem.* **50,** 1–7.

Wakabayashi, K., Ochiai, M., Saito, H., Tsuda, M., Suwa, Y., Nagao, M., and Suginura, T. 1983. Presence of 1-methyl-1,2,3,4-tetrahydro-β-carboline-3-carboxylic acid, a precursor of a mutagenic nitroso compound, in soy sauce. *Proc. Natl. Acad. Sci. U.S.A.* **80,** 2912–2916.

Wakabayashi, K., Takahashi, M., Nagao, M., Sato, S., Kinae, N., Tomita, I., and Sugimura, T. 1986. Quantification of mutagenic and carcinogenic heterocyclic amines in cooked foods. *Dev. Food Sci.* **13**, 363–371.

Waller, G. R., and Feather, M. S., eds. 1983. The Maillard reaction in foods and nutrition. *ACS Symp. Ser.* **215.**

Weisburger, J., Reddy, B. S., Hill, P., Cohen, L. A., and Wynder, E. L. 1980. Nutrition and cancer—on the mechanisms bearing on causes of cancer of the colon, breast, prostate, and stomach. *Bull. N.Y. Acad. Med.* **56**, 673–696.

Wiseblatt, L., and Kohn, F. E. 1960. Some volatile aromatic compounds in fresh bread. *Cereal Chem.* **37**, 55–66.

Wolform, M. L., Schlicht, R. C., Langer, A. W., Jr., and Rooney, C. S. 1953. Chemical interactions of amino compounds and sugar VI. The repeating unit in browning polymers. *J. Am. Chem. Soc.* **75**, 1013.

Wu, C. H., Russell, G. F., and Powrie, W. D. 1986. Paramagnetic behavior of model system melanoidins. *Dev. Food Sci.* **13**, 135–145.

Wynder, E. L., and Gori, G. E. 1977. Contribution of the environment to cancer incidence: An epidemiologic exercise. *J. Natl. Cancer Inst.* **58**, 825.

Yamada, M., Tsuda, M., Nagao, M., Mori, M., and Sugimuram T. 1979. Degradtion of mutagens from pyrolysates of tryptophan, glutamic acid and globulin by myeloperoxidase. *Biochem. Biophys. Res. Commun.* **99**, 766–769.

Yamaguchi, N. 1969. Antioxidative activities of browning reaction products and several reductones. *Nippon Shokuhin Kogyo Gakkaishi* **16**, 140–144.

Yamaguchi, N. 1986. Antioxidative activity of the oxidation products prepared from melanoidins. *Dev. Food Sci.* **13**, 291–299.

Yamaguchi, N., and Fujimaki, M. 1974a. Studies on browning reaction products from reducing sugars and amino acids. XV. Comparison of antioxidative activity of melanoidin with that of each tocopherol homologue and synergistic effect of melanoidin on tocopherol. *Nippon Shokuhin Kogyo Gakkaishi* **21**, 13–18.

Yamaguchi, N., and Fujimaki, M. 1974b. Studies on browning reaction products from reducing sugars and amino acids. XVI. Comparison of antioxidative activity and its synergistic effect of melanoidin with tocopherol on margarin. *Nippon Shokuhin Kogyo Gakkaishi* **21**, 280–284.

Yamaguchi, N., and Koyama, Y. 1967a. Studies on browning reaction products from reducing sugars and amino acids. III. Effect of extracts from biscuits and cookies by various solvents on the stability of fat. *Nippon Shokuhin Kogyo Gakkaishi* **14**, 106–109.

Yamaguchi, N., and Koyama, Y. 1967b. Studies on the browning reaction products yielded by reducing sugar and amino-acid. IV. Relationship between potassium ferricyanide-reducing power and stability of lard in cookies. *Nippon Shokuhin Kogyo Gakkaishi* **14**, 110–113.

Yamaguchi, N., Yokoo, Y., and Koyama, Y. 1964. Studies on the browning reaction products yielded by reducing sugar and amino acid. I. Effect of the browning reaction products on the stability of fats contained in biscuits and cookies. *Nippon Shokuhin Kogyo Gakkaishi* **11**, 184–189.

Yamaguchi, N., Koyama, Y., and Fujimaki, M. 1981. Fractionation and antioxidative activity of browning reaction products between D-xylose and glycine. *Prog. Food. Nutr. Sci.* **5**, 429–439.

Yamamoto, T., Tsuji, K., Kosuge, T., Okamoto, T., Shudo, K., Takeda, K., Iitaka, Y., Yamaguchi, K., Seino, Y., Yahagi, T., Nagao, M., and Sugimura, T. 1977. Isolation and structure determination of mutagenic substances in ʟ-glutamic acid pyrolysate. *Proc. Jpn. Acad.* **54B**, 248–250.

Yamashita, N., Shinohara, K., Jahan, N., Torikai, Y., Doira, H., and Omura, H. 1981. Mutagenic action of reductones on pupal oocytes of silkworm. *Eiyo to Shokuryo.* **34**, 367–371.

Yamazaki, I., Mason, H. S., and Piette, L. 1959. Identification of intermediate substrate free radicals formed during peroxidatic oxidations by electron paramagnetic resonance spectroscopy. *Biochem. Biophys. Res. Commun.* **1,** 336–337.

Yano, M., Hayashi, T., and Namiki, M. 1974. On the structure of the free radical products formed by the reaction of dehydroascorbic acid with amino acids. *Chem. Lett.* 1193–1196.

Yano, M., Hayashi, T., and Namiki, M. 1976a. Formation of free-radical products by the reaction of dehydroascorbic acid with amino acid. *J. Agric. Food Chem.* **24,** 815–819.

Yano, M., Hayashi, T., and Namiki, M. 1976b. On the formation of free radical products by the reaction of dehydroascorbic acid with amines. *Agric. Biol. Chem.* **41,** 951–957.

Yano, M., Hayashi, T., and Namiki, M. 1978a. Formation of free radical products by the reaction of dehydroascorbic acid or ninhydrin with aromatic amines. *Agric. Biol. Chem.* **42,** 83–87.

Yano, M., Hayashi, T., and Namiki, M. 1978b. Formation of a precursor of the free radical species in the reaction of dehydroascorbic acid with amino acids. *Agric. Biol. Chem.* **42,** 2239–2243.

Yen, G.-C., and Lee, T.-C. 1986. Mutagenic and nutritional effects of nitrite on Maillard browned casein. *Dev. Food Sci.* **13,** 539–548.

Yoshida, D., and Fukuhara, Y. 1982. Formation of mutagens by heating creatine and amino acids. *Agric. Biol. Chem.* **46,** 1069–1070.

Yoshida, D., and Matsumoto, T. 1978. Changes in mutagenicity of protein pyrolysates by reaction with nitrite. *Mutat. Res.* **58,** 35–40.

Yoshida, D., and Okamoto, H. 1980a. Formation of mutagens by heating creatine and glucose. *Biochem. Biophys. Res. Commun.* **96,** 844–847.

Yoshida, D., and Okamoto, H. 1980b. Formation of mutagens by heating the aqueous solution of amino acids and some nitrogenous compounds with addition of glucose. *Agric. Biol. Chem.* **44,** 2521–2522.

Yoshida, D.. and Okamoto, H. 1980c. Formation of mutagens by heating creatine and amino acids with addition of fatty acids. *Agric. Biol Chem.* **44,** 3025–3027.

Yoshida, D., Matsumoto, T., Yoshimura, R., and Mizusaki, T. 1978. Mutagenicity of amino-α-carbolines in pyrolysis products of soybean globuline. *Biochem. Biophys. Res. Commun.* **83,** 915–920.

Yoshida, D., Saito, Y., and Mizusaki, S. 1984. Isolation of 2-amino-3-methylimidazo[4,5[f]quinoline as mutagen from the heated product of a mixture of creatine. *Agric. Biol. Chem.* **48,** 241–243.

Yuferov, V. P., Froncsz, W., Kharitonenkov, I. G., and Kalmanson, A. E. 1970. Electron paramagnetic resonance study of free radical products of the reaction of ninhydrin with amino acids, peptides, and protein. *Biochim. Biophys. Acta* **200,** 160–167.

FOOD VERSUS BIOMASS FUEL: SOCIOECONOMIC AND ENVIRONMENTAL IMPACTS IN THE UNITED STATES, BRAZIL, INDIA, AND KENYA

DAVID PIMENTEL, ALAN F. WARNEKE, WAYNE S. TEEL,
KIMBERLY A. SCHWAB, NANCY J. SIMCOX, DAN M. EBERT, KIM
D. BAENISCH, AND MARNI R. AARON

College of Agriculture and Life Sciences
Cornell University
Ithaca, New York 14853

I. INTRODUCTION

Food and fuel are essential for human well being and economic development. Biomass energy (fuelwood, dung, crop residues, ethanol) is a major source of fuel in the world (Hall *et al.*, 1982, 1985; Dunkerley and Ramsay, 1983; Vimal and Tyagi, 1984; Pimentel *et al.*, 1986; Hall and de Groot, 1987). Fuel from biomass is especially important in developing nations, where at present about 90% of the energy needs of the poor is from various biomass sources (Chatterji, 1981). A total of 2.5 billion metric tons (t) of forest resources is harvested annually for a variety of uses, including fuel, lumber, and pulp (FAO, 1983a). About 60% of forest residues is harvested in developing nations, and about 85% of this is burned as fuel (De Montalembert and Clement, 1983). Fuelwood makes up about half (1.3 billion t) of the 2.8 billion t of biomass consumed annually worldwide; the remaining half consists of crop residues (33%) and dung (17%) (Pimentel *et al.*, 1986).

If, as projected, over half of the world's oil reserves will be used up by the year 2000, the long-term projection for fossil fuel is additional shortages and higher prices (CEQ, 1980; Crawford, 1987). Current low prices are temporary. The rise in oil prices from 1973 to date has affected all nations, especially developing nations. High fossil fuel prices and growing populations in developing countries have made it necessary for more people to rely on biomass in the form of fuelwood, crop residues, and dung for energy (Dunkerley and Ramsay, 1983; OTA, 1984; Sanchez-Sierra and Umana-Quesada, 1984). In the 8 years from 1972 to 1980, the cost of fuel imported by developing nations rose from 6 to 79 billion dollars (UN, 1983). Estimates are that the poor in developing nations either spend 15–40% of their income for fuel or invest considerable time in collecting biomass fuel (CSE, 1982; Hall, 1985).

Energy use, particularly fossil energy, has played an important role in increasing food production in the world. In the United States, for example, crop yields have increased about 3.5 times during the last 60 years (USDA, 1967, 1985). The fossil energy inputs to achieve this food increase have grown 40-fold or to an input of about 1000 liters of oil equivalents per hectare (Pimentel and Wen Dazhong, 1988). In China, a similar technological change led to a 2-fold increase in food production during the last 30 years, while fossil energy use increased nearly 100-fold or to an input of about 500 liters of oil equivalents per hectare (ha) (Wen Dazhong and Pimentel, 1984).

Energy and population growth are also interrelated. The major increase in human population growth rates during the last 300 to 400 years has coincided with the discovery and use of stored fossil energy resources such as coal, oil, and gas. Since about 1700, rapid population growth has closely paralleled the increased use of fossil fuel for agriculture and improving human health (Fig. 1).

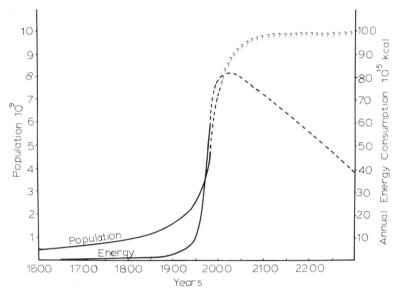

FIG. 1. World population and fossil energy use (——) and projected trends (----) for each (Environmental Fund, 1979; Linden, 1980; USBC, 1982; PRB, 1983).

Never in history have humans, by their sheer numbers, so dominated the earth's land, water, and biological resources. The current world population stands at more than 5 billion and increases by 270,000 each day, which is 83 million more people per year (PRB, 1986).

Associated with the escalating population are growing food shortages. Despite the growth in food production in all nations, food shortages exist in many regions of the world, especially in Africa. This is due both to the increase in the world population and to the unequal distribution of natural resources (CEQ, 1980; Brown et al., 1985). Presently, more than 1 billion humans arc malnourished, and the problem is becoming rapidly more severe (Latham, 1984).

Worldwide, efforts are being made to increase food supplies to help meet the needs of the rapidly growing world population. In addition to increasing fossil energy use for more fertilizers, irrigation, and pesticides, more arable land is being brought under cultivation. An estimated 10 million ha of new agricultural land are added to the total each year. Given that the world's arable lands are limited (Buringh, 1984; Larson, 1986), 10 million ha of forests are cut annually and the land converted to agriculture (Pimentel et al., 1986).

The prime cause of deforestation is the expansion of agriculture (Pimentel et al., 1986). The reduced productivity of the land forces farmers to remove more forests for agricultural production. In addition, the growing use of crop residues and dung as biomass fuels, in turn, causes more soil erosion and loss of vital soil nutrients by their removal from the natural soil cycle.

Erosion and other forms of environmental degradation in agriculture cause the loss of about 6 million ha of cropland each year because of lost productivity (UNEP, 1980; Dudal, 1981; Kovda, 1983; Stocking, 1985). With forests removed to replace this degraded agricultural land (Pimentel *et al.*, 1986), soil erosion is ranked as the most serious environmental problem in the world today (R. Revelle, personal communication).

In addition to soil degradation, water shortages exist in most nations of the world (Biswas, 1984). Nearly 80% of all water consumed annually in the world is for irrigation and agriculture (Biswas and Biswas, 1985). Groundwater aquifers are being mined of their water, and river waters are pumped so severely that, in some instances, their flows are reduced to a trickle (CEQ, 1980). In addition, contamination of vital water resources by fertilizers, sewage, and sediments is also reducing the usefulness and productivity of water resources.

Air pollution is also affecting agriculture, forests, and other vegetation in many parts of the world (CEQ, 1980). Declining amounts of tree cover have been associated with higher levels of atmospheric pollution, which has resulted in increased human disease (Sharma, 1987). Another contributor to human disease is wood smoke produced during cooking and heating with wood. Women and children in developing countries are particularly affected by the smoke, causing eye and lung infections and cancer (Sharma, 1987).

With forests and other vegetation being removed for agriculture, many kinds of plants and animals are being forced into extinction (Hanks, 1987). Reduced biological diversity looms as a serious threat to future agriculture, medicine, and genetic engineering because humans depend upon these biological raw materials (Myers, 1984). Thus, with biological resources declining along with the deterioration of land, water, and atmospheric resources, the state of the environment in all regions of the world appears to be declining.

Food and biomass fuel are interdependent because they require the same resources—land, water, and energy—for production. In addition, food can be converted into fuel and fuel converted into food. Conflicts exist today in the use of land, water, and other environmental resources for food and fuel (biomass energy) production because of resource shortages (Hall, 1985; Brown *et al.*, 1986). The objective of this article is to analyze (1) the benefits and costs of using land, water, and other environmental resources for food and various types of biomass fuel production as well as their interaction, (2) the role of socioeconomic development in the food/fuel interrelationships, (3) the causes of environmental problems in food and fuel production, and (4) the potential (if put into practice) of new technologies and practices for improving the use of biomass for food and fuel production.

II. BIOMASS RESOURCES

This section focuses on the use of biomass as both a food and an energy source in the United States, Brazil, India, and Kenya. These countries were selected because they represent different social and environmental conditions.

A. UNITED STATES

The total land area in the United States covers 9.17 million km² with a human population of over 241 million (Table I). Of the four nations, the United States is the largest in land area and second largest in total population. It has the lowest rate of population growth, but the largest per capita gross national product (GNP) (Table I).

Nearly one-half of the land area in the United States is used for crops and pastures (Table II). The forested area is also quite extensive, totaling 290 million ha. Despite the extensive area covered by biomass, biomass energy provides only about 4% of the total energy used in the United States (Tables II and III). The prime reason for the small percentage for biomass energy is because the United States uses so much fossil or commercial energy. Comparing the per capita use of biomass, the United States, however, ranks third—just ahead of India (Table II).

Fuelwood provides the major source of biomass energy in homes and factories in the United States, accounting for about 97% of the total (Tables III–VII). The second largest quantity of biomass energy used is bagasse in sugar production. The United States converts about 172 million t of biomass for energy use per year, and it has been projected that this quantity could be more than doubled to about 440 million t (ERAB, 1981). This large use of biomass for a fuel was

TABLE I

POPULATION, AREA, AND PER CAPITA GROSS NATIONAL PRODUCT

Country	Estimated population in 1986 (10⁶)[a]	Annual rate of increase (%)[a]	Surface area (10⁶ km²)[b]	Density (habitants/km²)	Gross national product (dollars per capita)[a]
United States	241.0	0.7	9.17	23	14,080
Brazil	143.0	2.3	8.51	17	1,870
India	785.0	2.3	3.28	239	260
Kenya	21.0	4.2	0.58	36	340

[a] PRB (1986).
[b] UN (1976).

TABLE II

LAND DISTRIBUTION BY USES AND POPULATION ENGAGED IN AGRICULTURE

Country	Total area (10⁶ ha)	Cropland (10⁶ ha)	Pasture (10⁶ ha)	Forests and woods (10⁶ ha)	Other land (10⁶ ha)	Percentage of population engaged in agriculture[a]
United States[b]	917	192	300	290	135	2.6
Brazil[c]	851	75	164	568	39	37.0
India[d]	328[c]	143[d]	12[d]	46[e]	127	62.0
Kenya[f]	58	2.3	4	2.4	48.3	75.0

[a] PRB, (1986).
[b] USDA (1985).
[c] FAO (1984).
[d] Bansil (1984).
[e] CSE (1985).
[f] FAO (1984).

projected to have some detrimental effect on food production and the environment.

B. BRAZIL

Brazil is the fifth largest country in the world, occupying a total area of 851 million ha. Its population is 143 million and is increasing at a rate of 2.3% per year (Table I). The per capita GNP is $1870.

The total annual biomass production in Brazil is slightly less than in the United States, followed by India and Kenya (Table V). Approximately 23% of the total annual biomass production in Brazil is being harvested as food and fiber (Table VI). Only 8% of its land, however, is devoted to crops, while 37% of Brazil's

TABLE III

CONSUMPTION OF COMMERCIAL ENERGY (10^{12} KCAL)

Country	Solid fuels[a]	Liquid fuels[a]	Natural gas[a]	Hydroelectric and nuclear[a]	Total	Per capita (10⁶ kcal)
United States[a]	4,300	7,775	4,475	1,825	18,375	76.6
Brazil[b]	57	383	19	132	591	4.1
India[b]	439	295	18	104	856	1.1
Kenya	0.8	9.9	0	1.6	12.3	0.6

[a] DOE (1983).
[b] UN (1986).

TABLE IV

METRIC TONS (10^6 DRY) OF BIOMASS ENERGY CURRENTLY USED[a]

Country	Fuelwood	Animal wastes	Bagasse and crop residues	Food grains, sugars, etc.	Total biomass	Metric tons per capita of biomass
United States[b]	166 (747)	1 (5)	4[c] (18)	1 (5)	172 (774)	0.72
Brazil	102[d] (459)	Negligible	46[e] (207)	10[e] (45)	158 (711)	1.1
India	124[f] (558)	38[g] (118)	64[g] (126)	>0	226[f] (855)	0.29
Kenya	20.4[e] (92)	11[e] (50)	1.5[e] (7)	>0	32.9[e] (148)	1.57

[a] Values in parentheses indicate energy equivalent if dry biomass were incinerated (10^{12} kcal).
[b] ERAB (1981).
[c] Mostly sugar cane bagasse.
[d] UN (1982).
[e] Meade and Chen (1977); FAO (1984).
[f] UN (1982).
[g] Derived from GI (1979).

population is engaged in agriculture. Forests cover 67% of the total land area (Table II). It has been estimated that the area of forests and woodlots in Brazil had decreased to 568 million ha in 1983 (FAO, 1984). The deforestation currently taking place is caused primarily by slash-and-burn agriculture rather than by commercial logging or cattle ranchers (Myers, 1986a).

Much of the remaining tropical rainforest has limited potential as a fuel source because it is located in remote areas and is not easily available to consumers. In fact, Brazil has been classified as a country that has a "deficit or acute scarcity" of fuelwood (Bogach, 1985). Fuelwood provides 22% of the country's total energy needs (Tables III and IV). Forests are not only important to Brazil as an energy source, but they also protect the land from soil erosion, reduce flooding, and minimize the silting of rivers, streams, and dams.

Currently, Brazil has the largest ethanol system in the world. The Brazilians produce 9.1 billion liters annually, primarily from sugarcane (Blum, 1985; Goldemberg et al., 1985). The United States produces only 2.4 billion liters of ethanol annually, primarily from corn grain (DOE, 1986). Approximately 19% of Brazil's current biomass energy is supplied by ethanol. Expansion of the sugarcane crop for ethanol production is associated with a decrease in the per capita production of domestic food crops. From 1974–1984, food production decreased 1.9%/year while sugarcane production increased 7.8%/year (de Melo,

TABLE V
ANNUAL BIOMASS PRODUCTION[a]

	United States		Brazil		India		Kenya	
	Land area (10⁶ ha)	Biomass production	Land area (10⁶ ha)	Biomass production	Land area (10⁶ ha)	Biomass production	Land area (10⁶ ha)	Biomass production
Arable land and production crops	192	1083	75	450	143	858	2.3	13.8
Pasture and grazing land	300	900	164	492	12	36	6.2	18.6
Forests	290	580	568	1136	46	92	2.4	94.8
Other	135	68	39	20	127	64	46.1	50.7[b]
Total area	917	—	851	—	328	—	57	—
Total biomass	—	2631	—	2098	—	1050	—	84.2
Total energy fixed (10¹⁵ kcal)	11.8		9.4		4.7		0.38	
Solar fixed energy per capita (10⁶ kcal)	59.2		104		6.0		18.1	
Biomass production (t/ha)	2.9		2.5		3.2			

[a] The average biomass yields per hectare were crops, 6 t; pastures, 3 t; forests, 2 t; and other, 0.5 t.

[b] Calculated using figures for woody biomass production given by O'Keefe et al. (1984) and assuming an annual nonwoody biomass production of 1 t/ha in arid grasslands.

TABLE VI

TOTAL ANNUAL AMOUNT OF SOLAR ENERGY HARVESTED IN THE FORM OF AGRICULTURAL

CROPS

AND FORESTRY PRODUCTS (DRY)

	United States		Brazil		India		Kenya	
	10^6 metric tons[a]	10^{12} kcal	10^6 metric tons[a]	10^{12} kcal	10^6 metric tons[a]	10^{12} kcal	10^6 metric tons[a]	10^{12} kcal
Corn	194	873	21	95	7.8	35	1.3	6
Wheat	71	320	1.8	8	45	203	0.1	0.5
Rice	6	27	9	41	91	410	0.03	0.1
Soybeans	51	230	16	72	8	4	—	—
Sorghum	22	99	0.3	14	12	54	0.15	0.7
Potatoes	16	72	0.4	18	2.4	11	0.1	0.5
Cassava	—	—	4.2	19	1.2	5	0.15	0.7
Vegetables	6	27	1.8	8	8.8	40	0.02	0.5
Fruits	5	23	4.9	22	3.9	18	0.15	0.7
Nuts	0.8	4	0.1	0.5	0.2	0.9	0.02	0.1
Oil seeds	9	41	2.0	9	18	365	0.13	0.6
Sugarcane	2.5	—	24.1	105	18	81	0.4	1.8
Sugar beets	2	27	—	—	—	—	—	—
Pulses	1	5	2.7	24	13	59	0.25	1.1
Oats	7	32	0.1	0.5	—	—	0.01	0.05
Rye	1	5	<0.1	<0.5	—	—	—	—
Barley	13	59	0.1	0.5	—	—	0.09	0.4
Total	407.3	1833	88.6	399	229.3	1032	2.9	13.1
Pasture and others	900[b]	4050	492[b]	2214	36[b]	162	19[b]	85
Forest industrial products	100[c]	450	40[d]	180	14[d]	63	0.8[e]	2.3
Totals	1407	6332	7590	2655	274	1235	22.4	101
Total per capita (t)	5.8		4.1		0.3		1.1	
Total per capita (10^6 kcal)	26.3		18.6		1.6		4.8	

[a] From data presented by the Food and Agriculture Organization (FAO, 1984).

[b] From Table V.

[c] USDA (1985).

[d] FAO (1983b).

[e] O'Keefe and Raskin (1985).

TABLE VII

FOREST UTILIZATION (10^6 t)

	Potential sustainable production[a]	Actual use		
		Industry	Fuelwood	Total
United States	580	191[b]	166[f]	357
Brazil	1136	40[c]	102[g]	142
India	92	14[c]	124[d]	138
Kenya	2.5	0.8[e]	19.6[e]	20.4[f]

[a] Assuming a net productivity of 2 t/ha.
[b] USDA (1985).
[c] FAO (1983b).
[d] See Table IV.
[e] O'Keefe and Raskin (1985).
[f] ERAB (1981).
[g] Bogach (1985).

1986). The increasing demands for fuelwood, construction lumber, and sugar-cane, combined with the effects of slash-and-burn agriculture, seem likely to have a significant negative impact on the quantity and quality of Brazil's tropical forests.

Following the 1973 oil crisis, Brazil embarked on an ambitious plan to produce ethanol from sugarcane and thereby reduce its dependence on foreign oil. To date, 45% of the total energy consumed comes from fossil fuel and 55% comes from biomass fuel (Tables III and IV).

C. INDIA

India's surface area is 36% that of the United States, but its population, at 785 million, is over three times as large (Table I). Of the four countries, India has the highest population density and the lowest GNP (Table I). If its population growth rate remains at 2.3%, by the year 2000 India can expect to have over 1 billion people.

The large population in India puts pressure on biomass resources to supply adequate food and fuel for the country. Of the total population, 80% is rural (Giriappa, 1986; Sharma, 1987), with 62% engaged in agriculture. The high population explains why 43% of the land, 143 million ha, is dedicated to crop production (Table II).

Although India will have to increase food production to meet population needs, it can increase its cropland only by removing its forests (Mishra, 1986; Sharma, 1987). Forest area in India, at 46 million ha, comprises only 14% of the country's total land area (Table II). It is estimated that India loses 1.5 million ha of forest land annually (CSE, 1985), and there is virtually no forest growth left below 2000 m (Myers, 1986b). The principal factors responsible for deforestation are population pressures from both humans and livestock (Sharma, 1987). Only 12 million ha, or 3.6% of India's total land area, is devoted to producing fodder (Table II), which forces the large population of livestock to graze on fallow and uncultivated wastelands as well as forest areas.

Besides utilizing biomass resources for food production, India relies heavily on biomass for energy. Biomass energy and fossil energy each comprise 50% of the energy consumption in the country, with the household sector utilizing nearly 90% of all biomass energy consumed (Tables III and IV). The predominant uses for biomass energy are cooking and lighting (GI, 1979). Bagasse, which is produced during the processing of sugarcane, is used by the sugar industry to provide heat and steam for the manufacture of sugar. India does not use food grains, sugars, or other biomass for ethanol production.

Wood is the primary source of biomass energy in India, comprising 55% of all biomass energy consumed, followed by bagasse and crop residues at 28% and animal dung at 17% (Table IV). Biomass energy use in India is similar to the world average, which is about 50% wood, 35% residues, and 15% dung. India's heavy reliance on fuelwood is alarming. The country utilizes 45% more fuelwood than the potential sustainable yield of its forest area (Tables V, VI, VII). It should be noted, however, that not all fuelwood in India is obtained from forests. About 22% of fuelwood is collected from nonforestland, such as privately owned plantations and woodlots, river banks, canals, roadsides, and areas around private houses (GI, 1979). Nevertheless, forests represent the greatest source of fuelwood in the country (GI, 1979).

In order to meet future food and fuel needs, India will have to utilize more of its biomass resources; however, it is unclear if the land can sustain such use. Of the total annual biomass currently produced, India already harvests 25% in the form of fuel (derived from Tables IV and V). This means that limited amounts of biomass resources can be used to meet future needs of the country's burgeoning population.

D. KENYA

Kenya occupies 582,650 km² of arid East Africa and has a population of 21 million people, and the population is growing at 4.2% per annum (Table I). Of the total land area, 4.2% supports forests and woodland, 4% is used for growing crops, and pastureland occupies another 7% (Table II). Parks and reserves occupy 4–5%, and developed areas such as villages and cities use 1% of the land. Semiarid savannas and rangelands occupy the remaining 80% of the land in Kenya.

Although 80% of Kenya's population lives on 20% of the land, resulting in densities of 500–900 people/km^2 on arable land (UNEP, 1981), only 15% live in urban areas, and 75% are engaged in agriculture (Table I). Per capita food production and caloric intake have decreased during the past decade, and in 1981 the daily per capita food supply was 88% of the minimum requirement of 2340 kcal/person/day necessary for the maintenance of health (Yeager and Miller, 1981). In 1982, Kenya imported 79,000 t of cereals and received another 115,000 t in aid. The per capita GNP in Kenya in 1986 was $340 (Table I).

Biomass provides the bulk of Kenya's energy needs (Tables III and IV). Fuelwood alone supplies 74% of the total annual energy requirements (O'Keefe and Raskin, 1985). Most of the wood consumed in 1980 (20.4 million t) was taken from trees growing on arable cropland, on grazing land, and in urban areas. Only 27% came from forests, yet this amount still exceeded the sustainable yield of the forests by over 50% (O'Keefe and Raskin, 1985). Consumption exceeded yields by 9.3 million t in 1980, causing depletion of the standing stocks. By 1985, 10.9 million t of fuelwood were expected to be taken from standing stocks yearly, resulting in a decrease of total standing stocks from 934.9 million t in 1980, to 885.4 million t in 1985 (O'Keefe and Raskin, 1985). Deforestation, due primarily to expanding agriculture but also caused by increased demand for fuelwood, is 1.6% per year (Molofsky et al., 1986).

In addition to wood, crop residues and dung are other important sources of biomass energy. Crop residues, including bagasse, amount to about 4.2 million t per year (Table IV). All bagasse is used in the sugar refining process. Of the other crop residues, about 30%, including 0.3 million t of woody residue from coffee and tea plantations, is used for energy (O'Keefe, 1983).

About 12 million t of dung are produced annually in Kenya. An estimated 0.6 million t are burned. A survey by Hosier (1985) found that animal dung is used by rural people when fuelwood supplies are insufficient, and then only for heating, not for cooking.

In 1982 the first power alcohol plant came on line at Muhoroni, Kenya (Stuckey and Juma, 1985). It utilizes molasses as its sugar source. (Another plant near Kisumu was discontinued after cost overruns had nearly tripled its initial $60 million cost.) The Muhoroni plant has a capacity to produce 64,000 liters/day. The cost per liter delivered to Nairobi is estimated at $0.57, including the cost of molasses, running costs, capital costs, and transport costs.

Of the total annual biomass production of 91.3 million t in Kenya, only 35.2 million t are produced on arable land, pastureland, and forests where four-fifths of the population lives (Tables IV and V). Of this, 62.5% is used for fuel and 8.2% is used for food. Additional expansion of Kenyan agriculture and increased consumption of woodfuel will be necessary through 2000 to support Kenya's rapidly growing population.

III.   SOLAR ENERGY USE

Biomass from forests and other sources is produced from incoming solar energy if temperature, soil, water, and biological resources are suitable for biomass production. In the United States a total of 14.2×10^{15} kcal of solar energy is collected as biomass each year (Table V). On a per-hectare basis this amounts to about an average of 3.0 t/ha/year (Table V). The average yields were 2.5 t/ha for Brazil, 3.2 t/ha for India, and 1.25 t/ha for Kenya. The low yield for Kenya is due to low rainfall.

How does the amount of solar energy collected annually in biomass compare with fossil energy consumed? The total quantity of commercial energy used in the United States is 18.4×10^{15} kcal (Table III). Thus, the United States is burning 30% more fossil energy than the total amount of solar energy captured by all the plant biomass in the nation! In India, the fossil energy consumed represents about 18.2% of the total solar energy captured by plant biomass; for Brazil, the percentage is 6.3%, and for Kenya the percentage is only 3.5% (derived from Tables III and V).

IV.   CONVERSION OF BIOMASS TO ETHANOL, BIOGAS, AND HEAT

The utilization of some forms of biomass for fuel requires conversion. Conversion often requires significant inputs of energy and may cause environmental and social problems. Energy inputs, environmental impacts, and social costs are assessed for ethanol, biogas, and heat energy systems in order to determine the net energy and economic returns for these systems.

A.   ETHANOL

The conversion of sugars and starches to ethanol by fermentation is a well known and established technology. Ethanol fermentation is carried out with yeast in an 8- to 12-hr batch process, which produces 8–10% ethanol by volume. The ethanol is then recovered by continuous distillation. The theoretical mass conversion efficiencies of sugar and starch to ethanol are 0.51 to 0.57 g ethanol/g of the sugar or starch substrate fermented. Usually about 90% of the theoretical yields from carbohydrate is achieved (some of the sugar and starch is consumed by the yeast population for its maintenance and growth). The yield of ethanol is about 1 liter per 2.7 kg of corn or per 14 kg of sugarcane (2.5 kg of sugar) (Tables VIII and IX).

The production of corn and sugarcane in the United States requires significant

TABLE VIII

INPUTS PER 1000 LITERS OF ETHANOL FROM U.S. CORN[a]

Inputs	kg	kcal (1000)	Dollars
Corn	2,700	3,259[b]	217[e]
Transport of corn	2,700	325[d]	32
Water	160,000[c]	90[c]	20
Stainless steel	6[c]	89[c]	10
Steel	12[c]	139[c]	10
Cement	32[c]	60[c]	10
Coal	660[c]	4,617[c]	40
Pollution costs	—	—	60[f]
Total		8,579	399

[a] Outputs: 1000 liters of ethanol = 5,130,000 kcal
[b] Table X.
[c] Slesser and Lewis (1979).
[d] Transport estimated to be 10% of production energy.
[e] $0.12/kg ($3/bu).
[f] Tables XII and XIII.

dollar and fossil energy inputs (Tables X and XI). This is important because the corn or sugarcane biomass constitutes one of the major energy and dollar costs in producing ethanol. For example, producing 1000 liters of ethanol requires 2700 kg of corn (Table VIII), which requires an average of slightly less than 0.5 ha of land (Table X). The energy needed to produce 6500 kg/ha of corn totals 7.8 million kcal at a cost of $523 (Table X). About 14,000 kg of sugarcane, which requires nearly ⅕ of a hectare (Table IX), is required to produce 1000 liters of ethanol. U.S. sugarcane yields an average of 81,000 kg/ha and requires 12.2 million kcal of energy and $1,059 to produce (Table XI).

Once the corn or sugarcane is harvested there are three sources of energy costs involved in its conversion to ethanol: transport to the plant, the conversion itself, and pollution control. These costs in both energy and dollar terms are given in Tables VIII and IX. It should be noted that these inputs are for a large, 200 million liter/year modern chemical plant. For corn, the largest energy inputs are for its production (3.3 million kcal) and for the coal (4.6 million kcal) used in the fermentation–distillation process (Table VIII). The total energy input to produce 1000 liters of ethanol is 8.6 million kcal, but the ethanol has an energy value of only 5.1 million kcal. Thus, a net energy loss of more than 3.0 million kcal occurs for each 1000 liters produced. The energy credit given for the distiller's grain by-product would reduce the net loss by about 700,000 kcal, but only if the distiller's grain is fed to ruminant livestock (ERAB, 1981).

About 54% of the cost of producing ethanol ($0.40/liter) in such a large plant

TABLE IX

INPUTS PER 1000 LITERS OF ETHANOL FROM U.S. SUGARCANE[a]

Inputs	kg	kcal × 1000	Dollars
Sugarcane	14,000	1,938[b]	167[b]
Transport of Sugarcane	14,000	400[c]	42
Water	125,000[d]	70	20
Stainless Steel	3[d]	45	10
Steel	4[d]	46	10
Cement	8[d]	15	5
Bagasse	1,900	7,600	—
Pollution Costs	—	—	60[e]
Total		10,114	$314

[a] Outputs: 1000 liters of ethanol = 5,130,000 kcal.
[b] Table XI.
[c] Estimated.
[d] Slesser and Lewis (1979).
[e] Tables XII and XIII.

TABLE X

ENERGY AND ECONOMIC INPUTS PER HECTARE
FOR CONVENTIONAL/CORN PRODUCTION
IN THE UNITED STATES[a,b]

	Quantity	10³ kcal	$/ha
Input			
Labor (hr)	10	7	50
Machinery (kg)	55	1,485	91
Fuel (liters)	115	1,255	38
N (kg)	152	3,192	81
P (kg)	75	473	53
K (kg)	96	240	26
Limestone (kg)	426	134	64
Corn seeds (kg)	21	520	45
Insecticides (kg)	1.5	150	15
Herbicides (kg)	2	200	20
Electricity (10³ kcal)	100	100	8
Transport (kg)	322	89	32
Total		7,845	$523
Output (yield)	6,500 kg	26,000	

[a] Pimentel et al. (1988).
[b] Output/input ratio (kcal) = 3.31.

TABLE XI

AVERAGE ENERGY INPUT AND OUTPUT PER HECTARE PER
YEAR FOR SUGARCANE IN LOUISIANA[a,b]

	Quantity/ha	10^3 kcal/ha	Dollars/ha
Inputs			
Labor	30 hr	21	150
Machinery	72 kg	1,944	119
Gasoline	54 L	546	15
Diesel	284 L	3,242	75
N (ammonia)	158 kg	3,318	84
P (triple)	97 kg	611	49
K (muriate)	149 kg	373	40
Lime	1120 kg	353	168
Seed	215 kg	802	215
Insecticide	2.5 kg	250	25
Herbicide	6.2 kg	620	62
Transportation	568.9 kg	146	57
Total		12,226	$1,059
Output			
Sugarcane	88,000 kg	24,618,000	
Sugar yield	6,600 kg		

[a] Ricaud (1980).
[b] kcal input/kcal sugar = 2.01.

is for the corn substrate itself ($0.22) (ERAB, 1981) (Table VIII). [At smaller plants with an annual production of 150,000 liters/year, the cost per liter approaches $0.66 (SF, 1982).] The next largest input is for coal to fuel the fermentation–distillation process, but this was only $0.04. These production costs include a small charge for pollution control ($0.06), which is probably a low estimate. Overall, the per-liter price for ethanol does not compare favorably with that for retail gasoline fuels which presently is between $0.20 and $0.25/liter.

Although the costs of producing ethanol using sugarcane are slightly lower than corn ($0.31/liter), the energetics are similar (Table IX). The total energy input for 1000 liters of ethanol using sugarcane is 10.1 million kcal. This value is about double the energy value of the ethanol (5.1 million kcal). However, there is no cost for the energy used in the fermentation–distillation process for ethanol produced from sugarcane because all of the required energy comes from bagasse by-product. The fuel energy from the bagasse is charged against the system (Table IX) because the bagasse could be used as an organic fertilizer or fuel source. Again, the pollution-control charge amounts to $0.06/liter, and this may be low. For the sugarcane system, 53% of the cost of producing ethanol is for the feedstock. For both corn and sugarcane it is clear that the cost of feedstock

TABLE XII

POLLUTION COSTS PER HECTARE
OF CORN PRODUCTION

Item	Quantity	Dollars/ha
Soil erosion	18 t	30[a]
Water runoff	50 mm	—
Fertilizers (N)	152 kg	—
Insecticides	2 kg	4[b]
Herbicides	4 kg	8[b]
Air pollutants		—
Total		42

[a] Calculated from data included in Clark (1985).
[b] Calculated from data included in Pimentel et al. (1980b).

dominates the system and makes the price of the end product dependent on the agricultural production costs.

The energy and dollar costs of producing a liter of ethanol (Tables VIII, IX, XII, XIII) include pollution costs. These costs add 10–15% to the overall costs of production. For example, producing a hectare of U.S. corn using conventional agricultural practices results in soil losses of about 18 t/ha/year. The total fertilizer and off-site environmental effects are calculated to be about $42/ha/year (Table XII). The other major cost is the pollution effect from pesticides, estimated to be about $12/ha/year. In total, these pollution impacts increase the cost of corn production about 13% (Table X).

Major pollution costs are also associated with the production of ethanol in the chemical plant. For each 1000 liters of ethanol produced using corn, 160,000

TABLE XIII

POLLUTION COSTS IN PRODUCING 1000 LITERS OF
ETHANOL

Item	Quantity	kcal × 1000	Dollars
Corn production	2,700 kg	3,259	17[a]
Effluent	160,000 kg		16[b]
Air pollutants			—
Total		3,259	$33

[a] Table XII.
[b] $0.10/1000 liters for sewage treatment.

TABLE XIV

INPUTS PER 1000 LITERS OF ETHANOL FROM BRAZILIAN SUGARCANE[a]

Inputs	kg	kcal × 1000	Dollars
Sugarcane	14,000	1,946[b]	172[b]
Transport of sugarcane	14,000	195[c]	24
Water	125,000	70[d]	20
Stainless steel	3	45[d]	10
Steel	4	46[d]	10
Concrete	8	15[d]	5
Bagasse	1,900	7,600	—
Pollution costs	—	—	60[e]
Total		9,917 kcal	301

[a] Outputs: 1000 liters of ethanol = 5,130,000 kcal.
[b] Table XV.
[c] Similar value used in Table VIII.
[d] Slesser and Lewis (1979).
[e] Tables XII and XIII.

liters of wastewater are produced. This wastewater has a biological oxygen demand (BOD) of 18,000–37,000 mg/liters depending on the type of plant (Kuby *et al.*, 1984).

All the ethanol data presented previously were for the United States. How does Brazilian ethanol production compare to these data? Overall, the ethanol production costs are slightly lower in Brazil than in the United States (Tables IX and XIV). The cost and energy inputs for sugarcane production in Brazil are similar to those in the United States (Tables XI and XV).

About 1.9 million kcal are required to produce 14,000 kg sugarcane feedstock for 1000 liters of Brazilian ethanol, which is similar to that in the United States (Tables IX and XIV). The total input to produce 1000 liters of ethanol is about 9.9 million kcal. This input is nearly double the yield of ethanol (5.1 million kcal). Thus, the most widely used process of producing ethanol in Brazil requires about 0.5 liter of imported fossil petroleum equivalent to produce 1 liter of ethanol (Table XIV). Others have reported that it takes about 1 liter of imported petroleum to produce 1 liter of ethanol (Chapman, 1983; Chapman and Barker, 1987).

The cost of producing 1 liter of ethanol was calculated to be $0.30 (Table XIV). This figure includes pollution costs of $0.06/liter. With this expense removed, the cost is $0.24/liter, which compares well with costs calculated by others who report a range of $0.23 to $0.27 (MME, 1987; J. Goldemberg, personal communication). This $0.30/liter does not include the subsidy charge that will add 20% to the cost (Nastari, 1983).

TABLE XV

AVERAGE ENERGY INPUT AND OUTPUT PER HECTARE PER YEAR
FOR SUGARCANE IN BRAZIL[a]

	Quantity/ha	10^3 kcal/ha	Dollars/ha[b]
Inputs			
Labor	210 hr[c]	157[d]	120
Machinery	72 kg[e]	1,944	119
Fuel	262 L[f]	2,635	131
N (ammonia)	65 kg[f]	1,364	42
P (triple)	52 kg[f]	336	27
K (muriate)	100 kg[f]	250	27
Lime	616 kg[f]	192	92
Seed	215 kg[e]	271[d]	70
Insecticide	0.5 kg[f]	50	5
Herbicide	3 kg[f]	300	30
Total		7,499	663
Output			
Sugarcane	54,000 kg[f]	15,120,000	
Sugar yield	3,672 kg		

[a] kcal input/kcal sugar = 2.02.
[b] Calculated based on quantity of inputs.
[c] Calculated from footnote b.
[d] Ghirardi (1983).
[e] Similar to Louisiana (Table XI).
[f] da Silva et al. (1978).

Note that sugarcane feedstock accounts for 56% of the total production costs and that the inputs include the costs for controlling pollution. The BOD of wastewater from Brazilian sugarcane-based alcohol plants is calculated to have an environmental impact equal to that of two-thirds of the wastes produced by the total human population in Brazil (Desai et al., 1980).

How much land is required to fuel one automobile if the automobile burned only ethanol? If we assume that the average U.S. automobile travels 16,090 km (10,000 miles) each year and gets 7 km/liter (USBC, 1985), then 2300 liters of gasoline will be required each year for an automobile. Using straight ethanol, the total in equivalent kcal would be 3,667 liters. Assuming a zero energy charge (no energy input) for the fermentation–distillation processes and charging only for the energy required to produce corn (Tables VIII, IX, and XIV), then 4.2 ha of land would be required to provide this much fuel (assumes 6500 kg/ha corn-grain yield, 1 liter net ethanol produced per 2.7 kg corn). In comparison, about 0.6 ha of cropland is used to feed each person in the United States (USDA, 1985).

Thus, more than 7 times more cropland would be required to fuel one automobile than to feed one person in the United States.

If all automobiles in the United States were fueled with ethanol based on the these assumptions, a total of 462 million ha of good cropland would be necessary. This is more than double the total arable land in the United States (Table II).

Making a similar calculation for Brazilian ethanol production, about 2.6 ha would be necessary to fuel one automobile (Tables XIV and XV). Therefore, if all of the automobiles in Brazil were fueled using sugarcane, a total of 26 million ha of cropland would be needed. This is more than one-third of the total cropland in production in Brazil today (Table II).

B. FUELWOOD AND OTHER SOLID BIOMASS FUELS

The oldest and simplest use for biomass fuel is cooking and heating, and the most common form of biomass used is fuelwood. In many environments where humans live, wood is readily available and can be easily cut and transported to their home. With careful manipulation, wood burns slowly and uniformly. It can be stored and protected from the weather easily and cheaply.

Wood is often processed into charcoal. The advantages of charcoal are that it is a clean-burning fuel and is lightweight for ease of transport. However, charcoal has several disadvantages. First, the conversion of wood into charcoal results in the loss of about 3 kcal of heat energy per 1 kcal of charcoal produced (Earl, 1975; Wood and Baldwin, 1985). Second, charcoal is dirty to handle and store.

In recent years fuelwood supplies have declined in many parts of the world, creating an effort on the part of farmers, governments, development agencies, and many others to promote growing trees as a way to improve the fuelwood supply (Allen, 1986). Generally, these efforts have been categorized under the titles *social forestry* and *agroforestry*. They are attempts to increase farmer access to wood supplies outside of traditional forest systems.

Community forestry or social forestry has received much publicity and has been favored by large donor organizations because they believe large forests have a greater visible impact than numerous, scattered, small-farm woodlots (T. N. Khoshoo, personal communication). However, these social or community forest projects have not been successful for several reasons (Allen, 1986; T. N. Khoshoo, personal communication). First, the people planting and caring for the trees do not have the same interest in these plantings as they have in their own tree plantings; thus, grazing animals and other activities are likely to destroy large portions of these forests. Second, harvesting is difficult to control and regulate. Typically, people who live near the forest harvest a large share of the wood. Third, many people who depend on the social forests as a necessity live too far away from them and must travel long distances to cut and transport their wood. This makes these social forests much less popular than farm woodlots (Allen, 1986).

Agroforestry has many definitions depending on the situation in which it is used, but simply put it is the deliberate management of trees on a given piece of land in association with crops, livestock, or a combination of the two (W. Teel, personal communication). In many cases it has been demonstrated that, although the productivity of a given component may decrease in an agroforestry system, the overall productivity of the system increases (Pimentel et al., 1987a). In one example interplanting legume trees with corn increased the yield of corn from 1000 kg/ha to 1500 kg/ha. At the same time a total of 2000 kg/ha of fuelwood was produced for use by the family (Pimentel et al., 1987a). This increased productivity is accomplished while reducing soil erosion rates from about 30 t/ha to only 1 t/ha (Nair, 1984; Lundgren and Nair, 1985). The control of erosion plus the extra nitrogen added to the land by the trees are the prime reasons for the 50% yield increase in corn grain.

Agroforestry should not be regarded as the only hope in terms of energy for the rural poor. It is simply one of the best options available. In certain situations agroforestry is not appropriate, especially in the rice-growing regions of India where population densities of people and animals make the survival of trees nearly impossible. In these situations people have had to find other sources of heat from the biomass available locally, which includes crop residues and dung.

Dung is burned when fuelwood is not available or is too expensive for the poor. However, burning dung causes several environmental problems. Dung has value both as a fertilizer and in protecting the soil from erosion. The amount of nitrogen in the manure and urine of milk cows is 19.5% by dry weight (Jewell et al., 1977). The amount of heat energy in that manure is 3.6 million kcal/t (Bailie, 1976). When dry dung is burned, about 195 kg of nitrogen fertilizer is lost for every metric ton. This nitrogen fertilizer costs $0.53/kg, or $103/t, and has an energy value of 2.87 million kcal/t. These values do not include the replacement costs for phosphorus, potassium, and calcium (since these are assumed to be recovered from the ash) or the loss to the soil of the organic material in the manure.

Crop residues have been proposed as an energy source (ERAB, 1981). However, many environmental problems are associated with the use of crop residues. The most serious is the removal of the protective vegetative covering, a layer that significantly decreases soil erosion and water runoff. For example, soil erosion rates may increase 90% when crop residues on soil surfaces are reduced from about 6 t/ha to only 0.5 t/ha (Mannering, 1984). Water run-off rates were reported to rise 10- to 100-fold when vegetative cover was removed from the land (USDA-ARS and EPA-ORD, 1976). In certain localized applications, on land that can tolerate some loss of organic material without an increase in

erosion, crop residues can be an energy source. With current agricultural practices in the United States and elsewhere in the world, little or no crop residue can
be harvested as fuel (ERAB, 1981; Pimentel *et al.*, 1981, 1987b).

Even though it is an efficient method of obtaining energy, one must remember
that burning straw is more complicated and costly than burning coal. It takes
many more work hours to tend and stoke the furnace to prevent clogging, to
control airflow to the chamber, to frequently clean the ash, and to add small,
constant amounts of fuel (Bailie, 1976). Although about 12.5 kg of crops residues equals 1 kg of fuel oil in energy terms, about double this is required to
obtain the same heat value because of the complication involved in burning straw
(OECD, 1984).

C. BIOGAS

Biomass material that contains large quantities of water can be effectively
converted into usable energy using naturally occurring microbes in an anaerobic
digestion system. These systems are presently active using feedstock dung and
certain plants such as water hyacinth (although production and harvesting problems are greater with the latter). The system used can be comparatively simple,
utilizing mesophilic bacteria with a total system cost of around $600 (W. Teel,
personal communication), or complex, 320-cow operations costing $120,000 or
more (SF, 1983). The basic principles for both are the same.

On a dairy farm or small cattle operation, the manure is loaded or pumped into
a sealed, corrosion-resistant digestion tank. It is usually held in the tank 14–28
days at temperatures around 30–38°C. In some digestion systems, the manure in
the tank is constantly stirred to speed the digestion process and assure that it is
evenly heated. During this period the mesophilic bacteria break down volatile
solids (VS) in the manure and convert them into methane gas (65%) and carbon
dioxide (35%). Small amounts of hydrogen sulfide may also be produced. This
gas is then drawn off through pipes and either burned directly (in the same way as
natural gas) or scrubbed to clean away the H_2S and used to generate electricity.
The cost breakdown for one system is given in Table XVI.

The amount of biogas produced by this system is determined by the temperature of the system, the volatile solids content, and the efficiency of converting them to biogas. This efficiency varies from 18% (Jewell and Morris, 1974) to
95% (Jewell *et al.*, 1977). Dairy cows produce 85 kg of manure for each 1000 kg
of live weight daily. The total solids in this manure are 10.6 kg, and of these 8.6
kg will be volatile solids. Theoretically, a 100% efficient digester would produce
625 liters of biogas from every kilogram of volatile solids added (calculated from
Stafford, 1983). The digester utilized for the data in Table XVII was 28.3 %
efficient, producing 177 liters of biogas/kg of volatile solids added. Thus, this
digester will produce 1,520 liters of biogas/1000 kg live weight daily. Note that

TABLE XVI

ENERGY INPUTS USING ANAEROBIC DIGESTION FOR BIOGAS

PRODUCTION

FROM 100 t WET (13 t DRY) OF CATTLE MANURE[a]

	Quantity	kcal (10^3)
Inputs		
Man-hours[b]	20 hr	—
Electricity	2234 kWh[c]	5,822[d]
Cement foundation[e] (30-year life)	0.9 kg[c]	2[f]
Steel (gas collector[e] and other equipment with 30-year life)	35 kg[c]	725[g]
Pumps and motors[h]	0.05 kg[c]	1[g]
Steel truck/tractor[b] for transportation (10-year life)	10 kg[c]	200[g]
Petroleum for transport[b] (10 km radius)	34 L[c]	340[i]
Total input		7090
Total output[j]		10,200

[a] The retention time in the digester is 20 days. The unit has the capacity to process 1,825 t (wet) per year. Note: the yield in biogas from 100 t is estimated at 10.2 million kcal. Thus, the net yield is 3.1 million kcal (Pimentel et al., 1978). The energy for heating the digester is cogenerated, coming from the cooling system of the electric generator.

[b] Estimated.

[c] Vergara et al. (unpublished data).

[d] 1 kWh = 860 kcal. Based on an energy conversion of fuel to electricity of 33%, thus 1 kWh = 2606 kcal.

[e] The digester was placed underground. Materials used for its construction were concrete and steel. Materials also include a gas storage tank.

[f] 1 kg of cement = 2000 kcal for production and transport (Lewis, 1976).

[g] 1 kg of steel = 20,700 kcal for mining, production, and transport (Pimentel et al., 1973).

[h] The design included three electrical devices: a motor to drive the agitator in the digester, a compressor to store gas, and a pump to supply hot water.

[i] A liter of fuel is assumed to contain 10,000 kcal. Included in this figure are mining, refining, and transportation costs.

[j] It was assumed that anaerobic digestion of manure takes place at 35°C with a solids retention time of 20 days. The temperature of the fresh manure is taken as 18°C and the average ambient temperature as 13°C. The manure is assumed to have the following characteristics: production per cow per day, 23.6 kg total; solids, 3.36 kg; biological oxygen demand (BOD), 0.68 kg. The digestion is assumed to transform 83% of the biodegradable material into gas. Gas produced is said to be 65% methane, and its heat of combustion is 5720 kcal/m^3 at standard conditions.

if the total heat value of the manure was used in calculating efficiency, then the
percentage efficiency would be only 5%.

Biogas has an energy content of about 5720 kcal/m³, compared to 8380
kcal/m³ for pure methane, because of the presence of carbon dioxide. Analyzing
the energy costs and the energy outputs for processing 100 t of manure (wet
weight) gives us a total of 10.2 million kcal produced, with a 7.1 million kcal
energy cost, for a net energy yield of 3.1 million kcal (Table XVI). Much of the
energy cost comes from the production of electricity to run the pumps and the
stirring system used to reduce the retention time in the digester and, thus, its size.
(The volume of the digester will be determined by the amount of manure produced by the animals during the retention time. In this example, with a retention
time of 14 days, it would be slightly over 75 m³.) It is assumed that this
electricity will be generated from the biogas and that the conversion efficiency of
this operation is 33%. The energy needed to heat the digester is cogenerated by
the electric generator via the use of the generator's cooling system as the heat
source. The net energy produced by the digester can either be used to generate
electricity for the farm or be used as a heat source for on-farm activities.

If it is not desirable to produce electricity from the biogas, the energy data
listed in Table XVI will change considerably, but other costs will be associated
with the changes. For instance, less energy will be lost in conversion to electricity if all of the energy is used directly by burning. However, compressing
biogas for use in engines will involve significant amounts of energy in addition to
scrubbing the biogas to remove hydrogen sulfide and water. Although material
costs are lowered if there is no generator or stirring mechanism on the digester,
the size of the digester must be increased because of the longer retention time
needed for complete digestion. Also, some of the biogas will have to be used to
heat the digester, perhaps as much as 610,000 kcal for every 100 wet tons of
manure digested (W. Vergara *et al.*, unpublished). The heat requirements were
calculated by including the heat losses to the surroundings, the heat associated
with the feed and the effluents, and the heat released by the biological reaction.
In the tropics the overall efficiency of biogas systems is enhanced because there
is no need to heat the system to keep the temperature in the 30–38°C range.

Dairy cattle are not the only source of manure for biogas systems. They are
used as a model since dairy animals are more likely to be located in a centralized
system, making the process of collecting and adding the manure to a digestion
system less time consuming and energy intensive than for range-fed steers, or
even for draft animals. Efficiencies of conversion vary not only from system to
system, but also in utilizing manure from different sources (Stafford, 1983).
Swine and beef cattle manure appears to yield more gas per kilogram of volatile
solids than does manure from dairy cattle. Poultry manure is also a good source,
but sand and other forms of heavy grit in this dung cause more pump maintenance problems and require more frequent cleanings of the digester.

Manure that exits the digester has the same fertilizer value as before it went in and has the advantage of less odor. It can be spread on fields in the same way and may be easier to pump if the initial pumping system used a cutter pump to break up stray bits of straw or long, undigested fibers. Biogas systems have the advantage of being able to adjust in size according to the scale of the operation. The pollution problem of manure in centralized dairy production systems, such as those in the United States, is the same whether or not it goes through a biogas generator.

In India the situation is different. There, a substantial percentage of the manure is burned directly as fuel in dried cakes. Burning utilizes a significantly higher percentage of the total energy in the manure, but results in a complete loss of nitrogen and the loss of substantial percentages of other nutrients. Whether or not biogas can be seen as a useful alternative in India and other countries is highly problematic in spite of the higher overall energy efficiency of the system.

D.   BIOGAS FOR SMALLHOLDERS

A general examination of the economics of biogas production in a rural area of a developing nation like Kenya or India shows that costs and benefits are mixed. The capital costs of constructing a simple biogas digester (such as that in Table XVII) with a capacity to process 8 t (wet) of manure per 20-day retention time, or 400 kg per day, are estimated to be between $2000 and $2500. Since the unit would have a usable life of 30 years, the capital costs are only $80/year.

If rural workers were to construct the biogas generator themselves, material costs might range from $300 to $600. At $400 for materials (without a charge for labor) the investment is only $14/year for the life of the digester.

A digester this size in India, where the cows average between 225–330 kg each, would require access to the manure from 20 cows. This manure will produce an estimated 2277 cubic meters of biogas/year at a conversion efficiency of 25% (Table XVII). The energy value of this gas totals 13.0 million kcal. Assuming $8.38/1 million kcal, the value of this much energy would be $109. If no charge is made for labor and dung and the capital cost is assumed to be only $14, the net return is $95. These costs are not equally as applicable to the Kenyan and Indian situations; in Kenya, it is more appropriate to assess energy replacement of biogas in terms of woodfuel. Using an average value of 4500 kcal/kg woodfuel (NAS, 1980), this amount of biogas would replace 3 t of wood; however, gas is generally more efficient when used for cooking, and the total amount of wood replaced might be double that figure.

Although the labor requirement for the biogas generator described here is only 5–10 min/day, the labor input for collecting and transporting biomass for the generator may be significant. If the source for the 400 kg of manure required for the digester was, on average, 3 km from the digester, it would take two laborers

TABLE XVII

ENERGY INPUTS FOR AN ANAEROBIC DIGESTER FOR

BIOGAS

PRODUCTION USING 8 t (1 t DRY) OF COW MANURE[a,b]

	Quantity	kcal
Output from 1 t biomass (dry)		
Methane gas	143 m^3	820,000[c]
Inputs for 1 t biomass		
Cement foundation (30-year life)	0.07 kg[d]	140[e]
Steel (30-year life)	0.33	7,000[f]
Total inputs		7,140
Net return/t dry biomass		812,840

[a] The retention time is 20 days without a means of storing the methane gas (Pimentel, unpublished data).

[b] Efficiency = (812,840 kcal output)/(4.7 × 10^6 kcal input) × 100 = 17.3%. The input is the energy content of manure if burned.

[c] It was assumed that anaerobic digestion of biomass takes place at 35°C with a solids retention time of 20 days. The temperature of the fresh biomass is taken as 21°C and the average ambient temperature as 21°C. The efficiency of the digester is 25%. Gas produced is said to be 65% methane and its heat of combustion is 5720 kcal/m^3.

[d] Vergara et al. (unpublished data).

[e] 1 kg of cement = 2000 kcal for production and transport (Lewis, 1976).

[f] 1 kg of steel = 21,000 kcal for mining, production, and transport (Pimentel et al., 1973).

working an 8-hr day to collect it, feed it into the digester, and return it to the fields where it could be utilized as a fertilizer. On a per-hour basis, the laborers would have to work for about $0.03 per hour for the biogas digester to have costs equal to the amount of gas produced. In some situations, especially in densely populated parts of a country, the amount of transport required might be less.

Although the profitability of small-scale biogas production may be low even without the charge for labor, biogas digesters have some advantages in rural areas. The biomass material can be processed and fuel energy can be obtained without losing the valuable nutrients (N, P, K, and S) that are present in the manure. Nitrogen and phosphorus are important limiting factors in tropical agriculture. The only loss in value that the manure has is due to the breakdown of fibrous material in it, making it an ineffective agent in the control of soil erosion (Pimentel, 1980).

When biomass is burned as a fuel, both nitrogen and other nutrients are lost to the atmosphere. The nitrogen in the biogas slurry (for the 146 t/year amounts discussed) would amount to approximately 3.7 t per year. This has an energy value of 77 million kcal and a cost (using a market price to $0.53/kg) of $1960 (USDA, 1985). The fertilizer value makes it worthwhile to use it as a biogas source rather than burn it as a primary fuel. If the nitrogen value plus the gas value is combined, then the return for the system is $6.42 for each hour of work, which is much better than $0.03/hr.

V. SOCIOECONOMIC ASPECTS

Promoters of biomass energy emphasize its benefits to the society, economy, and environment of the nation (Hall *et al.*, 1985; Sourie and Killen, 1986). Specifically, the creation of jobs, economic development, debt reduction, and the use of indigenous technology are cited as benefits. Many of these benefits, however, are often listed without a carefully documented assessment. In this section we attempt to make a detailed analysis of the socioeconomic benefits and costs of the Brazilian alcohol fuels program, which is frequently cited as demonstrating the benefits of biomass energy. In addition, some data on the socioeconomic impact of biomass energy use are presented for the United States.

A. BRAZIL

The Brazilian alcohol program, PROALCOOL, is held up as a model of how other developing countries could meet their fuel oil needs using their own renewable biomass resources, such as sugarcane. Alcohol production appeared to be an elegant solution to many problems faced by developing countries in the early 1970s. Import substitution made sense for many reasons, including the fact that it only required indigenous knowledge. Sugar had been cropped in Brazil since the earliest days of colonization, and Brazilians had conducted research on alcohol production. Since the concept of PROALCOOL sounded so sensible and the press coverage was so good, PROALCOOL moved ahead rapidly with little or no criticism.

Analyzing the socioeconomics of alcohol production is complicated. Not only must the relationship between the price and elasticity of demand for sugar, alcohol, and gasoline be carefully examined, but this also must be done in the context of often rapid inflation with the limited data provided by the Brazilian government. Although a total analysis is needed, we will focus our assessment on the costs of alcohol production in Brazil and the effects of alcohol production on food prices, food availability, and employment.

All accounts of the costs of alcohol production appearing in the literature suggest that the production costs are higher than the price Petrobras charges retailers (Ortmaier, 1981). Thus, the government must make up the difference. Of course, pricing depends on the world price for sugar and gasoline at any given time. The Ministry of Industry and Commerce (Ortmaier, 1981) published the statement that 56% of the cost (in 1980) of alcohol production is assigned to the purchase of sugarcane, yielding a situation in which the cost of production per liter is $0.33 (Ortmaier, 1981).

The high cost of production exceeding the price charged to consumers has necessitated government subsidies for alcohol producers. From 1976 to 1980, subsidies reached 61 billion cruzeiros, or about $490 million/year (Nastari, 1983). In turn, alcohol producers have been able to increase the value of their gross income by more than 200% between 1975 and 1980 (Nastari, 1983). Currently, subsidies are calculated to be about $180 million/year (Moreira and Serra, 1984). This subsidy contributes significantly to the debt of Brazil. However, this subsidy and ethanol production helps the government reduce the amount of foreign exchange expended to import oil. Brazil imports about 39 million liters, or $9 billion of oil annually, and has to pay an interest rate of about 10% per annum on all borrowed money (Moreira and Goldemberg, 1981). Thus, the production of 9.1 million liters of ethanol helps reduce the amount of oil imported and the interest on borrowed money. However, producing 1 liter of ethanol does not prevent 1 liter of oil being imported. As pointed out earlier, about 0.5 liter of oil equivalent has to be imported to produce 1 liter of ethanol.

A fundamental economic issue generated by the alcohol program is the relationship between alcohol production and the price and availability of food. This matter is usually discussed only in terms of the relative proportion of land in energy crops to land in food crops. The question is far more complicated, particularly in the case of a country such as Brazil with abundant cropland that can provide far more food than the population can consume. Despite this cropland, 25% of Brazil's population is malnourished (Calle and Hall, 1987). The issue is not how much food a country can produce, but the economic structure and how much food is available to the people.

Many factors determine the price and availability of foods, but an important factor is supply and demand of food. From 1971 to 1980, an increasing percentage of land was planted to sugarcane and export crops, including soybeans, whereas the percentage of land in food crops remained constant from 1976 on (Table XVIII). On a per-crop basis in the period between 1973 and 1980, black bean production declined by 16%, while sweet potato production declined 56% (OECD, 1984). During the period of 1976–1981, the total area planted for three basic staple crops—maize, rice, and black beans—remained stable at about 1.9 million ha (van der Pluijm, 1982). During this period the Brazilian population increased by about 15 million (PRB, 1977), thus increasing food demand by about 12%.

TABLE XVIII

TRENDS IN AREA UNDER SUGARCANE AND OTHER CROPS IN BRAZIL FROM 1971 TO 1980[a]

	1971–73	1975	1976	1977	1978	1979	1980
Alcohol production (10^6 liters)[b]	654	556	664	1,470	2,491	3,396	3,786
Area under sugarcane (10^3 ha)	1,830	1,969	2,093	2,270	2,391	2,537	2,607
Soybeans (10^3 ha)	2,507	5,824	6,417	7,070	7,782	8,256	8,766
Food crops (10^3 ha)[c]	24,659	25,837	28,036	28,270	26,922	27,542	28,030
Export crops (10^3 ha)[d]	12,951	15,566	14,526	16,730	17,789	18,408	18,949
Total cultivated area (10^3 ha)	37.3	42.0	43.3	45.7	45.5	46.8	47.9

[a] OECD (1984).

[b] Production from May of the year concerned until April of the following year.

[c] Rice, potatoes, beans, manioc, maize, wheat, bananas, onions.

[d] Cotton, groundnuts, cocoa, sissal, coffee.

In Sao Paulo State, where 70% of the alcohol is produced, significant changes have taken place in agriculture since the start of the PROALCOOL program. Sugarcane production increased by 1.1 million ha from 1968/69 to 1982/83, whereas food-crop-planted acreage declined by 0.4 million ha during the same period (excluding exported soybeans) (Calle and Hall, 1987). Most of the expansion (60%) in sugarcane acreage is reported to have come from pastureland. Thus, milk and meat supplies were also affected in addition to food crops. From 1968/69 to 1982/83, export-crop acreage increased by 0.2 million ha and also affected both food-crop and milk–meat production (Calle and Hall, 1987).

The stagnant levels of food production in Brazil overall and the growing demand for food led to reduced availability of (and high prices for) food (La Rovere, 1985). In 1976, riots broke out in Rio de Janeiro because of a shortage of black beans coupled with political and economic unrest (LAER, 1976; J. Goldemberg, personal communication). Only on the black market could one purchase 1 kg of black beans for the equivalent of a day's labor. This decline in black bean availability led to the importation of black beans from Chile. The increase in alcohol production and export crops was accompanied by a decline in per capita output of major staple food crops. At the same time, food prices increased more than the general inflation rate, an occurrence without precedent in Brazil's economic history (La Rovere, 1985).

Government incentives were provided to encourage alcohol production in Brazil. In terms of government support, only 28% of all rural producers receives economic credit (Burbach and Flynn, 1980). Small farmers who produce 75% of the country's basic staples receive only 5% of agricultural credit (LAER, 1977). Three of Brazil's major crops (black beans, manioc, and maize) received a total of 13% of government agricultural credit (LAER, 1979). The remaining subsidized credit was directed toward export crops and sugarcane–alcohol production.

An additional incentive to produce sugarcane and alcohol was provided by the rapidly growing value of land located near distilleries. Land prices in Brazil for producing sugarcane have risen to about $1500/ha (Ghirardi, 1983). With the income of the Brazilian laborer estimated to be about $1000/year, it would require many years for a laborer to save sufficient money to purchase even one hectare of land. Increased land values also encouraged smallholders, who tend to grow food for domestic consumption, to sell their land to large sugarcane growers (van der Pluijm, 1982). This resulted in more land concentrated in sugarcane. Since most distilleries were located near towns and urban centers, food production moved farther away from food consumers, increasing the energy costs of transport and leading to higher food prices.

Landless agricultural workers who live on the periphery of cities are called *boais-frias,* or cold meal eaters, in reference to the cold lunch they carry with them to work in the fields. These people accept almost any job they can find and may be trucked to rural areas each day to work in the fields (Desai *et al.,* 1980; Burbach and Flynn, 1980). Thousands of subsistence *moradores* were transformed into *boais-frias* during a period in which food in production for the domestic market was stable. *Moradores* provide the bulk of their own subsistence while *boais-frias* do not. Thus, the displacement of subsistence farmers meant that food production for domestic consumption that reaches the market must increase to enable these workers to eat as they did. This did not happen. Instead, 43% of the labor force (with 40% unemployment) now earns a minimum wage of about $92/month or about $0.57/hour; however, purchasing basic foods for a month costs a family three times this wage (Burbach and Flynn, 1980).

Related to the food vs. fuel question are jobs in sugarcane–alcohol production. If sugarcane production replaced a more labor-intensive crop or a crop providing year round employment, a net loss of jobs results. Most food production for domestic consumption was more labor intensive and less seasonal than alcohol production. As of 1975, 51% of land converted to sugarcane was previously planted in food crops (Ortmaier, 1981).

Sugarcane–alcohol production work is highly seasonal, resulting in at least 50% unemployment among sugar and alcohol workers during the 4 months when the job market is lowest (OECD, 1984). Only when sugarcane production was accompanied by diversified agricultural production could people find steady work; however, this was not the tendency.

The World Bank (1980) reported that one new job would be created for each 20,000 liters of alcohol produced and that 172,000 new jobs would be created if alcohol production was increased by about 7 billion liters [a similar trend was suggested by Pereira (1983)]. However, OECD (1984) reported that the number will be more like 27,700 jobs if the increase is by the large alcohol plants (120,000 liters of alcohol/day). Other analysts also reported that the employment increases were not impressive (Pluijm, 1982), with far fewer jobs created than the World Bank and the Brazilian government suggested.

The 25% of the population that is malnourished (Calle and Hall, 1987) and the 40% that is unemployed apparently have not benefited from the Brazilian alcohol program (Burbach and Flynn, 1980). The 25% malnourished and 40% unemployed contrast sharply with the 6.5% of the population who owns cars and have benefited from the subsidized ethanol program (South, 1984).

B. UNITED STATES

Although biomass production in the United States has certain problems (ERAB, 1980), increased employment may be a result of its use. For example, the direct labor inputs for wood biomass resources are 2–30 times greater per million kilocalories produced than for coal (Pimentel *et al.*, 1983a); thus, wages would be lower. A wood-fired steam plant requires 2–5 times more construction workers and 3–7 times more workers per plant. Total employment overall would be expected to increase from 5 to 20% depending on the biomass used and economy of the nation. For example, in the United States employment was projected to increase 5% if about 11% of U.S. energy needs were provided by biomass resources (Pimentel, 1977).

A shift to more biomass energy production in the United States and other nations would increase the occupational hazards of energy production (Morris, 1981). Significantly more occupational injuries and illnesses are associated with biomass production in agriculture and forestry than with coal (underground mining), oil, or gas recovery operations (OTA, 1980). Agriculture reports 25% more injuries per man-day than any other private industry (OTA, 1980). The total injury rate in logging and other forest industries averages annually about 25 per 100 full-time workers, whereas it is about 11 for bituminous coal mining (mostly underground) (BLS, 1978, 1979, 1980, 1981). In terms of a million kilocalorie output, forest biomass has 14 times more occupational injuries and illnesses than underground coal mining, and 28 times more than oil and gas extraction (BLS, 1978). Including the labor required to produce corn, about 18 times more labor is required to produce 1 million kcal of ethanol than an equivalent amount of gasoline (ERAB, 1981). This contributes to the higher price of ethanol.

Today, food and lumber products have a higher economic value per kilocalorie in their original form than when converted into heat, liquid, or gaseous energy (ERAB, 1980, 1981; OTA, 1980). For example, 1 million kcal of corn grain has a market value of $40, but when converted to heat energy it has a value of only $5. Producing liquid fuels (e.g., ethanol) is also expensive. A liter of ethanol now costs about \$0.40 to produce (Table VIII); nearly 70% of the cost of production is for the grain itself (ERAB, 1981).

Current subsidies help make gasohol competitive with gasoline. Federal and state subsidies may range as high as \$0.36/liter for U.S. ethanol (OTA, 1980). As a result, when production and subsidies are included, a liter of ethanol costs \$0.83, compared with the current \$0.15 cost of a liter of gasoline at the refinery (ERAB, 1981). Note that for the equivalent of 8000 kcal/liter of gasoline, a total of 1.5 liters of ethanol (5,310 kcal/liter), with a total value of \$1.25, would be needed.

The real cost to the consumer is greater than the \$0.83 needed to produce a liter of ethanol because 90% of all grain consumed in the United States is fed to livestock (Pimentel et al., 1980a). Therefore, shunting corn grain into ethanol will increase the demand for grains, resulting in higher grain prices. Higher grain prices will, in turn, raise the consumer prices of meat, milk, and eggs (ERAB, 1980).

VI. ENVIRONMENTAL IMPACTS

The removal of biomass from land for energy production increases the effects of wind and water degradation, flooding, and nutrient loss through topsoil erosion. It also affects wildlife communities by disrupting their natural ecosystems and threatens the health of some human populations. These and other threats to the environment from biomass energy production are assessed in the following sections.

A. SOIL EROSION PROBLEMS IN BIOMASS SYSTEMS

Land degradation by soil erosion is of particular concern to agriculturalists and foresters because soil re-formation is extremely slow. Under agricultural conditions, from 200 to 1000 years are required for the renewal of 2.5 cm, or 340 t/ha, of topsoil (Elwell, 1985; Hudson, 1981; Lal, 1984a,b; Larson, 1981; McCormack et al., 1982; Swanson and Harshbarger, 1964). This formation rate is the equivalent of about 1 t/ha/year (the range is 0.3–2 t/ha/year). Forest soil re-formation is slower than in agriculture and is estimated to take at least 1000 years to produce 2.5 cm (Curry, 1971).

Serious soil erosion occurs in most of the world's agriculture, including the United States (18 t/ha/year), Brazil (12–150 t/ha/year), and India (about 30 t/ha/year) (Table XIX). Thus, soil loss rates are from 12 to 150 times greater than the average soil formation rate of about 1 t/ha/year. Although no data for Kenya are available, two of us (D. P. and W. T.) have observed serious erosion on croplands in Kenya.

SELECTED EROSION RATES IN CERTAIN GEOGRAPHICAL REGIONS

Country	Erosion rate (t/ha-yr)	Comments	Sources
United States	18.1[a]	Average, all cropland	USDA (1980)
Midwest, deep loess hills (Iowa and Missouri)	35.6[a]	MLRA[b] #107, 2.2 million ha	Lee (1984)
Southern high plains (Kansas, New Mexico, Oklahoma, and Texas)	51.5[a]	MLRA[b] #77, 6.2 million ha	Lee (1984)
Brazil	150	Beans grown up and down slope	Silva et al. (1985)
	12	Beans grown with agroforestry	
India	25–30	Cultivated land[c]	DST (1980)
	28–31	Cultivated land	Narayana and Babu (1983), CSE (1982)
Deccan black soil region	40–100		
China	43	Average, all cultivated land	Brown and Wolf (1984)
Yellow River basin	100	middle reaches, cultivated rolling loess;	AAC (1980)
Java	43.4	Brantas river basin	Brabben (1981)
Belgium	10–25	Central Belgium, agricultural loess soils	Bollinne (1982; in Richter, 1983)
East Germany	13	1000-year average, cultivated loess soils in one region	Hempel (1951, 1954; in Zachar, 1982)
Ethiopia	20	Simien mountains, Gondor region	Lamb and Milas (1983)
Madagascar	25–40	Nationwide average	Randrianarijaona (1983); Finn (1983)
Nigeria	14.4	Imo region, includes uncultivated land	Osuji (1984)
El Salvador	19–190	Acelhuate basin, land under basic grains production	Wiggins (1981)
Guatemala	200–3600	Corn production in mountain region	Arledge (1980)
Thailand	21	Chao River basin	El-Swaify et al. (1982)
Burma	139	Irrawaddy River basin	El-Swaify et al. (1982)
Venezuela and Colombia	18	Orinoco River basin	El-Swaify et al. (1982)

[a] Indicates combined wind and water erosion, all others are water only.

[b] MLRA, Major land resource areas.

[c] Assumes that 60–70% of the 6 million t of topsoil lost is from cultivated land.

Worldwide degradation of agricultural land by erosion and other factors is causing the irretrievable loss of an estimated 6 million ha each year (Dudal, 1981; Kovda, 1983; UNEP, 1980). High erosion rates worldwide suggest that poor management practices are employed in agriculture. The absence of vegetative cover appears to be the prime cause of soil erosion (OTA, 1982). Thus, more biomass cover is needed on the land to protect soil from water and wind erosion. Row crops have the most serious erosion problems because they provide the least amount of biomass cover for soil protection. For instance, the conventional production of row crops such as corn and soybeans requires tilling the soil before planting. Tilling leaves the soil fully exposed to rain and wind erosion before sufficient crop cover develops to protect the soil.

The type of crop affects the amount of erosion that will occur on the land. Soybeans produce less biomass cover than corn during the growing season, and subsequent erosion rates on soybean land are greater than those of corn fields. For example, with conventional techniques on a loam soil with a 4% slope, soybean production resulted in 40.9 t/ha of erosion vs 21.8 t/ha for corn (Mannering et al., 1980). The surface cover after plowing was only 1% with soybeans and 7% for corn. Before plowing, 26% of the soil was covered with soybean residues, whereas 69% of the corn land was covered with corn stover. Soil cover was related directly to the amount of biomass produced by each crop: corn produces about 3 times the biomass produced by soybeans (15 vs 5 t/ha) (Lindstrom et al., 1979; USDA, 1983).

Close-grown row crops such as wheat and rape protect the soil from erosion better than row crops. Wheat grown on soil with a 4% slope is reported to have an erosion rate of about 14.1 t/ha/year (Fenster, 1973), approximately half of that for corn. After germinating, spring wheat has early, fast growth and develops a relatively dense stand of vegetation cover (150–200 plants/m²) that is capable of protecting the soil from rain and wind energy (Horner et al., 1960; Troeh et al., 1980). Rape is sown in a density similar to wheat, but establishes a stand more slowly than wheat and, thus, is less suitable in providing erosion protection (Adolphe, 1979).

Some crops, such as hay, provide nearly complete cover of the soil once the stand is established. These crops are usually grown as perennials and cover the soil all year for 5- to 10-year periods. For example, soil erosion rates for continuous alfalfa with a 6% slope were reported to be only 0.2 t/ha (Peterson and Swan, 1979). Contour grass strips are planted as a soil conservation measure because the dense vegetation cover is effective in collecting soil sediments carried down slope after a storm. Similarly, grass waterways convey water away from planted slopes with minimal loss of topsoil (Bennett, 1939; Beasley, 1972; Bosworth and Foster, 1982).

After vegetation cover, slope plays a major role in intensifying erosion rates from rainfall (Mills et al., 1986; Pimentel et al., 1987b). Typically, erosion rates

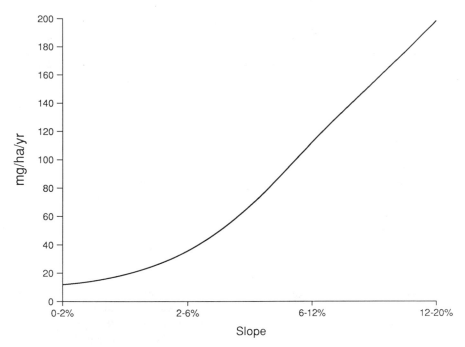

FIG. 2.   Increased soil erosion rates (mg/ha/yr) associated with rising land-slope percentages.

increase about 20-fold when slopes increase from 0 to 2% to the higher level of 12 to 20% (Fig. 2). Note that even on relatively flat land with slopes up to 2%, soil erosion rates ranged from 5 to 12 mg/ha/year.

These data emphasize the difficulty of producing potential biomass crops such as corn, sugarcane, wheat, and rape on sloping land. It should be emphasized that the high erosion rates for these potential crops resulted even when the biomass residues were left on the land. The erosion rates would have been significantly higher if these crop residues had been harvested for fuel (Pimentel *et al.*, 1981). For example, leaving 6.7 t/ha of corn residues on land will control erosion rates at 1–1.6 t/ha when no-till planting is employed; however, if 4–5 t/ha of residues are removed, soil loss is expected to increase 8 times (Table XX). This erosion rate is about 14 times greater than the soil re-formation rate (Pimentel *et al.*, 1987b). The production of forage and hay crops for energy might be possible on sloping land up to 12% if care is taken to maintain a dense stand of vegetation cover and biomass harvesting is carried out employing good management practices (ERAB, 1981). Without such practices to protect the soil, removing crop residues for biomass energy on slopes of 2% or greater would seriously degrade the world's soil resources.

Undisturbed forests often have a dense soil cover of leaves, twigs, and other

TABLE XX

PERCENTAGE OF SOIL LOSS FROM SEVERAL CONSERVATION TILLAGE SYSTEMS
COMPARED WITH CONVENTIONAL TILLAGE ON LAND WITH CONTINUOUS CORN CULTURE[a]

Tillage system	Surface residue after planting				
	1.1–2.2 t/ha	2.2–3.4 t/ha	3.4–4.5 t/ha	4.5–6.7 t/ha	Over 6.7 t/ha
Till–plant (chisel, disk)	89%	61%	48%	33%	20%
No till	71%	48%	33%	18%	8%

[a] Continuous corn with conventional tillage on land with a slope of 2% or more will suffer about 20 t/ha-yr soil erosion. Data from Mannering (1984).

organic material and have soil erosion rates that typically range from less than 0.1 to 0.2 t/ha/year (Megahan, 1972, 1975; Dissmeyer, 1976; Patric, 1976; USFS, 1977; Yoho, 1980; Patric et al., 1984). The combination of organic mulch, tree cover, and tree roots makes most natural forest soils, even on steep slopes of 70%, resistant to erosion and rapid water runoff.

Harvesting timber and pulpwood contributes to greater erosion when formerly covered land becomes exposed and tractors disturb the land in the clearing process. Typically, tractor roads and skid trails severely disturb 20–30% of the soil surface (Dyrness, 1965; Megahan and Kidd, 1972; Rice et al., 1972; Swanston and Dyrness, 1973; Dickerson, 1975; Klock, 1975; Megahan, 1975; Froelich, 1978). Harvesting techniques such as highland and skyline disturb 10–20%, and balloon harvesting disturbs about 6% of the land area (Dyrness, 1965; Ruth, 1967; Rice et al., 1972; Swanston and Dyrness, 1973). The heavy equipment compacts the soil, resulting in greater water runoff.

Compaction by tractor skidders harvesting ponderosa pine was found to reduce growth in pine seedlings from 6 to 12% over a 16-year period (Froelich, 1979). Water percolation in wheel-rutted soils was reduced for 12 years and in log-skid trails for 8 years (Dickerson, 1976). Lack of water is the major limiting factor in forest biomass production, as can be demonstrated with slash pine in Florida; pine growth over a 5-year period in the irrigated treatment was 80% greater than in the untreated control (Baker, 1973). Depending on slope, soil type, and climate, the effects of soil compaction on tree growth may last 8–16 years (Dickerson, 1976; Froelich, 1979).

The disturbed and compacted soil in the roadways and skid trails are the targets for future soil erosion. While erosion rates can be as high as 215 t/ha/year on severely disturbed slopes, average soil erosion per hectare of harvested forest ranges from 2 to 17 t/ha/year with long-term mean rates between 2 and 4 t/ha/year (Megahan, 1972, 1975; Kea, 1975; USFS, 1977; Yoho, 1980; Patric, 1976; McCashion and Rice, 1983). Although erosion from conventional logging can last for 20 years, most erosion ceases in about 5 years when vegetation cover becomes established (Megahan, 1972; Dickerson, 1976; Patric, 1976; Mc-Cashion and Rice, 1983). Erosion from forest harvesting is not large compared to row-crop production, but the effects can be long lasting because of the extremely slow rate of soil formation in forest ecosystems. The nutrients lost when topsoil is eroded also affect forest growth. Scraping off 3 cm of soil surface in various soil types reduces biomass production in ponderosa pine, Douglas fir, and lodgepole pine seedlings by as much as 5-fold (Klock, 1982).

Current practices in biomass food and fuel production result in serious soil erosion problems. As the need arises in countries such as Brazil to produce more biomass for energy, more land will have to be placed under cultivation. This increase in land for biomass energy may come from land previously used for food production (Pimentel et al., 1984). In countries expanding their biomass energy programs, farmers may be forced to clear forests or use poor-quality cropland in an effort to achieve the needed food production.

The utilization of poor-quality land for crops will intensify soil erosion. Because these marginal lands are often highly susceptible to erosion when planted to crops, the land will degrade rapidly and the farmers will again be forced to find land on which to grow crops.

New technologies and practices need to be implemented to control soil erosion and water run-off problems. Many effective soil and water conservation practices, such as rotations and strip cropping, exist today for immediate use (Pimentel et al., 1987a). Another old technology, agroforestry, is also receiving renewed attention (see page 204).

B. NUTRIENT LOSSES AND WATER POLLUTION ASSOCIATED WITH BIOMASS ENERGY AND EROSION

Rapid water runoff and nutrient losses occur when crop residues are harvested and rainfall erodes soils. For example, conventional corn production lost an average of about 5 cm/ha/yr more water than when corn was grown employing conservation practices (Pimentel and Krummel, 1987). Water quickly runs off unprotected soil because raindrops free small soil particles that, in turn, clog holes in the soil and reduce water infiltration (Scott, 1985). This water runoff transports organic matter, nutrients, and sediments.

In addition, the water-holding capacity and nutrient levels of soil decrease when erosion occurs. With conventional corn production, erosion reduced the volume of moisture in the soil by about 50% compared with no-till corn culture (Harrold et al., 1967). Similar findings of increased soil moisture volume were reported for corn grown in combination with living mulches (T. W. Scott, personal communication). Soil nutrient losses that occur with erosion also have a major negative effect on soil quality. In rich agricultural areas, 1 t of soil contains about 4 kg of N, 1 kg of P, and 20 kg of K (I. Buttler, personal communication). Using these soil nutrient values and an average U.S. erosion rate of 18 t/ha/yr, the average loss of nutrients per hectare of cropland would be 72 kg of N, 18 kg of P, and 360 kg of K.

When conservation technologies are employed by protecting the soil with residues and vegetation, increased crop yields result because water, nutrients, and soil organic matter are retained. In Texas, yields from cotton grown on the contour with ample soil protection were 25% greater than from cotton grown with the slope (Burnett and Fisher, 1954). Greater yields were also reported for experiments involving corn (12.5%) in Missouri (Smith, 1946) and for corn (12%), soybeans (13%), and wheat (17%) in Illinois (Sauer and Case, 1954). On land with a 7% slope, yields from cotton grown in rotation were increased 30%, while erosion was reduced by nearly 50% (Hendrickson *et al.*, 1963). In Nigeria, yields from corn grown by no-till under favorable soil and climatic conditions were 61% greater than from corn grown with conventional tillage (Wijewardene and Waidyanatha, 1984). In an experiment comparing tillage practices used on 22 consecutive maize crops grown on highly erodible Nigerian soils, the average grain yields from no-till plots were 20% higher than from conventional plots due to the accumulated effects of erosion-induced degradation of the unprotected soil (Lal, 1983).

Forests lose significant quantities of water, soil, and nutrients when cut and harvested. For instance, the surface water runoff from a forested watershed after a storm averaged 2.7% of the precipitation; after forest cutting and/or farming, water runoff rose to 4.5% (Dils, 1953). Clear felling of trees without harvest and without soil disturbance resulted in flood damage from high stream flow 10% more often than with the normal forest stand (Hewlett, 1979). Replacing natural forest growth with coppice forest regrowth was also found to increase annual stream flow about 10 cm above normal (Swank and Douglass, 1977). Nitrogen leached after forest removal may be 6–9 times greater than in forests with normal cover (Hornbeck *et al.*, 1973; Patric, 1980).

Large quantities of nutrients are also lost when crop residues themselves are removed and burned. On average, residues contain about 1% N, 0.2% P, and 1.2% K (Table XXI). When burned, the nitrogen is released into the atmosphere. Although one would expect to capture most of the P and K in the ashes, an estimated 70–80% of these nutrients are lost with the particulate matter that leaves with the burning process (Flaim and Urban, 1980). Thus, a relatively small percentage of the nutrients in crop residues would be conserved even with the intention of returning the ash residue to the cropland.

Water pollution may result when water is used during the process of converting sugarcane and corn grain into ethanol. In particular, the costs of disposing of the enormous amounts of stillage generated by alcohol production are not accounted for. The stillage from a 190 million liter/year (50 million gal/year)

TABLE XXI

NITROGEN, PHOSPHORUS, AND POTASSIUM
CONTENT OF CROP RESIDUES AND FUELWOOD

	Nutrient content (%)		
	N	P	K
Corn[a]	1.1	0.2	1.3
Rice[a]	0.6	0.1	1.2
Wheat[a]	0.7	0.1	1.0
Soybean[a]	2.3	0.2	1.0
Sugarcane[a]	1.0	0.3	1.4
Fuelwood[b]	0.12	0.01	0.06

[a] Power and Papendick (1985).
[b] Pimentel et al. (1983b).

ethanol plant utilizing corn as the feedstock has a BOD_5 (biological oxygen demand measured over a 5-day period) of 25,000–30,000 mg/liter. In Brazil, this liquid stillage is a serious pollution problem coming from ethanol producing plants (Yang and Trindade, 1978).

This poses significant energy, economic, and environmental problems for Brazil. Three main strategies have been suggested for dealing with this problem: (1) using the stillage as fertilizer, (2) evaporation of 50% of the liquid content and using the concentrated remains as animal feed, and (3) lagooning the waste. All three strategies are costly in terms of energy and money. Although the stillage has a fertilizer benefit to sugarcane production, it is only economical to use the stillage within a 3-km radius of the distillery (World Bank, 1980). This area could not absorb the stillage wastes generated each day.

C. AIR POLLUTION

The smoke produced when fuelwood and crop residues are burned is a pollution hazard because of the nitrogen, particulates, and other chemicals in smoke. A recent Environmental Protection Agency (EPA) report (1986) indicated that although only about 2% of United States heating energy comes from wood, about 15% of the air pollutants in the United States come from burning wood. Emissions from wood and crop-residue burning are a threat to public health because of the highly respirable nature of some of the 100 chemicals that the emissions contain (Pimentel et al., 1983a). Of special concern are the relatively high concentrations of potentially carcinogenic polycyclic organic compounds (POMs, e.g., benzo[a]pyrene) and particulates. Sulfur and nitrogen oxides, carbon monoxide, and aldehydes are also released, but usually in smaller quantities

(DOE, 1981; Morris, 1981). According to DOE in 1980, wood smoke contains "up to 14 carcinogens, 4 cocarcinogens, and 6 cilia toxic and mucus coagulating agents." Currently, concern is being expressed for people in developing nations who cook indoors in the presence of the smoke released from burning wood, dung, and crop residues.

The concerns of inhaling wood smoke have been under greater scrutiny in India particularly, where cooking is commonly done in inefficient *chullahs* without arrangements for removing the smoke from the house. Wood smoke, as mentioned, contains many air pollutants. Exposure to CO has been associated with poor fetal development and heart disease in Indian women (Sharma, 1987). In several parts of the country, daily cooking periods are as long as 6 hr, or 25% of the day. No doubt, women are routinely being exposed to gas and suspended particulate matter levels 10 times higher than safe public health levels (Sharma, 1987).

Air particulate amounts increased when dung was used in addition to or in place of wood as a fuel (CSE, 1985). However, biogas can be a healthier energy option for cooking. The gas is composed of methane, CO_2, hydrogen, and nitrogen, of which the calorific value varies depending on the percentage of methane content. In India, from 1000 to 1050 million t (Mt) of wet dung is available from 237 million cattle for producing the biogas. The 206 Mt/year of manure slurry provides about 1.4 Mt of nitrogen (N_2), 1.3 Mt of phosphate (P_2O_5), and 0.9 Mt of potash (K_2O) for the soil (Khoshoo, 1986). Approximately 330,000 biogas plants exist throughout India as of 1985, which shall result in saving 1.2 million t of wood equivalent each year (DNES, 1985).

Methanol and ethanol are also cooking fuel options. They are liquid fuels that can be made from wood or crops such as sugarcane and cassava, but the short supply of these crops makes the process expensive at this time (CSE, 1985). Some proponents of ethanol as an auto fuel indicate that it is "clean burning" if completely combusted because only CO_2 and water are emitted (Goldemberg *et al.*, 1985). In actual use, however, pure ethanol and methanol in automobiles yields increases of several fold in aldehyde emissions. This effect is pronounced in automobiles without catalytic converters (OTA, 1980).

Although the emissions from automobile exhaust may be reduced when burning ethanol as compared with gasoline fuel, the air pollution effects from ethanol are greater than gasoline when the total system is assessed. For example, approximately 700 kcal of diesel fuel are consumed to produce the 15 kg of sugarcane used to produce 1 liter of ethanol. Further, about 7600 kcal of bagasse are burned for the distillation process. Thus, 8300 kcal of air-polluting fuel are burned to produce 1 liter of ethanol that contains 5130 kcal. Thus, ethanol overall is a more serious air pollutant than gasoline, with an equivalent of 5130 kcal when the total system is analyzed. Location, however, may make a difference—ethanol is produced in the rural areas, whereas most of the ethanol is burned in cities.

D. BIOMASS HARVESTING, SOIL EROSION, AND PRODUCTIVITY

Harvesting biomass and increasing erosion adversely affects soil productivity by (1) reducing water availability and water-holding capacity, (2) removing nutrients (nitrogen, phosphorus, potassium, and calcium), (3) reducing organic matter, (4) restricting rooting depth as the soil thins, and (5) reducing soil tilth (OTA, 1982). In the southern United States, soil losses during the past 100–200 years have caused crop-biomass reductions ranging from 25 to 50% for crops such as corn, soybeans, cotton, oats, and wheat (Buntley and Bell, 1976; Langdale et al., 1985). Water is the major limiting factor for U.S. biomass production (Wittwer, 1981). Soil organic matter greatly enhances water infiltration rates. For instance, Wischmeier and Mannering (1965) found that runoff decreased 2.3 times because of improved infiltration when soil organic matter increased from 1 to 4%. When soils have been exposed and degraded by erosion, water infiltration may be reduced as much as 93% (Lal, 1976). Thus, water availability for crop production can be severely limited when insufficient biomass cover exists, soils erode, and soil organic matter decreases.

Water run-off and erosion rates increase when residues are removed or plowed under, as mentioned for conventional crop production. On average, an additional 5 cm/ha of water is lost under conventional cropping systems compared to production systems that employ conservation technology (Pimentel and Krummel, 1987). Each centimeter of added water in crop production has been demonstrated to raise corn yields between 130 kg/ha and 326 kg/ha (de Wit, 1958; Follett et al., 1978; Shalhevet et al., 1979; Hanks, 1983).

After water, shortages of soil nutrients (N, P, K, and Ca) and organic matter are the most important factors in limiting biomass productivity. Average soil erosion rates of 18 t/ha/yr on cropland remove 72 kg of N, 18 kg of P, 360 kg of K, and 180 kg of Ca in addition to any fertilizer nutrients that have been added on agricultural lands. However, erosion does not remove all of the components of the soil equally. Several studies have shown that the material removed by erosion is commonly up to 5 times richer in organic material than the soil left behind (Bennett, 1939). Organic matter is important to soil quality because of its effects on soil water-holding capacity, soil nutrients, soil structure, and cation exchange capacity. Organic matter is required in most soils for the formation of soil aggregates of desirable size, porosity, and stability (Greenland, 1981; Tisdall and Oades, 1982). Poor soil structure limits root growth and restricts the plant's capacity to obtain nutrients and water (Allison, 1973). Reducing soil organic matter from 3.8 to 1.8% was reported (using a model analysis) to lower the yields of corn by about 25% (Lucas et al., 1977).

Organic matter (crop residues) and the biota supply most of the nutrients available in soil; 95% of the nitrogen in surface soil and 15–80% of the phosphorus is in the soil organic matter (Allison, 1973). Nearly all of the remaining phosphorous in the mineral fraction is in a relatively unavailable, insoluble form, so most of the phosphorus entering plants, in the absence of fertilizer, is that made available by microbial breakdown of plant residues (Allison, 1973; Tate, 1984). It is also the primary source of energy for the essential soil biota (Allison, 1973; Volk and Loeppert, 1982). Clearly, soil erosion of organic matter and loss of residues may cause significant losses of nitrogen and phosphorous nutrients for biomass production.

E. OFF-SITE ENVIRONMENTAL EFFECTS FROM BIOMASS HARVESTING AND EROSION

In addition to reducing the productivity of the land, harvesting biomass and intensifying erosion and water runoff can cause several off-site environmental effects. For instance, water runoff in the United States is "delivering approximately 3 billion t/year of sediment to waterways in the 48 contiguous states" (NAS, 1974). About 60% of these sediments come from agricultural lands (Robinson, 1971; Highfill and Kimberlin, 1977; Larson et al., 1983). These off-site effects of erosion in the United States cost an estimated $6 billion annually (Clark, 1985). Just to dredge several million cubic meters of sediments from U.S. rivers, harbors and reservoirs costs an estimated $570 million each year (Clark, 1985). Sedimentation also reduces the useful life of reservoirs and costs the United States about $50 million/year (Robinson, 1971). An estimated 10–25% of new reservoir storage capacity in the United States is currently built solely to store sediments (Clark, 1985). In India, low-water flows and heavy siltation have reduced the storage capacity of reservoirs and cost $427 million in 1980 (Myers, 1986b).

Soil sediments, including pesticides and fertilizer nutrients, carried into rivers, lakes, and reservoirs from agricultural and forestlands adversely affect fish production (USDI, 1982). Sediments interfere with fish spawning, increase predation on fish, and destroy fish food (NAS, 1982). These sediments can also destroy estuarine and coastal fisheries and coral reefs (Begg, 1978; Alexander, 1979; Day and Grindley, 1981). In streams, aquatic damages from soil erosion on fish, other wildlife, water-storage facilities, and navigation have been estimated to be about $4.1 billion annually (Clark, 1985).

VII. CONCLUSION

Demand for food and biomass fuel is projected to intensify because of the rapidly growing world population, increasing affluence, and rising fossil fuel prices as oil and gas supplies continue to decline. This will exaggerate the shortages and conflicts in the food vs fuel issue.

Some balance, we believe, is possible in the food–fuel problem. This balance requires improving the supplies of food and, at the same time, improving the supply of biomass energy without disrupting food production. Within limits, this balance can be accomplished with (1) careful planning, (2) sound soil, water, and biological conservation policies, and (3) implementation of known sustainable agricultural and forestry technologies (Pimentel and Krummel, 1987).

One of the most serious problems in the food vs fuel issue is environmental degradation. Serious environmental problems with food–fuel production currently exist worldwide and include (1) soil erosion rates that are 10–150 times greater than soil formation, (2) water run-off rates that are 10 to 100-fold greater than when conservation practices are employed, (3) flooding and sedimentation effects that cost world society from $12 to $30 billion annually, (4) the loss of soil nutrients (N, P, K, Ca, etc.), that costs from $14 to $40 billion annually, and (5) the destruction of fish and other edible wildlife, which costs several more billion dollars each year.

Clearly, there is need for improved environmental policies to reduce soil erosion, water runoff, and the numerous other problems associated with biomass food and fuel production. Unfortunately, no government in the world has effective policies or legislation for controlling soil erosion and water runoff associated with biomass food and fuel production. This situation exists despite the fact that soil erosion ranks as the most serious environmental problem in the world today (R. Revelle, personal communication; Pimentel et al., 1987b).

Technologies, such as multiple rotation and contour strip cropping, are available today to manage effectively the vegetative cover of the land in order to protect agricultural and forest soils while preventing the loss of vital water and biological resources (Pimentel et al., 1987b). The economic benefits of controlling environmental degradation of soil and water resources are enormous for both farmers and society as a whole (Pimentel et al., 1987b). This is constantly being confirmed as we learn more about the complex relationships that exist among erosion, water runoff, and biomass production.

Other economic benefits could result from achieving a sound balance in biomass food and fuel production despite the fact that food is given higher priority by society and has higher monetary values than biomass fuels. There are clear implications for the development of biomass production technologies and environmental protection. Presently, the biomass fuel producer has fewer technologies available that can be used to protect soil, water, and biological resources because of the lower price of biomass fuel compared with food prices. Also, the low monetary value of biomass fuel reduces the incomes of farmers and laborers. All of these have a negative impact on society and the economy (Pimentel et al., 1984).

If governments subsidize biomass fuel production, as in Brazil and the United States with ethanol programs using sugarcane and corn grain, then a few producers may make enormous profits. In Brazil, revenues to sugarcane growers increased 200% with the ethanol program (Nastari, 1983).

The heavy subsidization of biomass fuel results in a higher priority given to biomass fuel than to food. The result is often reduced food production and higher food prices. Food shortages and high food prices affect society in many negative ways, including inadequate child nutrition. The poor commonly suffer the most when food costs rise. Also, without sound soil and water conservation policies, subsidizing biomass fuel can result in poorer management of soil, water, and biological resources (ERAB, 1981).

Other societal effects from biomass fuel programs include reducing the standard of living of the labor force, as happened in Brazil (van der Pluijm, 1982; OECD, 1984). In addition, the occupational risks in the labor force increase when biomass fuels are given priority over fossil fuels (Pimentel et al., 1984).

Both food and fuel are essential to society. Biomass fuels will have to play a greater role in the economies of most nations in the future. Although the use of biomass fuel has benefits to society, many social and environmental risks are associated with biomass fuel programs. Clearly, the trade-offs between the biomass food–fuel mix, social–economic needs, and the environment must be carefully assessed. Some balance in the biomass food–fuel complex can be achieved if the total system is examined and managed in a holistic manner.

REFERENCES

AAC. 1980. "Agricultural Almanac of China" (Zhonggue Nongye Nianjian). Agricultural Press, Beijing.

Adolphe, D. 1979. Canola. Canada's Rapeseed Crop. Publ. No. 56, prepared at the request of the Rapeseed Association of Canada. Shaw Printing Ltd., Winnipeg, Canada.

Alexander, W. J. R. 1979. Sedimentation of estuaries: Causes, effects and remedies. *Natl. Oceanogr. Symp., 4th, Cape Town, July.*

Allen, J. A. 1986. Fuelwood policies for Swazi nation land: Farm and community approaches for fuelwood production. M.S. thesis, Cornell University, Ithaca, New York.

Allison, F. E. 1973. "Soil Organic Matter and its Role in Crop Production." Elsevier, New York.

Arledge, J. E. 1980. Soil conservation at work: Guatemala's small farmer project. *J. Soil Water Conserv.* **35,** 187–189.

Bailie, R. C. 1976. "Technical and Economic Assessment of Methods for Direct Conversion of Agricultural Residue to Energy." West Virginia University, Morgantown.

Baker, J. B. 1973. Intensive cultural practices increase growth of juvenile slash pine in Florida sandhills. *For. Sci.* **19,** 197–202.

Bansil, P. C. 1984. "Agricultural Statistics in India." Oxford and ITSH Publishing, New Delhi.

Beasley, R. P. 1972. "Erosion and Sediment Pollution Control." Iowa State University Press, Ames.

Begg, G. W. 1978. The estuaries of Natal. Natal Town and Regional Planning Commission, Pietermaritzburg.

Bennett, H. H. 1939. "Soil Conservation." McGraw-Hill, New York.

Biswas, A. K. 1984. "Climate and Development." Tycooly International Pub. Ltd., Dublin.

Biswas, M. R., and Biswas, A. K. 1985. The global environment. Past, present, and future. *Resources Policy* **3**, 25–42.

BLS. 1978. Chartbook on occupational injuries and illnesses in 1976. Report 535. Bureau of Labor Statistics, U.S. Department of Labor, Washington, D.C.

BLS. 1979. Occupational injuries and illnesses in 1977. Summary. Report 561. Bureau of Labor Statistics, U.S. Department of Labor, Washington, D.C.

BLS. 1980. Occupational injuries and illnesses in the United States by industry, 1978. Bulletin 2078. Bureau of Labor Statistics, U.S. Department of Labor, Washington, D.C.

BLS. 1981. Occupational injuries and illnesses in the United States by industry, 1979. Summary. Bulletin 2097. Bureau of Labor Statistics, U.S. Department of Labor, Washington, D.C.

Blum, W. E. H. 1985. Land use in the humid tropics, exemplified by the Amazon Region of Brazil. *Appl. Geogr. Dev.* **25**, 71–87.

Bogach, V. S. 1985. "Wood as Fuel." Praeger, New York.

Bolline, A. 1982. Etude et prévision de l'érosion des sols limoneux cultivés en Moyenne Belgique. Thèse presentée pour l'obtention du grade de Docteur en Sciences Géographiques, Université de Liege (cited in G. Richter, 1983).

Bosworth, D. A., and Foster, A. B. 1982. "Approved Practices in Soil Conservation." Interstate Printers and Publishers, Danville, Illinois.

Brabben, T. E. 1981. Use of turbidity monitors to assess sediment yield in East Java, Indonesia. *In* "Erosion and Sediment Transport Measurement," pp. 105–113. Internatl. Assoc. Hydro. Sci. Publ. No. 133.

Brown, L. R., and Wolf, E. C. 1984. Soil erosion: Quiet crisis in the world economy. Worldwatch Paper No. 60. Worldwatch Institute, Washington, D.C.

Brown, L. R., Chandler, W. U., Flavin, C., Pollock, C., Postel, S., Starke, L., and Wolf, E. C. 1985. "State of the World 1985." Norton, New York.

Brown, L. R., Wolf, E. C., Starke, L., Chandler, W. U., Flavin, C., Postel, S., Wolf, E. C., and Pollock, C. 1986. "State of the World 1986." Norton, New York.

Buntley, G. J., and Bell, F. F. 1976. Yield estimates for the major crops grown on the soils of west Tennessee. *Tenn. Agric. Exp. Stn. Bull.* (561).

Burbach, R., and Flynn, P. 1980. "Agribusiness in the Americas," p. 104. Monthly Review Press, New York.

Buringh, P. 1984. The capacity of the world land area to produce agricultural products. Paper presented at Workshop Intecol and Institute of Mediterranean Agronomy, Zaragoza, Spain. January 30–February 2.

Burnett, E., and Fisher, E. C. 1954. The effect of conservation practices on runoff, available soil moisture and cotton yield. *Proc. Soil Sci. Soc. Am.* **18**, 216–218.

Chapman, D. 1983. "Energy Resources and Energy Corporations." Cornell Univ. Press, Ithaca, New York.

Chapman, D., and Barker, R. 1987. Resource depletion, agricultural research, and development. Paper prepared for U.S. National Academy of Sciences–Czechoslovak Academy of Sciences Workshop on Agricultural Development and Environmental Research, April 6–16, Ceske Budejovice, Czechoslovakia.

Chatterji, M. 1981. Energy and environment in the developing countries: An overall perspective and plans for action. *In* "Energy and Environment in the Developing Countries" (M. Chatterji, ed.), pp. 3–25. Wiley, New York.

CEQ. 1980. Global 2000 report to the President. Technical Report, Vol. 2. U.S. Government Printing Office, Washington, D.C.

Clark, E. H., II. 1985. The off-site costs of soil erosion. *J. Soil Water Conserv.* **40**, 19–22.

Crawford, M. 1987. Back to the energy crisis. *Science* **235**, 626–627.

CSE. 1982. "The State of India's Environment 1982." A Citizen's Report. Centre for Science and Environment, New Delhi.

CSE. 1985. "The State of India's Environment 1984–85." The Second Citizens' Report. Centre for Science and Environment, New Delhi.

Curry, R. R. 1971. Soil destruction associated with forest management and prospects for recovery in geologic time. *ASB Bull.* **18**, 117–128.

Day, J. H., and Grindley, J. R. 1981. The estuarine ecosystem and environmental constraints. *In* "Estuarine Ecology" (J. H. Day, ed.), pp. 345–372. Balkema, Rotterdam.

Desai, I. D., Tavares, G., de Oliveira, D., Douglas, A., Duarte, F. A. M., and de Oliveira, J. E. D. 1980. Food habits and nutritional status of agricultural migrant workers in southern Brazil. *Am. J. Clin. Nutr.* **33**, 702–714.

Dickerson, B. P. 1975. Stormflows and erosion after tree-length skidding on coastal plain soils. *Trans. Am. Soc. Agric. Eng.* **18**, 867–872.

Dickerson, B. P. 1976. Soil compaction after tree-length skidding in northern Mississippi. *Soil Sci. Soc. Am. J.* **40**, 965–966.

Dils, R. E. 1953. Influence of forest cutting and mountain farming on some vegetation, surface soil, and surface runoff characteristics. USDA Forest Station Paper No. 24, Southeast. For. Exp. Stn.

Dissmeyer, G. E. 1976. Erosion and sediment from forest land uses, management practices and disturbances in the southeastern United States. *Proc. Fed. Interagency Sediment. Conf.*, 3rd, *March 22–25, Denver* pp. 1-140–1-148.

DNES. 1984–1985. Annual Report, Department of Non-conventional Energy Sources, Government of India, New Delhi.

DOE. 1981. Wood combustion: State of knowledge survey of environmental, health and safety aspects. Mueller Associates, Baltimore. Rept. No. DOE/EY/10450-74, available from NTIS PC A07/MF/A01.

DOE. 1983. "Energy Projections to the Year 2010." Office of Policy, Planning, and Analysis, U.S. Department of Energy, Washington, D.C.

DST. 1980. Report of the Committee for Recommending Legislative Measures and Administrative Machinery for Ensuring Environmental Protection. Department of Science and Technology, Government of India.

Dudal, R. 1981. An evaluation of conservation needs. *In* "Soil Conservation, Problems and Prospects" (R. P. C. Morgan, ed.), pp. 3–12. Wiley, Chichester.

Dunkerley, J., and Ramsay, W. 1983. Analysis of energy prospects and problems of developing countries. Report to AID Bureau for Program and Policy Coordination. Resources for the Future, Washington, D.C.

Dyrness, C. T. 1965. Soil surface condition following tractor and high-lead logging in the Oregon Cascades. *J. For.* **63**, 272–275.

Earl, D. E. 1975. "Forest Energy and Economic Development." Clarendon, Oxford.

El-Swaify, S. A., Dangler, E. W., and Armstrong, C. L. 1982. "Soil Erosion by Water in the Tropics." Res. Ext. Ser. 024, College of Tropical Agriculture and Human Resources, University of Hawaii, Honolulu.

Elwell, H. A. 1985. An assessment of soil erosion in Zimbabwe. *Zimbabwe Sci. News* **19**, 27–31.

Environmental Fund. 1979. World population estimates. Environmental Fund, Washington, D.C.

EPA. 1986. National air pollutant emission estimates, 1940–1984. U.S. Environmental Protection Agency, Office of Air Quality Planning and Standards, Research Triangle Park, North Carolina.

ERAB. 1980. Gasohol. Report of the Gasohol Study Group, Energy Research Advisory Board, Washington, D.C.

ERAB. 1981. Biomass energy. Energy Research Advisory Board, Department of Energy, Washington, D.C.

FAO. 1983a. "1981 Production Yearbook of Forest Products." FAO, Rome.

FAO. 1983b. Country tables. Basic data on the agricultural sector. FAO, Rome (Microfiche 833041).

FAO. 1984. "Production Yearbook," Vol. 38. FAO, Rome.

Fenster, C. R. 1973. Stubble mulching. *Proc. Natl. Conf., Soil Conserv. Soc. Am.*, Ankeny, *Iowa* pp. 202–207.

Finn, D. 1983. Land use and abuse in the East African region. *Ambio* **12**, 296–301.

Flaim, S., and Urban, D. 1980. The costs of using crop residues in direct applications. SERI TR 353-513, Solar Energy Research Institute, Golden, Colorado.

Follett, R. F., Benz, L. C., Doering, E. J., and Reichman, G. A. 1978. Yield response of corn to irrigation on sandy soils. *Agron. J.* **70**, 823–828.

Froelich, H. A. 1978. Soil compaction from low ground-pressure, torsion-suspension logging vehicles on three forest soils. For. Res. Lab. Res. Paper 36, Oregon State University, School of Forestry, Corvallis, Oregon.

Froelich, H. A. 1979. Soil compaction from logging equipment: Effects on growth of young ponderosa pine. *J. Soil Water Conserv.* **34**, 276–278.

Ghirardi, A. G. 1983. Alcohol fuels from biomass in Brazil: A comparative assessment of methanol vs. ethanol. Ph.D. dissertation, University of California, Berkeley.

GI. 1979. Report of the Working Group on Energy Policy. Government of India, Planning Commission, New Delhi.

Giriappa, S. 1986. "Rural Energy Crisis." Himalaya Publ., Bombay.

Goldemberg, J., Moreira, J. R., Dos Santos, P. U. M., and Serra, G. E. 1985. Ethanol fuel: A use of biomass energy in Brazil. *Ambio* **14**, 293–297.

Greenland, D. J. 1981. Soil management and soil degradation. *J. Soil Sci.* **32**, 301–322.

Hall, D. O. 1985. Biomass: Fuel versus food, a world problem? *In* "Economics of Ecosystems Management" (D. O. Hall, N. Myers, and N. S. Margaris, eds.), pp. 207–226. Junk Publ. Dordrecht.

Hall, D. O., and de Groot, P. J. 1987. Introduction: The biomass framework. *In* "Biomass" (D. O. Hall and R. P. Overend, eds.), pp. 3–24. Wiley, Chichester.

Hall, D. O., Barnard, G. W., and Moss, P. A. 1982. "Biomass for Energy in the Developing Countries: Current Role, Potential, Problems, Prospects." Pergamon, Oxford.

Hall, D. O., Myers, N., and Margaris, N. S., eds. 1985. "Economics of Ecosystems Management." Junk Publ., Dordrecht.

Hanks, J. 1987. Human populations and the world conservation strategy. International Union for Conservation of Nature and Natural Resources, Gland, Switzerland.

Hanks, R. J. 1983. Yield and water-use relationships: An overview. *In* "Limitations to Efficient Water Use in Crop Production" (H. M. Taylor, W. R. Jordan, and T. R. Sinclair, eds.), pp. 393–411. American Society of Agronomy, Crop Science Society of America, and Soil Science Society of America, Madison, WI.

Harrold, L. L., Triplett, G. B., Jr., and Youker, R. E. 1967. Watershed tests of no-tillage corn. *J. Soil Water Conserv.* **22**, 98–100.

Hempel, L. 1951. Ueber Kartierungsmethoden von Bodenerosion durch Wasser. *Neues Arch. Niedersachsen* **26**, 590–598; *In* Zachar, D. 1982. "Soil Erosion. Developments in Soil Science," vol. 10. Elsevier, Amsterdam.

Hempel, L. 1954. Beispiele von Bodenerosion Karten im Niedersachsischen Bergland sowie Bermerkungen ueber Beruecksichtigung der Erosionsschaeden bei der Bodenschaetzung. *Neues Arch. Niedersachsen* **4–6**, 140–143; *In* Zachar, D. 1982. "Soil Erosion. Developments in Soil Science," vol. 10. Elsevier,

Hendrickson, B. H., Barnett, A. P., Carreker, J. R., and Adams, W. E. 1963. Runoff and erosion control studies on Cecil soil in the southern Piedmont. *U.S. Dept. Agric., Tech. Bull. No* (1281).

Hewlett, J. D. 1979. Forest water quality. An experiment in harvesting and regenerating Piedmont forest. Georgia For. Res. Pap., School of Forest Resources, University of Georgia, Athens.

Highfill, R., and Kimberlin, L. 1977. Current soil erosion and sediment control technology for rural and urban lands. *Proc. Natl. Symp. Soil Erosion Sediment. Water, Chicago* pp. 14–22.

Hornbeck, J. W., Likens, G. E., Pierce, R. S., and Bormann, F. H. 1973. Strip cutting as a means of protecting site and streamflow quality when clearcutting northern hardwoods. *Proc. N. Am. Soils Conf., 4th, Quebec* pp. 209–225.

Horner, G. M., Oveson, M. M., Baker, G. O., and Pawson, W. W. 1960. Effect of cropping practices on yield, soil organic matter and erosion in the Pacific Northwest wheat region. Bull. No. 1, Agric. Expt. Stn., Idaho, Oregon, and Washington and Agric. Res. Serv., USDA.

Hosier, R. 1985. Energy use in rural Kenya: Household demand and rural transformation. Beijer Institute, Royal Swedish Academy of Sciences, Scandinavian Institute of African Studies. Energy, Environment and Development in Africa No. 7, OAE. Stockholm, Uppsala.

Hudson, N.W. 1981. "Soil Conservation," 2nd Ed. Cornell Univ. Press, Ithaca, New York.

Jewell, W. J., and Morris, G. R. 1974. The economic and technical feasibility of methane generation from agricultural waste. *In* "Uses of Agricultural Wastes: Food, Fuel, Fertilizer" (R. J. Catania, ed.), pp. 132–164. Univ. of Regina Press, Saskatchewan, Canada.

Jewell, W. J., Davis, H. R., Gunkel, W. W., Lathwell, D. J., Martin, J. H., Jr., McCarty, T. R., Morris, G. R., Price, D. R., and Williams, D. W. 1977. Bioconversion of agricultural wastes for pollution control and energy conservation. Division of Solar Energy, ERDA. Natl. Tech. Info. Serv., Springfield, Virginia.

Kea, J. B. 1975. A study of soil erosion and sediment production rates on selected forestry operations in North Carolina. Forestry Note Number 16, Office of Forest Resources. Raleigh, North Carolina.

Khoshoo, T. N. 1986. Environmental priorities in India and sustainable development. Indian Science Congress Association, New Delhi.

Klock, G. O. 1975. Impact of five postfire salvage logging systems on soils and vegetation. *J. Soil Water Conserv.* **30,** 78–81.

Klock, G. O. 1982. Some soil erosion effects on forest soil productivity. *In* "Determinants of Soil Loss Tolerance," pp. 53–66. Am. Soc. Agron. Spec. Publ. No. 45, Soil Science Society of America, American Society of Agronomy, Madison, Wisconsin.

Kovda, V. A. 1983. Loss of productive land due to salinization. *Ambio* **12,** 91–93.

Kuby, W., Markoja, R., and Nackford, S. 1984. Testing and evaluation of on-farm alcohol production facilities. Acurex Corporation, Industrial Environmental Research Laboratory, Office of Research and Development. U.S. EPA, Cincinnati, Ohio.

LAER. 1976. Latin American Economic Report. October 22, **10,** 236.

LAER. 1977. Latin American Economic Report. July 15.

LAER, 1979. Latin American Economic Report. March 9.

Lal, R. 1976. Soil erosion problems on an alfisol in Western Nigeria and their control. IITA Monograph No. 1, October.

Lal, R. 1983. Erosion-caused productivity decline in soils of the humid tropics. *Soil Taxon. News* **5,** 4–5, 18.

Lal, R. 1984a. Productivity assessment of tropical soils and the effects of erosion. *In* "Quantification of the Effect of Erosion on Soil Productivity in an International Context" (F. J. Rijsberman and M. G. Wolman, eds.), pp. 70–94. Delft Hydraulics Laboratory, Delft.

Lal, R. 1984b. Soil erosion from tropical arable lands and its control. *Adv. Agron.* **37,** 183–248.

Lamb, R., and Milas, S. 1983. Soil erosion, real cause of Ethiopian famine. *Environ. Conserv.* **10,** 157–159.

Langdale, G. W., Denton, H. P., White, A. W., Gilliam, J. W., and Frye, W. W. 1985. Effects of soil erosion on crop productivity of Southern soils. *In* "Soil Erosion and Crop Productivity" (R. F. Follett and B. A. Stewart, eds.), pp. 252–271. American Society of Agronomy, Crop Science Society of America, and Soil Science Society of America, Madison, Wisconsin.

La Rovere, E. L. 1985. A south–south assault on the food/energy problem. *Ceres* **18,** 25–28.

Larson, W. E. 1981. Protecting the soil resource base. *J. Soil Water Conserv.* **36,** 13–16.

Larson, W. E. 1986. The adequacy of world soil resources. *Agron. J.* **78,** 221–225.

Larson, W. E., Pierce, F. J., and Dowdy, R. H. 1983. The threat of soil erosion to long-term crop production. *Science* **219,** 458–465.

Latham, M. C. 1984. International nutrition and problems and policies. *In* "World Food Issues," pp. 55–64. Center for the Analysis of World Food Issues, International Agriculture, Cornell University, Ithaca, New York.

Lee, L. K. 1984. Land use and soil loss: A 1982 update. *J. Soil Water Conserv.* **39,** 226–228.

Lewis C. W. 1976. Fuel production from biomass. Rept. No. 7, Systems Analysis Research Unit, Energy Studies Unit. Univ. Strathclyde, Glasgow.

Linden, H. R. 1980. 1980 assessment of the U.S. and world energy situation and outlook. Gas Research Institute, Chicago.

Lindstrom, M. J., Skidmore, E. L., Gupta, S. C., and Onstad, C. A. 1979. Soil conservation limitations on removal of crop residues for energy production. *J. Environ. Qual.* **8,** 533–537.

Lucas, R. E., Holtman, J. B., and Connor, L. J. 1977. Soil carbon dynamics and cropping practices. *In* "Agriculture and Energy" (W. Lockeretz, ed.), pp. 333–351. Academic Press, New York.

Lundgren, B., and Nair, P. K. R. 1985. Agroforestry for soil conservation. *In* "Soil Erosion and Conservation" (S. A. El-Swaify, W. C. Moldenhauer, and A. Lo, eds.), pp. 703–717. Soil Conservation Society of America, Ankeny, Iowa.

MME. 1987. Ava liaçaõ do Programa Nacional do Álcool. Comissão Nacional de Energia, Ministério de Minas e Energia, Brasilia.

McCashion, J. D., and Rice, R. M. 1983. Erosion on logging roads in northwestern California: How much is avoidable? *J. For.* **81,** 23–26.

McCormack, D. E., Young, K. K., and Kimberlim, L. W. 1982. Current criteria for determining soil loss tolerance. ASA Spec. Publ. No. 45, American Society of Agronomy, Madison, Wisconsin.

Mannering, J. V. 1984. Conservation tillage to maintain soil productivity and improve water quality. Agronomy Guide (Tillage) AY 222. Coop. Ext. Scrv., Purdue University, West Lafayette, Indiana.

Mannering, J. V., Nelson, D. W., and Johnson, C. B. 1980. Environmental impact of cropland agriculture on water quality. *In* "Assessment of Erosion" (M. deBoodt and D. Gabriels, eds.). Wiley, Chichester.

Meade, G. P., and Chen, J. C. P. 1977. "Cane Sugar Handbook." Wiley, New York.

Megahan, W. F. 1972. Logging, erosion, sedimentation—are they dirty words? *J. For.* **70,** 403–407.

Megahan, W. F. 1975. Sedimentation in relation to logging activities in the mountains of central Idaho. *In* "Present and Prospective Technology for Predicting Sediment Yields and Sources," pp. 74–82. Proc. Sediment–Yield Workshop, USDA, Sedimentation Laboratory, Oxford, Miss., Nov. 28–30, 1972. USDA Agr. Res. Serv., ARS-S-40.

Megahan, W. F., and Kidd, W. J. 1972. Effects of logging and logging roads on erosion and sediment deposition from steep terrain. *J. For.* **70,** 136–141.

de Melo, F. H. 1986. Brazil and the CGIAR centers: A study of their collaboration in agricultural research. CGIAR Paper #9. World Bank, Washington, D.C.

Mills, W. C., Thomas, A. W., and Langdale, G. W. 1986. Estimating soil loss probabilities for southern Piedmont cropping-tillage systems. *Trans. Am. Soc. Agric. Eng.* **29,** 948–955.

Mishra, R. K., ed. 1986. "India Towards 1990s." Patriot Publ., New Delhi.

Molofsky, J., Hall, C. A. S., and Myers, N. 1986. A comparison of tropical forest surveys. CO_2 Research Division, U.S. Department of Energy, Washington, D.C.

de Montalembert, M. R. and Clement, J. 1983. Fuelwood supplies in the developing countries. Forestry Paper No. 42. FAO, Rome.

Moreira, J. R. and Goldemberg, J. 1981. Alcohols—its use, energy and economics—A Brazilian outlook. *Resource Manage. Optim.* **1,** 231–279.

Moreira, J. R., and Serra, G. E. 1985. "The Brazilian National Alcohol Program—Incentives and Subsidies." International Institute of Environment and Development, California.

Morris, S. C. 1981. Health effects of residential wood fuel use. Brookhaven National Laboratory, Upton, New York.

Myers, N. 1984. Genetic resources in jeopardy. *Ambio* **13,** 171–174.

Myers, N. 1986a. Forestland farming in western Amazonia: Stable and sustainable. *For. Ecol. Manage.* **15,** 81–93.

Myers, N. 1986b. Environmental repercussions of deforestation in the Himalayas. *J. World For. Resource Manage.* **2,** 63–72.

Nair, P. K. R. 1984. Soil Productivity Aspects of Agroforestry. International Council for Research in Agroforestry (ICRAF), Nairobi, Kenya.

Narayana, D. V. V., and Babu, R. 1983. Estimation of soil erosion in India. *J. Irrig. Drain. Eng.* **109,** 419–434.

NAS. 1974. Productive agriculture and a quality environment. National Academy of Sciences, Washington, D.C.

NAS. 1980. Firewood crops: Shrubs and tree species for energy production. National Academy Press, Washington, D.C.

NAS. 1982. Impact of emerging agricultural trends on fish and wildlife habitat. National Academy of Sciences, National Academy Press, Washington, D.C.

Nastari, P. M. 1983. The role of sugar cane in Brazil's history and economy. Ph.D. thesis, Iowa State University, Ames.

OECD. 1984. Biomass for energy: Economic and policy issues. Organization for Economic Cooperation and Development, Paris.

O'Keefe, P. 1983. The causes, consequences and remedies of soil erosion in Kenya. *Ambio* **12,** 302–305.

O'Keefe, P., and Raskin, P. 1985. Fuelwood in Kenya: Crisis and opportunity. *Ambio* **14,** 220–224.

O'Keefe, P., Raskin, P., and Bernow, S., eds. 1984. Energy and development in Kenya: Opportunities and constraints. Energy, Environment and Development in Africa, I, OC. Beijer Institute, Royal Swedish Academy of Sciences, Scandinavian Institute of African Studies, Stockholm, Uppsala.

Ortmaier, E. 1981. The production of ethanol from sugarcane: Brazil's experiment for a partial solution to the energy problem. *Q. J. Int. Agric.* **20,** 265–278.

Osuji, G. E. 1984. The gullies of Imo. *J. Soil Water Conserv.* **39,** 246–247.

OTA. 1980. "Energy from Biological Processes," Vols. 1 and 2. Office of Technology Assessment, Washington, D.C.

OTA. 1982. "Impacts of Technology on U.S. Cropland and Rangeland Productivity." Office of Technology Assessment. Government Printing Office, Washington, D.C.

OTA. 1984. Technologies to sustain tropical forest resources. OTA-F-214, Congress of the United States, Office of Technology Assessment, Washington, D.C.

Patric, J. H. 1976. Soil erosion in the eastern forest. *J. For.* **74,** 671–677.

Patric, J. H. 1980. Effect of wood products harvest on forest soil and water relations. *J. Environ. Qual.* **9,** 73–80.

Patric, J. H., Evans, J. O., and Helvey, J. D. 1984. Summary of sediment yield data from forested land in the United States. *J. For.* **82,** 101–104.

Pereira, A. 1983. Employment implications of ethanol production in Brazil. *Int. Labour Rev.* **122,** 111–127.

Peterson, A. E., and Swan, J. B., eds. 1979. ''Universal Soil Loss Equation: Past, Present, and Future.'' Soil Science Society of America, Madison, Wisconsin.

Pimentel, D. 1977. Biomass energy conversion: Ecological, economic, and social constraints. Final Report for the Energy Research Analysis Division, National Science Foundation, Washington, D.C.

Pimentel, D., ed. 1980. ''Handbook of Energy Utilization in Agriculture.'' CRC Press, Boca Raton, Florida.

Pimentel, D., and Dazhong, W. 1988. Technological changes in energy use in U.S. agricultural production. *In* ''The Ecology of Agricultural Systems'' (C. R. Carroll, J. H. Vandermeer, and P. M. Rosset, eds.). MacMillan, New York, in press.

Pimentel, D., and Krummel, J. 1987. Biomass energy and soil erosion: Assessment of resource costs. *Biomass* **14,** 15–38.

Pimentel, D., Hurd, L. E., Bellotti, A. C., Forster, M. J., Oka, I. N., Sholes, O. D., and Whitman, R. J. 1973. Food production and the energy crisis. *Science* **182,** 443–449.

Pimentel, D., Nafus, D., Vergara, W., Papaj, D., Jaconetta, L., Wulfe, M., Olsvig, L., Frech, K., Loye, M., and Mendoza, E. 1978. Biological solar energy conversion and U.S. energy policy. *BioScience* **28,** 376–382.

Pimentel, D., Oltenacu, P. A., Nesheim, M. C., Krummel, J., Allen, M. S., and Chick, S. 1980a. The potential for grass-fed livestock: Resource constraints. *Science* **207,** 843–848.

Pimentel, D., Andow, D., Dyson-Hudson, R., Gallahan, D., Jacobson, S., Irish, M., Kroop, S., Moss, A., Schreiner, I., Shepard, M., Thompson, T., and Vinzant, B. 1980b. Environmental and social costs of pesticides: A preliminary assessment. *Oikos* **34,** 127–140.

Pimentel, D., Moran, M. A., Fast, S., Weber, G., Bukantis, R., Balliett, L. Boveng, P., Cleveland, C., Hindman, S., and Young, M. 1981. Biomass energy from crop and forest residues. *Science* **212,** 1110–1115.

Pimentel, D., Fried, C., Olson, L., Schmidt, S., Wagner-Johnson, K., Westman, A., Whelan, A. M., Foglia, K., Poole, P., Klein, T., Sobin, R., and Bochner, A. 1983a. Biomass energy: Environmental and social costs. Environ. Biol. Rept. 83-2, Cornell University, Ithaca, New York.

Pimentel, D., Fast, S., Gallahan, D., and Moran, M. A. 1983b. The energetic and environmental aspects of utilizing crop and forest residues for biomass energy. Final Report for U.S. Department of Energy, Washington, D.C.

Pimentel, D., Fried, C., Olson, L., Schmidt, S., Wagner-Johnson, K., Westman, A., Whelan, A., Foglia, K., Poole, P., Klein, T., Sobin, R., and Bochner, A. 1984. Environmental and social costs of biomass energy. *BioScience* **34,** 89–94.

Pimentel, D., Dazhong, W., Eigenbrode, S., Lang, H., Emerson, D., and Karasik, M. 1986. Deforestation: Interdependency of fuelwood and agriculture. *Oikos* **46,** 404–412.

Pimentel, D., Budowski, G., Fortmann, L., Gritzner, J., Reining, P., and Winterbottom, R. 1987a. Report on Agroforestry. AAAS Committee on Population, Resources, and the Environment. Draft.

Pimentel, D., Allen, J., Beers, A., Guinand, L., Linder, R., McLaughlin, P., Meer, B., Musonda, D., Perdue, D., Poisson, S., Siebert, S., Stoner, K., Salazar, R., and Hawkins, A. 1987b. World agriculture and soil erosion. *BioScience* **37,** 277–283.

Pimentel, D., Culliney, T., Buttler, I., Reinemann, D., and Beckman, K. 1988. Ecological resource management for a productive, sustainable agriculture. *In* "Food and Natural Resources" (D. Pimentel and C. W. Hall, eds.), in press. Academic Press, New York.

van der Pluijm, T. 1982. Energy versus food? Implications of macro-economic adjustments on land-use patterns: the ethanol programme in Brazil. *Bol. Estud. Latinoam. Caribe* (33), 85–106.

Power, J. F., and Papendick, R. I. 1985. Organic sources of nutrients. *In* "Fertilizer Technology and Use" (O. P. Engelstad, ed.), pp. 503–520. Soil Science Society of America, Madison, Wisconsin.

PRB. 1977. 1977 world population data sheet. Population Reference Bureau, Washington, D.C.

PRB. 1983. 1983 world population data sheet. Population Reference Bureau, Washington, D.C.

PRB. 1986. World population data sheet. Population Reference Bureau, Washington, D.C.

Randrianarijaona, P. 1983. The erosion of Madagascar. *Ambio* **12**, 308–311.

Ricaud, R. 1980. Energy input and output for sugarcane in Louisiana. *In* "Handbook of Energy Utilization in Agriculture" (D. Pimentel, ed.), pp. 135–136. CRC Press, Boca Raton, Florida.

Rice, R. M., Rothacher, J. S., and Megahan, W. F. 1972. Erosional consequences of timber harvesting: An appraisal. *Proc. Natl. Symp. Watersheds Transition, Fort Collins, June 19–22, Am. Water Resour. Assoc.* pp. 321–329.

Richter, G. 1983. Aspects and problems of soil erosion hazard in the EEC countries. *CEC Soil Erosion Conserv. Symp. Proc., Florence* pp. 9–18.

Robinson, A. R. 1971. Sediment: Our greatest pollutant? *Agric. Eng.* **52**, 406–408.

Rosillo-Calle, F. R., and Hall, D. O. 1987. Brazillian alcohol: Food versus fuel? *Biomass* **12**, 97–128.

Ruth, R. H. 1967. Silvicultural effects of skyline crane and high-lead yarding. *J. For.* **65**, 251–255.

Sanchez-Sierra, G., and Umana-Quesada, A. 1984. Quantitative analysis of the role of biomass within energy consumption in Latin America. *Biomass* **4**, 21–41.

Sauer, E. L., and Case, H. C. M. 1954. Soil conservation pays off. Results of ten years of conservation farming in Illinois. *Univ. Ill. Agric. Exp. Sta. Bull.* (575).

SF. 1982. Experts cooling to alternative fuels. *Successful Farm.* **80**, 13.

SF. 1983. 19,000 lb of milk and 850 kwh of electricity. James R. Borcherding. *Successful Farm.* **Dec.**, D-2-4.

Shalhevet, J., Mantell, A., Bielorai, H., and Shimshi, D. 1979. Irrigation of field and orchard crops under semi-arid conditions. International Irrigation Information Center, Volcani Center, Bet Dagan, Israel (distributed by Pergamon, New York).

Sharma, A. 1987. Resources and human well-being: Inputs from science and technology. Indian Science Congress Association, Calcutta.

da Silva, J. G., Serra, G. E., Moreira, J. R., Concalves, J. C., and Goldemberg, J. 1978. Energy balance for ethyl alcohol production from crops. *Science* **201**, 903–906.

Silva, J. R. C., Coelho, M. A., Moreira, E. G. S., and Neto, P. R. O. 1985. Efeitos da erosaõ na produtividade de dois solos da classe la tossolo vermelho-amarelo. *Cien. Agron. Fortaleza* **16**, 55–63.

Slesser, M., and Lewis, C. 1979. "Biological Energy Resources." Halsted, New York.

Smith, D. D. 1946. The effect of contour planting on crop yield and erosion losses in Missouri. *J. Am. Soc. Agron.* **38**, 810–819.

Sourie, J.-C., and Killen, L. 1986. "Biomass: Recent Economic Studies." Elsevier, New York.

South. 1984. *Third World Mag.* **Oct.** (48)

Stafford, D. A. 1983. Methane from farm wastes and energy recovery. *In* "Fuel Gas Developments" (D. L. Wise, ed.), pp. 1–17. CRC Press, Boca Raton, Florida.

Stocking, M. 1985. Erosion-induced loss of soil productivity: Trends in research and international cooperation. *Int. Conf. Soil Conserv., 4th, Maracay, Venezuela, Nov. 3–9*.

Stuckey, D., and Juma, C. 1985. Power alcohol in Kenya and Zimbabwe: A case study in the transfer of a renewable energy technology. UNCTAD/TT/61, UNCTAD Secretariat.

Swank, W. T., and Douglass, J. E. 1977. Nutrient budgets for undisturbed and manipulated hard-wood forest ecosystems in the mountains of North Carolina. *In* "Watershed Research in Eastern North America. A Workshop to Compare Results" (D. L. Correll, ed.), pp. 343–363. Vol. I, Feb. 28–March 3. Chesapeake Bay Center for Environmental Studies, Smithsonian Institution, Edgewater, Maryland.

Swanson, E. R., and Harshbarger, C. E. 1964. An economic analysis of effects of soil loss on crop yields. *J. Soil Water Conserv.* **19,** 183–186.

Swanston, D. N., and Dyrness, C. T. 1973. Managing steep land. *J. For.* **71,** 264–269.

Tate, K. R. 1984. The biological transformation of P in soil. *Plant Soil* **76,** 245–256.

Teel, W. 1984. "A Pocket Directory of Trees and Seeds in Kenya." KENGO, Nairobi, Kenya.

Tisdall, J. M., and Oades, J. M. 1982. Organic matter and water-stable aggregates in soils. *J. Soil Sci.* **33,** 141–163.

Troeh, F. R., Hobbs, J. A., and Donahue, R. L. 1980. "Soil and Water Conservation for Productivity and Environmental Protection." Prentice-Hall, New York.

UN. 1976. "Statistical Yearbook," Vol. 30. United Nations, New York.

UN. 1982. "Statistical Yearbook, 1980," Vol. 33. United Nations, New York.

UN. 1983. "Handbook of International Trade and Development Statistics." United Nations, New York.

UN. 1986. "Energy Balance and Electricity Profiles 1984." United Nations, New York.

UNEP. 1980. "Annual Review." United Nations Environment Programme, Nairobi, Kenya.

UNEP. 1981. "Environment and Development in Africa." Prepared by Environmental Development Action in the Third World (ENDA). Pergamon, Oxford.

USBC. 1982. "Statistical Abstract of the United States 1982," 103rd Ed. U.S. Bureau of the Census, U.S. Government Printing Office, Washington, D.C.

USBC. 1985. "Statistical Abstract of the United States 1985," 105th Ed. U.S. Bureau of the Census, U.S. Government Printing Office, Washington, D.C.

USDA. 1967. "Agricultural Statistics 1967." U.S. Government Printing Office, Washington, D.C.

USDA. 1980. "America's Soil and Water: Conditions and Trends." USDA Soil Conservation Service. U.S. Government Printing Office, Washington, D.C.

USDA. 1983. "Agricultural Statistics 1983." U.S. Government Printing Office, Washington, D.C.

USDA. 1985. "Agricultural Statistics 1985." U.S. Government Printing Office, Washington, D.C.

USDI, 1982. "Manual of Stream Channelization Impacts on Fish and Wildlife." U.S. Dept. of Interior, Fish and Wildlife Service. Biol. Serv. Program.

USFS. 1977. Generalized erosion and sediment rates for disturbed and undisturbed forest land in the Northeast. U.S. Forest Service, USDA.

USDA-ARS and EPA-ORD. 1976. "Control of Water Pollution from Cropland." EPA Report No. EPA-600/2-75-0266, ARS Report No. ARS-H-5-2. 2 vols. U.S. Government Printing Office, Washington, D.C.

Vimal, O. P., and Tyagi, P. D. 1984. "Energy from Biomass." Agricole Publ., New Delhi.

Volk, B. G., and Loeppert, R. H. 1982. Soil organic matter. *In* "Handbook of Soils and Climate in Agriculture" (V. J. Kilmer, ed.), pp. 211–268. CRC Press, Boca Raton, Florida.

Wen Dazhong, and Pimentel, D. 1984. Energy use in crop systems in northeastern China. *In* "Food and Energy Resources" (D. Pimentel and C. W. Hall, eds.), pp. 91–120. Academic Press, New York.

Wiggins, S. L. 1981. The economics of soil conservation in the Acelhuate River Basin, El Salvador. *In* "Soil Conservation: Problems and Prospects" (R. P. C. Morgan, ed.), pp. 399–415. Wiley, Chichester.

Wijewardene, R., and Waidyanatha, P. 1984. "Systems, Techniques and Tools. Conservation Farming for Small Farmers in the Humid Tropics." Department of Agriculture, Sri-Lanka and the Commonwealth Consultative Group on Agriculture for the Asia-Pacific Region.

Wischmeier, W. H., and Mannering, J. V. 1965. Effect of organic matter content of the soil on infiltration. *J. Soil Water Conserv.* **20,** 150–152.

de Wit, C. T. 1958. Transpiration and crop yields. *Versl. Landbouwk. Onderz.* (64.6).

Wittwer, S. 1981. New technology, agricultural production, and conservation. *Soil Conserv. Policies Symp., Zion, Illinois* **13,** (5/6).

Wood, T. S., and Baldwin, S. 1985. Fuelwood and charcoal use in developing countries. *Annu. Rev. Energy* **10,** 407–429.

World Bank. 1980. Alcohol production from biomass in the development countries. Washington, D.C.

Yang, V., and Trindade, S. C. 1978. The Brasilian gasohol program. *In* "Symposium Papers, Energy from Biomass Wastes," pp. 815–836. Institute of Gas Technology, Chicago.

Yeager, R., and Miller, N. N. 1986. "Wildlife, Wild Death: Land Use and Survival in Eastern Africa." State Univ. of New York Press, Albany.

Yoho, N. S. 1980. Forest management and sediment production in the South—a review. *South. J. Appl. For.* **4,** 27–35.

Zachar, D. 1982. "Soil Erosion." Elsevier, New York.

ADVANCES IN FOOD RESEARCH, VOL. 32

FACTORS INFLUENCING FOOD SELECTION IN THE AMERICAN DIET

CAROL I. WASLIEN

Nutrition and Food Science Program
School of Health Sciences
Hunter College
City University of New York
New York, New York 10010

239

I.   INTRODUCTION

A national priority to identify the factors which influence food selection was first recognized in 1941 by the National Academy of Science, National Research Council's Committee on Food Habits of American Populations when rationing of food supplies in the United States and Europe was deemed essential for winning World War II (Mead, 1962). It had been recognized by anthropologists that the various ethnic groups in the United States had distinctive patterns of food consumption and that income level and place of residence also influenced food selection. Recommendations were more easily formulated in the 1940s because the majority of the population came from Europe and their diets were fairly homogenous. Meat, bread, dairy products. and potatoes were important components of nearly all American diets. Although there were regional differences that reflected both the foods available locally and the predominate ethnic groups settling in the region, food habits and customs were reasonably predictable from one generation to the next. All three of the factors known to effect food habits—ethnicity, regionality, and habit or custom—tended to reinforce each other to limit variation within a group (Gibson, 1981); once the food habits of a given population had been described, this description could be expected to continue to be a useful index for predicting the foods selected by an individual.

Today, a new set of factors has begun to regulate food selection patterns, or foodways, that are reflective of the increased wealth and diversity of the U.S. population. These factors tend to create individual rather than group changes (Gibson, 1981), which reduces predictability. For the majority of the U.S. population, income is no longer the principal limiting factor of what foods are chosen; instead, the time available for food purchases, preparation, and consumption has become of paramount importance (Lipton, 1986). This new relative wealth has also provided the average consumer the luxury of being able to choose within a heirarchy of additional values permitting some individuals to chose foodways that protect the environment, others to choose to protect themselves from potential contamination, and still others to choose, hedonistically, to eat only what and when they desire. Improvements in food production and processing technology have also increased the variety of foods available nationwide, which inevitably has increased the diversity of foods in the American diet (Jerome, 1981). When technological innovation was combined with the greater exposure to new foods that travel and restaurant dining afforded through increased individual and family income, the range of new foods in the American diet was expanded even further. Although these new factors—the constraints of time, the selection from a wide range of value options, and the exposure to new foods—all tend to reinforce each other in the individual, they operate in different directions from ethnicity, regionality, and habit—the previously recognized sources of variation in food-choice behavior. They encourage experimentation, change, and diversity rather than consistency in the diets of traditional consumer groups.

All factors or constraints to food selection are entwined with the connotative attributes given to a food or meal. Senses of love and belonging, reward and status, hospitality and sophistication, or security and nurturing can be expressed through food selected for oneself and one's family and friends. The resulting foodways of an individual may thus be composed of a mixture of foods with conflicting attributes as one influential factor gains or loses precedence over another within this emotionally charged environment of food selection.

II. CHARACTERISTICS OF THE U.S. CONSUMING PUBLIC

In addition to these changes in the physical and social environment which influence food selection, there have been marked alterations in the demography and life-styles of U.S. consumers during the past 40 years. Some of these changes have had a marked influence on the nation's food-purchasing and consumption behavior.

A. HOUSEHOLD COMPOSITION

A major change has taken place in the composition of the household, the unit for most of the food consumption in the United States. Traditionally, the household has been a single, nuclear family consisting of a mother, a father, and 2 or 3 young children. The mother was responsible for most of the food purchases and food preparation, both of which were directed by the food preferences of the father (Bryon and Lowenberg, 1958). Children learned to prefer what was presented and approved by their mothers (Litman et al., 1964). In the past decade, the size of the typical American family has continued to shrink, from a mean of 2.9 in 1970 to 2.5 in 1985 (Raskin, 1979); it is expected to continue this decline in the coming decades. The biggest decrease has been in the number of large families with 4 or more children, which decreased from 37 to 26% of the total households (Putnam and Van Drees, 1984). Single-parent households with a child less than 18 years old have shown the biggest increase of any family category (Anonymous, 1982a) and are predicted to become more common than traditional two-parent households by the turn of the century (Anonymous,

1985a). There has also been a substantial increase in the percentage of single-person households as the number of people who never marry increases, divorced or widowed spouses choose not to remarry, and young people delay marriage; today, nearly 25% of all households consists of a single person (Exter, 1987). The biggest percentage increase within this category has been in the number of single men living alone.

B.   WOMEN EMPLOYED OUTSIDE THE HOME

Not only are there fewer typical households, but the mother in the typical family is no longer the sole purchaser and preparer of the family's food because more women have chosen or need to work outside of the home. More than 50% of today's married women are employed, and the typical family of a husband, nonworking wife, and a child less than 18 years old has fallen from 70% of households in the 1950s to 14% in the 1980s (Chou, 1986a). This increase in employed women is partly due to the increased education of women and their greater life expectancy. In the 1870s, a woman's average life expectancy was 50, the same as her age when her last child reached the age of 15 years and was ready to leave home. Thus her life was nearly over when she was no longer a full-time mother. With today's smaller families and improvements in health care, the average woman is 42 years old when her last child reaches the age of 15, and she can be expected to live another 30 years. Since she is no longer as dependent on a husband for child support, she is more able to work and to be independent (McKenzie, 1982). In many cases, this working woman relies on her husband and children to do many of the tasks she once did, such as food purchasing and preparation. She also chooses more easily prepared foods and eats more meals away from home, releasing time for more enjoyable activities, both to reduce the stress of combining the worlds of work, motherhood, and homemaker and to serve as a reward for achieving a higher income and greater status for herself in the community (Langer, 1986; Jackson *et al.*, 1985).

III.   FOOD PREFERENCE AND AGE OF THE CONSUMER

These changes in family composition and improvements in health care have resulted in an increase in the age of the U.S. consumer which has had important repercussions for foodways. Physiological changes which are known to occur as a person ages could influence food preference. In addition, neither a very young child nor a frail, elderly adult with chronic health problems has the mobility, shopping skills, and food preparation ability of younger adults. These changes have long been recognized by food marketers, but only recently has the demographic imperative attracted much notice (Chou, 1983).

A.   MATURATION OF SENSE OF TASTE AND FOOD PREFERENCES

The sense of taste and smell are important influences on the foods selected and eaten. However, the exact nature of the effects of these sensory functions on food preferences is unclear. It is well established that an infant has an innate, positive response to sweet taste that can be detected within days of birth (Food and Nutrition Board, 1985). The detection of, but indifference to, salt is also observed in infants, but a salt selection pattern closer to that of adults only appears in older children. With facial expressions, 2-year-old children show that they reject salty water, but they will eat more salted than unsalted carrots. Sour and bitter stimuli show less clear-cut developmental trends. Neonates grimace when sour or bitter substances are placed on their tongues, but, again, not until they are 2 years old do children appear to be able to differentiate between decrements in bitterness with an ability equal to that of adults (Lawless, 1985).

B.   MATURATION OF OLFACTION AND FOOD PREFERENCES

Olfactory ability is also present at birth as evidenced by a neonate's ability to pick out his or her mother's scent from a group by breast-pad odor alone. However, the strong reactions that adults have to the pleasantness and unpleasantness of odors do not appear until the child is 5 years of age. When young children were polled as to the positive or negative character of an odor, they tended to answer in the affirmative—e.g., that the odor of butyric acid was both good and bad. When forced to rank choices between odors, the closer they were in age to 7 years and older, the more they tended to respond as would an adult (Lawless, 1985).

Flavors that affect the oral trigeminal system tend to be rejected by children, but, in low doses, odors that affect the nasal trigeminal senses are reacted to in a rather nondiscriminatory manner. Very little is known of the child's response to the other factors which affect adult food preferences, such as texture, temperature, and appearance.

C.   LEARNED FOOD PREFERENCES

As the child reaches school age it is apparent that acquired rather than innate taste preferences are probably more important. Studies of 13 to 14 year olds showed that even a genetic ability to detect the taste of compounds did not influence flavor preferences, except for those who could taste phenylthiocarbamate and, thus, had an aversion to bitter-tasting foods such as beet and turnip greens (Jefferson and Erdman, 1970). Others, 9 to 15 year olds, seem to retain their early childhood preference for sweet tastes and to prefer sweet foods more and salty ones less than do adults (Plinar, 1983). When asked what foods they liked best from a list of foods served in the dining halls, young adult military personnel (mean age 25 years) were more likely to state a preference for sweet foods, although not necessarily sweet desserts; 40% of the 50 most preferred foods were sweet, while only 14% of the 50 least preferred were sweet (Meiselman, 1977).

1. Preference Development in the Family Setting

There is no doubt that the majority of adult food preferences is learned in the family setting. By age 2 to 4 years the young child has learned to eat what he or she is given or to refuse to eat as a mechanism for attracting attention (National Dairy Council, 1976). The child learns, mostly from the mother, that certain foods are "good" (vegetables) and must be eaten, even if they are not tasty, and that other, more tasty foods (candy, soft drinks) are "bad" or can only be eaten as a reward for being well-behaved (Litman et al., 1964). Several studies have shown that when preschool children and their parents were asked to rank fruit, vegetables, sandwiches, and snack foods in order of preference, there is a positive correlation between the choices of the child and his or her mother. This correlation was greater than that between the child and nonrelated mothers from the same subculture. However, there was no difference in the correlation between the preferences of the child and his or her father and between the child and nonrelated fathers from the same subculture, indicating that the mothers' preferences were a stronger influence for this age group (Plinar, 1983). For college-age students living at home, there continued to be a strong correlation between the food preferences of the mother and her children, but a significant relationship also began to appear between the preferences of the child and his or her father, with the highest correlations being in mother–daughter and father–son matchings. If the frequency of serving the food in the home during the preceeding 2 years was held constant, similar-sex child–parent correlations decreased but were still significant for both mothers and fathers. When the child's perceived food-preference response of the parent was held constant, there was also a significant reduction in the correlation. Thus, both the frequency of serving the food and imitation of the parents were causes for the similarity in preferences of children and their parents. The fact that a male child was more similar to his father and a female child to her mother also supported imitation of sex role as a source of variation in food preferences (Plinar, 1983).

2. Preference Development in the Social Setting

Learning by imitation does not occur just in the home. Experiments with children in day-care centers have shown that a younger child can be led to copy the food choices of an older child starting as early as 32 months of age even when a food is not preferred initially. For imitation to occur, the child must form a group identification and the prestige of that association must be favorable (Duncker, 1938). The child must discover for himself or herself that the beliefs of the group (or of the group leader, who is an authority for the group) are also appropriate for him or her (National Dairy Council, 1976). Others have shown that for lasting change to occur there must be some alteration in the connotative meanings associated with the food.

A multitude of apparently unrelated events specific for the individual can influence food preferences. Perceived danger (i.e., nausea) can create food aversions, while increased exposure, rapid satiety, or association with an already preferred food tends to enhance liking. Psychological states can also influence food aversions; both children and adults with a poor self-image and emotional problems tend to have an increased number of aversions (Gaugh, 1946).

D. METABOLIC FUNCTION AND FOOD PREFERENCES

Hedonic ratings of food by adults have been shown to be also influenced by metabolic status. Short-term caloric loading with glucose or with certain food combinations can reduce the pleasantness ratings for sweet sucrose solutions, while sustained caloric deprivation leads to enhanced pleasantness ratings for sweet stimuli (Drewnowski, 1984). The level of carbohydrate present in the food needed to produce the desired change in serotonin in the brain and the resulting sensations of relaxation and satisfaction may be a link in this preference behavior (Shiffman, 1986).

Obesity appears to influence taste preferences because obese adults have been shown to want more taste and odor from their food and will consume less of a food if it has a pronounced flavor or odor (Shiffman, 1986). When asked what foods they prefer, the obese tended to choose spicy and highly flavored foods (Drewnowski, 1984) that are main-dish items rather than desserts (Meiselman, 1977). Cognitive and attitudinal factors, of course, may underlie these judgments of food preference since obese individuals are likely to consider desserts as fattening and may be unwilling to admit their true preferences (Drewnowski, 1984). It is also possible that obese individuals develop higher set points for flavor satisfaction because they use certain foods to deal with uncomfortable states such as boredom, anger, and frustration. The amount of food needed to satisfy the flavor set point of an overweight adult might be only peripherally related to the amount perceived to be needed to satisfy another emotional goal.

E. LOSS OF SENSE OF TASTE AND SMELL WITH AGING

The number of taste buds and olfactory receptors decreases markedly with age. This causes the sensitivity of the senses of taste and smell to be diminished starting in the fifth and sixth decades of life, and possibly, increases the amount of flavor and odor needed to produce satisfaction (Shiffman, 1986). Foods also taste more sour and bitter. Superimposed on these aging changes may be more frequent nutrient deficiencies and a reduction in appetite brought on by increased illness and frequent medication, particularly in the frail elderly. Poor dentition and reduced peristalsis may necessitate modification in the texture of some foods as well. As the number of individuals in the United States who live beyond 75 years increases, the percentage of the total elderly who are advised to consume low-salt, low-sugar, and low-fat diets also increases, further limiting the range of acceptable foods in the diet of this segment of the population. In a national survey of households, the elderly who had to control their salt and calorie intakes represented one-half of the 30% of households who were concerned about nutrition (Haley, 1984).

IV. FOOD ATTITUDES AND AGE OF THE CONSUMER

A. INFLUENCE OF THE FAMILY SETTING

Neither innate taste detection nor learned taste preferences entirely determine what will be eaten by the child or adult; familiarity, positive associations with eating specific foods, and availability have a major impact on selection. The values and attitudes of the mother will determine, to a large extent, what foods are available in the household for consumption by preschool and school-age children, although the strength of this influence has eroded somewhat in recent decades because more mothers are employed outside of the home. A 1985 survey of 2000 women, primarily 18 to 65 years old and from households with more than two family members, showed that 50% of those surveyed agreed that there had been an increase in the number of meals eaten separately by family members in the past three years, and 44% said that there had been an increase in the number of meals eaten away from home by all family members (Fabricant, 1986). Often, the child makes his or her own breakfast [reported in 25% of the households in 1961 and continuing to increase (National Dairy Council, 1976)] and heats up his or her own dinner in the microwave oven after school (Sloan, 1985a; Brody, 1987). With the increase in working mothers and the constraints on the time available for food preparation, the concern of the mother has shifted somewhat from the preparation of appropriate foods for her children to the purchase of appropriate ready-made foods; the concern for the well-being of her child, however, has not diminished (Jackson *et al.*, 1985). And, in fact, the higher income of the two-wage household, as well as a perceived need to compensate for the lack of direct involvement in food preparation, has probably increased the demands by the mother for the health value in this food (McKenzie,

1982). In a 1983 survey of 200 mothers with children less than 12 years old from 200 cities across the United States, mothers said that they were "very concerned" about the health-promoting attributes of the food for their children (Sloan, 1985b). The prime nutrition concerns were the high salt, sugar, caffeine, and saturated fat contents in foods for their children. Many (57–73%) had limited the intake of foods high in these ingredients by their family. However, children were still allowed to determine what breakfast cereal was purchased in over 40% of the households. A good number felt that snack items, such as salty chips or cookies, were too high in salt, sugar, and preservatives. Mothers claimed to have limited the intake of these foods by their children; however, they were still common snack items and, when asked to state what features they considered most important in the purchase of snack foods, nutritional value was not mentioned and taste predominated. When asked to state which foods were most needed for a healthy child, vegetables and fruits were mentioned most often, followed by milk, meat, and whole-grain cereals. Mothers also considered fruit juice to be wholesome and nutritious; it was favored as an all-day beverage (Anonymous, 1982b) and followed milk closely as the "snack" beverage of choice (Sloan, 1985b).

As the child matures, his or her attitudes toward food reflect parental choice as well as the type of food training he or she has received at home (National Dairy Council, 1965). When households are very strict with little adjustment for the reactions of the child toward foods, a child tends to react by rejecting or liking foods which are different from those of his or her mother. Often, this rejection is in the form of outspoken opposition, which is a natural part of the maturation process leading to the abandonment of parental authority. In more lenient families where there is less of a barrier between generations, food enjoyment is common, with children more often imitating the food choices of their parents (National Dairy Council, 1965).

B.   INFLUENCE OF THE SOCIAL SETTING

The older child makes more of the food-consuming decisions today; not only is his or her mother employed outside of the home and he or she has some of the responsibility of food purchasing and preparation, but he or she also has an allowance or personal income, much of which is used for food purchases. Within this age category one finds very bizzare eating patterns, particularly among young teenage girls who place high value on sociability, on independence, on status, and on the enjoyment of food and eating as an end in itself. They tend to consider health as unimportant and to have poor food habits (Hinton et al., 1963). Their only health-related concern may be with a perceived excess in body weight, even for some who are underweight; these "overweight" girls tend to have very inadequate diets, to enjoy eating food less, and to place less value on health. Although smaller in number, the girls who place high value on health tend to have better diets. Girls who score best on emotional stability, conformity, adjustment to reality, and family relationships also miss fewer meals and have more varied and nutritious diets (Plinar, 1983). Other studies of 14- to 18-year-old Canadian girls indicated that the worst diets were seen in girls who skipped meals, were dieting or had dieted in the past, and were larger; all are indicative of the preoccupation of today's teenage girls with being slim (MacDonald et al., 1983). Teenage boys tend to be more health conscious than girls and rank health as the first consideration in food selection more often; this is followed by cost, sociability, enjoyment, independence, and status (McElroy and Taylor, 1966). For older teenage boys and girls, time is an important constraint influencing food selection and the decision of whether to eat or not; breakfast and the school lunch are often omitted because of the pressures of time (National Dairy Council, 1965).

The conflict between home training and other influences in the environment as the child matures can be demonstrated by open-ended questionnaires of children throughout this age spectrum. When 10 to 22 year olds were asked to list foods that were good for health reasons, foods they would consider part of a poor meal, or foods they would be praised for eating by their mothers, they listed milk, meat, and fruits (Litman et al., 1964). When asked which foods they preferred or would be scolded for eating by their mothers, they listed foods such as carbonated beverages, candy, and desserts. Thus, these teenagers and young adults had learned from their mothers what foods were desirable for health but were expressing their independence by not always considering them personally desirable.

But even older young adults (18 to 34 year olds), who should have learned for themselves the nutritional benefits of foods and who voiced a concern with health and fitness, occasionally wanted to pamper themselves with the foods they enjoyed (Hannejan, 1985). Sales of certain "reward foods" with higher added value, such as imported chocolates and specialty ice creams, have increased markedly in the past decade; advertising for these items has recognized this desire for self-indulgence by young adults and stresses the idea that you give yourself a treat (and not wait for someone else to recognize your accomplishments) by eating a candy bar or premium quality ice cream (Hannejan, 1985). Working women who are high-energy achievers and strive to continually improve themselves are particularly desirous of rewarding themselves (rather than waiting for praise as their mothers did) and use these small treats that make them feel pampered (Langer, 1986).

C.   HEALTH AS A VALUE IN FOOD SELECTION

From these examples of advertising ploys and the phenomenal increases in sales by candy and ice cream manufacturers, it is obvious that adults have many concerns other than health that direct their food choices. Cluster analyses of the answers to 10 questions regarding health, nutrition, finances, and time concerns collected by the Pennsylvania State University in a nationwide telephone survey of 967 women who were 20 to 59 years old revealed that nearly half were concerned about nutrition and food safety (Herrmann *et al.*, 1984). The younger women among those concerned about nutrition also were worried about being overweight, needed special diets, and had to consider their time and money more when making food purchasing decisions. These women (12% of the sample) tended to be less educated, to have lower incomes, to be from a minority group, and to be unmarried or separated parents. Another cluster of equal size with similar socioeconomic characteristics was far less concerned about nutrition, but equally concerned about time and financial constraints. A larger cluster containing older, better-educated, and higher income women expressed the most concern about nutrition but were also concerned with time, weight control, and special diets. This cluster represented nearly 25% of those surveyed. Time was an important constraint for all clusters.

The recognition of the importance of the health aspects of food has been increasing among the general U.S. population and not merely among mothers of young children. The U.S. Department of Agriculture (USDA) Continuing Survey of Food Intake by Individuals 19–50 years old for 1985 shows a substantial increase from the 1965 and 1977–78 National Food Consumption Surveys (NFCS) in the consumption of mixtures with small amounts of meat and large amounts of grain. This is thought to reflect the increased concern for nutrition and health resulting from the widespread dissemination of recommendations for reducing the intake of saturated fats made by the American Medical Association and the National Cancer Institute as well as by the U.S. Dietary Guidelines (Chou, 1986c).

Several studies have suggested that the elderly in the United States are the age group most concerned with the nutritional quality of their diets. Analyses of food attitudes and the frequency of intake of specific marker foods by well-educated, moderate-income, elderly men and women in Toronto suggest that the health-promoting characteristics of a food are its most important attributes (Fanelli and Stevenhagen, 1985). Of the 14 marker foods, 13 showed a high correlation between frequency of consumption and perceived health attributes. These attributes were a much stronger influence on the frequency of consumption than were perceived price, prestige, or convenience, although taste and familiarity were still the most important deciding factors in determining whether or not a given food would ever be consumed. It should be noted that most of the foods consumed in high frequency were also relatively easy to prepare and moderately inexpensive; also, there was a statistically significant correlation between the foods selected and the perceived ease and time required for the food's preparation by older women, indicating that time and price were probably still constraints for these individuals.

Analyses of the core group of foods eaten by the elderly in the 1977–78 NFCS demonstrated that there was very little income elasticity for the foods selected, i.e., that the lower income groups ate nearly the same foods as those with higher incomes. As in Toronto, the foods were all relatively inexpensive and easy to prepare (Akin *et al.*, 1986). A food-attitude survey done in Sacramento, California (using a wider array of foods with varying nutritional and price characteristics on consumers from a greater age range that included the elderly) indicated that health was an important concern for all ages but that price was more important to older than to younger consumers (Schutz *et al.*, 1986).

In a survey of expressed attitudes toward diet and foods in general, the elderly again showed greater concern for health and nutrition than did younger age groups. This concern was propagated by their fear of poor health and by the heightened public interest over nutrition in the past decade (Chou, 1984a). More than two-thirds of the consumers over 65 years of age claimed to have modified their meals at home to improve nutrition (Chou, 1984a). Many of the elderly also claimed to have increased their consumption of fresh fruits and vegetables because these were perceived to be more "natural," to "contain no preservatives," and, thus, to be "more healthy" (Chou, 1984b). Despite these health concerns, many elderly, for whom financial constraints were more critical than for younger adults, viewed spending less on food as an appropriate means of coping with financial pressures. They were willing and able to take the time to shop around to get the best buy because they are no longer employed or concerned with child care; what they bought was based on a time × money × health equation (Chou, 1984b). But they also paid more attention to perceived value (defined as freshness, reduced spoilage, and minimal package waste) and were more brand conscious and brand loyal than younger consumers (Chou, 1984b).

V. CHANGES IN MEAL PATTERNS WITH AGE

As part of the trend toward increased time constraints and the resulting demand for convenience, the location and time spent eating as well as the foods eaten have changed. The impact of these changes is probably most apparent in the meal patterns of teenagers and adults.

A. TEENAGERS

The typical meal pattern of three meals a day is becoming more atypical, particularly for young age groups in the United States. In the 1977–78 NFCS, 14% of the total individuals reported skipping breakfast, 23% skipped lunch, and over 60% snacked (Crocette and Gutherie, 1981). Children and teenagers snacked the most [59–70% snacked at least once in three days (Morgan, 1983)].

The amount of snacking positively correlated with per capita income (National Research Council, 1985). Teenagers tend to have erratic meal patterns and their meals are likely to contain unconventional foods which are quick and easy to prepare or available from the family refrigerator (Truswell and Darnton-Hill, 1981).

B.   YOUNG ADULTS

Today's young adults seem to have continued some of the irregularity of their teenage meal patterns; the 19- to 22-year-old age category was the most likely to skip breakfast in the 1977–78 NFCS (Crocetti and Gutherie, 1981). Restaurants have begun to cater to these younger patrons who are more affluent "grazers" and eat small meals several times a day away from home (Hannejan, 1985). But this carryover of teenage patterns is not exclusively limited to very young adults. A 1978 *Women's Day* Family Food Study indicated that among women 18 to 65 years old, predominantly from households with more than 2 family members, 34% skipped breakfast, 22% skipped lunch, and 19% skipped all regular meals and only ate or snacked when hungry (Anonymous, 1978). By 1985, a similar sampling of 2000 women for *Woman's Day* showed that 72% of the women skipped breakfast, 57% skipped lunch, 34% ate only when hungry, and 14% reported eating many small meals a day (Fabricant, 1986).

C.   MEAL TYPE VERSUS FOOD ATTRIBUTES

This shift in meal pattern has implications for the desirability of attributes in a food because the importance placed on a particular food attribute varies not only with the food but with the eating occasion and location as well. For example, a panel of young women with small children considered good taste to be the most important attribute for bread, but good nutritional properties the most important for ready-to-eat cereals because cereals were being used to replace less nutritious foods as snacks for children (Sloan, 1985a). On the other hand, the choice of a cereal-based snack by older children and adults was determined almost exclusively by its taste (Sloan, 1985a).

D.   MEALS AWAY FROM HOME

The number of meals eaten away from home (AFH meals) has markedly increased in the past decade as more women enter the work force with a subsequent reduction in the amount of time available for food preparation and an increase in family income (Langer, 1986). The greatest increase between the 1965 and 1977–78 NFCS was for the percentage of AFH meals by children 3–5 years. The greatest number of consumers of AFH meals were 23- to 34-years-old

men (27%) and 15- to 22-year-old women (25%), while the fewest AFH meals
(7–8%) were consumed by those over 75 years olds (Rizek and Jackson, 1980).
For all ages, the number of AFH meals positively correlated with per capita
income.

1. Effect of AFH Meals on Types of Foods Eaten

Cluster analysis of the foods eaten by 65 to 74 year olds from the 1977–78
NFCS showed that food intake patterns could be influenced by the number of
meals eaten away from home even in this group which had a low frequency of
such meals (Akin *et al.*, 1986). One cluster of men and one of women who
consumed fewer AFH meals ate significantly more nuts/seeds and salty snacks.
Another cluster of men and women consumed more sweetened milk products and
sugars/sweets. One cluster of women (45%) consuming more AFH meals was
more likely to consume animal fats and nonalcoholic beverages. For the younger
age groups, the consumption of AFH meals, particularly from fast-food restaurants, has an even more marked effect on meal pattern (Whelan, 1981), contributing significantly to the intake of saturated fat.

2. Location and Type of Meals AFH

The AFH meals are changing in type and locale as well as in consumer age
group. The fast-food industry has moved into many new outlets: college cam-
puses, hospitals, military bases, toll roads, retail stores, shopping malls, and
central city office buildings (Gallo, 1986). Convenience food retail stores have
also capitalized on the fast-food market and have added microwave ovens and
other foodservice equipment to expand their foodservice sales, so that their fast-
food sales have increased 50% from 1975 to 1985 (Gallo, 1986). Increasingly,
breakfast is being served in these fast-food outlets in addition to lunch and snacks
(Hannejan, 1985). Full-service restaurants have catered to this demand for convenience by providing gourmet delicatessens, bakeries, and full meals for take-
out customers (Anonymous, 1984).

Retail food stores have recently entered the competition for fast-food service
and take-out meals by providing in-store bakeries, delicatessens, and soup and
salad bars (Anonymous, 1982b). The produce section of the full-line grocery
store, where most of these new services are located, is the fastest growing
segment of the retail food business.

Full-service restaurants have been quicker than fast-food chains to change
their menus, if not their locations, to meet consumer preferences by adding
"lighter" items as well as chocolate and rich desserts (Chou, 1984b). The most
popular restaurant main-dish menu items in 1972 were fried chicken, roast beef,
spaghetti, and hamburgers (Anonymous, 1972). Since then, spaghetti has be-

come a more typical home-cooked meal and main-dish AFH meals are increasingly likely to include Mexican or Oriental dishes (Chou, 1986c). Mexican restaurants are the fastest growing restaurant type, particularly in the Southwest (Przybyla, 1986).

The attributes for food choice at AFH meals differ from those demanded for meals at home. The expressed order of importance of the criteria for the selection of an AFH meal eaten at a fast-food outlet was (1) taste, (2) price and convenience, and (3) nutritional composition (Whelan, 1981). The food selected at full-service restaurants was influenced most by perceived value and less by price; little thought was given to nutrition—although many customers claim to be selecting lighter foods than they did in the past (Anonymous, 1985e).

VI. ACTUAL FOOD SELECTION BY AGE GROUP

The food preferences of individuals reflect their unique combination of traditional practices, values, and attitudes. What is actually eaten will also reflect the availability of a food at a given time and place. The 1977–78 NFCS identified which foods were consumed by a significantly greater percentage of different age groups (Table I) and, thus, could be interpreted to be an acceptable part of the American diet. It also identified which foods were consumed significantly more times a day by age group (Table II) and may, thus, be interpreted to be foods that are considered foods most appropriate for that age group (Cronin *et al.*, 1982). As expected, the youngest group consumed the most whole milk each day,

TABLE I

FOODS MOST LIKELY CONSUMED BY PERSONS OF DIFFERENT AGE
GROUPS

Age group (years)	Foods
3–6	Potatoes, pasta, luncheon meat, dairy products
3–10	Noncitrus fruit, breakfast cereals, rice, nuts, sugar or sugar spreads
3–14	Candy
7–10	Whole milk, desserts, potato chips
7–17	Snack foods, condiments
15–17	Sugar-based and carbonated beverages
18–50	Salad dressings, low-calorie carbonated beverages
>50	Dark green vegetables, tomatoes, whole-grain bread, crackers, eggs, soups, cream or cream substitutes, coffee or tea

TABLE II

FOODS MOST FREQUENTLY CONSUMED BY AGE GROUPS

Age group (years)	Foods
3–6	Whole milk
3–10	Bread or cereals, milk products
11–14	Desserts
>15	Yeast breads, cream or cream substitutes
18–50	Sweets, carbonated beverages, low-calorie carbonated beverages
>51	Fruits, vegetables, noncitrus fruits, whole-grain bread, sugar or sugar spreads, table spreads, coffee or tea

although a greater percentage of elementary-school-age children were likely to consume milk (Cronin *et al.*, 1982). Children and teenagers were more likely to consume sugar-based and carbonated beverages and snack foods. Young adults appear to be the most weight-conscious because they consumed more salad dressing and low-calorie beverages, and those over 51 years of age appear to be the most concerned for health because they were more likely to consume fruits, vegetables, and whole-grain bread [although they still consumed the most coffee or tea, sugar or sugary spreads, and butter or margarine (Morgan, 1983)].

When examined for finer age differentiations for the near elderly (55–64 years), young elderly (65–74 years) and old elderly (over 75 years), this transition with age and increased concern for health was better demonstrated (Fanelli and Stevenhagen, 1985). Using the cut-off point of foods consumed by more than 25% of an age group daily and more than 50% at least once in 3 days, there were no changes with age in the foods included in the fruit category (orange juice, bananas, apples) or the bread–cereal category (white bread, crackers, whole-wheat bread, ready-to-eat cereal). In the two groups over 65 years, however, processed cheese was deleted from the protein sources (eggs, bacon, luncheon meat, ice cream, natural cheese), mayonnaise was deleted from the bread accompaniments category (margarine, butter, jam/jelly), beer was deleted from beverages (coffee, tea, whole milk, low-fat milk, cola), gravy and sugar substitutes were added to the condiments category (sugar, salad dressings), and soup was added to the vegetables (lettuce, potatoes, tomatoes). In the old elderly (over 75 years) cola was deleted from the beverages, green beans added to the vegetables, and cottage cheese substituted for natural cheese in the protein sources. These changes not only demonstrate the concern for the health attributes of food and the need to reduce the intakes of refined carbohydrates, salt, and saturated fats, but they also demonstrate which foods are considered irreplaceable by the elderly.

VII. EFFECTS OF CONSUMER SEX
ON FOOD SELECTION

Differences both in physiological response and in traditional family and work roles of men and women contribute to differences in food selection.

A. DIFFERENCES IN THE SENSES OF TASTE AND SMELL ON FOOD PREFERENCES

Women have a more accute sense of smell (Lemaire, 1985) and have a greater preference for tart taste (Laird and Breen, 1968) at all ages than men. These greater sensitivities and taste preferences possibly contribute to the greater number of food aversions (Eppright, 1947) as well as to the greater likelihood of the inclusion of fruit in their diet (1977–78 NFCS; Cronin et al., 1982) and their preference for fruit as a snack, while men prefer salty snacks (Anonymous, 1985b).

The majority of preferences is probably learned by imitation of the same-sex parent (Plinar, 1983). Children are taught which foods are appropriate for men and which are appropriate for women. Studies of young enlisted military men and women showed that 70% of the respondents could be identified as to sex by their food preferences, which was more than could be identified by either race or place of origin (Meiselman and Waterman, 1978). The best indicators were the preferences for beer and tossed green salad by men and women, respectively. Other differences in preferences included a significantly greater preference by men for eggs, breakfast meats, dinner meats, stews or extended meats, short-order foods, and pies. Women showed a significantly greater preference for appetizers, potatoes, vegetables, and fresh fruit.

B. DIFFERENCES IN FOOD VALUES AND ATTITUDES BY THE SEXES

During the past 10 years, there has been an increase in the number of households where men are the principle food preparers and shoppers. Many of the households with male food preparers are single-person households (61 vs. 13%), and an increased percentage of male food preparers are also either less than 25 years old or greater than 65 years old and live in central cities (Pearson et al., 1986). For a larger number of these households a majority of meals are eaten away from home (26 vs. 6%). For these food preparers, just as for women employed outside of the home (Langer, 1986), time is a major constraint so more meals are eaten away from home (Pearson et al., 1986) and convenience and take-out foods are popular (Pearson et al., 1986; Langer, 1986). Households from the 1977–78 HFCS with a female food preparer were more likely to have used hydrogenated vegetable fats, all-purpose flour, salad dressing, celery, fresh cabbage, and cucumbers, reflecting both an increased amount time available for food preparation and the preference for salads by women (Krondl *et al.*, 1982). Male food preparers were far less likely to purchase flour and more likely to purchase complex convenience foods like canned soup or frozen entrees. Male shoppers tended to be more brand loyal and less concerned with cost (Anonymous, 1985c). Although equally concerned about the nutritional content of what they eat (Anonymous, 1985d), they are less knowledgeable about nutrition than women with similar years of education (Wong *et al.*, 1982) and are less likely to have changed the food they eat at home or away from home to improve nutrition (Sloan and Powers, 1985).

In a survey of food-selection attitudes by more typical American households where a female was the principal food preparer, 51 men and women (moderately high-income, well-educated Caucasians with a mean age of 44 from a small, northern California town) were asked to rank 46 dairy and related-use foods for their perceived nutritional attributes (good for your health), for social (serve to guests) or basic attributes (needed even when on a diet, cheap, consumed at least once a day, good buy for the money), and for their appropriateness for various occasions (treats, specific meals, entertaining) (Bruhn and Schutz, 1986). Factor analysis of these attitudes identified meal-type dairy products (cheeses, cottage cheese, milks) as the highest ranking in nutritional attributes and treat foods (ice cream and sherbet, but *not* yogurt) as lower in nutritional attributes. This again indicates the perceived lesser importance of nutrition and the greater importance of taste for snacks. A mixture of treat foods (sherbet and ice cream), meal-type dairy products (hard cheeses), and nondairy foods (coffee) was highest ranking in social attributes, indicating a less clear-cut differentiation in the social or prestige rating of dairy foods. A mixture of treat foods (yogurt) and nondairy foods (tea) ranked highest in overall basic attributes. Yogurt, cottage cheese, and all the nondairy foods except beer and regular soda ranked high as foods good for dieting; whole milk, tea, and low-fat milk ranked high as cheap foods. Whole milk, cheddar cheese, and low-fat milk ranked highest as the best buys for the money, but milk was the only food that ranked high in being necessary to consume every day. Overall, social factors explained more of the variation in the appropriateness-for-use variables (as meals or treats) for men, and nutritional variables explained more of the variation in appropriateness-of-use variables for women, again supporting the greater concern of women for nutrition.

In a study of a similar but larger population, 338 men and women from Sacramento, California (who were moderately high-income, well-educated Caucasians with a modal age of 36–45 years), were asked to rank a wider range of 15 foods for more generalized food attributes (nutrition, price, brand, sensory properties). As a factor in food selection, sensory attributes ranked highest and brand lowest, with nutrition and price being intermediate and equal in importance

(Schutz *et al.*, 1986). The taste preference for a food showed a significant correlation with the other attributes. Nutrition was again a more important variable for main-course food items than for foods usually eaten as snack, and females tended to rank nutrition, brand, and sensory properties more highly as factors in food selection than did men.

Using another statistical procedure unconstrained for potential food selection factors (cluster analysis), the frequency of consumption of 13 beverages (milk, soft and hard drinks, coffee, and tea) was compared with life-style, values, and demographic indicators for 160 men and women 25 to 54 years old from a southern U.S. sample (Granzin and Bahn, 1982). The "available" cluster, those individuals who had a high consumption of ready-to-consume beverages (such as milk, regular soft drinks, milk shakes, punch, and health drinks kept in the refrigerator) was more likely to consist of younger females (mean age of 39 years) who placed a high value on the importance of religion and a low value on the importance of money, competition, and risk. They spent the most time on church work and the least time relaxing. The "adulterated" cluster, those who had a high consumption of modified products (such as diet sodas and decaffeinated coffee), was most likely to consist of older females (mean age of 48 years) who were married. They placed the least value on money and job satisfaction, an intermediate value on competition, religion, and risk, and spent the least time in team sports. The "caloric" cluster, those who had the highest consumption of beverages high in calories (such as soft drinks, beer, liquor, and milk shakes), was most likely to consist of young males (mean age of 30 years) who were most likely to live in a rural area and placed the highest value on risk and competition, the lowest value on religion, spent the least time on church work, and spent the most time relaxing, dancing, and in team sports. The "social" cluster, those who had a high consumption of beverages appropriate for a social setting (such as coffee, tea, wine), was equally likely to be male or female and was intermediate in age (mean age of 42 years). They placed the highest importance on money, intermediate importance on other values, and spent intermediate amounts of time on all activities. It would thus seem that the life-style (activities) and values of an individual can influence beverage selection and, probably, selection of other foods as well. These life-styles and values seem to be culturally allocated to male and female roles, with an overlap for only one cluster. It is probable that values affect life-style and that any food-selection pattern is secondary to these values and life-styles.

C.   DIFFERENCES IN ACTUAL FOOD SELECTION BY THE SEXES

The 1977–78 NFCS indicated that men were more likely to consume high-calorie items (whole milk, luncheon meats, grain-based desserts, sweets, and sweet spreads) and sandwiches, while women were more likely to consume low-calorie items (fruit, yogurt, coffee or tea, and low-calorie beverages). Men also ate significantly more white bread, milk, red meats, and grain-based desserts each day (Cronin *et al.*, 1982). Elderly men from Toronto were more likely to have eaten some of these same foods (soft drinks, hog dog buns) as well as baked beans and processed cheese slices, while women were more likely to have consumed low-fat milk, other cheeses, chicken, canned fish, and a variety of fruits and vegetables (Fanelli *et al.*, 1985).

VIII.   EFFECTS OF CONSUMER RACE ON FOOD SELECTION

A.   DIFFERENCES IN FOOD PREFERENCE BY RACE

The food preferences of blacks in the United States are a reflection both of the foods characteristic to the southern diet and of their countries of origin. Studies made of preferences for foods served in dining halls to young military personnel (Table III) showed that blacks had a greater number of preferences even when corrected for region of birth. The foods that best predicted race were mixtures with meat (e.g., stews and lasagna), which were preferred most by whites, and grits, which were preferred by blacks [both of these are also regionally specific foods (Meiselman, 1977)]. Later studies of similar populations by the same group (that used fewer categories of food) indicated that blacks preferred pork products, rice, green vegetables, fish, and fruit juice more than white military personnel and that whites preferred potatoes, beef, Italian and Mexican foods, and tomato juice more than did black military personnel (Meiselman and Waterman, 1978). Neither study identified the ethnic origins of the subjects; the selection of Italian or Mexican foods may reflect a biased sample of men and women of predominantly southern European or Hispanic origin.

The 1977–78 NFCS, which covered a greater age span and was more representative of the population in the continental United States, also demonstrated a preference among blacks for pork products, cooked cereals, and dark green vegetables, as indicated by a higher percentage of this group selecting these foods (Table IV), but only snack items and condiments were selected more frequently by whites. Other racial/ethnic groups, predominantly Hispanic and Asian, were more likely to consume legumes and peas, beef or pork, and greater amounts of fruits and vegetables or breads and cereals (Table V) (Cronin *et al.*, 1982). Blacks were less likely to consume dairy products, both as a percentage of the population and in the amount consumed.

B.   DIFFERENCES IN FOOD VALUES AND ATTITUDES BY RACE

Greater concern for health may be inferred from certain food intake patterns in white teenagers (or their parents), but this may also be a reflection of income. In

TABLE III

TASTE OR FREQUENCY PREFERENCES BY RACE/REGION

Race/region	Preference
Blacks	
Meat	Barbecued beef, braised liver and onions, grilled bologna, pepper steak, salmon, sausage links
Mixed	Stuffed cabbage, tuna salad sandwiches, macaroni and cheese
Vegetables	Mixed vegetables, succotash, carrot–raisin–celery salad, frozen lima beans, fried cabbage
Cereals/grains	Fried rice
Desserts	Bread pudding, pineapple sundaes, raisin cookies, raisin pie, vanilla wafers, yellow cake
Fruit juices	Grape, grapefruit, lemonade, pineapple, prune and fruit-juice mixtures
Sweetened Beverages	Grape flavored, grape soda, orange flavored, orange soda
Southerners	
Meat	Barbecued spareribs, chitterlings, fried fish, pork hocks
Vegetables	Cabbage, canned lima beans, collards, greens, sweet potatoes
Cereals/grains	Hominy grits, steamed rice
Desserts	Sweet-potato pie
Southern Blacks	
Meat	Pig's feet, pork chop suey
Whites	
Vegetables	Hash brown potatoes
Beverages	Milk, coffee, tomato juice
Northern Whites	
Vegetables	Carrot and celery sticks, tossed green salad

a study of the diet patterns of 1247 female adolescents from 8 southern states (McCoy *et al.,* 1984), use of vitamin supplements was significantly higher for white girls, although the highest intakes were for the girls from higher income families. Older girls, particularly black girls, were also more likely to add salt to their food at the table, a health practice which was felt to be of questionable merit in light of the high incidence of hypertension in black populations. A study done on northern young mothers (WIC program participants) in New York revealed that the black women tended to be less concerned about weight loss and, hence, were more likely to prefer less nutrient-dense foods. They also had more food

TABLE IV

FOODS CONSUMED BY RACIAL–ETHNIC GROUPS

Group	More likely to be consumed	Less likely to be consumed
Whites	Low-fat milk, nuts, grain- and dairy-based desserts, potato chips, condiments, candy, table spreads, salad dressings, cream/cream substitutes, coffee/tea, natural cheese	Quick breads, breakfast cereals, rice, poultry, eggs, sugar-based beverages
Blacks	Dark green vegetables, cooked cereals, bacon/salt pork	Noncitrus fruits, potatoes, whole-grain bread, milk, processed cheese, fats
Others	Dried beans/peas, beef, pork, soups	None

dislikes and ranked only a few foods higher than whites, some of which are more likely to be part of a southern diet (liver, corn bread, mincemeat pie) (Fetzer *et al.*, 1985). Studies in Washington, D.C., a city less removed from the traditional southern diet, indicated that blacks relied more on traditional food beliefs but had the same choices of foods considered to be wholesome; however, they did stress (more strongly than whites) the benefits of green vegetables (Wilson, 1973).

IX. EFFECTS OF ETHNIC ORIGIN ON FOOD SELECTION

As with blacks in the United States who have moved north, the persistence of the traditional diet in an immigrant population will be dependent on their access to the ingredients needed to make traditional foods, their exposure to other foods, and the time they have available for food preparation. If an ethnic group is sizable or in close proximity to the country of origin, there may be a sufficient market for the traditional food ingredients. If the immigrants were older adults at the time of immigration, they may be more likely to stay at home and would not be exposed to American foods at school or work. In addition, some traditional (nonstaple) foods can be more easily replaced than others in each culture, while other foods may have perceived close approximations. For instance, the Vietnamese in Washington, D.C., still eat rice every day, but at breakfast the rice has been replaced by breakfast cereals, and at lunch it has been replaced by bread or noodles (Tong, 1981). Fish and shellfish consumption has been reduced, but pork and organ-meat consumption still surpass beef. Vegetable consumption is

TABLE V

FREQUENCY OF FOOD CONSUMPTION BY RACIAL–ETHNIC GROUP

Racial–ethnic group	Consumed more often in a day	Consumed less often in a day
Whites	Ready-to-eat cereal, grain-based desserts, fats, coffee/tea	Meat, fish, poultry
Blacks	None	Milk, yogurt, cheese
Others	Fruits/vegetables, breads/cereals, skim milk	None

reduced because familiar vegetables are not available, and banana consumption is reduced because the bananas are not of the same type. Of the group surveyed, 40% said they had changed their food habits, and the major reason given was that women had to work outside of the home and there was no one available to do the more tedious food preparation needed for traditional cooking. The second reason given was the desire to adapt to the American life-style, and the third was that there was a difference in the foods available.

The relative inflexibility of the core diet (rice in the case of the Vietnamese) has been demonstrated for a variety of cultures. First-generation Armenians consume more cheese, yogurt, and lentils than second or third generation individuals, but these items are still an important part of the Armenian diet. Modifications have taken place in the ingredients in a food dish and in the preparation methods, with the raw fruit or bulgur, lentils, and barley preferred by first-generation Armenians being replaced by fruit juices and pasta by the third generation. When asked why traditional foods are not used, the first generation is most likely to reply, just as did the Vietnamese of Washington, that there is no one to prepare these foods or that they don't know where to get the ingredients, the second generation answers that traditional foods take too long to prepare or are too expensive, and only the third generation states that they don't like them and prefer American foods (Nalbandian *et al.*, 1981).

A. ASIAN ORIGIN

Asian (near, middle, and far east) and Hispanic immigrants share a belief in the health attributes of foods segmented into yin and yang, or cold and hot (Ludman and Morgan, 1984). Accordingly, yin (cold) foods are to be consumed to combat hot diseases (such as fever) and yang (hot) foods are eaten to counteract weakened conditions (such as anemia or during pregnancy). Since the same foods do not exist in every culture and each country has had varying degrees of mixture and acceptance of Western medicine, there will be varying degrees of adherence to the recommendations of these traditional beliefs. An analysis of Chinese populations living in the People's Republic of China, Hong Kong, and the United States revealed close agreement between these attitudes (about the necessity of a special dietary treatment for fever, anemia, and during pregnancy) in China and Hong Kong, but lesser agreement among Chinese populations in the United States. All three groups agreed with the tenets of yin and yang for treating fever and blood building but not with the recommendations for pregnancy. However, many of the foods recommended by yin and yang are the same as those favored by Western medicine. Also, the use of yin and yang is not always at the conscious level, so it is not possible to ask a person whether or not he or she is following the tenets of traditional medicine.

B.   HISPANIC ORIGIN

Other values that may affect the food habits held by some new immigrant populations are related to the belief in the locus of control over one's life. Mexican-Americans, for example, tend to believe more strongly in an external control over their lives, and this may lead them to believe that their satisfaction with a food product is independent of their own purchasing decisions (Saegert *et al.*, 1985). In some cases, questionnaires requiring a statement of food preference are of dubious value because it is considered inappropriate to state a preference, particularly among women in Eastern cultures. Immigrants may also be less willing to participate in surveys due to poor communication skills or distrust of the investigator, and, hence, are often underrepresented in national assessments.

When communication barriers and mistrust were overcome by direct visual contact with Hispanic investigators, Mexican-Americans from a small, south Texas town were found to favor familiar neighborhood food stores with convenient hours and lower prices more than Anglo-Americans from the same area. Although they voiced a stronger brand loyalty, they showed less brand loyalty in actual food purchases (Saegert *et al.*, 1985). The availability of special food products and Spanish-speaking store owners may have contributed to the preference for the neighborhood convenience stores.

Actual food selection by households of Hispanic ethnic origin from the 1977–78 NFCS indicated a relative reduction in money allocations for vegetables and food mixtures, condiments, or bakery products when compared with non-Hispanic households, and an increase in the percentage of the food budget allocated for cereals–rice–pasta, less expensive meats, and meat substitutes (eggs, beans, nuts) (Cronin *et al.*, 1982). This is also supported by studies of migrant populations in northern California where Mexican migrant families were shown to maintain or even increase their consumption of tortillas and beans while increasing their intake of ready-to-eat cereals and peanut butter (Dewey, 1984). Those who had been in the United States the longest tended to eat the most cheese, rice, and peanut butter (using wheat flour rather than corn tortillas), but they maintained the high intake of cereals and beans of their traditional diet. Most claimed to be eating more fruit and vegetables than when they were in Mexico, but they were still not eating enough to make their diets adequate in this food category. The children were more likely than other family members to eat new foods and were attributed with introducing new foods into the family's diet. Although a lower intake of fruits, vegetables, and meat and a higher intake of cereals and beans are traditional to the Hispanic diet, they are also characteristic of the diets of low-income groups in the United States. With increased income, the willingness to change these traditional diets to one with more meat and fruit has been amply demonstrated by other cultures [the Japanese being a striking example (Wenkam and Wolff, 1970)] and is probably true for Hispanic Americans as well, even though they remain the racial/ethnic population with the lowest income in the United States today and they are predicted to continue as such for some time.

X. EFFECTS OF REGION ON FOOD SELECTION

The higher consumption of fruits, vegetables, and whole-wheat bread by the residents of western states (Table VI) is a reflection of the western origin of the emphasis on vegetarian dishes and the introduction of Mexican and Oriental foods which started in that area (Chou, 1984b). It is also a relection of the large Hispanic and Asian communities that reside on the West Coast. The large ethnic Italian population on the East Coast probably explains the greater popularity of pasta. The foods consumed more frequently by southern households are also relected in the food preferences of military personnel from the South.

The regional differences in total food consumption also held true for snack selection. In the West, fruit was a more frequent choice (Table VII) as a snack, while pizza and sandwiches were preferred in the Northeast.

XI. EFFECTS OF URBANIZATION ON FOOD SELECTION

Adolescents are more able to break away from the family eating pattern in urban than in rural settings (Truswell and Darnton-Hill, 1981) and are exposed to food patterns of numerous ethnic groups, particularly if they come from East or West Coast cities. Hence, a major component of these ethnic diets, rice, is more likely to be consumed in central cities (Table VIII). On the other hand, the suburbs contain more higher income families and reflect the higher intake of

TABLE VI

FOODS CONSUMED BY PERSONS FROM DIFFERENT REGIONS

Region	Foods most likely to be consumed	Foods less likely to be consumed
Northeast	Citrus fruit, deep yellow vegetables, pasta, whole milk, processed cheese, soups	Dried beans/peas, quick breads, cooked cereal, sauces/gravies, bacon/salt pork
North central	Low-fat milk, desserts, potato chips, candy	Cooked cereal, rice, whole milk, poultry, eggs, carbonated beverages
South	Dried beans/peas, quick breads, cooked cereals, rice, poultry, eggs, sauces/gravies, bacon/salt pork, carbonated beverages, coffee/tea	Fruit, deep yellow vegetables, tomatoes, whole-grain bread, low-fat milk, yogurt, cheese, nuts, desserts, soups, potato chips, candy, fats
West	Noncitrus fruits, other vegetables, whole-grain bread, yogurt, natural cheese, nuts, candy, salad dressings, cream/cream substitutes	Pasta, potato chips, potato chips, carbonated beverages, coffee/tea

income-dependent foods (red meats, fruits, fats, and snacks). Nonmetropolitan areas have nearly the same pattern of intake as the South (as well as more nonworking wives, so foods requiring more preparation can be included).

Cluster analyses of the foods eaten by the elderly in the United States reveal that those clusters which are predominantly urban are also most likely to contain elderly men and women who consume more alcohol. For women, this group also consumes significantly less of other nutritious foods, such as fruits, vegetables, and whole grains, and thus tends to have an inadequate diet (Akin *et al.*, 1986). Urban men who consumed alcohol, however tended to have diets that were adequate in most nutrients.

TABLE VII

FREQUENCY OF FOODS CONSUMED BY PERSONS IN DIFFERENT REGIONS

Region	Consumed more times each day	Consumed fewer times each day
Northeast	Whole milk	None
North central	Yeast breads, coffee/tea	Noncitrus fruit, whole milk
South	None	Fruits, yeast breads, ready-to-eat cereals, milk, grain-based desserts, table spreads, coffee/tea
West	Fruits, vegetables	None

TABLE VIII

FOODS CONSUMED MORE OFTEN BY PERSONS LIVING IN DIFFERENT
TYPES
OF COMMUNITIES

Community type	Foods
Central cities	Rice, sugar-based carbonated beverages
Suburbs	Whole-grain bread, low-fat milk, processed cheese, red meats, nuts, desserts, potato chips, table spreads, salad dressings, low-calorie carbonated beverages
Nonmetropolitan areas	Dried beans/peas, quick breads, sauces/gravies

XII. EFFECTS OF INCOME ON FOOD SELECTION

The consumption of cereals increases in difficult times, thus a 2.7% increase occurred in cereal intakes in 1981 compared with 1% increase in overall food consumption. Cereals are an alternative to more expensive breakfast foods (Anonymous, 1982b), which may partially explain their increased consumption. Meat is an example of a food with relatively high income elasticity (Chou, 1986c). Up until 1977, beef consumption had been growing at 2.5%/year for the previous 25 years after which it began to decrease. Consumption increased with increases in per capita income and decreased as the cost of beef increased relative to beef substitutes. In the 1970s, the average per capita income rose to a level where total meat consumption plateaued, poultry prices decreased, and, hence, beef consumption began to fall. If corrected for inflation between 1979 and 1984, income dropped 9% for families with one wage earner and 2% for two-wage families. The youngest families showed the greatest drop (18%), and only the elderly had an increase (Chou, 1986a). Health concerns do not appear to be as important as economic factors in explaining this fall in beef consumption (Lipton, 1986).

In the 1977–78 NFCS (Table IX), high-income families tended to allocate a greater percentage of their income to beverages and expensive meats and a lesser percentage to vegetables, cereals–rice–pasta, bread, milk–cheese, less expensive meats, eggs–beans–nuts, or fats–oils–sugars–sweets (Cronin *et al.*, 1982). These higher income families tended to also have higher intakes of beef, milk, desserts, and alcohol but similar intakes of poultry, eggs, cereals, and legumes (with the highest income groups three times the skin milk intake and three times the sirloin steak intake).

TABLE IX

FOODS MOST OFTEN CONSUMED BY PERSONS
OF DIFFERENT INCOME LEVELS

Per capita income (dollars)	Foods most likely consumed
<5,000	Rice
<9,999	Eggs, table spreads
5,000–9,999	Dried beans/peas
>10,000	Fats, salad dressings
>15,000	Cheese
>20,000	Noncitrus fruits, other vegetables, whole-grain bread, natural cheese, beef, grain- and dairy-based desserts, potato chips, condiments, candy, fats

XIII. CONCLUSION

The marked changes that have occurred in the makeup of the U.S. population in age, life-styles, and ethnic and racial mixtures, together with the rapid changes that can arise with greater wealth and rapid advances in food technology, demand research methodologies that can consider multiple factors simultaneously and are still rapid enough to make predictions before the population has changed again. We no longer have the luxury of being able to describe the dietary practices of small, homogenous populations using one factor at a time. Techniques are needed which can take advantage of rapid, computerized statistical procedures using well-described, diverse population samples. These appraisals must consider not only physiological, regional, or cultural variations in the population, but also include variations in values and life-styles.

The information on the factors influencing the food selection of some of the rapidly growing minority groups in the United States as they become acculturated is limited. A great deal of descriptive information on the traditional diets of isolated population groups is available, but how and why diets of new and longer term residents are modified throughout the United States is lesser known. The Hispanic HANES (Health and Nutrition Examination Survey) recently completed should bring more information on nutrition status, but more attempts, together with questions that can identify the factors that influence dietary changes, are needed to incorporate these minorities into the National Food Consumption Survey.

REFERENCES

Akin, J. S., Guilkey, D. K., Popkin, B. M., and Fanelli, M. T. 1986. Cluster analysis of food consumption patterns of older Americans. *J. Am. Diet. Assoc.* **86**, 616–624.

Anonymous. 1972. Menu census. *Inst. Vol. Feed.* **70**, 67.

Anonymous. 1978. First Woman's Day Family Food Study. Yankelovich, Skelly and White.

Anonymous. 1982a. Households and families, March 1981. *Family Econ. Rev.* **3**, 37–40.

Anonymous. 1982b. State of the industry. *Food Eng.* **Aug.**, 75–90.

Anonymous. 1984. Trends in food choices. *Focus Food Markets, Cornell Coop. Ext.* **Apr. 30.**

Anonymous. 1985a. Marketplace. *Food Eng.* **Aug.**, 34.

Anonymous. 1985b. What you eat between meals depends on where you live, survey says. *J. Am. Diet. Assoc.* **85**, 604.

Anonymous. 1985c. Who's manning the cart? *Consumer Union News Dig.* **10**, 3.

Anonymous. 1985d. Study shows nutrition concern slipping. *Milling Baking News* **June 4**, 48–49.

Anonymous. 1985e. Consumers are choosing nutritious menu items. *Food Eng.* **Nov.**, 26.

Brody, A. L. 1987. Packaging: Into the microwave—and out. *Cereal Foods World* **32**, 829.

Bruhn, C. M., and Schutz, H. G. 1986. Consumer perceptions of dairy and related-use foods. *Food Technol.* **Jan.**, 79–85.

Bryon, M. S., and Lowenberg, M. E. 1958. The father's influence on young children's food preferences. *J. Am. Diet. Assoc.* **34**, 30–35.

Census of manufacturers. 1985. *Cereal Foods World* **30**, 359.

Chou, M. 1983. Consumer research—slicing the golden apple. *Cereal Foods World* **28**, 471.

Chou, M. 1984a. Consumer research—selling to older Americans. *Cereal Foods World* **29**, 633.

Chou, M. 1984b. Consumer research—the food industry's bell-weather. *Cereal Foods World* **29**, 739.

Chou, M. 1986a. Consumer research—the challenge of demographic changes. *Cereal Foods World* **31**, 562.

Chou, M. 1986b. Consumer research—who buys baked goods? *Cereal Foods World* **31**, 323.

Chou, M. 1986c. Consumer research—grain products regain popularity. *Cereal Foods World* **31**, 906.

Crocette, A. F., and Gutherie, H. A. 1981. Food consumption patterns and nutritional quality of U.S. diets: A preliminary report. *Food Technol.* **Sept.**, 40–49.

Cronin, F. J., Krebs-Smith, S. M., Wyse, B. W., and Light, L. 1982. Characterizing food usage by demographic variables. *J. Am. Diet. Assoc.* **81**, 661–673.

Dewey, K. G. 1984. Combining nutrition research with nutrition education—dietary changes among Mexican-American families. *J. Nutr. Educ.* **16**, 5–7.

Drewnowski, A. 1984. Obesity and taste. *Curr. Concepts Perspect. Nutr.* **3** (2).

Duncker, K. 1938. Experimental modification of children's food preferences through social suggestion. *J. Abnormal Social Psychol.* **33**, 489–507.

Eppright, E. S. 1947. Factors influencing food acceptance. *J. Am. Diet. Assoc.* **23**, 579–587.

Exter, J. 1987. Changes in the American population. *Am. Demograph.* **March,** 15–20.

Fabricant, F. 1986. Food notes: Women and food. *New York Times,* July 9.

Fanelli, M. T., and Stevenhagen, K. J. 1985. Characterizing consumption patterns by food frequency methods: Core foods and variety of foods in diets of older Americans. *J. Am. Diet. Assoc.* **85**, 1570–1577.

Fetzer, J. N., Solt, P. F., and McKinney, S. 1985. Typology of food preferences identified by Nutri-Food Sort. *J. Am. Diet. Assoc.* **85**, 961–965.

Food and Nutrition Board. 1985. What is America eating? *CLS Lifelines. Natl. Res. Council* **11**, 6–7, 13–14.

Gallo, A. E. 1986. Food marketing—from farm to table. *Natl. Food Rev.* **35**, 1–5.

Gaugh, H. G. 1946. An additional study of food aversions. *J. Abnormal Social Psychol.* **41**, 86–90.

Gibson, L. D. 1981. The psychology of food: Why we eat what we eat when we eat it. *Food Technol.* **Feb.**, 54–70.

Granzin, K. L., and Bahn, K. D. 1982. Personal values as an explanation of food usage habits. *Home Econ. Res. J.* **10**, 401–410.

Haley, R. 1984. Nutrition concerns. *New York Times,* December 5.

Hannejan, K. 1985. New product analysis. *Food Eng.* **Oct.**, 65–88.

Herrmann, R. O., Warland, R. H., and Feick, L. F. 1984. Patterns of nutrition concerns and dietary constraints among adult women. *J. Am. Diet. Assoc.* **84**, 1478–1480.

Hinton, M. A., Eppright, E. S., Chadderdon, H., and Wolins, L. 1963. Eating behavior and dietary intakes of girls 12 to 14 years old. *J. Am. Diet. Assoc.* **43**, 223–227.

Jackson, R. W., McDaniel, S. W., and Rao. C. P. 1985. Food shopping and preparation: Psychodemographic differences of working wives and housewives. *J. Consumer Res.* **13**, 110–113.

Jefferson, S. C., and Erdman, A. M. 1970. Taste sensitivity and food aversions of teenagers. *J. Home Econ.* **62**, 604–608.

Jerome, N. 1981. The U.S. dietary pattern from an anthropological perspective. *Food Technol.* **Feb.**, 37–53.

Krondl, M., Lau, D., Yurkiw, and Coleman, D. H. 1982. Food use and perceived food meanings of the elderly. *J. Am. Diet. Assoc.* **80**, 523–527.

Laird, D. A., and Breen, W. J. 1939. Sex and age alterations in taste preferences. *J. Am. Diet. Assoc.* **15**, 549–550.

Langer, J. 1986. Changing demographics: Stimulus for new product ideas. *J. Consumer Market.* **30**, 35–43.

Lawless, H. 1985. Sensory development in children: Research in taste and olfaction. *J. Am. Diet. Assoc.* **85**, 577.

Lemaire, W. H. 1985. Food in the year 2000. *Food Eng.* **May,** 90–110.

Lipton, K. L. 1986. Meat, poultry and dairy: What does the future hold?. *Natl. Food Rev.* **35**, 6–11.

Litman, T. J., Cooney, J. P., and Stief, R. 1964. The views of Minnesota school children on food. *J. Am. Diet. Assoc.* **45**, 433–437.

Ludman, E. K., and Morgan, J. M. 1984. Yin and yang in the health-related food practices of three Chinese groups. *J. Nutr. Educ.* **16**, 3–5.

McCoy, H., Kenney, M. A., Kirby, A., Disney, G., Ercanli, F. G., and Glover, E. 1984. Nutrient intakes of female adolescents from eight southern states. *J. Am. Diet. Assoc.* **84**, 1453.

MacDonald, L. A., Wearring, G. A., and Moase, O. 1983. Factors affecting the dietary quality of adolescent girls. *J. Am. Diet. Assoc.* **82**, 260.

McElroy, J., and Taylor, B. 1966. Adolescents' values in selection of food. *J. Home Econ.* **58**, 651–655.

McKenzie, J. 1982. Social changes and the food industry. *Nutr. Rev. Suppl.* **40**, 13–17.

Mead, M. 1962. Cultural change in relation to nutrition. *In* "Malnutrition and Food Habits" (A. Burgess and R. F. A. Dean. eds.), pp. 50–56. Tavistock, London.

Meiselman, H. L. 1977. The role of sweetness in the food preference of young adults. *In* "Taste and Development: The Genesis of Sweet Preference" (J. M. Weiffenbach, ed.), pp. 10–20. National Institute of Dental Research, DHEW Pub. No. (NIH)77-1068, USDHEW, NIH, MD.

Meiselman, H. L., and Waterman, D. 1978. Food preferences of enlisted personnel in the armed forces. *J. Am. Diet. Assoc.* **73**, 621–629.

Morgan, K. J. 1983. The role of snacking in the American diet. *Cereal Foods World* **28**, 305–306.

Morgan, K. J., and Johnson, S. R. 1985. Food shopping patterns and nutritional quality of diets. *Cereal Foods World* **30**, 839–844.

Nalbandian, A., Bergen, J. G., and Brown, P. T. 1981. Three generations of Armenians: Food habits and dietary status. *J. Am. Diet. Assoc.* **79**, 694–700.

National Dairy Council. 1965. Factors influencing adolescent food habits. *Dairy Council Dig.* **36**, 1–4.

National Dairy Council. 1976. "A Sourcebook on Food Practices with Emphasis on Children and Adolescents." B 026 (6).

Pearson, J. M., Capps, O., and Axelson, J. 1986. Convenience food use in households with male food preparers, *J. Am. Diet. Assoc.* **86**, 339–343.

Plinar, E. 1983. Family resemblance in food preference. *J. Nutr. Educ.* **15**, 137–140.

Przybyla, A. E. 1986. America's passion for spices. *Food Eng.* **June**, 70–78.

Putnam, J. J., and Van Drees, M. G. 1984. Changes ahead for eating out. *Natl. Food Rev.* **26**, 15–17.

Raskin, B. 1979. Militant consumers—a hard sell for bakery foods. *Bakery* **June**, 88–100.

Rizek, R. L., and Jackson, E. M. 1980. Current food consumption practices and nutrient sources in the American diet. Consumer Nutrition Center–Human Nutrition, Sci. & Ed. Ad., USDA, Hyattsville, MD.

Saegert, J., Hoover, R. J., and Hilger, M. T. 1985. Characteristics of Mexican-American consumers. *J. Consumer Res.* **12**, 104–108.

Schutz, H. G., Judge, D. S., and Gentry, J. 1986. The impor

tance of nutrition, brand, cost and sensory attributes to food purchase and consumption, *Food Technol.* **Nov.**, 79–82.

Shiffman, S. S. 1986. Recent findings about taste: Important implications for dieters. *Cereal Foods World* **31**, 300.

Sloan, A. E. 1985a. Consumers and nutrition—a challenge for the food industry. *Cereal Foods World* **30**, 638–640.

Sloan, A. E. 1985b. Boomers. *Food Eng.* **Nov.**, 62–63.

Sloan, A. E., and Powers, M. E. 1985. A consumer survey on cereal grains: Their products, technology, and nutrition. *Cereal Foods World* **30**, 641–643.

Tong, A. 1981. Refugees: A positive force in the community. *Annu. Meet. Am. Home Econ. Assoc., 72nd, Atlantic City.*

Truswell, A. S., and Darnton-Hill, I. 1981. Food habits of adolescents. *Nutr. Rev.* **39**, 73–88.

Wenkam, N. S., and Wolff, R. J. 1970. A half century of changing food habits among Japanese in Hawaii. *J. Am. Diet. Assoc.* **57**, 29–32.

Whelan, E. M. 1981. Fast food and the American diet. American Council Science & Health, New York.

Wilson, C. S. 1973. Food habits: A selected annotated bibliography. *J. Nutr. Educ.* **5(1)**, Supp. 1, 41–71.

Wong, H., Krondl, M., and Williams, J. I. 1982. Long-term effect of a nutrition intervention for the elderly. *J. Nutr. Elderly* **8**, 31–34.

INDEX